Safe, Sane and Consensual

Safe, Sane and Consensual

Contemporary Perspectives on Sadomasochism

Darren Langdridge
Open University, UK

and

Meg Barker
Open University, UK

First published in 2007
Paperback published in 2013 by
PALGRAVE MACMILLAN

Palgrave Macmillan in the UK is an imprint of Macmillan Publishers Limited,
registered in England, company number 785998, of Houndmills, Basingstoke,
Hampshire RG21 6XS.

Palgrave Macmillan in the US is a division of St Martin's Press LLC,
175 Fifth Avenue, New York, NY 10010.

Palgrave Macmillan is the global academic imprint of the above companies
and has companies and representatives throughout the world.

Palgrave® and Macmillan® are registered trademarks in the United States,
the United Kingdom, Europe and other countries.

ISBN 978–0–230–51774–5 hardback
ISBN 978–1–137–33837–2 paperback

This book is printed on paper suitable for recycling and made from fully
managed and sustained forest sources. Logging, pulping and manufacturing
processes are expected to conform to the environmental regulations of the
country of origin.

A catalogue record for this book is available from the British Library.

A catalog record for this book is available from the Library of Congress.

Contents

Notes on Cover Image

The person depicted in the image on the front cover writes:

Collaborating on this project has been life changing for me. I am much more accustomed to being on the other side of the process, as a journalist, critic and academic, in the position of connoisseurship, expertise, rather than the body to be scrutinised. I have never been involved with pictures like this before as a subject/producer.

The most striking experience has been that of choosing to place myself in a new and intimidating position, collaborating with a partner to work some magic, to queer the stability of categories of photographer, subject, top, bottom, expert and amateur. Willingly giving over some of my power to the photographer.

The result amazes me. I have never seen myself look this powerful and beautiful.

For now, putting my name to this image feels too risky. The (scary) moment has arrived to release our work and my image into the world.

Alex Miller writes:

This picture brings together two paths I've been exploring for some years now: taking pictures of people, and my abilities and desires in BDSM. A camera is an instrument of power, of seeing and of exposure, and I know from my own experience that this is why many people hate having their picture taken.

So usually, when I'm working on making a portrait of someone with my camera, I reverse that power flow as much as I can. I try not to hide behind the camera, I work slowly to help them relax, we chat, I don't tell them how to move or pose, but ask them how they would like to be seen. I show them the pictures immediately, and destroy those that they don't like (digital imaging is a wonderful thing)

So recently it occurred to me: what happens if I do the opposite, and with a person who also consciously chooses to give that power to me?

The editors of this volume offered me a push towards finding out, and the answer, it seems, is something really quite powerful. These are not pictures that I have 'taken', but images that we have created together. I am amazed at the results.

Alex Miller and her collaborator are very grateful to SM Dykes Manchester, and a couple of their members in particular.

Thank you for the rope and for the inspiration.

Notes on Contributors

Mlle Alize began her fascination with the BDSM scene in 1996 while attending university. She was initially drawn to the scene by the clothes and the concept of Goddess worship and chivalry. Mlle Alize started her professional involvement in the scene in 1998. As her involvement in the scene grew, so did her philosophies regarding BDSM. In 2004, Mlle Alize attended and graduated from the Academy of SM Arts under the tutelage of Mme. Cléo du Bois. Mlle Alize is currently based in Washington, DC, where she has 1800 sq ft of play space. She currently works with both couples and individuals. She also writes several columns focusing on female sexuality and adult toys/products.

Meg Barker is a Senior Lecturer in Psychology at the Open University, UK and a practising sex and relationship therapist. In addition to this book, Meg Barker and Darren Langdridge have published academic collections on non-monogamous relationships and counselling and psychotherapy. They also co-edit the journal *Psychology & Sexuality* and have contributed material on BDSM to the British Psychological Society guidelines on working with sexual and gender minorities. Meg co-organises the Critical Sexology seminar series and has published on representations of BDSM, constructions of dominant women, and is part of a current project exploring the lived experience of submissive men. Meg's previous research on sexualities and relationships has been published in several journals and books and has culminated recently in a general audience book *Rewriting the Rules* (2012), which has a website: www.rewriting-the-rules.com.

Robin Bauer lives in Brussels and is a Lecturer in Gender & Science Studies and Queer Studies in various German universities. He recently completed his PhD thesis on queer BDSM practices and communities in sociology at the University of Hamburg. He has published numerous articles on BDSM, transgenderism, polyamory and gender & science studies curricula, seeking to combine his activism with his academic work. As camp manager of a gay men's SM camp in Denmark he is probably the first transman to be in a leading position within the gay men's BDSM community in Europe.

Andrea Beckmann is Senior Lecturer in Criminology at the University of Lincoln, UK and a social pedagogue. Her academic interests are in the areas of 'sexual deviance' and the broader realm of the politics of the 'body' and 'truth' as well as in other areas of social theory. She also researches and publishes critical accounts of the impact of neoliberalism and the new managerialism on education and other conditions of domination. Andrea is the elected British representative of the European Group for the Study of Deviance and Social Control. Andrea is the author of various publications on consensual 'SM' that have attracted international recognition. Her book *The Social Construction of Sexuality and Perversion: Deconstructing Sadomasochism* (2009, Palgrave Macmillan) was nominated for the The Bonnie and Vern L. Bullough Book Award, which recognizes outstanding scholarship in the field of sexology.

Robert V. Bienvenu II is Team Leader of the Community-Academic Consortium for Research on Alternative Sexualities and Chair of the CARAS Research Advisory Committee. A sociologist who lives in the Washington, DC area, his forthcoming book addresses the historical development of fetish and SM subcultures in the United States.

Eric Chaline is a journalist, editor, translator and commercial non-fiction writer with a special interest in gay BDSM sexualities in the UK. He completed his doctorate at London South Bank University, and is currently rewriting his thesis, 'From Sexual Outlaw to Sexual Consumer: Gay BDSM in the UK, 1950s to the Present', for the general reader. His gay BDSM-related publications include 'Researching sexual difference: A survey of gay SM in the UK', *Lesbian & Gay Psychology Review*, and 'The Construction, Maintenance, and Evolution of Gay SM Sexualities and Sexual Identities: A Preliminary Description of Gay SM Sexual Identity Practices', *Sexualities*.

Grant Denkinson calls himself male, bisexual and polyamorous. He lives in Leicester with his partner, two housemates and three pet rats. He works with computers in physics and astronomy and is in advanced clinical training as a psychotherapist. He's been a bit of an activist type, mainly around sex, sexuality and relationships and is now taking some time away from that to find time for learning, thinking and just living.

He gets around mainly by bicycle and on trains and likes to cook good vegan food.

Lisa Downing is Professor of French Discourses of Sexuality at the University of Birmingham, UK. She is the author of numerous books, articles and chapters on sexuality studies (particularly critical accounts of 'perversion' and 'paraphilia'), gender studies, and cultural studies, including: *Desiring the Dead: Necrophilia and Nineteenth-Century French Literature* (2003) *The Cambridge Introduction to Michel Foucault* (2007), and *The Subject of Murder: Gender, Exceptionality, and the Modern Killer* (2013). Her publications as co-editor include *Perversion: Psychoanalytic Perspectives/Perspectives on Psychoanalysis* (with Dany Nobus, 2006) and *Queer in Europe: Contemporary Case Studies* (with Robert Gillett, 2011). She is currently co-authoring a critical study of the diagnostic concepts of sexologist John Money and their cultural, medical and political influences. She co-organises the Critical Sexology seminar series with Meg Barker and Robert Gillett and convenes postgraduate programmes and staff research in Sexuality and Gender at Birmingham.

Dossie Easton is one of the most prolific writers on the subject of SM. Her books, written with colleague Janet W. Hardy (aka Catherine A. Liszt), include *The New Topping Book* (2003), *The New Bottoming Book* (2001), *When Someone you Love is Kinky* (2000), and *Radical Ecstasy* (2004). Dossie is a licensed marriage and family therapist specialising in relationship issues and alternative sexualities in San Francisco. She worked in the mental health system in the US for ten years including three years at a battered women's shelter. She also teaches on relationship and SM skills, techniques and philosophy, and is a poet and performer. She was one of the founding members of the Society of Janus (San Francisco's SM support and educational organisation) and leads a community linking SM and spirituality.

Camel Gupta is a mental health worker, independent researcher and journalist. Camel worked for several years in a voluntary capacity for Threshold Women's Mental Health Initiative, providing support and listening to a broad range of clients. A member of several working groups concerning LGBT mental health, Camel has written on sexuality, BDSM, safe space and mental health for a number of publications, writes about visual culture, contemporary art and performance, and has an MA in Visual Cultures from Goldsmiths' College, University of London.

William Henkin is a licensed psychotherapist and a board certified sex therapist who has worked and taught extensively in the altern- ative sex and gender communities for more than 30 years. A past- president of the San Francisco chapter of the Society for the Scientific Study of Sexuality, a member of the Ethics Committee of the World Professional Association for Transgender Health (formerly HBIGDA), and adjunct faculty at the Institute for Advanced Study of Human Sexuality, Dr. Henkin's publications include articles, chapters, or monographs on BDSM, bisexuality, infantilism, transgender identity issues, dissociative identity disorder, creativity, sex addiction, and mind-body integration. Author or co-author of more than a dozen books including *The Rocky Horror Picture Show Book* and *Consensual Sadomasochism: How to Talk About It and How to Do It Safely* (with Sybil Holiday), Dr. Henkin conducts his private practice in San Francisco, California.

Alex Iantaffi is an Assistant Professor, at the Program in Human Sexu- ality, Department of Family Medicine and Community Health, at the University of Minnesota, USA. He is also a licensed marriage and family therapist, who originally trained in the UK as a systemic psychother- apist, and he is the Editor-in-Chief for the *International Journal of Sexual and Relationship Therapy*. His therapeutic work is currently focused on transgender and gender non-conforming youth, and their families. Alex has conducted research, and published on gender, disability, Deafness, education, sexual health, HIV prevention, trans* issues, polyamory, and BDSM. His scholarly work has been increasingly focused on issues of intersectionality and sexual health disparities. He is currently Principal Investigator for a study, funded by the National Institutes of Health (NIH), on Deaf Men who have Sex with Men (MSM), HIV testing and prevention, and technology. Alex is also an activist, writer, parent, and knitter who still believes that the personal is indeed political.

Peggy J. Kleinplatz is Professor of Medicine and Clinical Professor of Psychology at the University of Ottawa, Canada. She is a clinical psycho- logist, Board Certified in Sex Therapy, Sex Education and as a Diplomate in Sex Therapy. Since 1983, she has been teaching Human Sexuality at the School of Psychology, University of Ottawa, where she received the Prix d'Excellence in 2000. Her clinical work focuses on eroticism and transformation. Her current research focuses on optimal sexuality, with a particular interest in sexual health in the elderly, disabled and margin- alized populations. She is the editor of *New Directions in Sex Therapy:*

Innovations and Alternatives (2012), and with Charles Moser, of *Sadomas-ochism: Powerful Pleasures.*

Darren Langdridge is Head of Department of Psychology at the Open University, UK, Honorary Professor of Psychology, Aalborg University, Denmark and a UKCP accredited existential psychotherapist. In addition to this book, Darren Langdridge and Meg Barker have published academic collections on non-monogamous relationships and counselling and psychotherapy. They also co-edit the journal *Psychology & Sexuality* and have contributed material on BDSM to the British Psychological Society guidelines on working with sexual and gender minorities. Darren is the author of *Phenomenological Psychology: Theory, Research and Method* and *Existential Counselling and Psychotherapy*, as well as numerous papers on sexualities, the construction of 'the family' and existential psychotherapy. He is currently working on his next book entitled *Sex-Sexuality-Citizenship: Beyond the Boundaries of Belonging.*

Charles Moser is Chair of the Department of Sexual Medicine at the Institute for Advanced Study of Human Sexuality, San Francisco, USA. He is Board Certified in Internal Medicine and a Fellow of the American College of Physicians. He maintains a private practice in San Francisco specializing in Internal Medicine and Sexual Medicine (the sexual aspects of medical concerns and the medical aspects of sexual concerns). He has authored or co-authored over 40 scientific papers or books.

Kathy Sisson is an independent scholar in California. She is on the Board of Directors of the Society for the Scientific Study of Sexuality and currently serves as program chair for its western region. She is also on the Board of Advisors for the Woodhull Freedom Foundation, an international sexual advocacy organization. Her research focuses on alternative sexualities. Portions of her article appeared previously in *American Sexuality Magazine* and are reprinted here with permission. Copyright © 2005 National Sexuality Resource Center/San Francisco State University. (shift to Acknowledgements)

Sophia was born in Somerset, UK, in 1972 and was educated at the University of Manchester. She has been active in the bisexual and queer BDSM communities in Britain since 1990 and has also been involved in the civil rights campaign to decriminalise consensual BDSM. Sophia is polyamorous, bisexual and identifies as a switch. She lives in London in a poly household and works in the media. Her other academic interest is the archaeology of late mediaeval monasteries.

Richard Sprott received his Ph.D. in Developmental Psychology from UC Berkeley in 1994. He is adjunct faculty in the Department of Human Development at California State University, East Bay, and Executive Director of CARAS – Community-Academic Consortium for Research on Alternative Sexualities. CARAS is dedicated to the support and promotion of excellence in the study of alternative sexualities, and the dissemination of research results to members of alternative sexuality and research communities and to the general public. Being a community-based research organization, the focus of CARAS depends on partnerships and the involvement of different alt-sex communities, with an emphasis on alt-sex communities that are currently ignored or understudied, such as BDSM and polyamory.

Matthew Weait is Professor of Law and Policy and Pro-Vice-Master (Academic Partnerships) at Birkbeck College, University of London, UK. His research, which has its roots in the voluntary and policy work he has done in the field over the past decade, centres on the impact of law on people living with HIV and AIDS, and on theories of responsibility (especially in criminal law). Matthew has published widely in these areas and his monograph *Intimacy and Responsibility: the Criminalization of HIV Transmission* was published in 2007.

Megan Yost is an Assistant Professor of Psychology at Dickinson College in Pennsylvania, USA. She is a feminist social psychologist by training, whose research focuses on gender and human sexuality. She is particularly interested in understanding psychological connections between power and sexuality predictors of sexual violence, the influence of gender on sexuality and people's lived experience related to gender expression, sexual orientation and diverse sexual practices.

Part I
Introducing Sadomasochism

1
Sadomasochism: Past, Present, Future

Darren Langdridge and Meg Barker

Sadomasochism (SM) occupies an extraordinary place within the popular imagination with it variously represented as madness, criminality and/or comedy (Langdridge & Butt, 2004; Wilkinson, 2009). Few other sexual practices/identities can lay claim to such a complex or worrying array of representations. This is not stable as much is in flux when it comes to SM, however, with: challenges to the inclusion of SM in psychiatric nosologies (such as the American Psychiatric Association Diagnostic Manual); legal challenges to and defence against prohibitive legislation (the UK extreme pornography act); and popular consumption of SM through the publishing sensation that is 'Fifty Shades of Grey' by E. L. James (discussed further below). SM is a highly emotive topic of considerable contemporary relevance and this book seeks to map out and critically interrogate the terrain for the interested reader.

Psychological and Psychiatric Perspectives

The 'psy-professions' have lain claim to much of the terrain when it comes to SM, playing a critical part in locating this practice/identity within the public realm (Taylor, 1997). Psychological and medical perspectives on sadomasochism (SM) have historically been concerned with explaining it as a form of psychopathology. In the past, studies of SM have been concerned with acts which are furthest away from common practices, that result in physical harm, or even death, and that are clearly non-consensual. Psycho-medical analyses of such acts are then generalised to all consensual sadomasochistic sexual acts. Even today, authors on SM often base their analyses on the small number of SMers they have seen personally as psychotherapy clients[1] along with public accounts of severe acts of sadism (such as those perpetrated by

TRASGRESSING   VS.   COERCIVE

serial murderers) (e.g. Welldone, 2002), rarely drawing any clear distinction between acts which are transgressive and those which are coercive (see Denman, 2004).

Sexual sadism and masochism are still classified as psychiatric disorders within both the Diagnostic and Statistical Manual of the American Psychiatric Association (DSM – IV) and the International Classification of Diseases (ICD-10), despite the lack of evidence that SMers are any more psychologically unhealthy than others (Gosselin & Wilson, 1980; Moser & Levitt, 1987). Like homosexuality some twenty years ago, sadomasochistic sex is considered alongside rape and child sexual abuse as individual sexual pathology in need of explanation, treatment and cure (see Kleinplatz & Moser, this volume for a fuller critique of this).

New stories of SM

Recently, however, there has also been growing interest amongst social scientists in exploring the meaning of sadomasochism in non-pathological ways (for instance, Barker & Gill, 2012; Beckmann, 2001, 2009; Deckha, 2011; Langdridge, 2005, 2006, 2007; Langdridge and Butt, 2004, 2005; Newmahr, 2011; Powls & Davies, 2012; Ritchie & Barker, 2005; Stiles & Clark, 2011; Taylor, 1997; Taylor and Ussher, 2001). This research has sought to understand the stories that SMers themselves tell of their lives and sexual practices rather than relying on pathologising psycho-medical explanations. Much of this research has emerged, at least in part, out of the growth of SM communities themselves. Such groups are increasingly calling for the freedom to express their identities and/or to engage in SM practices, and perhaps for even wider public acknowledgement and recognition of SMers' rights as citizens, similar to the calls that have been made around lesbian, gay and bisexual sexualities (see below and Langdridge, 2006). As noted previously (Langdridge, 2007: 282), a number of factors appear to have led to the growth of new SM stories and communities including:

the growth of urbanisation and industrialisation enabling autonomous personal lives to develop; oppressive State interference in people's personal lives and the resistance that this engenders; changes in communication and the mass media; the emergence of individual stories of personal suffering, pain and then triumph; the (very recent) rise of positive psychotherapeutic and medical professionals encouraging the stories; and the development of an interactive social world ready to hear the stories.

This is, of course, in addition to the simple need people have to find others who share similar sexual identities and desires. Stories of SM have certainly proliferated within and outside communities centred on these identities/practices over the last twenty years or so. There are increasing numbers of SMers sharing their own stories using forums such as social gatherings, community events and commercial venues, and – particularly – online networks lists and websites. Many of the stories which reach beyond the communities to the outside world are watered down, 'mainstreamed' and deeply de-sexualised – often focussed on an SM aesthetic rather than anything anyone involved in SM would identify as something they do (Weiss, 2006) – but still there is increasing public awareness (see Barker, Iantaffi & Gupta, this volume, and Wilkinson, 2009). The growth of communities with people supporting and organising themselves has led to demands for research that is congruent with the phenomenology of the participants themselves and this book is a further attempt to honour that demand.

Public awareness of SM is also developing. Representations of SM have been increasingly prevalent in popular culture for a decade or more: in commercials, music, and movies, notably 'Secretary' which was perhaps the first mainstream film to seriously depict sadomasochistic main characters in an empathic manner, rather than just using SM imagery in a relatively restrictive manner (Weiss, this volume; Wilkinson, 2009). Mainstream sex shops such as Ann Summers have stocked fluffy handcuffs, riding crops and whips alongside underwear, vibrators and costumes, although there is a strong sense – in such shops and in the related parties – of the importance of policing the boundary between acceptable 'spicy sex' and 'real SM' (see Barker Gupta & Iantaffi, this volume).

However, it was with the publication of E. L. James' hugely popular trilogy of erotic novels 'Fifty Shades of Grey' in 2012 that SM has taken a central role the popular imagination. It is interesting that this series began life as fan fiction from the 'Twilight' series of books and movies. Turning the protagonists from vampire and virgin to dominant and potential submissive not only made it possible for James to sell the books, but also enabled the erotic pain/pleasure and power dynamics that many enjoy within vampire, and other romance and horror, fiction, to be more openly recognised as a (relatively) acceptable part of someone's sexuality. These books, and their impact, are just beginning to be considered academically, with a spate of journal special issues, books and conferences. As with 'Secretary' it is notable that SM is made safer by being embedded within a very traditional heteronormative romance narrative Downing (2013), and as with the·inclusion of SM equipment within mainstream sex shops, it is interesting that the female protagonist is responsible for policing a boundary between sexy 'kinky fuckery' and dangerous, pathological 'real SM'. It remains to be seen, though, whether the immense popularity of 'Fifty Shades' will open up the possibility for other fictional stories of SM to make their way into the mainstream.

In the following section we highlight four key debates concerning SM that span the personal and political. Whilst there are many topics worthy of further research and discussion, we would argue that these issues are particularly important and likely sites for future scholarship within the field. We follow this with a discussion of terminology and an outline of the structure of the book.

Contemporary debates

Feminism and consent

In academic circles, SM continues to occupy a central role in many debates in the social sciences, from the feminist sex wars in the 1970s through to present day debates about consent and violence, as well as mental health, diagnosis and psychopathology. Consent, for example, is a particularly problematic concept (See Downing, this volume) and one that has been troubled in an important way by feminist scholarship. The liberal notion of consent at the heart of much sadomasochistic practice has been critiqued by a number of feminist theorists who have argued that the idea of a contract, highlighted in SM, continues to be used to mask the operation of sexual power particularly in relation to hetero-patriarchy. And furthermore, these conditions may well be internalised and replayed in sadomasochistic relationships such that SM "eroticises the crude power difference of gender which fuels heterosexual desire, reinforcing rather than ending it" (Jeffreys, 1996: 86). However, as Moore and Reynolds (2004: 32–33) point out:

> The claim that consent is meaningless under hetero-patriarchy is epistemologically flawed. It is based on a false universalism whereby all men oppress all women... Whilst claiming, on the one hand, to be woman-centred and committed to fighting women's oppression by listening to women's voices... on the other hand, they dismiss

the accounts of women who report positive experiences of heterosexuality.

The same can be said for SM, with women's voices – in the forms
of women SMers – being apparently irrelevant to the radical feminist
theoretician. For the radical feminist it appears that there is an inherent
incompatibility between SM and feminism whether the SM takes place in
an 'opposite-sex', 'same-sex' or gender queer context. Whilst there is not
the space to engage fully with this issue here the most obvious counter to
this particular radical feminist position, mentioned above by Moore and
Reynolds (2004), concerns the way in which one voice is given priority
over another. In this case, the voice of the radical feminist drowns out
the voice of the woman SMer. As Ritchie and Barker (2005) highlight in
their work with women SMers, SM has the potential to reveal or even
subvert traditional gender dynamics with women themselves being able
to work with consent in a way that recognises the influence of hetero-
patriarchy and the potential impact this may have on their identities
and practices (see also Bauer, this volume). The debates will undoubtedly
continue on this topic and many more as SM troubles and is troubled
by important issues in sexualities and gender studies, and there are
intriguing emerging moves amongst feminist academics working in this
field, and SM community writers, to occupy a both/and rather than
either/or position regarding liberal and radical feminist positions (Baker
& Gill, 2012; Barker, forthcoming 2013; Downing, 2013). It is hoped
that this book will contribute to the ongoing development of such
debates.

SM and abuse

Related to the previous topic are issues surrounding SM and abuse.
Those who are critical of SM practices, including the radical feminists
mentioned above, have historically linked SM to abuse in multiple ways,
often by claiming that SM itself is inherently abusive; by putting SM
on a continuum with coercive and abusive behaviours such as rape and
murder; and by assuming that those who practice SM do so because they
have a history of abuse. Like SM community members, academics taking
a non-pathologising stance towards SM have tended to directly counter
the position of 'SM is always abuse' by clearly distinguishing between
SM and abuse, and by providing evidence against links between SM and
childhood abuse and/or harmful/criminal behaviour (Barker, Iantaffi &
Gupta, 2007; Kleinplatz & Moser, 2006).

Recently this area has been complicated by a number of high-profile online writers from within SM communities who have, themselves, taken a more critical stance towards SM practices (see Barker & Gill, 2012). Whilst retaining the position that SM is not, per se, dangerous, pathological or abusive, they have questioned the simplistic assumptions of the SM mantra 'safe, sane and consensual', and even the more cautious alternative 'risk-aware consensual kink' (Barker, Gupta & Iantaffi, this volume). One key argument is that, in taking the position that 'SM is never abuse' (to counter the view that it is always abuse), and in insisting that consent is always present, some SM communities have unwittingly created an environment where abusive and non-consensual behaviours, when they do occur, are hidden, and those who speak about them are silenced. With projects like 'consent culture' and 'safe/ward', there are moves towards more sophisticated understandings of consent as a collective responsibility, as an active, ongoing, relational negotiation (rather than simply an individual not 'saying no' or safewording), and as something which is limited by wider cultures of consent toxicity and social power dynamics within which everyone is located (Barker, forthcoming 2013). Such moves towards more 'critically informed kink' (Barker & Gill, 2012) within heterosexual/pansexual US/UK SM communities echo the understandings of consent and power present in Bauer's European dyke+queer communities (this volume).

SM as therapy

An interesting counterpoint, or perhaps more accurately, *extension to* discussion of SM and abuse concerns the therapeutic value of SM. Meg Barker, Camel Gupta and Alex Iantaffi (this volume) discuss this with a particular focus on the potentials and pitfalls of such narratives. We have also engaged in dialogue about this same issue within the context of the legitimacy of silencing already silenced sexualities (Barker & Langdridge, 2010). And most recently, Danielle Lindemann (2011) has contributed to this debate with her empirical study of professional dominatrices and their perception of the therapeutic value of SM. So, what is at stake here?

Central to debates about SM as therapy is the question of whether this exemplifies the positive potential of SM or further reinforces the perception of SM as psychopathology, the result of childhood abuse and/or some other pathology. Whilst there is no evidence of greater mental health problems or distress amongst SMers than non-SMers (see, for instance, Kleinplatz & Moser, 2006; Richters et al., 2008) the story will go, "If these practices are therapeutic then surely the people that are drawn to them are in need of therapy and therefore damaged?" So, are stories of SM being psychotherapeutically beneficial something to be celebrated and encouraged (in the sense of coaxing and coaching the production of a new sexual story – Plummer, 1995) or something to be worried about and discouraged/critiqued at this politically sensitive time for SM communities? The challenge for researchers – as with the stories of abuse within SM mentioned above – is that this question raises deeply troubling questions about our right to embrace/critique stories that are clearly in evidence (and indeed, growing) within SM communities: we discuss this point further in Barker & Langdridge (2010).

Lindeman (2011) highlights three further issues with the discourse of SM as therapy, in the context of her empirical study of SM pro-dommes where this story was clearly voiced by most of her participants. The first is how the pro-dommes in her study were effectively performing emotional labour for their touch- (and sometimes, talk-) starved clients, a role traditionally ascribed to women, which supports and reproduces existing societal gender relations, and which has potentially wider implications within SM communities given the slippage between expectations on pro-dommes and on dominatrices in general (Barker & Gill, 2012). Whilst this may be a salient point for (female) pro-dommes, it might be argued that there are examples of differently gendered displays of emotional labour within the broader SM scene. This does, however, remain an interesting point for further investigation. Lindeman (ibid) also raises the curious (and peculiarly modern) question of whether professional SM workers might need to be licensed to practice (raising a raft of further issues), given their avowed status as 'mental health workers' rather than 'sex workers'. It seems highly unlikely that arrangements will be put in place for this in Europe but it is not out of the question in North America, where one might imagine a legal case against a pro-dom/domme should they be perceived to have damaged a person's mental-health (whilst claiming to provide therapeutic services). Finally, Lindeman (ibid) raises the thorny issue of how some of her pro-domme participants felt they might thought to be absolving their clients for beliefs and actions that they found morally repugnant. Race play and Nazi scenes, child abuse play, and misogynist scenes for instance, are not as rare as one might assume and may, therefore, provide challenges not only for professional SMers but also others approached to play out such scenes. Such activities might be therapeutically valuable for some people but is it right to engage with them and what might be the consequences of doing so? How should we approach such activities as clinicians working in a non-pathologising way with our clients? And, how might we seek to represent such things to the wider public, if we wish to at all?

There is clearly much more work needed exploring SM as therapy, as there is with SM and abuse and the gender politics of SM, and we expect that this will continue to be the case for the foreseeable future. In many ways, these issues all intersect, with questions of consent and feminism frequently playing into concerns about SM as abuse and the therapeutic value of SM at times difficult to distinguish from abuse. It is difficult to tackle these issues when there remains so much prejudice and misinformation about SM but we think it is time that all of us who seek to challenge oppression of SMers face this challenge head on rather than shirk our responsibility to care and, if necessary, fight for one another.

Citizenship and belonging

If we move beyond the personal (inflected by the political) towards the political (inflected by the personal), SM occupies an important position as a marker of the boundaries of sexual citizenship (Langdridge, 2006). From the case of Operation Spanner (see Langdridge, 2006; Weait, this volume), in which 16 gay men in the UK were convicted in 1990 for engaging in consensual sadomasochistic sex, to the recent attempts at prosecutions under the UK's extreme pornography legislation (Section 63 of the Criminal Justice and Immigration Act 2008) for representations of fisting, we can see a continuing battle over the boundaries of acceptability with SM. People who engage in SM practices have been and continue to be excluded from full citizenship in the UK, and as a result subject to medical and legal sanction and intervention. SM exists on the very outer limits of the 'charmed circle' of acceptable sexual practices/identities (Rubin, 1984) and is thus subject to continuing policing by the state. Beyond the state there also continues to be prejudice with a lack of acknowledgement by the wider public, though perhaps this is slowly changing. Questions of citizenship are, therefore, a central issue for both the theory and practice of SM (see Langdridge, 2006 and 2013, for more on this).

There are many challenges facing SMers seeking full sexual citizenship such that they have the same rights and responsibilities as those engaged in more traditional sexual practices, that are endorsed and supported by the state through legislation (and recognised as acceptable by the wider public). Challenges faced here include: the way in which SM might be perceived as too sexual; the fragmentation of SM with some embracing it as an identity and others engaged in it as part of their wider sexual repertoire; and the thrill of dissidence where part of the appeal of SM that comes from being 'Other' may be lost with full citizenship (Langdridge, 2006). When we examine the claims made by SMers themselves what emerges are many different, frequently opposed, positions with no simple model of political progress that will satisfy them all. One theoretical attempt to address this seemingly unresolvable tension is by engaging with both claims for citizenship *and* claims for transgression thus:

> A dialectical relationship between citizenship (ideology) and transgression (utopia) may provide a way of recognizing the different needs of community members in SM and other communities. That is, those that want recognition, rights and responsibilities can make their claims for integration, identities and citizenship and with this, work to queer citizenship from within, while those that wish to remain outside, for the attendant thrill that this provides, can work to queer the project from the outside as transgressors or sexual outlaws. Langdridge (2006: 386).

Much more needs to be worked through here, however, with both the theory and practice of SM and its relationship to (sexual) citizenship. The complexity of SM is that it means so many different things to so many people. It might be nothing more than a slight extension or variation to more normative sexualities (as we might see in 'Fifty Shades of Grey') or something apparently so extreme that SMers are at risk of the full force of the state through legal and medical intervention. And finally, it involves some people who desperately want to live within the law and be accepted by a wider public and other people who would fight tooth and nail to remain forever a sexual outlaw. There are no easy answers here but instead a wealth of possibilities and a wealth of challenges to normative understandings of (sexual) citizenship.

Terminology

This book seeks to provide further discussion and debate about SM amongst and between psychologists, other social scientists, legal and medical scholars. Our understanding of SM is broad and includes all sexual identities and practices involving pain play, bondage, dominance and submission, and erotic power exchange. Whilst the book represents many different perspectives, it is limited to work that moves away from pathological explanations of SM identities and practices. Instead, the book presents work which seeks to understand the world as it appears to the practitioner him or her-self, along with writing that explores some of the complex intellectual issues that arise from these identities/practices without simply resorting to extant pathological explanations.

Authors use different terms for SM throughout, including SM, S&M, S/M or BDSM (a broader term which stands for bondage and discipline, domination and submission, and sadomasochism), and it is probably worth spending a little time here explaining some of this terminology. We have left authors to define their own terms in each chapter rather than using the same term throughout because they may be using a word to refer to a particular subset of activities. Also, some feel that it is important to separate out S and M as two distinct practices/identities (sadism and masochism) whilst others feel that bringing them together in the word sadomasochism suggests that one is not possible without the other.

Similarly, various words are used for the different participants or positions in SM. Generally 'sadist', 'dominant', 'dom/domme', and 'top' are used for the person in the position of power or the one giving out the stimulation and 'masochist', 'submissive', 'sub', and 'bottom' are used for the person with less power or the one on the receiving end. A 'switch' is someone who takes both kinds of roles. Often the words 'dominant' and 'submissive' are used for more psychological SM (e.g., that involving humiliation or servitude) and 'top' and 'bottom' for more physical (e.g., that involving pain or other sensations), although there is also often overlap between the two. SM activity may be referred to as 'play' or a 'scene' and non-SM sex may be termed 'vanilla'. Sometimes those who take part in SM are referred to as SM practitioners, although others prefer terms like 'SMers', since many in the SM communities view SM as an identity they have whilst others see it as an activity they practice[2]. As mentioned above, a key phrase adopted by very many people engaging in SM is SM as 'safe, sane and consensual' (SSC), describing the core conditions for SM play. More recently, use of the acronym RACK (risk aware consensual kink) has grown in popularity, in recognition of the fact that no activity is 100% safe (implied in SSC), alongside a move to question the need to warrant a person's sanity for choosing to engage in SM practices. We are keen to emphasise the diversity of SM practices and identities as well as experiences involved and motivations for taking part, which may differ widely between individuals and even within the same person on different occasions. For those unfamiliar with the terminology and variety of practices around SM the chapter by Moser and Kleinplatz in this book is likely to be very helpful. In this chapter the authors seek to provide a nosology of the variety of practices/scenes that may be involved in SM.

Structure of the book

The chapters that follow were written for the first publication of this book in hard back in 2007. Whilst we have updated and expanded this introduction, the following chapters remain the same as they were in 2007. They were cutting edge then and remain so now in 2012. We have raised some further contemporary issues in our introduction but believe that what follows still represents some of the most significant scholarship in the field, providing an important point of reference for all people wishing to explore SM from a non-pathologising perspective.

The book begins with four chapters concerned with cultural, normative, psychiatric and legal issues. This includes an analysis of the history and cultural basis of SM (Sisson), a nosology of SM practices (Moser and Kleinplatz), a critical examination of the psychiatric classification of SM (Kleinplatz and Moser) and an important theoretical discussion of the current legal situation in the UK (Weait). This is followed by a section that explores new (non-pathological) psychological and/or other theoretical understandings of different aspects of SM including an existential exploration of pain play (Langdridge), a meditation on SM, spirituality and transcendence (Beckmann) and a critical examination of safety discourses around SM practices (Downing).

Following these chapters is a section presenting empirical research on the topic. This begins with a quantitative investigation into the sexual fantasies of SM practitioners (Yost), followed by a study of gay male SM scripts (Chaline) and an analysis of the ways in which BDSM may be used to queer gender (Bauer). We then include a section on psychotherapy and SM, which includes pieces on emerging narratives of SM itself as therapeutic (Barker, Iantaffi and Gupta), and related pieces on Jungian shadow play (Easton) and possible beneficial aspects of role play (Henkin). The book ends with a section exploring potential links between academic work on S/M and activism in this area with a piece on an important initiative in San Francisco developing links between sexual communities and academic researchers (Sprott and Bienvenu), a discussion of the development of SM training tools (Barker) and a chapter comprising a number of pieces representing 'voices from the communities' (Sophia, Denkinson, Alize, Green).

The book includes contributions from academics, practitioners and activists in the UK, USA, Canada, and Continental Europe and represents some of the most cutting-edge work in the field by leading

scholars. We hope this work is of interest to academics and practitioners working in the social sciences and beyond and that this
important non-pathological work will help to further the emerging
positive agenda for future work on this fascinating yet much maligned
topic.

Notes

1. This fails to acknowledge that this is a biased subset of individuals who are
   likely to be experiencing problems in general.
2. See Langdridge (2006) for more on this distinction.

References

Barker, M. (forthcoming 2013). Consent is a grey area? A comparison of understandings of consent in *Fifty Shades of Grey* and on the BDSM blogosphere.
Sexualities.

Barker, M. & Gill, R. (2012). Sexual subjectification and Bitchy Jones's Diary.
Psychology & Sexuality, 3(1), 26–40.

Barker, M., Iantaffi, A & Gupta, C. (2007). Kinky clients, kinky counselling? The
challenges and potentials of BDSM. In L. Moon (Ed.) *Feeling Queer or Queer
Feelings: Counselling and Sexual Cultures*. pp. 106–124. London: Routledge.

Barker, M. & Langdridge, D. (2009). Silencing accounts of already silenced sexualities. In R. Ryan-Flood & R. Gill (Eds.) *Secrecy and Silence in the Research Process:
Feminist Reflections*. pp. 67–79. London: Routledge.

Beckmann, A. (2001). 'Deconstructing Myths: The Social Construction of "Sadomasochism" Versus "Subjugated Knowledges" of Practitioners of Consensual
"SM"' *Journal of Criminal Justice and Popular Culture*, 8(2), 66–95.

Beckmann, A. (2009). *The Social Construction of Sexuality and Perversion: Deconstructing Sadomasochism*. Basingstoke: Palgrave Macmillan.

Denman, C. (2004). *Sexuality: A Biopsychosocial Approach*. London: Palgrave.

Deckha, M. (2011). Pain as culture: a postcolonial approach to S/M and women's
agency. *Sexualities*, 14(2), 129–150.

Downing, L. (2013). Safewording!: Kinkphobia and gender normativity in *Fifty
Shades of Grey*. *Psychology & Sexuality*, 4(1), 92–102.

Gosselin, C. & Wilson, G. (1980). *Sexual Variations: Fetishism, Sadomasochism and
Transvestism*. London: Faber and Faber.

Jeffreys, S. (1996). Heterosexuality and the desire for gender. In D. Richardson
(Ed.) *Theorising heterosexuality*. Buckingham: Open University Press.

Kleinplatz, P. & Moser, C. (2006). *Sadomasochism: Powerful Pleasures*. London:
Routledge.

Langdridge, D. (2005). Actively dividing selves: S/M and the thrill of disintegration. *Lesbian & Gay Psychology Review*, 6(3), 198–208.

Langdridge, D. (2006). Voices from the margins: SM and sexual citizenship.
Citizenship Studies, 10(4), pp. 373–389.

Langdridge, D. (2007). The time of the sadomasochist: Hunting with(in) the
'tribus'. In S. Seidman, N. Fischer & C. Meeks (Eds.) *Introducing the New Sexuality
Studies* [First published in hardback as *Handbook of the New Sexuality Studies* in
2006]. London: Routledge. pp. 280–287.

Langdridge, D. (2013, forthcoming). *Sex, Sexuality, Citizenship: Beyond the Boundaries of Belonging.* New York: Oxford University Press.

Langdridge, D. & Butt, T. (2004). A Hermeneutic Phenomenological Investigation of the Construction of Sadomasochistic Identities. *Sexualities*, 7(1), 31–53.

Langdridge, D. & Butt, T. W. (2005). The erotic construction of power exchange. *Journal of Constructivist Psychology*, 18(1), 65–73.

Lindemann, D. (2011). BDSM as therapy? *Sexualities*, 14(2), 151–172.

Moore, A. & Reynolds, P. (2004). Feminist approaches to sexual consent: A critical assessment. In M. Cowling & P. Reynolds (Eds.) *Making sense of sexual consent.* Aldershot: Ashgate.

Moser, C. & Levit, E. E (1987). An explanatory-descriptive study of a sadomasochistically oriented sample. *The Journal of Sex Research, 23,* 322–337.

Newmahr, S. (2011). *Playing on the Edge: Sadomasochism, Risk, and Intimacy.* Bloomington, IN: Indiana University Press.

Powls, J. & Davies, J. (2012). A description review of research relating to sadomasochism: considerations for clinical practice. *Deviant Behavior*, 33, 223–234.

Richter, J., de Visser, R.O., Rissel, C.E., Gruhlich, A.E. & Smith, A.M.A. (2008). Demographic and Psychosocial Features of Participants in Bondage and Discipline, "Sadomasochism" or Dominance and Submission (BDSM): Data from a National Survey. *Journal of Sexual Medicine*, 5, 1660–1668.

Ritchie, A. & Barker, M. (2005). Feminist SM: A contradiction in terms or a way of challenging gendered dynamics through sexual practice? *Lesbian & Gay Psychology Review*, 6(3), 227–239.

Rubin, G. (1984). Thinking sex: notes for a radical theory on the politics of sexuality. In C. Vance (ed.) *Pleasure and Danger: Exploring Female Sexuality* (pp. 267–319). London: Routledge.

Stiles, B.L. & Clark, R. (2011). BDSM: a subcultural analysis of sacrifices and delights. *Deviant Behavior*, 32, 158–189.

Taylor, G. W. (1997). The Discursive Construction and Regulation of Dissident Sexualities: The Case of SM, in J. M. Ussher (1997) *Body Talk: The Material and Discursive Regulation of Sexuality, Madness and Reproduction.* London: Routledge.

Taylor, G. W. and Ussher, J. (2001). Making Sense of S&M: A Discourse Analytic Account. *Sexualities*, 4(3), 293–314.

Weiss, M. (2006). Mainstreaming kink: the politics of BDSM representations in U.S. popular media. In P. Kleinplatz, & C. Moser, (Eds.) *Sadomasochism: Powerful Pleasures.* (pp. 103–132) Binghamton, NY: Haworth Press.

Welldon, E. V. (2002). *Ideas in Psychoanalysis: Sadomasochism.* Cambridge: Icon Books.

Wilkinson, E. (2007). Perverting Visual Pleasure: Representing Sadomasochism. *Sexualities*, 12(2), 181–198.

2
The Cultural Formation of S/M: History and Analysis*

Kathy Sisson

S/M's cultural visibility has increased dramatically over the past three decades. Recent corporate advertising campaigns from Saks Fifth Avenue, Continental Airlines and Ikea have featured S/M motifs and iconography. S/M themes punctuate bestselling books (*The Sexual life of Catherine M.*, 2001), mainstream movies (*Secretary*, 2002) and popular music (Madonna's *Erotica*, 1992). Contemporary fashion has embraced black leather, boots, collars, chains and other apparel evocative of S/M. Internet sites with explicit S/M content are readily accessible. And sexuality sections of most major bookstores feature manuals explaining S/M to potential participants.

Researchers continue to debate the prevalence of S/M behaviour (Hunt, 1974; Levitt, 1971). However, extant S/M research estimates 5–10% of the US population, or over 14 million individuals, currently engage in S/M activities (Kinsey, Pomeroy, Martin & Gephard, 1953; Moser, 1988; Reinisch with Beasley, 1990). Despite this cultural visibility and prevalence, the history of S/M practice and its relation to the larger culture remain relatively unstudied.

The utility of studying sex as part of the larger culture became apparent in the 1980s with the emergence of social constructionism (Irvine, 1994; Parker & Aggelton, 1999; Weeks, 1985). Researchers have applied theoretical, constructionist models to study a variety of sexual minority groups: gay and lesbian (D'Emilio, 1983; Rich, 1986; Rubin, 1984; Weeks, 1981), AIDS victims (Parker, Herdt & Carballo, 1991) and adolescents

---

* This chapter was first published as Sisson, K. (2005). The cultural formation of S/M: History and analysis. *Lesbian & Gay Psychology Review*, 6(3), 147–162. Thanks to the BPS for permission to reprint this article.

(Irvine, 1994). But to date no study has employed a cultural theory approach to explore the history and formation of the contemporary S/M phenomenon. This chapter draws upon previous theoretical contributions to provide a brief overview of sexual cultural theory and to present a new theoretical model of cultural function and formation. It then utilizes this model to frame a historical overview of S/M practice as it evolved from the sixteenth century to the present and to analyze S/M's role in contemporary culture. The chapter focuses primarily on American S/M history and culture, but references international and UK S/M cultural developments as well. It will conclude with recommendations for the utility of the model in organizing and understanding the historical evolution of other sexual minority communities which remain similarly under-researched.

Sexual culture theory

A sexual culture may be defined as a collective system of meanings and practices that emerges from historically specific social and psychological conditions (D'Emilio, 1983; Hostetler & Herdt, 1998; Padgug, 1979). Sexual cultures issued from nineteenth-century modernization processes (Herdt, 1997; Rubin, 1984). In contemporary Western society, multiple sexual cultures (also referred to as 'subcultures') emerge, proliferate and co-exist alongside the monogamous, reproductive heterosexual paradigm (Hostetler & Herdt, 1998; Taylor, 1996). Sexual cultures may be viewed as 'performing' certain functions for their members and evolving through discernable stages (Herdt, 1997; Hostetler & Herdt, 1998; Weeks, 1981). A new theoretical model of sexual culture function and formation which synthesizes previous scholarship follows.

Sexual culture function model

Sexual culture functions may be summarized as (1) demarcating boundaries between the sexual culture ('inside')[1] and the larger, paradigmatic culture ('outside'), (2) providing a story of origin and historical context, (3) establishing a code of behaviour which prescribes appropriate and inappropriate conduct, (4) creating a system of shared meanings about specific desires and behaviours, (5) providing a means of social reproduction that allows newcomers to access and participate in the sexual culture and (6) generating sexual identity.

One aspect of sexual identity, therefore, would be its generative relationship with sexual culture (Herdt, 1997; Hostetler & Herdt, 1998; Irvine, 1994; Rubin, 1984; Taylor, 1996; Weeks, 1981). Sexual identity may be defined as a template for organizing sexual desires and subject–object relationships (Herdt, 1997). Sexual identity formation emerges from the confluence of multifaceted personal and social phenomena, including sexual cultures (Hostetler & Herdt, 1998), personal narratives (Plummer, 1995), sexual experiences (Plummer, 1995), educational processes and social interactions (Weeks, 1981). From the mid-nineteenth to the mid-twentieth century, a binary sexual identity schema based sexual identity on the sex of the object choice, limiting available sexual identities to homosexual or heterosexual (Herdt, 1997; Hostetler & Herdt, 1998). In the latter half of the twentieth century, individuals began constructing new sexual identities based primarily on individual subjectivity, transgender and queer being perhaps the most visible (Connell & Dowsett, 1992; Hostetler & Herdt, 1998).

Sexual culture formation model

Delineating stages of sexual culture evolution, while artificially imposing order on inchoate historical events, provides a useful organizational framework. The stages of sexual culture evolution may be summarized as: (1) contacts – discrete individuals sharing common desires locate and establish contact with each other; (2) networks – contacts expand to form loosely linked assemblages of like-minded individuals; (3) communities –networks merge and coalesce into unaffiliated, regional associations based on face-to-face interactions, sharing common interests, ideology and public spaces; (4) social movements – communities grow and, often galvanized by the harassment and discrimination that accompany increasing social visibility, gather the economic, political and social momentum necessary to support effective activist campaigns; and (5) sexual cultures – ultimately, the communities and social movements expand and merge within a shared system of meaning and practices; a new sexual culture takes its place alongside the dominant sexual culture as one of an increasing number of twentieth-century sexual cultures.

Historical overview of S/M practice: cultural formation

This paper defines S/M as a broad range of consensual, erotic, interpersonal interactions involving the administration and reception of pain and/or the enactment of dominant and submissive power dynamics. Historical evidence suggests that behaviours imitative of those we contemporarily identify as S/M have occurred for millennia (Brandt,

1963; Ellis, 1905; see also Eulenberg, cited in Ellis, 1905; Keuls, 1985; Taylor, 1996). However, historical accuracy precludes imposition of modern terminology and concepts on behaviours transpiring with different meanings in different contexts (Herdt, 1997; Padgug, 1979). The words 'sadism' and 'masochism' entered the lexicon in 1886 in Krafft-Ebing's *Psychopathia Sexualis* (Krafft-Ebing, 1886/1953); Freud coined the term 'sadomasochism' in 1905 in *Three Contributions to the Theory of Sex* (Freud, 1905/1938). Therefore this paper designates behaviours resembling contemporary S/M practice that occurred prior to these dates as 'S/M-type' behaviour.

Up until the 1940s, no clear distinction between sexual orientation and S/M practice appears in the literature. A distinct gay male leather community developed in the USA in the 1940s and much has been written about its formation (Rubin, 1994, 1997). Distinct heterosexual and lesbian S/M communities emerged in the 1970s. Due in large part to the vituperous feminist sex wars during the second wave of feminism, a considerable literature on lesbian S/M communities exists as well (e.g. Califia, 1981). I suggest that these three distinct S/M communities, gay, lesbian and heterosexual, co-exist today as part of the larger S/M sexual culture. However, a paucity of data exists regarding the development and characteristics of heterosexual S/M communities and culture. In its historical overview from the 1940s to the 1980s, this chapter focuses on the formation of a primarily heterosexual S/M community, although same-sex interactions quite likely transpired between some of its members.

Stage 1: contacts (1600s–1900s)

Historical evidence of contacts between individuals engaging in S/M-type behaviour dates from the seventeenth century and proliferates up through the turn of the twentieth century. Medical literature from seventeenth-century Europe referenced flagellation as a means to shorten the male refractory period and as a remedy for erectile dysfunction and female lack of desire (Boileau, 1700/1903; Eulenberg, cited in Ellis, 1905; Meibomius, 1639/1718). Popular works, such as *The Presbyterian Lash* (anon., 1661), *Venice Preserved* (Otway & Kelsall, 1682/1969) and *The Virtuoso* (Shadwell, Nicolson & Rodes, 1676/1992), associated flagellation with sexual pleasure, the latter positioning it in an English brothel.

Ellis describes whipping as a 'well-known ... sexual stimulant' in England (1905: 133) by the eighteenth century. Brothels specializing in S/M-type interactions began to appear in the major cities of Europe, and S/M-type motifs grew increasingly prevalent in eighteenth-century literature. Cleland's *Fanny Hill* (1748/1986) described an incident of mutual whipping between a prostitute and client in an English brothel. In *Confessions* (1782/1953), Rousseau attributes his sexual masochism to childhood whippings. And the Marquis de Sade's works describe a plethora of S/M-type behaviours, some of which transpired in Parisian brothels.

The nineteenth century's significant social transformations modernized human sexuality (Herdt, 1997; Rubin, 1984). The shift from agrarian to urban social organization provided individuals with newfound anonymity, privacy and contact with diverse populations and behaviours. Industrialization gave rise to dramatized power relations. Secularization, consumerism, the rise of the middle class and increased leisure time all contributed to new concepts of individual subjectivity, including sex and gender. And many scientists and scholars began turning their attentions to sex research.

Brothels specializing in S/M-type interactions flourished across Europe and in certain American urban centres in the nineteenth century. Some proved quite lucrative; Theresa Berkelely's flagellation brothel in England reportedly made $20,000 in eight years (Tannahill, 1982).

Nineteenth-century literature containing S/M-type themes grew increasingly popular. *Venus Schoolmistress* (anon., 1830) references Berkeley's flagellation brothel. *The Pearl* (anon., 1870), an erotic magazine widely circulated in upper class society, included stories of flagellation. *The Lustful Turk* (anon., 1828) described sexual dominance and 'violent, aggressive sexuality ... a good example of nineteenth century pornography with Sadian overtones' (Beck, 1999: 386).

Although these and similar works with S/M-type themes attained widespread popularity, Krafft-Ebing's publication of *Psychopathia Sexualis* (1886) brought 'sadism' and 'masochism' squarely into the cultural discourse and cultural consciousness. *Psychopathia Sexualis* conferred typology, aetiology and pathology on previously unremarkable sexual behaviours and desires. Prior to its publication, S/M-type behaviour was considered neither sick nor sinful, regarded often as a medical curiosity, if at all (Bullough, 1977; Levitt, 1971). It captivated mainstream readers and catapulted sadism and masochism into the public arena. Krafft-Ebing described sadism and masochism as individual phenomena, a precedent followed by subsequent sexologists until the late 1960s, when social scientists observed that S/M was no longer an isolated, individual behaviour, but rather had become a social phenomenon (Gephard, 1969). *Psychopathia Sexualis* also popularized the binary sexual identity schema based on gender or sex of object choice – homosexual and heterosexual.

Stage 2: networks (1900s–1970s)

Nineteenth-century social developments led to the beginning of the modern American S/M phenomenon – the formation of S/M practitioner networks. Changes in early twentieth-century S/M practice also facilitated network formation. Privatization, novel materials and behaviours and new contact strategies were particularly integral.

The locus of S/M practice shifted from flagellation brothels to private homes and parties in the first two decades of the twentieth century. Flagellation brothels' role diminished. In the USA, the first sexual revolution and World War I made non-commercial sex more acceptable and available. Law enforcement agencies in both Europe and the USA began suppressing brothel prostitution. Although a corresponding rise in street prostitution included S/M-oriented prostitution (Bienvenu, 1998) and some brothels specializing in S/M interactions maintained successful clandestine operations, S/M practice moved increasingly into the private arena.

The materials and practices American S/M practitioners employed at these private parties also shifted in the first few decades of the twentieth century. Flagellation brothels offered a fairly narrow range of practices centred on spanking and flagellation with various contrivances (Bienvenu, 1998). They employed 'soft media' – materials such as fur, satin, velvet and silk (Bienvenu, 1998). By the 1930s, S/M practitioners' range of behaviours had expanded to involve elaborate restraints, specialized equipment, highly stylized fashion and electrical and medical technology (Bienvenu, 1998). The materials they incorporated shifted to 'hard media' – such as leather and metal (Bienvenu, 1998). These S/M products tended to be expensive and early S/M practitioners were generally affluent (Bienvenu, 1998). In subsequent decades, practitioners also incorporated rubber and latex.

S/M practitioners' primary contact strategy was carefully worded advertisements placed in underground magazines. Code words and veiled references to 'discipline' conveyed an S/M-oriented subtext to like-minded individuals (R. Roberts, personal communication, 2000). As small networks of S/M practitioners began to form, face-to-face referrals also integrated an increasing number of aficionados (Bienvenu, 1998).

Most early American S/M practitioner networks formed around the producers of S/M-related products (Bienvenu, 1998). A small number of east coast artists, photographers, artisans, writers and publishers provided S/M apparel, equipment, catalogues, mail order services and erotica. Most were practitioners themselves and their S/M products were often a sideline to the production of equestrian and burlesque supplies (Bienvenu, 1998).

A fetish 'family tree' of S/M erotica producers began forming in the 1930s with Charles Guyette's emergence as a prominent S/M erotica producer. Guyette sold S/M photography and equipment through under-the-counter sales in his theatrical supply store and by mail order in underground catalogues. He anchored the earliest network of American S/M practitioners and provided support for subsequent generations of S/M producers (Bienvenu, 1998). His widespread social interconnectedness and influence on successive generations of S/M producers facilitated S/M network formation for the next three decades. Certain contemporary S/M producers and practitioner networks trace their origins back to Guyette's enterprise (Bienvenu, 1998).

In the 1940s, mainstream 'cheesecake' magazines (men's magazines featuring scantily clad, voluptuous women) began incorporating S/M iconography, which dramatically expanded the early S/M producers' cultural visibility. Although Guyette had attained prominence in underground S/M networks, his audience remained relatively small; cheesecake magazines reached hundreds of thousands of mainstream consumers a month. Robert Harrison published several popular cheesecake magazines containing S/M-themed art, photographs and advertisements from a second generation of S/M producers, many of whom Guyette sponsored (Bienvenu, 1998).

Harrison's successful publications provided venues for John Coutts, Irving Klaw and Leonard Burtman to debut as second-generation S/M producers. Artist, photographer and writer John Coutts emerged from Guyette's social circle and went on to publish *Bizarre* magazine, an explicitly S/M-oriented magazine, from 1946 to 1956. Irving Klaw, primarily a photographer, achieved notoriety with his fetish photographs of Bettie Page, many of which appeared in Harrison's magazines. Klaw also made the first bondage film in 16 mm in 1949. Leonard Burtman trained as a photographer with Harrison, and by the early 1950s, had established a fetish publishing empire that survived into 1980s (Bienvenu, 1998). Each of these artists and businessmen continued to sponsor successive generations of S/M producers (Bienvenu, 1998).

Greg Day also rose to prominence as a private practitioner and wealthy patron in the interconnected social networks from the late 1930s to the 1960s. He shared close friendships with Guyette and Coutts and social relationships with most of the other S/M producers (Klaw apparently limited himself to business relationships) (Bienvenu, 1998). Day hosted numerous private play parties at his home in New York which were attended primarily by couples (Bienvenu, 1998). Other wealthy practitioners and patrons began equipping their homes with S/M paraphernalia and dungeons, but Day remained the most visible private practitioner. Offshoots of his social circle still exist in contemporary east coast S/M circles (Bienvenu, 1998).

The public visibility of S/M iconography increased with its presence in mainstream cheesecake magazines, but the fear of discrimination, harassment and legal prosecution compelled the S/M producer/practitioner networks to remain underground. A number of S/M producers were imprisoned on obscenity charges and driven out of business by the burden of continuous legal investigations from the Post Office, FBI, state and local law enforcement agencies and social morality groups (Bienvenu, 1998). In efforts to avoid prosecution, S/M producers began censoring themselves, withholding images that included pubic hair, heel heights over three inches and men and women together in sexual situations (Bienvenu, 1998).

Burtman was the only early S/M producer with sufficient resources and legal advisors to survive these investigations (Bienvenu, 1998). His nationwide S/M erotica distribution network included mail order catalogues, correspondence publications, books, magazines, photographs and the first 35 mm mass-distributed fetish feature film, *Satan in High Heels*. His expansive social circle included Harrison, Day, Klaw, Guyette, Coutts, as well as professional dominatrices, transsexual stage performers and numerous private practitioners (Bienvenu, 1998). Like Klaw, Burtman's photographs of Bettie Page helped leverage him into popular culture and, in the 1960s, he successfully transitioned into mainstream pornography.

Legal prosecution of US S/M producers intensified in the 1950s, until the Warren Court began its increasingly liberal obscenity interpretations. *Roth v. U.S.*, 354 U.S. 476 (1957), narrowed definitions of obscenity and added the 'prurient interest' criterion. *Manual Enterprises Inc. v. Day*, 370 U.S. 478 (1962), added 'patently offensive' to obscenity criteria. *A Book Named "John Cleland's Memoirs of a Woman of Pleasure" v. Attorney General of Massachusetts*, 383 U.S. 413 (1966), rearticulated these rulings and established three criteria for determining obscenity: (1) that the dominant theme of the material taken as a whole appeals to a prurient interest in sex, (2) that the material is patently offensive because it affronts contemporary community standards and (3) the material is utterly without socially redeeming value. (In *Miller v. California*, 413 U.S. 15 (1973), the Burger Court added the 'SLAPS' test to obscenity criteria, ruling that only material lacking serious literary, artistic, political or scientific value could be characterized as obscene.)

These rulings changed law enforcement agencies' policies and facilitated the growth of an increasingly explicit pornography industry. S/M iconography began appearing in popular pornographic movies, magazines and books, and a burgeoning pornography industry engulfed many small, independent S/M erotica producers. Yet, despite the Warren Court's rulings, the FBI and Post Office continued investigating and charging the remaining small S/M erotica producers with obscenity (Bienvenue, 1998). Attempting to thwart these investigations, small publishers masked their S/M-themed works as pseudo-scientific, psychological essays on human sexual behaviour (R. Roberts, personal communication, 2000). But ultimately, independent S/M producers became increasingly disadvantaged in the marketplace.

Several technological and marketing shifts in the 1960s further eroded the small, independent S/M producers' roles. S/M equipment and apparel became cheaper and easier to mass-produce with the introduction of PVC and less expensive, more versatile leather. 'House of Milan' opened in the USA as the first public retail outlet for fetish clothes and equipment, a precedent which led to the increasing availability of S/M products.[2] And mass media's increasing role as cultural choreographer facilitated the popularization of fetish as fashion. Haute couture designers and photographers, particularly Yves St. Laurent, Helmut Newton and Vogue, began featuring S/M motifs, PVC and leather into their work. Television shows introduced characters clad in latex and leather, most notably Emma Peel in *The Avengers*.

Stage 3: communities (1970s–1980s)

The 1960s' cultural shifts facilitated the formation of S/M communities in the early 1970s. Communities began forming around nascent S/M support groups. Two of the earliest groups remain the largest in the USA: The Eulenspiegal Society (TES) formed in New York in 1971 and the Society of Janus (SOJ) formed in San Francisco in 1974. Although both groups began as pansexual S/M support organizations, their memberships became increasingly heterosexual within the first several years of their formation. The HIV/AIDS crisis in the 1980s further divided the gay, lesbian and heterosexual S/M communities. The following discussion focuses on San Francisco S/M community formation which, while distinct, is also illustrative of S/M cultural formation patterns occurring more generally throughout the decade.

Society of Janus and San Francisco S/M community formation

Cynthia Slater, a bisexual, professional dominatrix (Weymouth, 1999), organized SOJ. She drew initial members from pre-existing, unaffiliated S/M networks – primarily gay men from the leather community (Weymouth, 1999). These early members' goals were to develop an educational S/M support group and to sponsor regular S/M 'play parties' (parties at which S/M practitioners socialize and engage in S/M interactions). They established rules of conduct and guidelines for S/M interactions, conducted orientations for new members and began providing educational programs on safety and techniques (Weymouth, 1999). Initially SOJ members met in private apartments, and SOJ remained underground for the first several years. By the late 1970s, SOJ secured meeting space in a number of different public venues, ranging from bar backrooms to liberal churches and sex clubs and gradually emerged into public view.

SOJ encountered organizational obstacles in addition to the ideological and personality conflicts endemic to most embryonic organizations. It attracted a disproportionate number of men to women and found it difficult to increase female membership. Women comprised roughly one-ninth of members regularly attending early meetings; the dearth of female members extended well into the 1980s (Weymouth, 1999). To encourage female participation, in 1976 SOJ formed a women's outreach group called Cardea (Weymouth, 1999). Cardea arranged venues for S/M-curious women to socialize, ask questions and explore their S/M interests.[3] SOJ also solicited potential female members by posting flyers, advertising in local magazines and face-to-face referrals (Weymouth, 1999).

Additionally heterosexual S/M practitioners, having emerged from the small, covert, S/M practitioner networks of the preceding decades, were reluctant to 'come out' about their S/M interests and risk legal persecution or the loss of social privilege (Weymouth, 1999). Gay men from the leather community had been out about their S/M orientations for decades and were seemingly less concerned (Weymouth, 1999). But, by the mid-1980s, heterosexual male and female membership began to increase; SOJ's composition shifted; and gay, lesbian and heterosexual S/M practitioners moved into discrete communities.

Stage 4: social movement (1980s–1990s)

By the early 1980s, the public visibility of SOJ, other S/M organizations and S/M sexuality in general began increasing considerably. Several
social phenomena in the ensuing decade politicized the discrete gay,
lesbian and heterosexual S/M communities, and by the end of the 1980s,
these communities coalesced into a larger social movement, demanding
to participate in the cultural sexual discourse. Influences in the 1980s
included a rapid expansion in S/M's local, national and international
cultural visibility, the HIV/AIDS crisis, a second wave of technological
change and the emergence of S/M activism.

Cultural visibility

Locally, in the San Francisco Bay Area, the cultural visibility of S/M
communities grew rapidly in the 1980s. Other S/M organizations began
forming and holding S/M play parties, meetings, orientations and educational programs. In 1982, SOJ began publishing a monthly calendar to
keep practitioners informed of the increasing number of Bay Area S/M
community events (Weymouth, 1999). A public television documentary,
One Foot Out of the Closet (1980), was the first television program in San
Francisco to investigate S/M (Weymouth, 1999). Its conclusion that S/M
practitioners were not especially different from any other group 'cracked
open the bubble of the underground' (K. Sunlove in Weymouth, 1999:
20), bringing S/M practice and practitioners new public visibility. Several
S/M events debuting in San Francisco in the 1980s have become urban
tradition. The annual Folsom Street Fair is perhaps the most renown. The
fair, a five-block celebration of the leather/S/M communities, originated
in 1984; it now ranks as the third largest public gathering in California,
attracting 400,000 aficionados from across the globe (Mickic, 2005).
SOJ and other S/M organizations sponsor charity fundraising events
during the fair. In 1986, SOJ also provided its first organized contingent
in the Gay Freedom Day Parade and continues the annual tradition.
Flea markets, bondage beauty pageants, slave auctions and a variety of
special play parties debuting in the 1980s occur regularly throughout
the Bay Area.

Nationally and internationally, S/M support groups proliferated,
organized and coalesced with increasing economic, social and political power in the 1980s. The National Leather Association formed in
1986 to provide information about S/M, support for political activism
and outreach education for law enforcement and the media. In 1989,
Tony DeBlase designed the leather flag, a continuing symbol for the

leather/S/M community worldwide. The Leather Archives and Museum, devoted to preserving and documenting S/M history, opened in Chicago in 1996. The National Coalition of Sexual Freedom (NCSF), a US-based non-profit S/M and sexual minority advocacy organization, formed in 1997. S/M conventions even began booking conference space in corporate hotels and holding play parties in the hotel ballrooms.

Media presence and technological change

S/M's media presence increased dramatically in the 1980s and 1990s. The S/M communities' proliferation and coalescence generated increasing media attention and commerce of its own, and corporations began to recognize the marketing appeal of S/M iconography and narratives. Mainstream publishers released S/M-themed books, no longer disguised as pseudo-psychological studies. Memoirs, scientific research, instructive/educational manuals and essays about various aspects of S/M appeared in libraries and on mainstream bookstore shelves. Major studios produced a number of popular movies incorporating S/M themes and iconography: *9 ½ Weeks* (1986), *Blue Velvet* (1986), *Basic Instinct* (1992), *Exit to Eden* (1994), *Pulp Fiction* (1994), *Paris France* (1994) and *8 mm* (1999). And corporate advertising campaigns (Haagen-Dazs ice cream, Ma Griffe perfume, Boddington's beer) incorporated S/M iconography as they pursued innovative marketing strategies that transmogrified risk into commodity for an audience jaded by mainstream sexual imagery (Beckmann, 2001).

The second wave of technological change centred on the Internet. With Internet access, individuals unable or unwilling to access established S/M organizations could acquire wide-ranging information about S/M. The Internet provided new contact strategies, cyber venues and chat rooms for like-minded individuals to meet and even play online. It also spawned the formation of 'munches', frequent, informal gatherings, usually convened in local restaurants, for individuals with S/M interests to meet and socialize. The first munch was organized on the Web in 1992 by an American woman who later became a SOJ member (Weymouth, 1999). The concept took hold and munches now flourish nationally and internationally.

Other technological and marketing shifts also impacted S/M's cultural expansion. Inexpensive, readily available plastics and power tools made home production of S/M equipment and apparel more feasible. And mass-produced, commercial S/M products proliferated, made ever more accessible through online sales and explicit mail order catalogues.

HIV/AIDS and S/M activism

In San Francisco, in the early 1980s, the increase in heterosexual male SOJ members changed the groups' focus and composition; and by mid-decade, the HIV/AIDS epidemic intensified the emigration of gay, lesbian and heterosexual S/M practitioners into discrete communities. SOJ's new heterosexual members brought widely divergent S/M interests, some of which fell outside the original gay male members' definitions of S/M (Weymouth, 1999). When the HIV/AIDS crisis erupted, some heterosexuals feared contracting the disease from gay men at S/M play parties, and gay men felt increasingly less welcome at pansexual S/M events (Weymouth, 1999). As heterosexual membership increased, gay male membership declined and many gay men returned to the leather community. Pansexual S/M events virtually disappeared and the larger Bay Area S/M community lost scores of its most knowledgeable leaders to HIV/AIDS. By the mid-1980s, SOJ was primarily a heterosexual organization (Weymouth, 1999). However, the HIV/AIDS crisis also raised sexual minority communities' political consciousness, galvanizing and politicizing particularly the gay and lesbian communities nationally and internationally. S/M activism emerged from the confluence of the HIV/AIDS crisis, S/M's growing public visibility, S/M organizations' more voluble public voice and S/M practitioners' escalating experiences with discrimination and legal prosecution. S/M activism has focused on public education, legal prosecution and, more recently, mental health issues.

As S/M's cultural visibility has grown, its practitioners have encountered a corresponding increase in discrimination, harassment and legal prosecution on consent, obscenity and assault charges. NCSF conducted the *National Violence and Discrimination Survey* of S/M, leather and fetish communities in 1998. It found that of 1017 respondents, 36% reported incidents of harassment and/or violence and 30% reported incidents of discrimination involving employment and/or child custody (National Coalition for Sexual Freedom, 1998). NCSF's *Incident Response Overviews* from 2002 and 2003 suggest these experiences continue. Other S/M practitioners have reported loss of employment, child custody privileges and security clearances (Moser, 1988). S/M activists work to educate the public, law enforcement and media about S/M in order to reduce such incidents. Two particular areas of interest are (a) legal prosecution and (b) depathologization.

(a) Recent legal cases involving S/M have focused on consent and obscenity issues. Contemporary S/M organizations promote and share the behavioural code, 'safe, sane and consensual' (Brame, Brame & Jacobs, 1996; Miller & Devon, 1995). According to S/M community standards, only consensual S/M interactions constitute S/M; non-consensual interactions constitute abuse (Brame, Brame & Jacobs, 1996; Miller & Devon, 1995; Moser & Madeson, 1996). Therefore legal cases interpreting consent bear directly on S/M practitioners' ability to engage in their desired behaviour. Recent consent-related cases have raised two intertwined issues: whether consensual S/M interactions constitute assault, and whether an individual can legally consent to assault.

In England, in 1980, the judge in the Spanner trial convicted five gay men practicing consensual S/M of serious assault. The House of Lords upheld the convictions on appeal, declining to make an exception in existing English law that allows individuals to consent to assault or bodily harm in the service of public benefit (surgery, contact sports, military training) (Farshea, 1999). Moreover, under English law, individuals who consent to receptive S/M may be charged having aided and abetted the assault on their own person (Farshea, 1999; see also Chaline & Pendal, 2005).

Jovanovic and Attleboro were seminal US cases involving consent and assault issues and served to politicize S/M communities nationwide. The judge in the 1998 Jovanovic case also ruled that consent was no defence to assault. However, an appeals court overturned the ruling on evidentiary grounds. Oliver Jovanovic recently filed suit against New York City for false arrest and malicious prosecution. In the 2000 Attleboro case, a woman was charged with possession of a dangerous weapon (a wooden spoon) and assault, despite the testimony of her partner that their interactions were consensual. The charges stemmed from a police raid of a private party in Attleboro, MA. After considerable publicity the charges were eventually dropped. The highest-level recent obscenity case appears destined for the US Supreme Court. *Nitke v. Ashcroft*, filed by the NCSF in 2001, challenges the use of 'local community standards' to define obscenity on the Internet. The clause is part of the 1996 Communications Decency Act. Testimony concluded in late 2004. The ruling is pending and both sides have already declared their intention to appeal.

The harassment and legal prosecution levelled against S/M practitioners has galvanized and politicized S/M communities nationally and internationally. Just as Stonewall politicized the gay and lesbian rights movement, these events and cases have impelled S/M community activists to begin advocating for equal protection under the law and freedom from discrimination. In pursuit of these goals, S/M activists have recently turned their energies to interrogating the mental health profession's diagnoses of sexual sadism and sexual masochism as pathology.

(b) The American Psychiatric Association diagnoses sexual sadism and sexual masochism as paraphiliac sexual disorders (APA, *Diagnostic and Statistical Manual of Mental Disorders – DSM-IV-TR, 2000*). However, several researchers have challenged the assumption that S/M practitioners exhibit poor mental health or are markedly different than the general population in ways other than their sexual preferences. Gosselin, Wilson and Barrett administered the Eysenck Personality Questionnaire to 57 S/M-identified women and found that, although the women showed 'high psychoticism, low neuroticism and high libido traditionally associated with a stereotypic "male" image...this is not to say that the behaviour of S/M women should be regarded as pathological...' (1991: 14–15). Breslow (1987) conducted studies of dominants/sadists, masochists/submissives, and S/M practitioners who assume both roles. He administered the Rotter's Internal vs. External Locus of Control and Burger and Cooper's Desirability of Control Inventories and found that all three groups believed 'that they are capable of exercising control over their environment', as measured by the former, and 'fell into the category of high desire for control' on the latter (Breslow, 1987: 999). In general, belief in one's ability to control one's environment indicates more positive level of mental health (Yalom, 1980).

Moser concludes that although 'S/M practitioners, like members of any other sexual orientation, can have psychiatric problems...they have not been shown to have any particular psychiatric problems or even any unique problems associated with their orientation' (1998: 53, 57). He also notes that the *DSM-IV-TR's* diagnostic criteria for paraphiliac behaviour is so broad as to apply to nearly everyone (Moser, 2001). Moser and others are currently working to have sexual sadism, sexual masochism and the other paraphilias removed entirely from the DSM (Moser, 2002; Moser & Kleinplatz, 2005).

Iconoclastic researchers suggest that diagnoses of mental illness are essentially social constructions used to control behaviour not conforming to the cultural norm (Levine & Troiden, 1988; Moser, 2001;

Szasz, 1974). DSM diagnoses influence the criminal justice system, the medical profession, public policy, the media and public opinion. Culturally the pathologization of consensual S/M may impede social acceptance of a sexual outlet that research indicates may be benign for many practitioners. Individually pathologization may contribute to internalized, negative self-images among S/M practitioners. Echoing the removal of homosexuality from the DSM in 1973, researchers, clinicians and activists are beginning to challenge the DSM diagnosis of sadism and masochism.

Stage 5: sexual culture (2000 to present)

The model of cultural function and formation this paper proposes defines sexual culture as a collective system of meanings and practices which emerges from historically specific social and psychological conditions. It posits that sexual cultures evolve through a five-stage developmental sequence and perform certain functions for their members. The preceding historical overview suggests that S/M cultural formation has been inextricably linked with the surrounding social and psychological climate and conforms to the proposed cultural formation model. Additionally S/M communities and organizations appear to perform the functions predicted by the cultural function model. Therefore this paper suggests that an embryonic S/M sexual culture emerged in the late 1990s. The following analysis summarizes the ways in which the S/M communities and organizations comprising S/M sexual culture perform the cultural functions.

Cultural functions

Contemporary S/M communities and organizations provide certain cultural functions for their members. In various ways, they: (1) demarcate boundaries, (2) provide a story of origin, (3) establish codes of behaviour, (4) create a system of shared meanings, (5) provide a means of social reproduction and (6) generate sexual identity.

First, boundaries between inside and outside S/M culture create 'safe' spaces for practitioners to acknowledge publicly their S/M interests and to engage in S/M practice. S/M support groups, play parties, S/M conventions, S/M-oriented public events, S/M-friendly businesses, S/M-friendly therapists and S/M-themed publications and art all provide non-judgmental, protected environments for S/M practitioners. Second, many S/M organizations, including SOJ, chronicle their stories of origin in written and oral histories. Email lists devoted to discussing S/M/leather history exist online. Scholars and S/M practitioners have

written numerous books and articles on historical aspects of S/M practice. The Leather Archives and Museum's stated mission is to document
and preserve S/M/leather history. And the Museum of Sex in New York
mounted an historical overview of S/M at its opening in 2002. Third,
the overarching credo of S/M behaviour, safe, sane and consensual, is
widely recognized and respected by S/M practitioners (Brame, Brame &
Jacobs, 1996; Easton & Liszt, 2000; Miller & Devon, 1995). Guidelines
for S/M interactions, including preliminary negotiations about what will
transpire, a 'safe word' which halts or slows S/M play and 'aftercare'
arrangements for monitoring participants' post-play reactions, are de
rigueur (Easton & Liszt, 2000; Wiseman, 1996). Individuals known to
violate the guidelines are often marginalized by local S/M communities
and expelled from S/M events (Brame, Brame & Jacobs, 1996).

Fourth, S/M practitioners share a system of meanings about their
sexual behaviour, 'which are culturally produced, learned and reinforced by participation in the S/M subculture' (Weinberg, 1987: 51–52).
S/M interactions are understood to be consensual, collaborative and
mutually defined; and they occur within a context of sexual expression,
role-play and fantasy (Patrias, 1978; Weinberg, Williams & Moser,
1984). Fifth, to facilitate new members' entry to S/M culture, many
S/M organizations offer orientation meetings and mentoring programs.
Orientations usually provide a history of the organization, a forum for
questions and explanations about its rules, guidelines and educational
and social resources. Mentoring programs pair new members with
more experienced members to smooth the integration process. The
system of munches also provides safe and supportive environments for
newcomers, as well as public access for the curious. Finally, researchers
theorize that sexual identity generates in relation to sexual culture,
through historical and personal narratives, social interactions, educational processes, exclusionary boundaries and culturally specific vocab-
ularies (Herdt, 1997; Hostetler & Herdt, 1998; Irvine, 1994; Plummer,
1995; Rubin, 1984; Taylor, 1996; Weeks, 1981). Accordingly this paper
posits that S/M as a sexual identity generates in relation to contemporary
S/M's cultural functions and is available as one of the new, post-modern
sexual identities based on internal subjectivity. Akin to Hostetler and
Herdt's (1998) observations about queer identity and culture, S/M
practitioners may move fluidly in and out of the various roles available
within S/M culture[4]; and they may hold S/M as one of multiple, simultaneous sexual identities or as a primary, more fixed sexual identity
that takes priority over their partners' sex or gender (Califia, 1994;
Moser, 1998). Akin to Plummer's (1995) suggestion about the role of

personal narrative in sexual identity formation, S/M practitioners draw upon narratives forged in a complex nexus of S/M cultural experiences to constitute their chosen, and changeable, S/M sexual identities.

S/M's role in contemporary culture

S/M practice and the cultural conditions in which it evolved over the past two centuries share a reflexive relationship. Nineteenth-century social transformations created a fertile environment for the formation of S/M practitioner networks and the subsequent formation of S/M sexual culture. As work moved from home to industry, new power relations emerged between employer and employee, and complex power dynamics became a ubiquitous feature of modern society. Social organization and sexuality grew increasingly complex as well. New possibilities for lifestyles, sexual relations, employment, leisure time and autonomy gave impetus to the formation of a variety of new social networks. As S/M practice and ideology became more publicly visible, it, in turn, impacted on the larger culture.

Several researchers have explored the nexus of this modernization process and S/M practice. Baumeister (1988) observed that increasingly complex social conditions of modernization created anxiety and pressure as individuals shouldered new responsibilities, public personas, decisions and competition. He suggested that masochistic interactions may have provided temporary relief. Masochistic interactions would provide 'a temporary and powerful escape from high-level awareness of self as an abstract, temporally extended, symbolically constructed identity, to a low-level, temporally constricted awareness of self as physical body, focusing on immediate sensations (both painful and pleasant) and on being a sexual object' (Baumeister, 1988: 54). By temporarily adopting a masochistic identity, individuals could escape the 'burden of selfhood' and achieve respite from the demands of modern society.

Gephard (1969) also related S/M practice to the increasing complexity of industrialized society. He suggested that 'sadomasochism ... seems the monopoly of well-developed civilizations' and that 'it may be that a society must be extremely complex and heavily reliant upon symbolism before the inescapable repressions and frustrations of life in such a society can be expressed symbolically in sadomasochism' (Gephard, 1969: 80). Weinberg (1994) suggests six prerequisite social criteria for the institutionalization of S/M interests into S/M culture: embedded power relations, social acceptance of aggression, unequal power distribution, leisure time, imagination and creativity.

However, these theories do not fully account for the late twentieth-century's dramatic acceleration of S/M cultural formation. Other theorists have suggested that unique twentieth-century social conditions may have facilitated this stage of S/M's cultural development. McClintock (1993) suggests S/M is a uniquely well-suited sexuality for post-modern, post-procreative society because it flaunts socially constructed power, gender roles, identity and eroticism. McClintock proposes several ways in which S/M accomplishes this: (1) S/M subverts reified social power relations by creating and enacting exaggerated power roles and by appropriating the privilege to punish; (2) S/M challenges the boundaries of sanctioned gender role behaviour by allowing either gender to assume dominant and submissive roles; (3) S/M mocks the concept of a unitary, fixed identity by allowing participants to move fluidly in and out of an S/M sexual identity and by facilitating participants' adoption of various fantasy and S/M roles; and (4) S/M deconstructs the paradigm of genitally oriented eroticism by utilizing non-genital, non-erogenous sites on the body for sexual arousal.

Foucault (1982) observed that in post-sexual revolution, post-procreative societies, sexual encounters are easily arranged, eliding the novelty, uncertainty and tension that leant drama to sexual interactions in the past. In this context, he viewed S/M as a power game to heighten sexual intensity. Lee (1979) also viewed S/M sex as a game, as the epitome and ritualization of recreational sex. The ritualized nature of S/M may also help explain S/M culture's late twentieth-century appeal. The 1960s initiated a period of social upheaval that extended to the century's close. The Vietnam War and Watergate eroded pubic trust in political leaders. The civil rights movement radically reorganized racial relations. The sexual revolution undermined traditional concepts of interpersonal, romantic relationships. The second wave of feminism ushered in new types of gender relations. The gay and lesbian rights movement challenged the hegemonic heterosexual paradigm. A new sexual identity schema based on individual subjectivity confounded the established binary – homosexual or heterosexual – sexual identity system. Post-modern, social constructionist and deconstructionist theory eroded the comfortable foundation of objective truth. HIV/AIDS created terror around genitally oriented sexual behaviours. The traditional ideologies crumbled and chaos lurked in the rubble. The ritual of S/M interactions, the exaggerated, clearly defined power roles, the explicit codes of conduct, the liturgic, 'theatrical iconography of punishment and expiation' (McClintock, 1993: 106), may provide

S/M practitioners with a temporary reimposition of order amidst late twentieth-century social turbulence.

It appears that the tumultuous late twentieth century has also created a mainstream consumer populace receptive to avant-garde representations of transgression, power, sexuality and risk. To this end, corporate America has profited from its appropriation of S/M iconography into fashion, art, media, literature, retail and entertainment. Coburn (1977) described the phenomenon as 'S/M chic'. S/M scenes and innuendos appear in movies ranging from *Naked Gun 33 1/3* to *Secretary*. Certain celebrities (Madonna, Angelina Jolie) feel comfortable openly discussing their S/M interests. Vogue, Jean-Paul Gaultier and Helmut Lang bring S/M iconography to haute couture. Popular fashion integrates black leather, boots, collars and other apparel evocative of S/M practice. Mainstream media openly discuss S/M topics. And the Internet offers a myriad of websites, chat rooms and newsgroups specializing in various aspects of S/M.

This proliferation of S/M iconography in mainstream culture mirrors the emergence of S/M as a sexual culture. Over the last three decades, the public visibility of S/M iconography and ideology has increased dramatically. This has been due, in part, to S/M communities' increasing organizational strength and S/M practitioners' increasing advocacy. However, transformative social events occurred simultaneously, which created a culture increasingly receptive to S/M iconography and ideology. The reflexive relationship S/M practice has shared with the surrounding social conditions for the past two centuries has culminated in a trend toward the 'mainstreaming' of S/M.

Conclusion

Future research is recommended to investigate the impact that cultural receptivity to S/M iconography and ideology may have on S/M practice. Will S/M practice lose some or all of its stigma? Will the mainstreaming of S/M dilute the sexual heat of taboo for some practitioners? Will engaging in S/M behaviour become a more permissible sexual outlet? Will more individuals experiment with S/M? Will S/M culture's shared meanings and range of behaviours shift?

SM also initiates speculation about the nature of sexual cultures in general. How would achieving the goals most sexual minority activists share – ending discrimination, obtaining equal protection under the law and securing freedom to engage in private, consensual sexual interactions – affect their various sexual communities? How would sexual cultures that position themselves outside, or in opposition to, the hetero-sexual, monogamous, 'vanilla' paradigm assimilate greater mainstream acceptance? How would newly enfranchised sexual cultures respond to other formative sexual minority cultures' advocacy for a voice in the cultural discourse?

Other sexual minority networks and communities have acquired public visibility in recent years, greatly facilitated by the Internet. National and international networks of aficionados engage in furry sex, plushy sex, messy sex, crush fetishes, balloonism and many other under-studied sexual practices.[5] Whether their roles in the larger culture will eventually match the one S/M practice has played remains unclear. However, studying sexual minority practices leads to a broader under-standing of human sexuality in general. This chapter presents a new theoretical model of cultural function and formation, which proved useful in framing a history and analysis of S/M cultural formation. Its utility in this undertaking recommends it as a model for organizing and understanding the historical evolution of other sexual minority communities, which remain similarly understudied.

Notes

1. The 'inside' spaces normalize and facilitate particular sexual behaviours and expressions of desire. These desires are both sexual – the subjective, individual erotic drive – and social – the larger, human desire for collective acceptance and belongingness.
2. One of the most enduring links between successive generations of S/M produ-cers, House of Milan's original catalogue was published by Burtman, and his cousin, Yogi Klein, was its principal cofounder (Bienvenu, 1998). House of Milan's successor company, HOM, publishes contemporary fetish erotica in California.
3. In 1978, Cardea morphed into another all-female S/M support group, SAMOIS. These two groups anchored the formation of San Francisco's lesbian S/M community.
4. S/M practitioners self-identify by numerous labels. Top/bottom, dominant/submissive, master/slave, sadist/masochist and switch are perhaps the most common. Most practitioners identify as switch, meaning they alternate between the dominant and submissive roles (Breslow, Evans & Langley, 1985, 1986; Moser, 1988; Spengler, 1977).
5. The variety of human sexual expression seems infinite. Furry and plushy sexuality involves anthropomorphism: in furry sex, individuals engage in sexual interactions wearing animal costumes; plushy sexuality involves sexual contact with stuffed animals. Messy sexuality involves slathering various substances – often food, but also including mud, oil, paint, and so on – over the body. Crush fetishes involve sexual gratification from witnessing female feet crush insects. Balloonism is the eroticization of rubber balloons.

References

American Psychiatric Association (1994). *Diagnostic and Statistical Manual of Mental Disorders* (4th ed.). Washington, DC: APA.

Baumeister, R. (1988). Masochism as escape from the self. *Journal of Sex Research*, 25(1), 28–59.

Beck, M. (1999). The pornographic tradition: Formative influences in sixteenth-to nineteenth-century European literature. In J. Elias, V. Elias, V. Bullough, G. Brewer, J. Douglas & W. Jarvis (Eds) *Porn 101: Eroticism, Pornography, and the First Amendment* (pp. 369–395). Amherst, NY: Prometheus Books.

Beckmann, A. (2001). Deconstructing myths: the social construction of 'sado-masochism' versus 'subjugated knowledges' of practitioners of consensual 'SM'. *Journal of Criminal Justice and Popular Culture*, 8(2), 66–95.

Bienvenu, R. (1998). *The Development of Sadomasochism as a Cultural Style in the Twentieth Century United States*. Unpublished doctoral dissertation, Indiana University, Indiana.

Boileau, J. (1903). *With Rod and Whip: A History of Flagellation among Different Nations* (Unknown Trans.). USA: Medical Publishing Company. Original work published 1700.

Brame, G., Brame, W. & Jacobs, J. (1996). *Different Loving: The World of Sexual Dominance and Submission* . New York, NY: Villard.

Brandt, P. (1963). *Sexual Life in Ancient Greece*. New York, NY: Barnes & Noble.

Breslow, N. (1987). Locus of control, desirability of control, and sadomasochists. *Psychological Reports*, 61, 995–1001.

Breslow, N., Evans, L. & Langley, J. (1985). On the prevalence and roles of females in the sadomasochistic subculture: Report of an empirical study. *Archives of Sexual Behavior*, 14(4), 303–317.

Breslow, N., Evans, L. & Langley, J. (1986). Comparisons among heterosexual, bisexual, and homosexual male sadomasochists. *Journal of Homosexuality*, 13(1), 83–107.

Bullough, V. (1977). *Sin, Sickness and Sanity: A History of Sexual Attitudes*. New York, NY: Garland Publishing.

Califia, P. (1981). A personal view of the history of the lesbian S/M community and movement in San Francisco. In SAMOIS (Eds) *Coming to Power* (pp. 243–281). Boston, MA: Alyson Publications.

Califia, P. (1994). *Public Sex: The Culture of Radical Sex*. San Francisco, CA: Cleis Press.

Chaline, E. & Pendal, J. (2005). Spanner: S/M, consent and the law in the UK. *Lesbian & Gay Psychology Review*, 6(3), 283–287.

Cleland, J. (1986). *Fanny Hill*. London: Penguin Books. Original work published 1748.

Coburn, J. (1977). S&M. *New Times*, 4, 43–50.

Connell, R. & Dowsett, G. (1992). The unclean motion of the generative parts: Frameworks in Western thought on sexuality. In R. Connell & G. Dowsett (Eds) *Rethinking Sex: Social Theory and Sexuality Research* (pp. 179–196). Melbourne: Melbourne University Press.

D'Emilio, J. (1983). Capitalism and gay identity. In A. Snitow, C. Stansell & S. Thompson (Eds) *Powers of Desire: The Politics of Sexuality* (pp. 100–116). New York, NY: Monthly Review Press.

Easton, D. & Liszt, C. (2000). *When Someone You Love Is Kinky*. San Francisco, CA: Greenery Press.

Ellis, H. (1905). *Psychology of Sex*. New York, NY: Random House.

Farshea, K. (1999). *A Spanner Information Site* [on-line]. Available: http://www.commex.org/whatever/spanner/spanner.html.

Foucault, M. (1982). Sexual choice, sexual act: An interview with Michel Foucault. *Salmagundi*, 58/59, 10–24.

Freud, S. (1938). *Three Contributions to the Theory of Sex* (A. Brill, Trans.). New York, NY: Random House. Original work published 1905.

Gephard, P. (1969). Fetishism and sadomasochism. In J.H. Masserman (Ed.) *Dynamics of Deviant Sexuality* (pp. 71–80). New York, NY: Grune & Stratton.

Gosselin, C., Wilson, G. & Barrett, P. (1991). The personality and sexual preferences of sadomasochistic women. *Journal of Personality Individual Differences*, 12, 11–15.

Herdt, G. (1997). *Same Sex, Different Cultures: Exploring Gay and Lesbian Lives*. Boulder, CO: Westview Press.

Hostetler, A. & Herdt. G. (1998). Culture, sexual lifeways, and developmental subjectivities: Rethinking sexual taxonomies. *Social Research*, 65(2): 249–290.

Hunt, M. (1974). *Sexual Behaviour in the 1970s*. New York, NY: Dell Books.

Irvine, J. (1994). Cultural differences and adolescent sexualities. In J. Irvine (Ed.), *Sexual Cultures and the Construction of Adolescent Identities*. Philadelphia, PA: Temple University Press.

Keuls, E.C. (1985). *The Reign of the Phallus: Sexual Politics in Ancient Athens*. Berkeley, CA: University of California Press.

Kinsey, A.C., Pomeroy, W.B., Martin, C.E. & Gephard, P.H. (1953). *Sexual Behaviour in the Human Female*. Philadelphia, PA: W.B. Saunders.

Krafft-Ebing, R. (1953). *Psychopathia Sexualis: A Medico-forensic Study* (V. Robinson, Trans.). New York, NY: Pioneer Publications. Original work published 1886.

Lee, J. (1979). The social organization of sexual risk. *Alternative Lifestyles*, 2(1), 69–100.

Levine, M. & Troiden, R. (1988). The myth of sexual compulsivity. *Journal of Sex Research*, 25(3), 347–363.

Levitt, E. (1971). Sadomasochism. *Sexual Behaviour*, 1(6), 69–80.

McClintock, A. (1993). Maid to order: Commercial fetishism and gender power. *Social Text*, 37, 87–113.

Meibomius, J. (1718). The *Use of Flogging: A Treatise on the Use of Flogging in Medicine and Venery* ('A Physician', Trans.). Paris: C. Unsinger. Original work published 1639.

Mickic, N. (2005). *Folsom Street Fair 2005* [on-line]. Available: http://www.folsomstreetfair.com/fair-faq.php.

Miller, P. & Devon, M. (1995) *Screw the Roses, Send Me the Thorns: The Romance and Sexual Sorcery of Sadomasochism*. Fairfield, CT: Mystic Rose Books.

Moser, C. (1988). Sadomasochism. *Journal of Social Work and Human Sexuality*, 7, 43–56.

Moser, C. (1998). S/M (sadomasochistic) interactions in semi-public settings. *Journal of Homosexuality*, 36(2), 19–29.

Moser, C. (2001). Paraphilia: A critique of a confused concept. In P. Kleinplatz (Ed.) *New Directions in Sex Therapy: Innovations and Alternatives* (pp. 91–108). Philadelphia, PA: Brunner-Routledge.

Moser, C. (2002). Are any of the paraphilias in the DSM mental disorders? *Archives of Sexual Behaviour*, 31(6), 490–491.

Moser, C. & Kleinplatz, P.J. (2005). DSM-IV-TR and the paraphilias: An argument for removal. *Journal of Psychology and Human Sexuality*, 17(3/4), 91–109.

Moser, C. & Madeson, J. (1996). *Bound to be Free: The S/M Experience*. New York, NY: Continuum Publishing Company.

National Coalition for Sexual Freedom (1998). *Violence and Discrimination Survey* [on-line]. Available: http://www.ncsfreedom.org/library /viodiscrim-survey.htm.

National Coalition for Sexual Freedom (2002 & 2003). *Incidence Response Overview* [on-line]. Available: http://www.ncsfreedom.org/library/index.htm.

Otway, T. & Kelsall, M. (1969). *Venice Preserved*. Lincoln, NE: Nebraska University Press. Original work published 1682.

Padgug, R. (1979). Sexual matters: On conceptualizing sexuality in history. *Radical History Review*, 20, 3–23.

Parker, R. & Aggelton, P. (Eds) (1999). Introduction. *Culture, Society and Sexuality: A Reader*. London: UCL Press.

Parker, R., Herdt, G. & Carballo, M. (1991). Sexual culture, HIV transmission, and AIDS research. *Journal of Sex Research*, 28, 1.

Patrias, D. (1978). *The Sociology of Secret Deviation: The Case of Sadomasochism*. Unpublished doctoral dissertation, New York University, New York.

Plummer, K. (1995). *Telling Sexual Stories: Power, Change and Social Worlds*. London: Routledge.

Reinisch, J. with Beasley, R. (1990). *The Kinsey Institute New Report on Sex: What You Must Know to be Sexually Literate*. New York, NY: St. Martin's Press.

Rich, A. (1986). Compulsory heterosexuality and lesbian existence. In A. Rich, *Blood, Bread and Poetry: Selected Prose 1979–1985*. New York, NY: Norton & Company.

Rousseau, J. (1953). *The Confessions of Jean-Jacques Rousseau* (J. Cohen, Trans.). London: Penguin. Original work published 1782.

Rubin, G. (1984). Thinking sex: Notes for a radical theory of the politics of sexuality. In C. Vance (Ed.) *Pleasure and Danger: Exploring Female Sexuality*. London: Pandora Press.

Rubin, G. (1994). *The Valley of the Kings: Leathermen in San Francisco, 1960–1990*. Unpublished doctoral dissertation, Michigan: University of Michigan.

Rubin, G. (1997). Elegy for the valley of kings: AIDS and the leather community in San Francisco, 1981–1996. In M.P. Levine, P.M. Nardi & J.H. Gagnon (Eds) *In Changing Times: Gay Men and Lesbians Encounter HIV/AIDS* (pp. 101–144). Chicago, IL: University of Chicago Press.

Shadwell, T., Nicolson, M. & Rodes, D. (1992). *The Virtuoso*. Lincoln, NE: Nebraska University Press. Original work published 1676.

Spengler, A. (1977). Manifest sadomasochism of males: Results of an empirical study. *Archives of Sexual Behaviour*, 6, 441–456.

Szasz, T. (1974). *The Myth of Mental Illness*. New York, NY: Harper & Row.

Tannahill, R. (1982). *Sex in History*. New York, NY: Stein & Day.

Taylor, T. (1996). *The Prehistory of Sex*. New York, NY: Bantam Books.

Weeks, J. (1981). Discourse, desire, and sexual deviance: Some problems in a history of homosexuality. In K. Plummer (Ed.) *The Making of the Modern Homosexual*. London: Hutchinson.

Weeks, J. (1985). *Sexuality and Its Discontents: Meanings, Myths and Modern Sexualities*. London: Routledge & Kegan Paul.

Weinberg, T. (1987). Sadomasochism in the United States: A review of recent sociological literature. *Journal of Sex Research*, 23, 50–69.

Weinberg, T. (1994). Research in sadomasochism: A review of the sociological and social psychological literature. Annual Review of Sex Research, V, 257–278.

Weinberg, M., Williams, C.J. & Moser, C. (1984). The social constituents of sadomasochism. *Social Problems*, 31(4), 379–389.

Weymouth, T. & Society of Janus (1999). *Society of Janus: 25 Years* [on-line]. Available: http://www.soj.org/articles.html.

Wiseman, J. (1996). *S/M 101: A Realistic Introduction*. San Francisco, CA: Greenery Press.

Yalom, I. (1980). *Existential Psychotherapy*. USA: Basic Books.

3
Themes of SM Expression

Charles Moser and Peggy J. Kleinplatz

SM (also known as BDSM, i.e. Bondage and Discipline, Dominance and Submission and Sadism and Masochism) is a term used to describe a variety of sexual behaviours that have an implicit or explicit power differential as a significant aspect of the erotic interaction. Of course there are other sexual interactions or behaviours that have an implicit power differential, but that power differential is not generally eroticized in non-SM interactions. Sex partners may even disagree if a particular interaction or relationship constitutes SM, each seeing it from a different perspective. The boundaries between SM and non-SM interactions are not always clear, which is why self-definition is crucial for understanding SM phenomena.

Colloquially the set of SM inclinations has been referred to derisively as an interest in 'whips and chains', but is much more complex and varied than suggested by that description. Practitioners use both numerous academic terms and jargon (e.g. S/M, B/D, WIITWD [i.e. what it is that we do], D/s, Bondage, Leather, Kink) to refer to these interests. They have been labelled controversially in the psychiatric literature with diagnostic labels such as Paraphilia, Sadomasochism, Sexual Sadism, Sexual Masochism and Fetishism. There is no evidence that the descriptions in the psychiatric literature resemble the individuals who self-identify as SM participants or that SM participants understand the implications of adopting the psychiatric terms as self-descriptors.

Judging from the proliferation of SM themes in sexually explicit media, references in mainstream books, film and the news media, as well as academic studies and support groups, it is reasonable to conclude that SM is an important sexual interest for a significant number of individuals. To further the study of SM, it is important to understand the range of SM activities and different subtypes of practitioners.

This chapter is an attempt to discuss the range and types of SM themes commonly identified in SM practice. It is our hope that understanding the different manifestations of SM will lead to a more complete understanding of this genre of sexual expression. Throughout this chapter we will use quotes from SM practitioners. These were obtained during fieldwork for other research projects; no new investigation was undertaken for this chapter.

Serious study of SM or, for that matter, any set of sexual proclivities reveals precisely how diverse sexual behaviour is. However, the range of sexual behaviours (limited only by human, physical capacities) is dwarfed by the range of sexual *fantasies* and *desires* which are unlimited.

The set of SM themes delineated below is an introduction to some of the more common manifestations of SM interactions. It is important to recognize though that the finely detailed nuances of a given individual's desires can never be understood, no matter how carefully one observes, without also listening attentively to the individual's erotic hopes and dreams (Kleinplatz, 2001, 2006). These are unique to each participant and would be infinitely more difficult to categorize. Simply stating that this person is into 'humiliation' while that one wants 'to be possessed' does not begin to capture the individual or interpersonal experience. The inadequacy of labels to convey the subtlety of the meanings embedded in a given fantasy or interaction becomes especially glaring when confronted with two or more SM participants, each involved in superficially similar behaviours (e.g. being bound and flogged) but wherein each seeks an entirely different experience (Kleinplatz, 2001, 2006).

The subjective aspects of SM require their own taxonomy. Motives and intentions are complex and cannot ever be deduced from observation alone. Given that the range of intentions is as vast as imagination itself, a taxonomy of the inner world of SM participants is beyond the scope of this chapter.

Roles

At the most basic level, SM practitioners adopt either dominant or submissive roles or given roles at different times. Individuals who choose the dominant role often refer to themselves as 'top', 'master', 'mistress', 'domme', 'owner', 'S', 'dom', 'dominatrix', 'sadist', among other terms. Those who adopt submissive roles often use the terms 'bottom', 'slave', 'sub', 'subbie', 'property', 'm', 'owned', 'masochist', and so on. Those individuals who are interested in both roles are called 'switches' or 'flexible' (or in some circles, more archaically as 'versatile'). The terms 'top' and 'bottom' are also used to describe non-SM sex acts; for example, when gay men engage in anal intercourse, they may refer to the inserter as the 'top' and the insertee as the 'bottom'.

Our choice to use the terms 'dominant' and 'submissive' was at least partially arbitrary (relying upon convention) and in the hopes of mini-mizing confusion for the reader. Many SM practitioners feel strongly about the terms used to describe their interests and at least some will object to our choice. Nevertheless we believe we have chosen the most descriptive and least offensive option.

Individuals who adopt a particular label do not necessarily participate in the same, associated activities, nor does use of the same label by two people imply that they assign identical meanings to their labels. SM practitioners often argue amongst themselves about what these labels actually mean and about differences between these labels. There are clearly regional differences, differences among groups, differences due to sexual orientation and between men and women. For example, some people would say that a 'masochist' is interested primarily in physical sensations, a 'submissive' is primarily interested in psychological domin-ation (but with limits) and a 'slave' is primarily interested in providing service or in experiencing psychological domination without limits. In reality, the same individual could adopt any of these terms, without any change in behaviour.

It is not rare for some individuals to take on unusual identities or disavow any SM identity regardless of their behaviour (see Plante, 2006). For example, 'dominant bottoms' are individuals who direct their part-ners to stimulate them in specific ways under the former's control (e.g. 'give me five strokes with a cane on the left buttock'). Others engage in spanking while insisting that their activities are in no way related to SM (Plante, 2006). Some individuals 'top from the bottom', meaning they subtly direct the scene.

Commonalities

SM interactions or relationships characteristically begin with negoti-ation, wherein the limits (i.e. what is forbidden) are discussed. Isolated interactions almost always involve this negotiation process, but once a relationship has been established the negotiations are reinstituted when changes in the relationship or a desire to change the focus of their inter-action are contemplated. Limits can be subdivided into 'hard limits' (never to be tested) and 'soft limits' (where some exploration is permis-sible). Transgressing someone's limits is a serious faux pas in the SM community. The negotiation process is an important part of establishing a relationship. Many participants and groups have standard limits, for example, no children, blood, 'scat' (i.e. faeces) or permanent marks. There are limits that are rarely mentioned, but nevertheless, communicated. For example, while the fantasy of being sold as a slave is common, few 'slaves' are permanently sold or given to another. When relationships end, 'slaves' negotiate the termination of their relationships and are usually released (Dancer, Kleinplatz & Moser, 2006).

SM is said to have five common features (Weinberg, Williams & Moser, 1984): the appearance of dominance and submission, role-playing, mutual definition, consensuality and a sexual context for the individual.

The emphasis here is on the *appearance* of dominance and submission, because the actual power in the relationship is much more subtle. The power dynamics are much more complex than one person simply being in charge while the other follows his or her lead. *Role-playing* involves the assumption of specific roles that give the appearance of dominance and submission.

Mutual definition refers to the way the participants jointly define the relationship or interactions. Although they do not necessarily call their activities SM or some similar term, they recognize that such behaviours differ from 'vanilla' (i.e. non-SM) relationships. Someone who self-defines as dominant cannot go around barking orders at acquaintances or strangers and survive in our society. Similarly, submissives who say they are always submissive do not fall to their knees in front of strangers without some negotiation. There are venues where there are agreed-upon rules and the participants do not necessarily negotiate explicitly; rather, one's presence conveys agreement to participate. Theses venues often use symbols (e.g. coloured ribbons) to indicate the specific liberties allowed; negotiation is needed for other acts not covered by the accepted rules.

SM is *consensual* by definition. Just as the difference between consensual coitus and rape is consent, the difference between SM and violence is consent. Non-consensual acts are criminal.

By our definition, SM involves a *sexual* element or context. There are people who do not define their activities as sexual; for the purposes of this chapter, we are not including them in this discussion.

Bondage

One method of exerting power is to restrict the movements of the other partner. Some individuals prefer specific materials (e.g. rope, chains) or manner of bondage (e.g. tight bondage which prevents any movement or looser restraints to allow struggling). Other materials commonly used include plastic wrap, strips of cloth, masking tape and string or twine. Usually great care is taken to prevent blood supply disruption or nerve compression from being affected. Some individuals like to fight, squirm and try to escape; others find the experience comforting and relax into it. In some cases, one is restrained by solely psychological suggestion. For example, being told not to move may suffice or being tied in a manner from which the person could, theoretically, free him or herself.

Some bondage is applied over clothes, but complete or partial nudity is common. For some, the added vulnerability of being naked is important whereas for others, it is the process of being bound that is erotic. Sometimes the genitals are covered by the bondage and at other times they are made conspicuously vulnerable. Being bound implies an inability to escape which is heightened by the vulnerability of being touched intimately. For others, the inability to touch one's genitals when contact is desired creates a different type of vulnerability.

In some cases, the bondage is focused on a specific part of the body such as breasts or wrists. Specialized devices exist to specifically bind wrists, thumbs, ankles and so on. This genre includes devices that prevent sexual access (e.g. chastity belts, gags, butt plugs) or which serve as a reminder that the submissive is no longer in control of those bodily areas. In some cases, the primary purpose is to prevent the wearers from stimulating themselves; in other situations it prevents individuals from sexual liaisons with others. In still other situations, it reminds submissives of the control the dominants have and their dependence on their dominants.

Some bondage occurs in conjunction with clothing. For example, there are belts that lock and prevent removal of clothes. Similarly locks can be used to prevent the undoing of zippers or buttons. It is also possible to make a rope or chain harness that does not typically prevent access or limit motion, but the wearer knows that it *could* be used to immobilize him/her. Others enjoy the aesthetic look of these devices and wear them as fashion statements. Still others use them as reminders of the nature of their relationships or status differences. In this genre, piercings, whether permanent or temporary, can be used as an element of bondage. Some individuals would include corsets, similar garments and extreme high heels as elements of bondage. They can be worn by both sexes, prevent movement and restrict certain functions (e.g. sitting, walking, taking a deep breath).

The setting or equipment used can also serve as an important aspect of the eroticism. To be tied in a semi-public place (e.g. an SM party) or in a place where he/she can be discovered (e.g. a mountain trail) is important for some. Others find that how they are positioned is the key aspect, for example, having one's legs spread or buttocks displayed can be crucial. Some individuals especially enjoy being bound to large devices made for such purposes (i.e. a 'T'- or 'X'-shape). Being bound to a bed is common and several commercial and homemade devices are available to facilitate this.

Some individuals enjoy being enclosed in a device that does not restrict their personal movement but prevents escape. Cages are a primary example of these devices but, more simply, a cuff with a long tether would allow movement about a room or an apartment but prevent submissives from leaving the area. Similarly leashes can prevent someone from wandering too far from the holder. Body sacks (i.e. large cloth bags that can be tied to prevent escape) are also popular.

For some the process of being tied or tying someone up is the essential turn-on. After the person is immobilized, he/she is quickly untied. An entire evening may be spent tying and retying someone in different configurations. For others, it is the feeling of being immobilized that is erotic. In such instances, the submissive would not be untied until after the scene (i.e. erotic interaction) is completed. Some individuals sleep in some type of bondage every night.

There is a style of bondage called Shibari or Japanese bondage where the aesthetic of the bondage is important. Shibari practitioners practice tying someone up to be able to do it quickly, with a flourish, and to make sure the knots and ropes follow certain aesthetic principles.

Another specialized style of bondage involves suspension – tying the person so that they are suspended in air. Obviously this requires appropriate equipment and special safety considerations.

It is considered extremely bad form (not to mention dangerous) to leave the immobilized person alone. In case of fire or other emergency, quick release mechanisms incorporated into the bondage or special scissors are available to free the person quickly. For some individuals, SM without bondage is unthinkable and for others it is a special occasion when the participants have adequate time for preparation and execution of an elaborate tableau.

Discipline

Some individuals' arousal is linked to the notion of being disciplined for violation of pre-arranged rules. One aspect of this is referred to as 'corporal punishment' although the discipline can be psychological rather than physical. An important component of these scenarios is mutual agreement that the dominant partner can and should discipline the submissive partner. Sometimes the submissive partner feigns resistance and needs to be 'forced' and at other times submits 'willingly'. The submissive partner may deliberately 'provoke' the 'warranted' discipline. However, at other times, discipline is meted out for its own sake, despite the absence of 'need' for punishment or infraction of rules.

Although dominants may appear to be imposing their will on 'unwilling' submissives, by definition, all SM is consensual; if the submissive were not willing, the act would be an assault and legally actionable; this is actually quite rare in organized SM communities. In the feigned 'unwilling' situation, the submissive wants to be subdued and fights being overpowered. In almost all cases, the submissive will lose, but there are instances when the tables are turned. Also switches may use these struggles as a mechanism for deciding who will play which role, in which case roles may switch several times during an encounter.

Discipline can take the form of spankings, paddling, whipping, caning or the use of other implements. Psychological discipline, including standing in the corner, denial of privileges and 'humiliation' also occur. The dominant is expected to be in control of the extent of the punishment, the pain inflicted and the severity of any marks left. A dominant who loses control would not be thought of highly. It is not uncommon for the dominant to apologize for an errant blow that leaves an unwanted mark or accidentally hits an area without prior agreement.

Another type of discipline has a military style. Individuals often choose to join an organization or group that requires members to 'earn' privileges and respect by adhering to a specific code. These are found in both male/female and homosexual/heterosexual contexts. Uniforms and other symbols meant to show membership in the group are earned by the participants. This structure is sometimes useful in helping members develop useful personal traits (e.g. responsibility, cleanliness, honesty). It is not uncommon for these groups to sponsor community service in one form or another or to come to the assistance of individuals in need.

There is a historical precursor of these militaristic groups which is referred to as 'Old Guard' (see Baldwin, n.d.). The modern SM movement traces its organizational inceptions to gay motorcycle clubs that began after World War II. After the war, many GIs returning to the USA recognized their homosexuality and decided to reside in larger cities. Some of these men found the black leather motorcycle chic to be particularly attractive. In addition, some of these men were also interested in

SM. The use of the term 'Leather' as a synonym for SM traces its roots to these groups. The Old Guard had a rank order structure, borrowed from their common military experience, though they were closer in appearance to the 'Rebel without a Cause' genre.

Dominance and submission

SM interests generally do not predict whether someone is dominant or submissive in daily life. The stereotype of the powerful businessman who hires a dominatrix to humiliate him is more the exception than the rule. There is no shortage of powerful businessmen who want to be dominant during sex as well as at work. Professional submissives are available (Sisson & Moser, 2005) and some businessmen – among others – do use their services. Low-income men usually cannot afford to hire either a professional submissive or dominant, whether male or female.

The feeling of being either dominant or submissive in a relationship can be the source of eroticism and create the atmosphere for specific sexual or SM acts. Common scenarios include 'owner' (i.e. 'master' or 'mistress')–'slave', 'teacher–student' and 'adult–child' (only involving chronological adults) role-plays. Although these role-plays can be maintained throughout the duration of the relationship, they are clearly different from the reality of actual parent–child or teacher–student relationships. For example, in general, teachers do not cane students, let alone as a prelude to engaging in a variety of sex acts. Similarly real slave owners tend not to treat their slaves as cherished objects (Dancer, Kleinplatz & Moser, 2006).

Some participants use these roles as a fleeting element of a sexual interlude, often lasting for just a few minutes. The rest of the relationship is devoid of SM role-play. For others, the role-play provides the context for the SM and, sometimes, even for the relationship itself. That is, they find the roles create the erotic backdrop for the relationship; without these roles the partner would cease to be attractive.

In the same way that some individuals want sex to occur in the context of a committed relationship, some individuals want their SM to occur in the context of a committed SM relationship. The context of the relationship assumes many different forms. For example, some submissives want to be seen as treasured possessions, trading obedience for being taken care of and nurtured. Some might, for example, comment that they like old-fashioned relationships, with the male as head of the household. Similarly female-dominant relationships have the same style, with the man worshiping the woman on the pedestal. Variations of the treasured possession theme occur in same-sex LGB (lesbian, gay, bisexual) relationships.

Many submissives will report that they are looking for 'my one', that is, the person to whom he/she can be utterly devoted. Once they have found 'the one', they will be obedient in exchange for care. They will report they love their dominants in a romantic context. Others define their devotion in terms of being the maid, chauffeur or abject slave. They expect to be treated as an inferior and without expecting romantic love in return. One ritualized type of male-dominant and female-submissive relationship is called 'Gor', styled after the science fiction novels of John Norman. In these relationships, chattel slaves (usually women) have no rights or privileges; Goreans believe that male dominance and female submission constitute the natural order. Nevertheless slaves are disciplined for misbehaviour – not sexual reasons. A well-trained slave wants to please her master and demonstrate her obedience.

Another stylized form of male dominance and female submission is known as 'Christian Kink', based on the religious belief that men should be heads of the household. 'Domestic Discipline' has a similar bent, except that either partner can be the disciplinarian. Similar themes are played out in same-sex LGB relationships.

Another theme involves a parent–child relationship, though in sexualized form. 'Daddy–boy' (also spelled 'boi'), 'Daddy Dom' (usually involving a female submissive being treated as a little 'princess') and 'Mommy–girl' (also spelled 'grrl') relationships occur. Of interest, the 'Mommy–boy' dynamic is less common and often cast as an 'adult–baby' relationship. Even though these terms denote the gender of the participants, one cannot infer the sex of the participants from this language; lesbians often employ the 'male' terms and some men use the 'female' terms. Adopting any of these terms does not mean that participants' relationships are necessarily founded on identical premises – just that some individuals find some aspects of the genre resonate for them.

There is no indication that these individuals are searching for minors or re-enacting incestuous acts from their childhood. Some individuals fantasize about being slaves at hard labour. There are reports of individuals who have done this for weeks at a time, but we are unaware of anyone who does this on an ongoing basis. The common theme in all these relationships is a clear power dynamic that resonates with the participants.

Symbols

However an SM relationship is characterized, symbols of the relationship and commitment are often used. This is similar to how non-SM relationship participants exchange rings, pins, other jewellery and often marriage vows. These symbols and rituals include rings (both for fingers and for pierced body parts), collars, formal ceremonies, being marked (e.g. by wearing a collar, being pierced, tattooed, scarification by cutting or branding), signing contracts and protocol agreements.

The giving or receiving of a collar can be an elaborate process. Individuals will discuss the meaning of a collar to them at length. If the relationship ends, there are discussions of what to do with the collar, how it should be returned, and so on. Although there are several symbols that suggest an SM relationship, wearing them can signify a fashion statement or that the individual has an interest in SM, but not necessarily that the person is involved in an SM relationship. Often one cannot discern if someone is dominant or submissive from dress or comportment. Submissives stating that they are 'collared' indicate that they are involved. It is usually appropriate to ask if the symbol denotes the person is in a relationship, similar to the etiquette surrounding a woman in a singles bar who is wearing a wedding ring. In some cases, an individual can have a 'vanilla' relationship, but still be searching for an SM partner or vice versa.

SM participants often sign a contract to seal their relationship formally. Some of these contracts are quite brief; others are very detailed, spelling out the rights and obligations of both parties. Some of these contracts form part of a ritual, signed in front of friends and resembling a wedding ceremony.

One aspect of these contracts concerns protocol, that is, the way the submissive addresses the dominant partner. Some of these styles (e.g. calling one's dominant 'My Lordship' or 'My Ladyship') can be humorous even to other SM practitioners. Some submissives always refer to themselves in the third person. In written communication, they capitalize their dominants' names or pronouns and use lowercase letters for submissives. This can lead to written statements such as 'A/all of Y/you attending O/our party...'

Tattooing or other body modification is not uncommon among young people today, whether members of the SM community or not. Usually it is a statement about themselves and/or a ritual commemorating commitment (e.g. tattooing one's girlfriend's name on one's arm) or a significant event in one's life (e.g. joining the Marines). It seems logical that a significant SM relationship or a confirmation of one's role could be similarly acknowledged.

Physical pain

Many people are under the impression that SM is primarily about individuals who either like to give or receive pain. In fact, the pain or intensity that is part of SM is a specific type of pain. Random pain or pain produced outside of an SM context is rarely erotic or desired. Some clueless individuals believe that a 'masochist' would like to be handled roughly or subjected to painful stimuli outside of a particular SM relationship. This type of behaviour is considered boorish at best and may elicit a violent reaction from the 'masochist'.

Some SM practitioners do not experience the stimulation as painful and call it 'intensity'. There are 'intensity junkies' who desire very specific types of intensity. It is well known that sexual arousal alters pain perception, elevating pain thresholds over 80% (Komarisuk & Whipple, 1984; Whipple & Komarisuk, 1985, 1988); what would hurt in a non-erotic context does not hurt or 'hurts so good' when aroused. The best non-SM example of this is the 'hickey' or love-bite. Someone biting your neck when aroused feels different from someone biting your neck in an unaroused state. Individuals who are not involved in SM often engage in activities that can be considered physically or emotionally painful. Examples of this include long-distance running and enrolment in a graduate program, both of which often involve considerable exertion, pain and sacrifice.

For many participants, it is not pain per se that is arousing but rather the idea of pain. As one stated, '*Actual* pain gives me no pleasure, yet the *idea* of pain does, *if inflicted by way of discipline and for the ultimate good of the person suffering it*' (Ellis, 1936: 90). A respondent in previous research once commented, 'I do not get turned on because my lover spanks my ass. I get turned on seeing him get turned on spanking it. It is about the power exchange, force and most importantly a mental state that makes me put his desires and needs ahead of my own'.

SM practitioners often have very specific types of sensations that they are seeking. Some prefer 'thuddy' sensations that result from blows from a paddle versus the 'stingy' characteristic of blows from a cane. Other specific types of pain involve needles, tickling and electricity (e.g. from a TENS unit). Practitioners sometimes have very specific preferences in implements, rejecting even somewhat similar implements. Within a dominant–submissive relationship, the submissive partner may be 'rewarded' with the use of a preferred implement and 'punished' with the use of a non-preferred implement.

One can withstand more intense sensation if the stimulation is slowly escalated, soft blows slowly increasing in strength rather than starting at a point that is perceived as painful from the outset. Conversely light spankings that are not painful can sensitize the skin over the course of a scene, leave marks and by the end are perceived as painful. Some stimuli are easy to endure for a short time, but are more difficult with longer applications even without a change in intensity (e.g. tickling).

There are preferences not only for specific types of stimulation but also for stimulation of particular body parts. 'CBT' (i.e. 'cock and ball torture'), 'cunt torture', breasts, nipples, 'bastinado' (i.e. stimulation of the soles of the feet) are particular foci of attention. Sometimes the focus is on a very particular variety of stimulation (e.g. groin kicking), separate from other types of CBT.

It is reported that in Japan, there are businesses that cater only to painful stimulation of the nose, but it is rare to find anyone interested in that type of stimulation in North America or Europe. The theme of the stimulation can also be important. Medical scenarios lead to some specific types of stimulation that the individual seeks within the context of that particular scenario but are rarely of interest when in other settings.

Stimulation can be intense and sometimes marks are left. Most commonly marks consist of a redness of the skin that goes away in a few minutes to hours. More intense blows may cause superficial bruising (i.e. breakage of small, surface blood vessels) and may lead to more pronounced redness. Such marks usually last for days. Deeper bruising leads to the proverbial black and blue marks which also last for days. More extensive bruising over a larger area would obviously last longer.

On occasion there is a desire to place a permanent mark. The motivation behind this is multifactorial: the mark may symbolize a commitment, the seriousness of the relationship, a remembrance of a special time or confirmation of the ability of the submissive partner to endure the pain of placement. For some it has other purposes and does not need to be placed as part of an SM scene.

Permanent marks can be placed in a variety of ways. Knives or scalpels are used to make designs. If the scar is meant to be more prominent, after healing, the scar is retraced with the knife or scalpel. Occasionally cigarette or cigar ash is rubbed into the wound to increase the scarring. Branding, that is, burning the skin, is also used. Brands tend to spread (become less distinct over time) and are less common as SM symbols. Some individuals have been re-branded to overcome the fading of the original brand.

Tattooing is another popular way to mark someone. The tattoo may only consist of the dominant's name or initials but some submissives have a generic tattoo that says 'slave' or 'property of...' to emphasize the SM nature of the relationship. Designs depicting scenes such as a person kneeling, in bondage, or crossed whips/canes are also popular. Dominants also get tattoos to signify their interests; tattoos such as 'MASTER' or a picture of an individual in a dominant pose are common.

Temporary piercing is also done for the pain or intensity of sensations. Piercings can be made permanent by introducing jewellery (typically a bar or ring) into the flesh. From these rings, other jewellery or a tag can be hung to indicate ownership or status. Temporary piercings rarely become infected. Permanent piercings can become infected, more likely in some sites rather than others. Surprisingly genital piercings rarely become infected, while nipple and umbilical piercings can take months to heal.

Humiliation

'Humiliation' is among the most difficult aspects of SM play to describe accurately. What is devastatingly humiliating to one person is not humiliating at all to the next person. In previous research, one respondent revealed that he wanted to be forced to drink his dominant's urine. He felt that the urine was the 'distillate of the body' and this was a way of ingesting the essence of his dominant's being. Of note, he was interested in drinking only his dominant's urine and felt that being forced to drink someone else's urine would be humiliating. This anecdote illustrates that what is and is not perceived as humiliating depends on the individual and/or relationship.

Contact with urine is relatively common, contact with faeces is less common and contact with vomit is rare. Another form of humiliation is enacted by prohibiting the submissive from washing or bathing. Control of elimination is relatively common, either by requiring the submissive to ask permission or being forbidden from urination or defecation. Along the same lines, but not necessarily experienced as humiliating, is having to ask the dominant for permission to have an orgasm.

It can be seen as humiliating to be required to call your partner 'Master' or 'Lady' or to always refer to yourself in the third person. Denial of various adult prerogatives can be perceived as humiliating. Examples include control over how the submissive dresses, being forbidden from wearing certain articles of clothing, requiring nudity or having the submissive's food chosen. Forcing a submissive to wear particularly feminine clothing can be humiliating to gay, bisexual or straight men as well to some bisexual and lesbian women. Other methods of setting the tone include shaving the pubis, not letting the submissive sit on the furniture – only on the floor – and requiring public displays of respect (e.g. kneeling, bowing, curtsying). The subjective experience, of course, is unique to each individual.

Sometimes the humiliation is related to the possibility of discovery. Writing something derogatory on the submissive's body in a place that is usually hidden by clothing can accomplish this type of humiliation. Similarly requiring that a man wear bright red toenail polish when he is going to a gym, leaving him open to pointed questions, being shunned by others or being propositioned could be humiliating.

Some physical acts could be seen as humiliating, for example, analingus, face slapping and foot licking. Nevertheless activities previously considered to be humiliating can become socioculturally normative and accepted behaviours, thus losing their power to confer a particular feeling state; fellatio and cunnilingus are excellent examples of the historical shift in social construction from aberrant and therefore demeaning status to standard and commonplace. In some cultures, being the receptive partner during anal coitus is considered humiliating, although in other cultures the same behaviour occurs without any implication of humiliation.

One very interesting form of humiliation is 'cuckholding' or being a 'cuck'. In this situation, a heterosexual couple seeks another man (the cuckholder) to have sex with the female partner. The male submissive (the cuck) is usually the target of a variety of disparaging comments about his masculinity. He is often made to watch the cuckholder have sex with the female partner. Some of these women are dominant and the sex between the cuckholder and the woman is devoid of SM between them. In other cases, the female partner is also submissive and she and the cuckholder have their own SM relationship. In some cases, the cuck is 'forced' to be 'bisexual' and engages in sex acts with the cuckholder as well or is required to perform oral sex on the woman after the cuckholder has ejaculated in her vagina (or anus). This fantasy is prevalent enough for couples who seek other partners to indicate sometimes that they are not interested in being cuckholded.

Race relations in the USA provide the backdrop for one variation of the cuck fantasy in which an African-American man is sought out specifically to be the cuckholder for a Caucasian couple. Less frequently, African-American couples specifically seek out Caucasian cuckholders. A particularly extreme form of this fantasy is the 'cuck' who fantasizes about having the woman impregnated by the cuckholder. In these cases, the cuck accepts parental responsibility of the cuckholder's offspring. Although this particular fantasy is common among those with an interest in this genre, we can find no case of it actually occurring.

There are several other roles that can be seen by others as humiliating including infantilism (i.e. role-play of being a child or infant), even when these roles have divergent meanings to participants. Infantilism is similar to transvestism, in which participants derive erotic arousal or a sense of comfort from dressing in the garments associated with the role. Similarly 'pony play' and other animal play can be seen by observers as humiliating, although the participants derive either erotic arousal or a sense of comfort from assuming the animal role. This is different from 'furrysex', in which two or more partners dress in animal costumes to have sex; the dressing is not necessarily erotic but the idea of having sex as an animal is arousing. In furrysex, the individual adopts a mix of human and animal characteristics, like a cartoon character, rather than trying to assume the role of an actual animal.

Society, in general, does not support humiliation of categories of individuals, so it is not uncommon to have groups founded around some principle that allows for the 'humiliation' of one class of individuals by another. There are male supremacy and female supremacy groups, groups created along racial lines and military-themed groups.

Fetishes

A fetish is characterized by sexual arousal to an inanimate object. In the professional literature, a fetish is distinct from partialism; the latter involves a strong sexual attraction towards a part of the body. Technically one can be a shoe fetishist or foot partialist or both. Within the SM community, both possibilities are merged together and referred to as a fetish. Individuals who enjoy SM accessories often describe their interests as fetishes. They find wearing or touching the preferred articles highly arousing. The articles themselves are rarely arousing, but if they are worn by a partner, it heightens the partner's attractiveness and heightens the eroticism of the sex. For example, pantyhose can be a fetish object, but brand new pairs, never worn, rarely become a focus of erotic interest. The same pantyhose worn by the participant or a partner can elicit a strong erotic response. Similarly an article of clothing that reminds the person of a partner or a specific erotic interlude can become a fetish object.

Common fetish objects include leather, latex and corsets. At some parties, all guests are required to wear the appropriate fetish material. Several glossy magazines cater to different fetishes, such as smoking, leather, rubber, feet, and so on. The fetish aspect of some SM groups or events has led some discerning participants to comment derisively that it occasionally appears as though S&M stood for Stand and Model. It is not uncommon for several fetishes to be combined. The configuration of women wearing corsets, smoking cigars and with a focus on their feet can be particularly intriguing to some.

It should be noted that the term 'fetish' is usually applied to unusual objects or body parts. Feet are uncommon fetish targets as compared to breasts. Nevertheless there is a similar 'fetishistic' breakdown of attraction to large breasts, small breasts, male breasts, lactating breasts, pierced nipples, and so on. This variation demonstrates the range of diversity in erotic patterns and the nuances that are inherent in the process.

Relationships

Most people believe that SM relationships usually consist of one dominant partner and one submissive partner. In fact, there is no typical SM couple and all combinations of relationships are possible. Sometimes relationships are comprised of two dominants or two submissives. In these situations, the individuals either take turns playing the desired role or a third party (or another couple) becomes involved. In some cases, the new partner joins the couple as a permanent member (creating a triad or poly group) or their participation can be as part of a secondary relationship. Dominance and submission may also be fluid; many dominants will explore submission under the right circumstances and submissives will consider being dominant.

Relationships consisting of two dominant partners living together do exist; usually there is no overt SM play between the dominant partners. Often the dominant partners will have other relationships (whether long term or casual) with submissive partners. In deference to the primary relationship, these other relationships may have restrictions imposed (e.g. no coitus, no kissing on the lips, control over the number of times the submissive is seen) that serve to reinforce the primary relationship.

The dominant partners may play with a submissive, together or separately. In some dominant–submissive relationships, the submissive partners may have their own submissives. They often define themselves as dominant, but submissive to their dominant. Sometimes the decision to be dominant or submissive is based upon other criteria, such as being submissive to men and dominant to women or how attractive the partner is. The desire for sexual contact with a particularly attractive partner could lead a dominant to take the submissive role. Occasionally one partner uses being dominant to attract partners for the other dominant. It is rare, but not unheard of for a submissive to serve more than one dominant regularly. On occasion an individual is submissive to one partner and that person is submissive to another, resulting in the submissive being submissive to both, but with a rank order.

Male submissives may be willing to engage in SM activities with another man ('forced bi') if a woman is present. Female submissives may wish to explore their own bisexuality but enjoy the security of an experienced male dominant to 'direct'. Male–male and female–female couples do attract other partners of both sexes. The idea of having two dominants of the same sex can be erotic.

It is not unusual for one or both partners to define themselves as switches, formally acknowledging that they are interested in both roles. SM roles within the couple often switch, but some couples maintain their roles within the couple and switch outside the relationship. There are also couples among whom the dominant uses the submissive partner to seduce another dominant as portrayed in the classic SM novel, *The Image* (de Berg, 1956/1966). When the new dominant is sufficiently trained, the dominant partner in the original couple becomes his/her submissive. Some dominants seek out submissive partners and then 'order' the submissives to dominate them. Submissives, wary of this possibility, often reject switches as prospective partners or state unambiguously that they are seeking only completely dominant partners.

Couples among whom both are submissive do exist. They often try to please the other by taking turns being dominant, but typically dislike it. They may choose to be submissive to the same person or couple, as this allows them time together and sharing. Occasionally the dominant will control their sexual interactions with each other, even if not present.

Some couples are comprised of an SM-identified partner and a 'vanilla' partner. This state of affairs often results from attempts to live an SM-free life, but after years of attempting unsuccessfully to suppress the SM inclinations, they come to accept them. Often the vanilla partner is aware of outside, SM-oriented relationships and either actively supports them or just prefers to avoid confronting the issue. There are, of course, individuals who surreptitiously engage in these relationships without their partners' knowledge.

Some couples actively seek to have a permanent third partner join them on a full-time basis to form a triad. These relationships can be in the form of a 'V' (vee) or a 'Δ' (triangle or delta). In a V relationship, two of the three partners do not interact with each other sexually. In a Δ, all partners interact sexually. In some triads, both submissives or both dominants are equal in status. In other relationships, an 'alpha' and 'beta' partner or designation exists, conferring different status to different members.

Larger groups also exist, including 'quads', 'constellations' and 'houses'. Quads are comprised of four individuals, along the same lines as a triad. Constellations are groups with many people who have different roles and connections with each other. Houses usually have one person or couple who is the organizer or who actually leads the group. The sexual and SM relationships can become complex very quickly.

SM couples meet and date just as non-SM couples do. They meet through introductions, dating services, in non-SM situations, or at SM events. They occasionally date several people, without committing to anyone. Others view SM play as demonstrating serious commitment. Due to the possibility of running into a partner who has dubious intentions (whether dominant or submissive), in the larger, more public and organized SM communities, potential partners may be vetted in a number of ways. Past partners may be interviewed, initial meetings are arranged and set in public places and these meetings occur without the assumption of any role. Occasionally a friend acts as a chaperone. A first 'play date' may occur at a public SM event/party which allows for safety via observation by others.

That said, one-night stands are not uncommon. One safety measure is to pre-arrange a 'safe call'. The submissive partner leaves contact information with a friend as to where he/she will be and with whom. That person is supposed to notify the police if the submissive does not call by a designated time. Obviously safety is important, but many experienced SM participants who have had numerous partners do not report experiencing any serious problems.

Discussion

This chapter is a beginning. The themes discussed here, that is, roles, bondage, discipline, dominance and submission, symbols, physical pain, humiliation, fetishes, SM relationships and their commonalities, hardly provide an exhaustive description of SM interests and behaviours. The challenge of developing a definitive taxonomy of SM activities, interactions, meanings and other phenomena is hampered by the complexity of SM – or for that matter any other sexual interest.

For sexologists studying SM, the challenge is heightened by the recognition that roles, fantasies, activities and relationships do not necessarily correspond with one another. Most SM practitioners would recognize the themes described above as descriptive of their sexuality, even if a particular theme is not part of their own sexual patterns or desires. Correspondingly it is fascinating that the same sexual interests can be expressed in such divergent manners. Our field is in need of a model parsimonious enough to account for both the minute and huge differences among individuals who profess to have the same general sexual interests.

Some people engage in the sorts of behaviours and relationships described above without defining themselves as SM participants. There are also individuals who never enact these SM themes themselves, but nonetheless self-identify as SM practitioners. Sexologists will also need to develop models comprehensive enough to conceptualize all of these patterns.

SM is an understudied area of sexology. One reason for this has been the difficulty in defining what types of behaviours and interests are subsumed under SM, how to differentiate them from other sexual and non-sexual interests and behaviours. We hope this chapter will help to demystify SM and will aid psychotherapists, healthcare professionals and others in appreciating the range and intricacy of SM themes and their practitioners.

References

Baldwin, G. (n.d.). *The Old Guard (The History of Leather Traditions)*. Retrieved December 20, 2006, from http://www.tdl.com/%7Ethawley/oldgd.html.

Dancer, P.L., Kleinplatz, P.J. & Moser, C. (2006). 24/7 SM slavery. *Journal of Homosexuality*, 50(3/4), 81–101.

de Berg, J. (1966). *The Image*. (Patsy Southgate, Trans.). New York, NY: Grove Press, Inc. Original work published 1956.

Ellis, H. (1936). Love and pain. *Studies in the Psychology of Sex: Vol. I, Part 2* (pp. 66–188). Philadelphia, PA: F.A. Davis.

Kleinplatz, P.J. (2001). A critique of the goals of sex therapy or the hazards of safer sex. In P.J. Kleinplatz (Ed.) *New Directions in Sex Therapy: Innovations and Alternatives* (pp. 109–131). Philadelphia, PA: Brunner-Routledge.

Kleinplatz, P.J. (2006). Learning from extraordinary lovers: Lessons from the edge. *Journal of Homosexuality*, 50(3/4), 325–348.

Komarisuk, B.R. & Whipple, B. (1984). Evidence that vaginal self-stimulation in women suppresses experimentally-induced finger pain. *Society for Neuroscience Abstracts*, 10, 675.

Plante, R. (2006). Sexual spanking, the self, and the construction of deviance. *Journal of Homosexuality*, 50(3/4), 59–79.

Sisson, K. & Moser, C. (2005). Women who engage in S/M interactions for money: A descriptive study. *Lesbian & Gay Psychology Review*, 6(3), 209–226.

Weinberg, M.S., Williams, C.J. & Moser, C. (1984). The social constituents of sadomasochism. *Social Problems*, 31(4), 379–389.

Whipple, B. & Komarisuk, B.R. (1985). Elevation of pain threshold by vaginal stimulation in women. *Pain*, 21(4), 357–367.

Whipple, B. & Komarisuk, B.R. (1988). Analgesia produced in women by genital self-stimulation. *Journal of Sex Research*, 24, 130–140.

4
Is SM Pathological?*

Peggy J. Kleinplatz and Charles Moser

Are sexual sadism and sexual masochism [SM] pathological? To some, even the question must seem absurd. It is already a foregone conclusion. Sexual sadism and sexual masochism have been classified as pathological by the various editions of the major psychiatric nosologies, currently the *Diagnostic and Statistical Manual of Mental Disorders (DSM-IV-TR*, APA, 2000) and the *ICD-10* (i.e. the *International Classification of Diseases* produced by the World Health Organization). Popular opinion would indicate that SM seems 'weird' or 'sick'. But by what criteria should we be making such determinations and who should be designated to make these assessments?

One of the difficulties in designating any set of proclivities as pathological is the lack of criteria for what constitutes 'normal' or 'healthy' sexuality. Although there are some parameters for normal physiological responses, sexology is sorely lacking in models covering the spectrum of sexual interests, desires and behaviours, that are problematic to 'normal' and 'optimal' sexuality. The lack of objective criteria makes it all too easy for mental health professionals to rely upon predominant cultural values to guide assessments (Moser & Kleinplatz, 2002, 2005). Also missing are ways to distinguish 'inherently' problematic interests from the problems caused by discrimination against sexual minorities.

At present, Western clinicians tend to think of 'normal' sexuality as monogamous, procreation-oriented intercourse, featuring the heterosexual, young (but not too young) and able-bodied. Attempts to regulate human sexuality, to greater or lesser degree, have always been with us, but have caused great hardships to sexual minorities. Although 2000 years of Christian history dictated prohibitions against sexual sins, chief among

* This chapter was first published as Kleinplatz, P. & Moser, C. (2005). Is S/M Pathological? *Lesbian & Gay Psychology Review*, 6(3), 255–260. Thanks to the BPS for permission to reprint this article.

these was lust – sex for its own sake. During the Victorian era, new social domination by the natural sciences evoked the need to justify oppression, repression and suppression of human sexuality in pseudoscientific terms; thus there was an emphasis on 'science' and 'social hygiene', even if the same old taboos were now justified in new terms.

Over the last 100 years, a wide variety of sexual 'disorders' have gone in and out of fashion and, correspondingly, in and out of psychiatric focus. These include nymphomania, satyriasis, masturbation, oral sex, homosexuality, hypersexuality, sexual addiction and the entire category of unusual sexual interests known collectively as the 'paraphilias'. This latter category includes sexual sadism and sexual masochism. Some of these were quietly removed from the psychiatric nosologies, others with great fanfare (e.g. the controversial removal of homosexuality from the *DSM* by the APA in 1973) while still others, including SM, continue to be classified as pathological. But other than social convention, by what criteria are behaviours to be judged as pathological?

Originally, the *DSM* was based in psychoanalytic theories of psychopathology. Currently the *DSM* is intended ' . . . to be neutral with respect to theories of etiology' (APA, 2000: xxvi), based on objective observation, and able to support its statements with empirical research. However, various critiques have questioned whether science can ever be value-free (e.g. Dineen, 1999; Kutchins & Kirk, 1997). Even when we attempt to rely on allegedly empirical criteria, the application of them requires human judgement.

For example, some would claim that statistical criteria are important. However, this line of reasoning, even if it were to be applied consistently – and it is not – is irrelevant. Uncommon phenomena or attributes might be considered more worrisome, but there are many rare entities that are perfectly normal (e.g. an IQ of 160, a natural blonde). Masturbation and a preference for oral sex were deemed pathological at one time even though they were widespread. Correspondingly many pathological conditions are quite common (e.g. cancer, hypertension, hypercholesterolemia). This criterion of prevalence is questionable. Nevertheless SM is not rare. Statistics on its prevalence are typically estimates. Kinsey, Pomeroy, Martin and Gebhard (1953) found that 22% of the men and 12% of the women in their sample had at least some erotic response from sadomasochistic stories, and 50% of men and 55% of women reported having at least some erotic response to being bitten. Janus and Janus (1993) reported that 14% of men and 11% of women in their sample had personal experience with sadomasochism. More recently Renaud and Byers (1999) found that 65% of Canadian university students have fantasies of being tied up and 62% have fantasies of tying up a partner.

Distress and dysfunction/impairment

The *DSM* uses the criteria of distress and impairment/dysfunction: 'Fantasies, behaviors, or objects are paraphilic only when they lead to clinically significant distress or impairment (e.g. are obligatory, result in sexual dysfunction, require participation of nonconsenting individuals, lead to legal complications, interfere with social relationships)' (APA, 2000: 568).

According to the *DSM*, there is little evidence of distress (APA, 2000: 566): 'These individuals are rarely self-referred and usually come to the attention of mental health professionals only when their behavior has brought them into conflict with sexual partners or society'. Furthermore, when distress is manifest, it may result primarily from social stigma surrounding SM. This phenomenon is akin to internalized homonegativity in gay and lesbian individuals (Kleinplatz & Moser, 2004; Nichols, 2006). The recommended 'treatment' is to validate the distress rather than to 'cure' the SM desires (Moser, 2001).

As for impairment, this criterion is particularly noteworthy in illustrating the social biases that continue to pervade the *DSM*. For example, the *DSM* considers it a sign of impairment if SM is 'obligatory'; why single out some behaviours as pathological when required for sexual fulfilment and not others? Why not decree that people who require heterosexual intercourse to reach orgasm are pathological? Actually that was precisely the case during the 1950s when women who 'failed' to achieve orgasm during intercourse were labelled 'frigid'. Both increases in scientific knowledge – including knowledge based in self-report data – and changing social mores led to expanding visions of female sexuality. In any case, Langevin, Lang and Curnoe (1998) demonstrated that most people sexually aroused by the paraphilias are also aroused by more 'conventional' sexual stimuli. The exclusivity criterion is thus unsustainable either theoretically or empirically.

The next sign of impairment is that the paraphilia 'results in sexual dysfunction'. There is no data to support this assertion, particularly as worded, so as to suggest a causal link. Given the high prevalence of sexual dysfunction in population studies, it is striking that SM participants are *not* presenting in therapists' offices more often.

The stipulation that a diagnosis of sexual sadism or sexual masochism requires participation of nonconsenting individuals is similarly odd on several levels: This criterion refers to a crime (i.e. a conflict between the individual and society) which is specifically excluded from the definition of a mental disorder. It is all too easy for societies to criminalize and pathologize socially unacceptable behaviour. It is to the APA's credit that they objected to just such mis-use of psychiatry to pathologize and thereby silence dissent in the totalitarian regimes. More fundamentally this criterion suggests a basic misunderstanding of SM. One of the basic tenets of SM organizations is that all activities be 'safe, sane and consensual'. Any violation of the consent imperative is unacceptable within SM communities (Wright, 2006).

The next two indications of impairment, that SM 'lead[s] to legal complications' or 'interfere[s] with social relationships' are equally fraught with bias. Of course any stigmatized behaviour may lead to legal or social problems. Indeed SM participants do suffer legal complications; they lose custody of children; they lose their jobs; they lose security clearances. In court cases, the expert witness for the opposition often states, 'We would not be here if SM were not a disorder and a psychiatric diagnosis'. This is circular reasoning. One must grapple with whose problem is really in evidence in such cases – that of the actor or that of the perceiver?

This final sign of impairment, that is, 'interference with social relationships', is worthy of special attention. It brings forth many of the myths about SM participants which are then used to justify their need for psychotherapy. The commonality is the notion that SM participants are unable to maintain 'normal' intimate relationships, referred to in the *DSM* as 'the capacity for reciprocal, affectionate sexual activity' (APA, 2000: 567). They are also described as having 'pair-bonding disorders' (Schwartz & Masters, 1983) and 'courtship disorder' (Freund, 1990). However, there is no evidence that individuals involved in SM have greater difficulty establishing intense, intimate relationships than other people, nor that SM relationships are pathological. Furthermore roughly half of all American marriages end in divorce (National Center for Health Statistics, 2005). The average American couple may not be any more 'healthy' or 'successful' than the average SM relationship.

SM activity is often construed as evidence of sex used in service of affect regulation, self-medication, escapism, acting out and sexual addiction (Carnes, 1991; Goodman, 1992; Hastings, 1998; Levine, Risen & Althof, 1990). This criticism presupposes that mental health professionals have some idea of what proper uses of sexuality ought to be; again the implication is that sex ought to be reserved for 'sexual' purposes (i.e. tension release, orgasm, procreation) in the context of normative, monogamous, heterosexual relations. It is noteworthy that mental health professionals often refer to behaviours as 'acting-out' or 'escapist' when these forms of behaviour make the disapproving professional uncomfortable. This sort of terminology tends to be employed when certain forms of sexual expression are disturbing to us. This language is also used when mental health professionals act as agents of social control, providing clinical justifications for pathologizing what the broader society finds distasteful.

What is conspicuously absent from the clinical discourse is the subjective meaning(s) of SM as described by participants. Instead of pathologizing SM or reifying viewers' and clinicians' visceral clutch, consider the accounts of participants who indicate that indeed some SM may be growth-enhancing, just as any kind of sex can be disturbed or disturbing, life-affirming or growth-enhancing. SM participants often describe their experiences as 'coming home' (Kleinplatz, 2006).

But it is wrong to hurt people ... isn't it?

Notwithstanding the lack of empirical evidence of psychopathology among SM participants, the visceral clutch is overwhelming when contemplating giving or receiving pain or enacting dominant–submissive role-plays. It seems 'sick' to get aroused by hurting people or by being subjected to pain. But we attach different interpretations to pain in different situations, based on our intuitive understanding of pain mechanisms as well as because of moral judgements. Pain is regarded and, indeed, processed differently depending on the participants' state of consciousness. The meanings we attach to a given 'painful' event (e.g. athletic competition, ballet performance) help to shape experience. For example, one's mindset affects perceptions of pain in childbirth. An 18-year-old who had endured an unplanned pregnancy, giving birth alone, with no childbirth education will have a significantly longer labour and require significantly more analgesia and anaesthesia than a well-prepared woman who has a partner and anticipates the birth of her baby eagerly. Does it 'hurt' in both cases? Obviously it does, but it is not the pain that is front and centre for the latter woman. Many people commonly engage in activities which could be construed as painful by the naïve observer but which are not experienced that way by the participant, for example, long-distance running. In addition, levels of sexual arousal influence perceptions of pain. Pleasurable stimulation elevates pain thresholds over 80% and orgasm over 100% (Whipple & Komarisuk, 1985, 1988). Even the SM participant who 'likes' pain does not necessarily enjoy it in a dentist's chair any more than the average person would.

Context modulates experience. Notably the emergency rooms are hardly overflowing with people hurt in SM scenes. It is essential to attend to that context before determining what is truly harmful versus that which produces intense sensation but causes no danger. Sports injuries are far more likely to lead to emergency room visits but weekend athletes are not automatically diagnosed with mental disorders. Sports are acceptable, even given all the inherent risks. Not unlike SM, participation in sports requires informed consent. In SM, consent is utterly crucial (Wright, 2006).

It is precisely this context which illuminates the real basis for the discomfort surrounding the 'pain' of SM as perceived in our society and as reified in psychiatric and legal codes. In nonsexual situations, Western society often tolerates and even supports pain-producing activities. British law has specifically exempted boxing, football, military service and, in previous years, parental chastisement from legal liability notwithstanding the pain involved; these activities are judged to be in the public interest (White, 2006). By contrast, in the infamous Spanner case in the UK, the defendants were SM participants, arrested for their 'violent' acts, who claimed exemption given their mutual consent and well-being. The Spanner case put consent on trial. In appeal after appeal, British courts refused to accept consensual sexual pleasure as a valid exception to the rules prohibiting acts of violence; presumably unconventional sexual pleasure among men was not seen as in the public good (White, 2006). This case highlights the underlying discomfort with SM, such that we criminalize and pathologize that which we collectively cannot abide. When pain relates to sex, then it is pathologized.

Ironically the emerging empirical evidence indicates that it is not typically the pain which provides arousal in SM interactions but what it represents – the exchange of power. Cross and Matheson (2006) found no evidence of psychopathy, escapism or any form of psychopathology among SM participants. Instead Cross and Matheson found that power play provided the primary motivation and source of fulfilment.

Conclusions

In the absence of theory or research demonstrating what constitutes 'normal' sexuality, it is all too easy to pathologize the unconventional based on prevailing social currents. SM is particularly liable to being stigmatized in societies uneasy with sexual pleasure for its own sake. Individuals who are labelled and treated as mentally ill are entitled to feel significant distress about perceptions of them; that distress does not signify psychopathology per se. The discomfort that SM induces in others does not justify the legal and clinical opprobrium typically meted out to sexual minorities. There is no evidence to demonstrate that SM, however common or uncommon, creates personal distress or dysfunction for participants or otherwise endangers consenting individuals any more than occurs in the course of other, socially sanctioned pastimes. As such, one can only conclude that SM is not pathological. Clinical integrity requires that SM be removed from future editions of the *DSM* and *ICD*.

References

American Psychiatric Association (2000). *Diagnostic and Statistical Manual of Mental Disorders* (4th ed., text revised). Washington, DC: American Psychiatric Association.

Carnes, P. (1991). *Don't Call it Love*. New York, NY: Bantam.

Cross, P. & Matheson, K. (2006). Understanding sadomasochism: An empirical examination of four perspectives. *Journal of Homosexuality*, 50(2/3), 133–166.

Dineen, T. (1999). *Manufacturing Victims*. London: Constable.

Freund, K. (1990). Courtship disorder. In W.L. Marshall, D.R. Laws & H.E. Barbaree (Eds) *Handbook of Sexual Assault: Issues, Theories, and Treatment of the Offender* (pp. 195–207). New York, NY: Plenum.

Goodman, A. (1992). Sexual addiction: Designation and treatment. *Journal of Sex & Marital Therapy*, 18(4), 303–314.

Hastings, A.S. (1998). *Treating Sexual Shame: A New Map for Overcoming Dysfunction, Abuse, and Addiction*. Northvale, NJ: Jason Aronson.

Janus, S. & Janus, L. (1993). *The Janus Report*. New York, NY: Wiley.

Kinsey, A.C., Pomeroy, W.C., Martin, C.E. & Gebhard, P.H. (1953). *Sexual Behavior in the Human Female*. Philadelphia, PA: W.B. Saunders.

Kleinplatz, P.J. (2006). Learning from extraordinary lovers: Lessons from the edge. *Journal of Homosexuality*, 50(2/3), 325–348.

Kleinplatz, P.J. & Moser, C. (2004). Towards clinical guidelines for working with BDSM clients. *Contemporary Sexuality*, 38(6), 1–4.

Kutchins, H. & Kirk, S.A. (1997). *Making Us Crazy*. London: Constable.

Langevin, R., Lang, R.A. & Curnoe, S. (1998). The prevalence of sex offenders with deviant fantasies. *Journal of Interpersonal Violence*, 13(3), 315–327.

Levine, S.B., Risen, C.B. & Althof, S.E. (1990). Essay on the diagnosis and nature of paraphilia. *Journal of Sex & Marital Therapy*, 16(2), 89–102.

Moser, C. (2001). Paraphilia: A critique of a confused concept. In P.J. Kleinplatz (Ed.) *New Directions in Sex Therapy: Innovations and Alternatives* (pp. 91–108). Philadelphia, PA: Brunner-Routledge.

Moser, C. & Kleinplatz, P.J. (2002). Transvestic fetishism: Psychopathology or iatrogenic artifact? *New Jersey Psychologist*, 52(2), 16–17.

Moser, C. & Kleinplatz, P.J. (2005). *DSM-IV-TR* and the paraphilias: An argument for removal. *Journal of Psychology & Human Sexuality*, 17(3/4), 91–109.

National Centre for Health Statistics (2005). Available: http://www.cdc.gov/nchs/fastats/divorce.htm. Accessed on 20/8/05.

Nichols, M. (2006). Psychotherapeutic issues with 'kinky' clients: Clinical problems, yours and theirs. *Journal of Homosexuality*, 50(2/3), 281–300.

Renaud, C.A. & Byers, E.S. (1999). Exploring the frequency, diversity and content of university students' positive and negative sexual cognitions. *Canadian Journal of Human Sexuality*, 8(1), 17–30.

Schwartz, M.F. & Masters, W.H. (1983). Conceptual factors in the treatment of paraphilias: A preliminary report. *Journal of Sex & Marital Therapy*, 9(1), 3–18.

Whipple, B. & Komarisuk, B. (1985). Elevation of pain threshold by vaginal stimulation in women. *Pain*, 21(4), 357–367.

Whipple, B. & Komarisuk, B. (1988). Analgesia produced in women by genital self-stimulation. *Journal of Sex Research*, 24, 130–140.

White, C. (2006). The Spanner trials and the changing law on sadomasochism in the UK. *Journal of Homosexuality*, 50(2/3), 167–187.

Wright, S. (2006). Discrimination of SM-identified individuals. *Journal of Homosexuality*, 50(2/3), 217–231.

5
Sadomasochism and the Law

Matthew Weait

Introduction

In their essay on the jurisprudence of Robert Cover, Sarat and Kearns (2001) ask whether law can ever make peace with violence. The reason for, and essence of, the question is the fundamental paradox that while law purports to substitute itself for violence – in the form of a civilized, and civilizing, alternative – it retains, and depends on, an immanent violence of its own. Cover, alone among his contemporaries, recognized the importance of revealing and reaffirming the fact that the violence embedded within the concept of 'legitimate force' was, and remained, violence: that the concept of the lawful use of violence amounted to nothing but a cunning (and effective) sleight of hand performed by the positivist conjuror. For Cover, the adverse physical and psychic consequences to the person which can, and often do, flow from the interpretation of a legal text are such that superficially attractive and convincing assertions about the neutrality (pacifism?) of the interpretive process or about the text itself are in fact illusory: a real effect perhaps, but one produced by smoke and mirrors.

Cover believed that the co-ordinated form of violence which constitutes law was an achievement, in the sense that it represented the obverse of undisciplined private violence. For him, the dominant liberal tradition which seeks to obscure the violence of law is one that denies an important political truth about law and its social function:

As long as death and pain are part of our political world, it is essential that they be at the center of law. The alternative is truly unacceptable – that they be within our polity but outside the discipline of collective decision rules and the individual efforts to achieve outcomes through those rules.

(Cover, 1986: 1628)

Such a vision does not lead Cover to conclude that the interpreters of legal texts (e.g. judges) and those whose office requires them to implement their interpretations (e.g. criminal justice professionals) are, and can only ever be, necessarily violent; far from it. He believed that judicial violence should, and could, be exercised sparingly – that tolerance could be achieved and heteronormativity celebrated and affirmed. In this chapter, I question, among other things, whether – in the context of the 'violence' that sadomasochism ('S/M') represents for law and the 'violence' that law metes out on those who identify as sadomasochists – Cover's optimism is well-placed, and why – because the answer to the question is a resounding, if complex, 'no' – that might be.

Some context: what does the law have to say about S/M?

First things first: S/M is not a crime. It would be absurd to contend otherwise, since the only satisfactory (if irreducibly circular) definition of a crime is something that is contrary to the criminal law; and although there are dimensions, or aspects, of S/M that may provoke a criminal law response, there is no 'law against' being a sadist or a masochist or against what might be thought of as the core elements of S/M relationships (domination, submission, ritualized humiliation, the eroticization of the giving and receiving of pain). To the extent that those in S/M relationships observe the behavioural boundaries that the law places on all adult human beings of full mental capacity, there is no question, but what such people do and how they do it is up to them. But – and it is, of course, a big but – the 'problem' is that an S/M identity (just as any other identity) may entail a form of expression which brings it into conflict with the norms of a society for whom that identity is exceptional – whether that exceptionality is couched in terms of psychological abnormality, sexual perversity or immorality. And since law's concern (within states based on governance under the rule of law) is with the maintenance of general standards of conduct – with the normative project of how all of us *should* behave towards each other and as members of a community – those whose identity and its expression challenges those normative standards will, necessarily, find that identity and its expression regulated and limited or (in certain circumstances) repressed and subject to a coercive, punitive response.

The problem, more simply put, is that although we may conceive of ourselves – especially at the dawn of the twenty-first century and in the developed world – as having certain inviolable rights that the state should not be able to infringe, the reality is that those rights are to be asserted within a framework of governance at whose core are the liberal ideas of negative liberty and the harm principle: the idea that we may do anything that we are not specifically proscribed by law from doing and that the only legitimate limit on such proscription is harm to others. The impacts of the inter-relationship between rights and these principles for those committed to an S/M lifestyle, who derive pleasure from representations of S/M or who participate in S/M sex, are various but they include – in English law – the following.

First, it may be against the law to engage in S/M which takes place in a particular location over a period of time (which, given the 'underground' nature of S/M, the fact that it may involve a group of participants,[1] and the need for sessions to be pre-arranged or organized, is not uncommon). The common law offence of 'keeping a disorderly house'[2] – which requires proof of persistent or habitual use of premises for indecent[3] acts – was used against one of the appellants, and aiding and abetting the commission of the offence against another, in the notorious and important Operation Spanner case (*R v Brown*).

Second, the publication[4] of obscene[5] and the communication[6] of obscene or indecent images (in still or video form) that do in fact, or appear to, represent S/M may result in the imposition of criminal liability. Although there appears not to be any recently decided cases in English law that address the meaning of indecency and obscenity in the context of representations of S/M, taking photographs and video recordings of S/M have been central to a number of important criminal cases, both in the UK[7] and in the USA[8] since they have provided the evidence upon which prosecutions on charges of assault and wounding have been based. Furthermore the UK Government recently conducted a *Consultation on the Possession of Extreme Pornographic Material* (Home Office, 2006),[9] which provoked widespread concern from civil liberties and sexual freedom groups, especially organizations representing the interests of those involved in S/M, because the initial proposals would have made it an offence to possess pornographic[10] material whose content depicted 'serious sexual violence' and 'serious violence in a sexual context'. Even though the government, in the face of significant concern and opposition that this would effectively proscribe the possession of images of consensual S/M, has decided to adopt the phrase 'serious violence', and a threshold that would be met only by images of 'acts that appear to be life threatening or are likely to result in serious, disabling injury', it is clear that the representation of S/M remains a politically contentious topic and that possession of certain extreme forms of S/M pornography will result in the criminalization of those for whom this provides a form of erotic satisfaction.

Lastly, and most critically for the purposes of this chapter, the very conduct in which people involved in S/M engage – what might be thought of as the core means of expressing an S/M identity – may result in the imposition of liability if it comprises 'violence' amounting in law to actual or grievous bodily harm or wounding. In what follows, I will explore in some detail the reasons the English courts have given for imposing liability, usually through the denial of the defence of consent, however genuine that consent may be.

Bodily harm

On the face of it, English criminal law adopts a straightforward and relatively unproblematic approach to the classification of those interferences with other people's bodies that justify state punishment. Starting from the very low threshold of battery (which means any unlawful touching), it graduates through the unlawful infliction of actual bodily harm (which means causing any hurt or injury that is more than merely 'transient or trifling') to the unlawful causing of grievous (i.e. really serious[11]) bodily harm. It also imposes liability on those who unlawfully wound, a term which means the breaking of both the outer and inner layers of the skin.[12] These degrees and types of interference, it should be noted, only attract criminal liability if they also meet the condition of *unlawfulness*. This condition ensures that, for example, bodily interference that occurs in the context of self-defence does not attract liability.[13] It also means – critically – that no liability arises where the defendant is, or would be,[14] allowed to raise the defence of consent and that defence is, or would be, successful. As we shall see, it is because consent (where it is available) operates in law as a way of determining whether a person has exercised an autonomous choice to be touched, injured or wounded – and so cannot be said to have been harmed in any meaningful sense – that it renders lawful what would otherwise be criminal. For now, however, it is important to think a little more critically about what is meant by bodily harm in the context of S/M, and how the courts have characterized it.

The first thing to note is that the law's approach to bodily harm is based on a relatively blunt (if superficially appealing) descriptive premise: that we exist, in our embodied selves, as intact, integrated, autonomous physiological and psychological systems. This makes it easy to conceive of bodily harm as anything that disrupts the smooth operation of those systems (a broken leg, a ruptured spleen, being infected with disease, suffering psychological illness). These observable disruptions to the functional equilibrium which bodies are treated as having may then be categorized according to the degree of adverse impact that they have on them, thereby enabling the idea of offence seriousness and the grading of punishments. This rough and ready approach to bodily harm, manifest in the Offences Against the Person Act 1861, is one that may cause no difficulty in the paradigm case of injury sustained by stabbing, shooting, punching and kicking during aggressive and unwanted confrontation; but by focusing on the disruptive consequences and effects of one person's actions on the body of another it fails, necessarily, to reflect the parties' inter-subjective understanding of what those consequences and effects may mean *for them*. This, of course, is unsurprising given – as I have explained above – that the function of law in a community is to articulate and maintain norms of behaviour of general application. This means that objective standards are inevitable. But where, as in S/M, it is precisely the inter-subjective meaning of acts and effects that matter to the participants, the necessity of objectivity and the absence of any sensitivity to context or meaning creates substantial difficulties.

Those difficulties stem, in part, from the complex relationship found in law between the concepts of harm, injury and violence. Because the paradigm case that the law confronts is unwanted physical interference and because one of the functions of law is to protect – for paternalistic reasons – the interests of those subject to such interference, it is all too easy for the courts both to frame any conduct that causes adverse physical or psychological consequences as *violence* and the consequences themselves on the 'victim' as *harm* – a term that is not simply descriptive but carries with it a strong sense of moral wrong. This construction of harm is readily apparent in, for example, the language of the Court of Appeal and the House of Lords in the judgments in *R v Brown*.[15] This, it will be recalled, was the case that arose out of Operation Spanner – where a number of men who had met for a number of years to engage in consensual S/M were arrested and charged with a range of offences, primarily under the Offences Against the Person Act 1861, after the police seized videos depicting their activities. In the words of the Lord Chief Justice:

> The appellants belonged to a group of sadomasochistic homosexuals who willingly and enthusiastically participated in the commission of acts of violence against each other for the sexual pleasure which it engendered in the giving and receiving of pain.

That 'violence' comprised some fairly hardcore activities, and it is important, if we are to understand the context in which arguments concerning the legal response to S/M have been framed, to be clear what those activities involved. For example:

> Count 5:... [the appellants] branded a man 'A' with Laskey's initials using a wire heated by a blow lamp. Scarring from those injuries remains. Matches were taped to the victim's nipples and the navel and having been set alight were then doused.
> Count 6:... This involved [the appellants] in what can best be described as genital torture, including hitting the victim's penis with a ruler and holding his testicles with a spiked glove. Map pins were inserted into the buttocks of one of the victims...
> Count 12:... The victim had his body hair shaved. He was hit with stinging nettles. He had 36 cuts to his back and buttocks causing blood to flow...
> Count 14:... The victim had hot wax dripped into the urethra of his penis. The penis was burned with a candle flame and then a syringe needle was inserted...
> Count 17:... [a co-defendant] had his penis nailed to a bench. He was caned, hit and rubbed with a spiked strap, then cut with a scalpel by [one of the appellants]. There were five lateral cuts together with further cuts to [one of the co-defendant's] scrotum. There was a free flow of blood...
> Count 28: The victim... had his penis hit and rubbed with sandpaper, then his scrotum was clamped and pinned to a board with three pins. His foreskin was nailed to a board.[16]

Reading these counts, as text and at a critical distance, it is not difficult to see how those for whom S/M is not central to sexual identity or practice would interpret the conduct of the appellants as violent or the effects of their actions as harms, nor, by extension, how the judiciary – notwithstanding its recognition that these activities were engaged in willingly and enthusiastically – would characterize them as involving 'torture'. It is worth quoting at length from the leading judgment in the House of Lords of Lord Templeman:

> The assertion was made on behalf of the appellants that the sexual appetites of sadists and masochists can only be satisfied by the infliction of bodily harm and that the law should not punish the consensual achievement of sexual satisfaction. There was no evidence to support the assertion that sado-masochist activities are essential to the happiness of the appellants or any other participants but the argument would be acceptable if sado-masochism were only concerned with sex, as the appellants contend. In my opinion sado-masochism is not only concerned with sex. Sado-masochism is also concerned with violence. The evidence discloses that the practices of the appellants were unpredictably dangerous and degrading to body and mind and were developed with increasing barbarity and taught to persons whose consents were dubious or worthless.[17]

He continues:

> In principle there is a difference between violence which is incidental and violence which is inflicted for the indulgence of cruelty. The violence of sado-masochistic encounters involves the indulgence of cruelty by sadists and the degradation of victims. Such violence is injurious to the participants and unpredictably dangerous. I am not prepared to invent a defence of consent for sado-masochistic encounters which breed and glorify cruelty...[18]

And he concludes:

> Society is entitled and bound to protect itself against a cult of violence. Pleasure derived from the infliction of pain is an evil thing. Cruelty is uncivilized...[19]

Violence, degradation, barbarity, cruelty, cult, evil – it is clear that for Lord Templeman at least (and those other judges in the majority in *R v Brown*, though in not quite such ascerbic terms) the bodily harm inflicted in the context of S/M is not something that is, or should be, understood as the participants themselves might understand it or wish it to be understood. It is certainly not primarily 'sexual' (an important point, since were the conduct to be treated as such, denying the defence of consent as a matter of principle would be far more problematic[20]). To the extent that the English legal position of characterizing S/M as violence (one that is shared in other common law jurisdictions[21]) is one that serves to protect masochists or 'bottoms' whose limits are not respected or who would otherwise find it difficult to bring charges in cases of non-consensual violent sex which the 'top' argues was consensual, even those uneasy about the potentially oppressive consequences on sadistic 'tops'[22] may acknowledge it to be one that reflects a defensible position.[23] And it is also the case, given the fundamental difficulty a liberal legal system has in both seeking to preserve individual freedoms and protecting its subjects from harm – a difficulty that generates the most profound paradox in the context of S/M – that the pragmatic precautionary position which the courts have adopted is the least worst option. This, however, does not provide a satisfactory answer to the deeper factors informing the law's response, ones that go to the heart of why it is that it should adopt such a forceful, uncompromising and moralizing approach when there exist so many other contexts in which the deliberate or incidental infliction of injury is sanctioned. It is to those reasons that we now turn.

Autonomy and consent

Autonomy is foundational to societies in which the principles of governance and adjudication are informed by the tenets of liberalism and the rule of law. At its moral-philosophical heart lies the notion that to flourish and realize one's full potential every person is to be conceived of as an individual, as an end in oneself rather than as a means to the ends of others, whether those others be individuals or the state. Conceived of as a cognitively aware, rational agent, the autonomous person is free to make choices, whether those choices are intimate or economic, private or public. Where those choices produce benefits the autonomous person may legitimately treat these as his/hers to enjoy; where they result in disbenefits (e.g. punishment for those who choose to offend), he/she must bear responsibility for them. Literally understood, autonomy means self-government. In the context of offences against the person, it carries with it the idea that every person is entitled to be free from undesired and unjustified physical interference. However, where a person consents to what would otherwise be an assault, there is – on one reading – no harm caused because he/she is exercising his/her autonomy; and where law recognizes the defence of consent, it does so because it acknowledges that there exists a domain in which people should be allowed to act free from the threat of criminal liability, for to conclude otherwise would result in a significant diminution of fundamental human freedoms (in this context, the 'right' of a 'top' in an S/M relationship or encounter to rely on the consent of a 'bottom' partner, and the 'right' of that partner to give that consent).

In many contexts the law does recognize that the fact of consent to injury, or to the risk of injury, should operate as a bar to criminal charges, even where the injury sustained is – or could be – substantial. The most commonly cited example is that of contact sports. In contact sports, the causing of physical injury may either be intentional (as in boxing) or incidental (as in rugby). The traditional, judicial, reason for this is that such sport is part of our shared 'culture' and that injuries sustained within its confines (i.e. within the rules of the sport in question) are not something with which the courts should be concerned or should interfere with. Physical engagement of this kind, whatever its consequences, is valued by many – and by respecting the right of people to participate the courts are merely reflecting the 'zeitgeist'. It is a position that has a long pedigree, as can be seen from this extract from an early nineteenth century text on the criminal law:

> ...If death ensue from such [sports] as are innocent and allowable, the case will fall within the rule of excusable homicide; but if the sport be unlawful in itself or productive of danger, riot, or disorder, from the occasion, so as to endanger the peace, and death ensue; the party killing is guilty of manslaughter.... Manly sports and exercises which tend to give strength, activity and skill in the use of arms, and are entered into merely as private recreations among friends, are not unlawful; and therefore persons playing by consent at cudgels, or foils, or wrestling are excusable if death ensue. For though doubtless it cannot be said that such exercises are altogether free from danger; yet they are very rarely attended with fatal consequences; and each party has friendly warning to be on his guard. And if the possibility of danger were the criterion by which the lawfulness of sports and recreations was to be decided, many exercises must be proscribed which are in common use, and were never heretofore deemed unlawful... But the latitude given to manly exercises of the nature above described, when conducted merely as diversions among friends, must not be extended to legalise prize-fighting, public boxing matches and the like, which are exhibited for the sake of lucre, and are calculated to draw together a number of idle disorderly people... And again, such

meetings have a strong tendency in their nature to a breach of the peace...[24]

It is clear from this that a sharp distinction is to be made between those activities which exhibit athleticism for its own sake and those that have baser motives. More importantly for present purposes is the fact that such sport affirms the values associated with masculinity itself. The existence, in competitive sport – its essence, perhaps – of a victor and vanquished, is something that mirrors broader, conservative, notions of what being masculine is and should be. To be injured fighting and to lose, when one's goal is the same as one's opposition, is not shameful or barbaric – it is to be applauded. How much more of a threat, then, to the common law and the traditions it seeks to uphold is S/M – where the objective of one partner (at least as this is understood in the judicial mind) – is to experience the erotic potential of pain and injury: consciously to seek submission, and to 'lose'? The same point may be made in relation to non-essential cosmetic surgery. Although it is uncontentious that people should be entitled to consent to wounding (for that is what the surgeon's scalpel inflicts) where this is necessary for our health, it is less evident that surgery purely for the purpose of vanity should be sanctioned: less evident, that is, unless we recognize that most, if not all, cosmetic procedures are ones undertaken in search of a notion of feminine or masculine 'perfection' (perter, larger breasts; slim hips; longer penises; more defined chests). For those who seek to modify themselves in accordance with prevailing notions of feminine and masculine archetypes, the law has nothing to say. In contrast, injury to the genitals or breasts, scarring, branding – damage, no less – produce none of the socially or culturally approved outcomes that those procedures enable. Nor, and this is perhaps even more illuminating, does the law have anything to say where injuries are sustained outside these established contexts, but where they nevertheless affirm established gender roles. In *R v Wilson* a man was convicted under section 47 of the Offences Against the Person Act 1861 as a result of branding his wife's buttocks with his initials. Having been heard after *R v Brown* (in which branding had also been the basis of some of the charges) it might reasonably be thought that wife's consent would not provide him with a defence – and this is what the trial judge concluded. The Court of Appeal, however, quashed the conviction. Russell LJ was trenchant in his criticism of the prosecution and of the wider implications of criminalizing such behaviour. In his view, the facts before him were entirely different from *Brown*. The wife had not merely consented to the injury, she had instigated it (as if this was not the case in S/M sex). He quoted approvingly the husband's statement in police interview that his wife had said she wasn't 'scared of anybody knowing that I love you enough to have your name on my body'. The branding was, the judge thought, no different from tattooing – which had been the husband's original intention. This would have been lawful, and so, therefore, should this be. Russell LJ concluded:

> Consensual activity between husband and wife, in the privacy of the matrimonial home, is not, in our judgment, a proper matter for criminal investigation, let alone prosecution.

The distinction drawn by the judge with *R v Brown* rests explicitly on the cultural dimensions of the case. The branding took place within a marriage. The injury was a symbolic one that represented the traditional subordination of wife to husband. It marked his ownership of her. It represented the positive value of fidelity. It took place in their matrimonial home. The fact that the injury itself was physically no different in fact from that which was inflicted on some of the men in *Brown* is not the relevant consideration. It was not the product of aggression, nor done for sensual gratification, nor witnessed by others (other than the doctor who reported the injury to the police), nor was it inflicted in a specially constructed dungeon. In short, the injury affirmed, rather than challenged, heteronormative sexuality.[25]

These cases demonstrate, I believe, that the criminal law conceives of autonomy not as a value that it should strive to protect at all costs, but rather as one which it can and should protect if and only if it is expressed in a particular way, for particular reasons, and that those reasons are consonant with the broader cultural values which law seeks to protect and affirm. More critically perhaps – and this requires a closer and more creative reading of the courts' approach – the law will acknowledge the validity of consent to injury, and so permit the defence of consent, where that injury is not one in which pleasure is taken. For what distinguishes the courts' response to injury in sport or surgery as compared with S/M, or the branding in *R v Brown* with that in *R v Wilson*, is not simply their relative value or context but the presence or absence of sensual gratification. Those who seek to knock each other out in the boxing ring try to avoid pain; those who seek cosmetic modification do so under anaesthetic; for Mrs Wilson, the branding was something to be endured. But in *R v Brown*, the injury was of the essence – it was an aesthetic, sensuous, desired experience for the men who consented to the injury. And why should this make a difference? Because law – in the last analysis – depends for its authority on the assumption that human beings will seek to minimize the risk of being hurt, deprived of liberty, subjected to the degradation of captivity. Those who participate willingly in S/M are thus, at least at a symbolic level, law's gravest threat. Not only do tops place themselves in the position of the law (by inflicting the pain and/or injury that will satisfy their desire) but bottoms ridicule the power of law by actively enjoining the top to engage in the discipline and ritual humiliation upon which the law depends for its authority.[26] Put in the strongest of terms, it is possible to argue, as Bataille (1962) has done, that the erotic – in which the body is, literally, wasted – is a threat to law, and since it is the most extravagant of erotic practices, in which blood may be lost simply for the thrill of it, S/M represents the most fundamental expression of that threat: the embodied, sensuous, articulation of autonomy at the expense of the power of law[27]:

> ... everything to do with eroticism and infamy play their part in turning the world of sensual pleasure into one of ruin and degradation. Our only real pleasure is to squander our resources to no purpose, just as if a wound were bleeding away inside us; we always want to be sure of the uselessness or the ruinousness of our extravagance. We want to feel as remote from the world where thrift is the rule as we can. That is hardly strong enough; we want a world turned upside down and inside out. The truth of eroticism is treason.
>
> (Bataille, 1962: 166–167)

S/M and privacy rights[28]

For those who practise S/M sex, one of the most intuitively appealing claims is that it is an aspect of their private lives, and so beyond the legitimate reach of the state. Just as other dimensions and expressions of sexuality (such as homosexuality) should be free from interference, because they are intrinsic to a person's identity, so – it is often claimed – should the expression of a sexuality of which S/M forms a part (to whatever extent, of whatever kind and to whatever degree). There are, however, two significant problems with claims grounded in privacy. First, despite immediate appearances to the contrary, privacy is a complex and fiercely contested and problematic concept – politically, legally and philosophically. This means that arguments for freedom to practise S/M grounded in privacy should, if they are to be persuasive, be coherent, well argued and take into account competing rights claims and also acknowledge the non-radical, conservative and (potentially) oppressive dimensions of such arguments. Second (and more practically), there exists, at least within English and European Human Rights law, no right to privacy as such. At the very most, there exist a number of limited and context-specific circumstances in English law in which a person's privacy will be protected, and – so far as European human rights jurisprudence is concerned – the 'right' is a qualified one, subject to numerous and important exceptions, to respect for private life, not to private life or privacy as such.

Let us take each of these two aspects of privacy in turn, dealing first with the problematic meaning of privacy itself. To claim that an aspect of oneself or one's behaviour is private is to make two kinds of claim. The first is that there is something about one's identity, relationships, behaviour and so on – that is so fundamental that it merits recognition and respect for its own sake. The second is that because of its importance the particular dimension of privacy in question should be protected from external interference, and that such protection is both legitimate and necessary. Privacy claims are, thus, about freedom *from* (a particular threat) and freedom *to* (engage in a particular activity or mode of being) and comprise both positive and negative liberties. Privacy may also be understood in consequentialist, or teleological, terms (as important because it promotes certain individual or social benefits) or deontological ones (because it respects core human values, such as dignity and freedom of expression). For feminists, this mode of analysis is problematic because it implies the existence of a non-public domain – comprising the personal, sexual, reproductive, domestic, relational and familial dimensions of people's (and especially women's) lives – which has resulted both in its exclusion from mainstream political debate and legislative reform and in the oppression of and discrimination against those who – for socio-cultural and economic reasons – have been in some sense relegated to live their lives in that domain (see O'Donovan, 1985). In much the same way, liberal analyses and critiques of privacy that focus on the extent to which the state should have access to the private lives of people have been criticized for organizing their assumptions about personhood around a presumption of autonomy, rather than one grounded in interdependency and connectedness (see Nedelsky, 1989, 1990, 1993).

Framing the legitimacy of S/M sex within a discourse of privacy therefore raises a number of difficult issues. First, any claim is based on the suggestion that there is something akin to an S/M identity or sexuality, of the same kind as a homosexual identity – means (if it is to mean anything at all) that the expression of that identity should be respected by law. So in the same way that respect for homosexual identity necessitates that those who engage in consensual same-sex relations are free from legal sanctions, so respect for S/M sexuality requires the same. The difficulty, explored above, is that whereas same-sex sexual behaviour does not entail violence or the infliction of injury (as the law conceives of these), S/M sex may do so; and to the extent that the freedom to express S/M sexuality in this way, to this degree, is understood as *constitutive* of that sexuality, this renders privacy claims difficult, if not impossible, to argue for because they entail a claim to be free to do physical harm and a freedom from punishment in the event that such harm is caused. Second, because this kind of privacy claim depends largely on the assertion of a protected domain of properly called 'private' life, it risks grounding the legitimacy of S/M sex within a discourse that has – far from being liberatory – been implicated in the oppression of women. This is not the place to engage in a detailed discussion or critique of this important point.[29] It is, however, necessary to acknowledge that there exists a lively debate among feminist legal theorists and activists as to whether S/M is empowering or disempowering to women. For some, the transgressive opportunities that S/M provides means that it enables women (whether lesbian or heterosexual) to assert their sexual agency in ways that more 'vanilla' forms of sex cannot (see Ardill & O'Sullivan, 2005; Chancer, 1982, 1992), while for others, S/M merely serves to reproduce the violence that is emblematic of heterosexual men's domination of women (see Superson, 2005).

The more general point is that to conceive of S/M as belonging to the 'private sphere' has the effect of affirming the primacy of individual autonomy and self-determination, masculine values that can all too easily slide into a neo-liberal or libertarian politics that denies the legitimacy and importance of the relational, social and collective dimensions of morality, ethics and law.[30]

Although its meaning is no doubt fluid over time, the symbolic and normative power of 'the private' as a category that frames our perceptions of the world ensures its continued use in the distinctions drawn in law, and nowhere is this clearer or more relevant in the present discussion than in *Laskey v UK*,[31] the litigation before the European Court of Human Rights that followed on from, and was based on the same facts as, the decision of the House of Lords in *R v Brown*.

In *Laskey v UK*, the issue before the court was whether there had been a violation in the applicants' right to respect for private life under Article 8 of the European Convention on Human Rights, which states

(1) Everyone has a right to respect for his private and family life, his home and his correspondence.

(2) There shall be no interference by a public authority with the exercise of this right except as is in accordance with the law and is necessary in a democratic society in the interests of national security, public safety or the economic well-being of the country, for the prevention of disorder or crime, for the protection of health or morals or for the protection of the rights and freedoms of others.

This right, which is enforceable in the UK *via* the Human Rights Act 1998, is one that significantly increases privacy protection for individuals since there is no legally recognized right to privacy as such in English law.[32] It is, however, a qualified right – as the exceptions and limitations in Article 8(2) make clear; and while the Court in *Laskey* held that the criminal proceedings against the applicants had constituted an interference by a public authority with their right to respect for private life, it also held that the interference was in accordance with law and pursued the legitimate aim of protecting health and morals within the meaning of Article 8(2). The success of the application therefore turned on whether the interference was 'necessary in a democratic society'.

In addressing this question, the court emphasized that the UK had a wide margin of appreciation when determining the scope and application of the criminal law, particularly in matters relating to personal morality and its regulation through law. Although it had been accepted that Article 8 was engaged, the court determined that not every kind of sexual activity which took place behind closed doors was of a kind that would fall within the right to respect for private life. In its view, it was at least open to question whether sexual activity which involved a group of people, the recruitment of new members, the creation of specially equipped rooms and the shooting of videos ought properly to be treated as private within the meaning of Article 8. Similarly the court was unpersuaded by the applicants' argument that their conduct was a manifestation of their sexuality, that the participation was truly consensual, that no one other than members of the group observed their activities, that no infection had resulted or permanent injury been caused, and that no complaints to public authorities had ever been made. Nor was it persuaded by the suggestion that concerns about moral corruption were speculative and that they were being targeted as a result of their homosexuality. Accordingly it held that the only relevant question was whether the state was entitled to criminalize the infliction of physical injury – irrespective of context – and concluded that it was. For the court a democratic society is one that depends on the imposition of limits to behaviour, and those limits are not ones to be decided unilaterally by individuals or groups of individuals, even where such determination is exercised in the context of consensual activity experienced by participants as expressive of identity and sexuality and therefore of their embodied autonomy.

It remains open to question whether the decisions in *R v Brown* and *Laskey v UK* are ones that would stand, especially given the decision in *R v Wilson* (there is a strong argument that the inconsistency of the decisions amounts to discrimination on grounds of sexual orientation under Article 14 of the Convention[33]); but as the law stands, it is reasonably clear that the right to respect for private life is not one that will protect those whose private life involves the infliction of injury in the context of expressing an S/M identity. And, on the basis of the analysis and critique presented in this essay, this makes perfect sense. Because one of the functions of the criminal law is to set out generally applicable benchmark standards against which people may legitimately be judged, and because those standards incorporate, in principle, the values of the society in which they apply, it would be bizarre in the extreme if the law were to abrogate its own jurisdiction – its authority to judge – through deference to claims of privacy. To do so would, in effect, result in the affirmation, at its own expense, of true individual autonomy – of self-determination beyond the law. More significantly here, it is not merely the value that we place in our bodily integrity which the law mirrors in its refusal to allow us to consent to injury, even where that might be experienced in the context of S/M as an expression of love, care and affection (Inness, 1992). Instead its regulation of the public/private distinction reflects its critical interest in sustaining and reinforcing the legitimacy and desirability of certain other values, conceptual categories, identities, relationships and behaviours.

Concluding remarks

I stated at the outset of this chapter that S/M is not, as such, against the law; but in its extravagant eroticism, its manifestation of a desire that challenges the very logic upon which law depends, its parodic subversion of punishment, authority, power, domination and submission, its aesthetics, its playfulness and its disregard for the body which the courts see it as their duty to protect, it is in a very real sense against the law. It is against the law because it is an erotics of anarchy, of treason and an inversion of all that the law and a liberal legal system stands for. At the same time, and somewhat paradoxically, S/M – in its justificatory deployment of the language of liberalism (of consent, freedom, choice) – is a practice, lifestyle and identity that exists at the limit point of liberalism itself. To engage in S/M is, in this theoretical sense at least, an 'edge-play' of the purest form. To be a practitioner of S/M is to be a resistance fighter, to assume an identity and to express that identity in a way which is, literally, incomprehensible to a moderate and moderating legal system which sees its responsibility as one of sustaining traditional heteronormative values. At the level of the individual case the question of the legality of S/M may be framed in the technical language of the defence of consent, the meaning of a disorderly house or the scope of a Convention right; but conceived of more broadly, it is a question that goes to the heart of the function of law itself.

Notes

1. It was formerly the case in English law that a criminal offence was committed when more than two men engaged in homosexual activity (though no such prohibition existed with respect to women). The European Court of Human Rights held, in *Adt v UK* (2001) 31 E.H.R.R. 33, that criminalizing gay group sex *per se* (on a charge of the then offence of gross indecency) was a violation of Article 8 of the European Convention on Human Rights (the right to respect for private life).
2. 'A house does not acquire the legal character of disorderliness because disorder occurs on one occasion. The essence of the mischief is the continuity which exists where the use of premises for a given unlawful purpose becomes notorious.' (*Moores v D.P.P.* Times, April 25, 1991 (QBD); see further comment (1992)).
3. Indecency is a notoriously elusive term in English law, and where a case turns on its meaning in a particular context it is treated as a question of fact for the jury to determine applying their common sense and understanding of the term.
4. The Obscene Publications Act 1959 (see below, Note 5) applies only to the *publication* of *obscene* material (which may be visual, written or audio in nature). In contrast, the Protection of Children Act 1978 applies to the taking, making, possession and distribution of indecent photographs and pseudo-photographs of children. Proving obscenity is far harder than merely having to establish indecency.
5. An article is obscene for the purposes of the Obscene Publications Act 1959 'if its effect …is…such as to tend to deprave and corrupt persons who are likely, having regard to all relevant circumstances, to read, see or hear the matter contained or embodied in it', and a person publishes an obscene article who 'distributes, circulates, sells, lets on hire, gives, or lends it, or who offers it for sale or for letting on hire; or…in the case of an article containing or embodying matter to be looked at or a record, shows, plays or projects it, or, where the matter is data stored electronically, transmits that data' (as

amended by the Criminal Justice and Public Order Act 1994, Sch. 9, para. 3). See, further, Edwards (1998).

6. Section 85 of the Postal Services Act 2000 provides, *inter alia*: '(3) A person commits an offence if he sends by post a postal packet which encloses – (a) any indecent or obscene print, painting, photograph, lithograph, engraving, cinematograph film or other record of a picture or pictures, book, card or written communication, or (b) any other indecent or obscene article (whether or not of a similar kind to those mentioned in paragraph (a)). (4) A person commits an offence if he sends by post a postal packet which has on the packet, or on the cover of the packet, any words, marks or designs which are of an indecent or obscene character'. The maximum penalty on indictment for these offences is a fine and 12 months imprisonment. The meaning of indecency under the Postal Services Act is wider than that under the Obscene Publications Act 1959 (where there is a requirement that the material have a tendency to 'deprave and corrupt') and is a matter solely for the jury to determine. See further, Parpworth (2006).

7. *R v Brown* [1994] 1 AC 212.

8. *People v Samuels* 58 Cal. Rptr. 439 (1967) (California Court of Appeal). For comment see Harvard Law Review (1968).

9. See http://www.homeoffice.gov.uk/documents/cons-extreme-porn-3008051/Gvt-response-extreme-porn2.pdf.

10. The proposed definition of 'pornographic' is material produced solely or primarily for the purpose of sexual arousal.

11. *DPP v Smith* [1961] AC 290.

12. *JJC (A Minor) v Eisenhower* [1983] 3 All ER 230.

13. *R v Mowatt* [1968] 1 QB 421.

14. I say 'or would be' because there are numerous contexts in which the judicial acceptance of the legitimacy of consent to significant injury means that it is unlikely, if not inconceivable, that the point would fail to be tested in court (e.g. consent to necessary surgery by a qualified doctor).

15. [1994] 1 AC 212 (HL).

16. *R v Brown* (1992) 94 Cr App R 302, at 305 to 307 (CA).

17. *R v Brown* [1994] 1 AC 212 at 235.

18. *Ibid* at 236.

19. *Ibid* at 237.

20. In rape, for example, the absence of consent is definitional (i.e. contained in the very definition of the offence itself – s 1, Sexual Offences Act 2003). This means that although questions might arise as to what counts as consent, there could be no conviction where a jury determined that there was in fact consent. The same principle applies in the context of indecent assault, where the presence of consent to a touching that would otherwise be considered indecent negates any liability. The central issue in *R v Brown*, in contrast, was the availability of the defence of consent in the context of offences such as those in the Offences Against the Person Act 1861 (a matter for the appellate courts), where the absence of consent is not definitional and falls to be decided on the basis of public policy.

21. See, for example, *R v Welch* (1995) 101 CCC (3d) 216, 43 CR (4th) 22g (OCA) (Canada); *People v Jovanovic* 263 AD 2d 182, 700 NYS 2d 156.

22. It is potentially oppressive because to deny the defence of consent on the basis that S/M constitutes nothing other than violence would make it possible for 'bottoms' who had in fact consented to injury to seek prosecutions if the relationship were to end or for other reasons.
23. For a more comprehensive discussion of this position, see Hanna (2001).
24. East, *Pleas of the Crown* (1803) vol. 1, Chap. v, paras 41 and 42, pp. 268–270.
25. The position adopted by the courts is somewhat different when there is a significant risk of serious or life-threatening injury, even when this takes place within a heterosexual relationship (see *R v Emmett* (unreported, 18th June 1999). See also, in the context of indecent assault, *R v Boyea* (1992) 156 JP 505).
26. It is also worth noting that for a social institution which is grounded in the importance of clear verbal communication, the existence of safe words (where 'no' means 'yes', but 'blue' may mean 'stop') establishes S/M as a direct assault on the logic upon which the law relies.
27. I explore these ideas more fully elsewhere (Weait, 1996).
28. See also Weait (2005).
29. For further discussion, see Hoople (1996).
30. O'Donovan's analysis is hugely influential, but has been criticized by those who argue that it is inconsistent with the fact that law sustains the private domain *via* its indirect regulation (see Graycar, 1987–1988; Olsen, 1985). See also Boyd (1997).
31. *UK* (1997) 24 EHRR 39.
32. This is most graphically apparent in *R v Brentwood Borough Council, ex. p. Peck* [1997] The Times, 18 December, where it was held that there was no right to privacy where a local authority released video footage of the applicant's suicide attempt. The law does recognize privacy in some contexts (e.g. the conditions for applying for search warrants under s. 15 of the Police and Criminal Evidence Act 1984, and the right to access personal information held by public bodies under the Freedom of Information Act 2000).
33. On this point see the opinion provided by counsel for the Spanner Trust: http://www.spannertrust.org/documents/opinion.pdf.

References

Ardill, S. & O'Sullivan, S. (2005). Upsetting an applecart: difference, desire and lesbian sadomasochism. *Feminist Review*, 80(1), 98–126.
Bataille, G. (1962). *Eroticism*. London: Marion Boyars.
Boyd, S.B. (Ed.) (1997). *Challenging the Public/Private Divide: Feminism, Law, and Public Policy*. Toronto: University of Toronto Press.
Chancer, L. (1982). From pornography to sadomasochism: Reconciling feminist differences. In R.R. Linden *et al.* (Eds) *Against Sadomasochism: A Radical Feminist Analysis* (pp. 79–93). East Palo Alto, CA: Frog in the Well.
Chancer, L. (1992). *Sadomasochism in Everyday Life*. New Brunswick, NJ: Rutgers University Press.
Comment (1992). Keeping a disorderly house – a common law offence. *Criminal Law Review*, Jan, 49–50.
Cover, R.M. (1986). Violence and the word. *Yale Law Journal*, 95, 1601–1629.

Edwards, S. (1998). On the contemporary application of the Obscene Publications Act 1959. *Criminal Law Review*, December, 843–853.

Graycar, R. (1987–1988). Review of Katherine O'Donovan, sexual divisions in law. *Journal of Family Law*, 26, 265–274.

Hanna, C. (2001). Sex is not a sport: Consent and violence in the criminal law. *Boston College Law Review*, 42, 239–290.

Harvard Law Review (1968). Note: Assault and battery – consent of masochist to beating by sadist is no defense to prosecution for aggravated assault. *Harvard Law Review*, 81, 1339–1342.

Hoople, T. (1996). Conflicting visions: SM, feminism and the law. *Canadian Journal of Law and Society*, 11(1), 177–220.

Inness, J.C. (1992). *Privacy, Intimacy and Isolation*. New York, NY: Oxford University Press.

Nedelsky, J. (1989). Reconceiving autonomy: Sources, thoughts and possibilities. *Yale Journal of Law and Feminism*, 1(1), 7–16.

Nedelsky, J. (1990). Law, boundaries and the bounded self. *Representations*, 30, 162–189.

Nedelsky, J. (1993). Reconceiving rights as relationship. *Review of Constitutional Studies*, 1(1), 1–26.

O'Donovan, K. (1985). *Sexual Divisions in Law*. London: Weidenfeld and Nicolson.

Olsen, F. (1985). The myth of state intervention in the family. *University of Michigan Law Review*, 18, 835–864.

Parpworth, N. (2006). Sending obscene or indecent material through the post. *Justice of the Peace*, 170(21), 384.

Sarat, A. & Kearns, T.R. (2001). Making peace with violence: Robert Cover on law and legal theory. In A. Sarat (Ed.) *Law, Violence and the Possibility of Justice* (pp. 49–84). Princeton, NJ: Princeton University Press.

Superson, A. (2005). Deformed desires and informed desire tests. *Hypatia*, 20(4), 109–126.

Weait, M.J. (1996). Fleshing it out. In L. Flynn & L. Bentley (Eds) *Law and the Senses* (pp. 160–175). London: Pluto Press.

Weait, M.J. (2005). Harm, consent and the limits of privacy. *Feminist Legal Studies*, 13(1), 97–122.

Part II
Theorising Pain and Injury

6

Speaking the Unspeakable: S/M and the Eroticisation of Pain

Darren Langdridge

Whilst pain is not a feature of all sadomasochistic practice, it certainly plays an important part in S/M for some. A variety of explanations have been put forward for the seemingly counterintuitive erotic appeal of pain play. Most explanations have attempted to locate cause in psychopathology (see Taylor, 1997, for a review). One exception and, to date, the most convincing, is the explanation based on physiology and the close relationship between pain and pleasure centres (Sack & Miller, 1975). However, even here, much is lost with the reduction of intensely intersubjective phenomena to physiology. In this chapter, I explore the appeal of pain play and attempt to provide greater understanding of this particular aspect of S/M, by engaging with ideas from Scarry's (1985) *The Body in Pain*. In the process, I aim to offer an important caveat to Scarry's arguments about torture and the unmaking of the world. In her insightful analysis of torture, Scarry (1985) argues that pain involves the 'shattering of language'. That is, pain is almost uniquely inexpressible in language and as a consequence, for Scarry (1985), it is inextricably implicated in political and perceptual complications, and ultimately the unmaking of the world. I take her arguments about the structure of torture, and specifically the way in which it involves the double experience of agency and disintegration of consciousness, and – through the critical dual addition of pleasure and consent – argue that these (along with a fusion of bodily horizons) are key aspects of the appeal of pain play in S/M.

S/M and pain

Pain is probably most often identified as *the* constitutive component of S/M in lay representations of this particular sexual practice/identity.

There is, of course, much more to S/M than simply the intersection of pain and pleasure through sex (see Moser & Kleinplatz, Chapter 3). Pain may not play any part in an S/M scene and may be something actively avoided by people engaging in S/M. However, for some who practice S/M pain is an important – indeed, sometimes central – aspect of their S/M play. The relationship between pain and sex is one that appears to most trouble wider public understandings (see Langdridge, 2006; Weait, Chapter 5), principally because discourses of pain invariably focus on the inherently aversive nature of pain (Scarry, 1985), with the consequent need for avoidance of stimuli leading to pain. This discourse may be pervasive but represents only one way of understanding pain and furthermore is actually at odds with physiological explanations, which provide some support (in terms of providing a neurological foundation) for meanings in which pain may be actively sought out as part of our sexual repertoire.

Psycho-physiological studies of S/M, or rather, more specifically S/M concerned with pain, have sought to identify possible relationships between pain and pleasure centres. Ellis (1903) argued that different states of arousal are effectively indistinguishable such that pain can be experienced as pleasure and therefore, in these terms, S/M may be thought a normal aspect of our sexual lives. Since this time, a number of other writers have sought to understand the appeal of pain in S/M through an examination of psycho-physiological features. For instance, Sack and Miller (1975) argue that it is vital to understand pain phenomenologically given the extensive evidence of individual and cultural differences in pain responsivity and understandings of the psychology of pain, its effects and management. As Mains (1991) points out, at a very basic level pain will trigger the production of opiate-like chemicals in the brain, which release endorphins, resulting in a chemical 'high'. For Mains, therefore, pain is *in itself* pleasurable. This 'high' may also further enhance sexual pleasure and/or sexual excitation and therefore increase the ability to tolerate/enjoy pain.

Whilst these psycho-physiological explanations are undoubtedly useful and refreshingly non-pathological, they leave a great deal to be understood about the possible pleasures to be found in pain play. First, the arguments about the close relationship between neurological centres for pain and pleasure apply to all people and yet only a minority seek to explore this aspect of their sexuality. Second, and perhaps most importantly, these explanations reduce inherently complex intersubjective experiences to neurology. Such reductionism invariably results in the loss of fundamentally meaningful emergent properties such that the phenomenon – as lived – is lost. This is particularly apparent with S/M where there is so much more to pain scenes than simply the application of a pain stimulus during and/or for sexual arousal. There is, therefore, still a need to explore and provide possible theoretical understandings for the appeal of pain in S/M. In the remainder of this chapter, I seek to do just this, drawing on one of the most well-regarded phenomenological studies of pain – albeit one concerned with non-consensual torture – *The Body in Pain* by Elaine Scarry.

Scarry: *The Body in Pain*

Scarry's (1985) book is an important meditation on embodiment, the inexpressibility of pain and the way in which the deliberate infliction of pain – through torture – results in the unmaking of a person's world.[1] To this end, Scarry draws on a wide variety of materials in support of her phenomenology, including classic and contemporary literature, information from Amnesty International, medical research, religious writing and beyond. This results in a rich portrait of the effects of pain on a body and it is this heavy understanding that I describe briefly below before moving on to explore these arguments in more detail in the context of consensual S/M.

One of the key aspects of pain explored by Scarry is that pain is almost uniquely inexpressible in language. One's own pain is immediately and self-evidently present, almost impossible to ignore. For the person observing another in pain, however, it is almost impossible to grasp the full experience of that pain: one can remain totally ignorant and even with great effort only apprehend a shadow of what is being experienced. As a consequence, pain as experienced becomes an example of certainty whilst pain as observed becomes an example of doubt. This 'unsharability' is, at least in part, the result of the difficulty that comes from expressing pain, from communicating painful experience in language. Scarry (1985: 4) quotes Virginia Woolf thus:

> English, which can express the thoughts of Hamlet and the tragedy of Lear has no words for the shiver or the headache...The merest schoolgirl when she falls in love has Shakespeare or Keats to speak her mind for her, but let a sufferer try to describe a pain in his head to a doctor and language at once runs dry.

Furthermore this inexpressibility becomes ever more prevalent and incalculably more difficult with severe and prolonged pain. But, as Scarry points out, physical pain[2] is not simply inherently difficult to articulate:

it is also something which actively destroys language through a resultant recourse to a state anterior to language, the verbalisations of the baby before it has acquired language.

One of the key features of pain – in many, if not most, circumstances – that leads to this inexpressibility is that it lacks a referent. That is, in direct contradiction to the principle of intentionality – the central principle of phenomenology – outlined by Husserl (1900/1970), pain has no correlation with the external world. Intentionality in this sense refers to the fact that whenever we are conscious (aware), we are always conscious of something: there is always an object of consciousness. We do not simply feel love but rather love for someone or something: likewise we do not simply see or hear but rather see or hear something. Our consciousness (and therefore body) is thus turned out on the world, always in an intentional relationship with objects in the world such that we enter the shared world of experience (see Langdridge, 2007, for more on this). Pain, however, is not of or for anything, having no referential quality. It almost uniquely speaks to the heart of phenomenology, challenging the very core of this philosophy, trapping us in an egocentric predicament. That is, since pain is not intersubjective – being uniquely private – it is not part of the lifeworld. As such, pain represents experience that is not shared – not turned out on the world – and therefore not readily accessible to others.

In spite of the difficulty in giving voice to pain, there have been attempts – especially within medicine – to find ways of speaking pain. For whilst it is difficult to give voice to pain – given the absence of any clear referential quality to pain – it is not impossible. Perhaps the clearest and most successful attempts to articulate pain have come from medicine: here are people seeking to understand the subtlety of painful experience in order to better diagnose and treat those in pain. Through the development of various pain scales it has become possible, to some extent, to make visible solely interior events. Furthermore those working to end pain and suffering on a grand scale (such as Amnesty International) also attempt to find the language to communicate the suffering of pain from one person to others.

One of the consequences of the inexpressibility of pain concerns power and its political (and personal) consequences: in particular the power of one over another that comes about through the deliberate non-consensual infliction of pain through torture. Scarry (1985: 12) asks the question:

How is it that one person can be in the presence of another person in pain and not know it – not know it to the point where he himself inflicts it, and goes on inflicting it?

That is, how can one human being torture another, accepting that in most cases the infliction of pain is not driven by what psychiatrists term 'psychopathy' but rather through political will? The distance between people that is possible through the inexpressibility of pain – the inherently unknowable quality of another person's pain – is clearly key in understanding the ability of people to inflict such cruelty: for if we could feel the pain of the other, understand its consequences in our bodies, we would almost certainly find it impossible to torture another person.

A number of key features of torture in particular are also identified by Scarry, including the complex relationship between self and other, especially with respect to agency, the blurring of inside and outside – private and public – and the way in which torture results in the disintegration of consciousness through the constriction of the world of the tortured and expansion of the world of the torturer. I take these structural aspects of the body in pain – the structure of torture – and use them below as a heuristic for better understanding the appeal of sadomasochistic pain play.

The eroticisation of pain

Before continuing to explore in detail how Scarry's analysis may illuminate our understanding of the appeal of pain in S/M, it is important to highlight some of the key differences between consensual pain play in S/M and non-consensual torture. These differences are not only important in ethical/moral terms but also for the way in which they may provide a critical differentiation between apparently similar experiences such that one is pleasurable and the other deeply distressing.

First, there is a clear difference between S/M and torture with regard to consent. Consent is central to S/M (see Langdridge, 2006; Moser & Kleinplatz, Chapter 3; Weait, Chapter 5) and whilst this may be complex[3] it remains the key distinguishing feature between S/M and torture. People enter into S/M scenes voluntarily, in most cases fully aware of the consequences of their contracted relationship. In torture – discussed by Scarry – consent is notably absent and the infliction of pain is a deliberate act of cruelty without regard for the agency of the victim and their wishes to be involved or not. The second clear difference between S/M and torture involves the meaning of the acts for the parties involved. People within S/M scenes enter into such contracts for the pleasure (however broadly conceived) that they may experience. That is, the participants themselves mutually define the meanings of the acts that are perpetrated. Of course that is not to say that different parties may not experience events differently but, regardless, the meaning is their own. In torture, the meaning of violent acts is clear but, due to the lack of consent, restricted to the particular violent context within which they occur. The possibility of re-construing these acts is limited by the removal of agency from the victim.

Of note is the way in which consent acts to maximise the possibility of violent acts being understood in the participant's own terms, providing an opening-up of meaning. It is possible, of course, that pleasure may be experienced in non-consensual acts of violence but this often involves complex and problematic feelings of intrapsychic conflict, discomfort and dis-ease. Within S/M pain play multiple complex meanings are possible for often apparently simple acts of violence. A cut not only produces pain but also offers a sense of release, an exchange of power, a feeling of trust, loss of selfhood and so on: the possibilities are almost limitless. This ability to find meaning is founded on the consensual nature of the activities being played out, often explicitly negotiated and even if not, invariably thought through before, sometimes during, and very often after. Perhaps the key feature of consent in this context is the sense of agency that it engenders. That is, we take responsibility for the meaning of sexual experience (which may – of course – include the temporary abdication of responsibility itself) and can therefore conjure up multiple meanings such that apparently aversive acts become thoroughly pleasurable. This is taken up further below through discussion of pain and the language of agency.

Understanding the appeal

The double experience of agency and dissolution of inside/outside

As mentioned above, whilst ordinarily there is no language of pain, through ongoing attempts to find a language of pain, we have found some ways of verbalising pain, albeit one that is necessarily fragmentary and incomplete. Scarry points out that these attempts to find a language of pain – from medics, campaigners, lawyers and others – repeatedly return to the same linguistic set, one centred on the symbolic imagery of weaponry or what Scarry refers to as 'the language of agency'. Ironically this language can not only be used to ameliorate or end pain – through the actions of medics, lawyers and campaigners – but also perversely be used to further hurt others, keep pain invisible and actively destroy the social world in which we live.

The language of agency is essentially familiar and concerns the way in which we attempt to conjure up shared meaning through the 'as if' structure in language: by the attribution of agency to an external agent (like a weapon) or the attribution of agency to an internal agent through perceived bodily damage. The language of agency is common: 'it feels like someone is stabbing my arm with a knife', 'it feels as if my brain is swollen and throbbing'. There is a clear attempt to create a referential quality to the experience of pain, to attribute agency to something. Of course there may be occasions where there is the presence of an external weapon or internal damage but this is not important, the point is that in both cases (where there is a clear object of agency and those where there is not) the felt experience of pain can only be communicated by the same language of agency, by the externalisation and objectification of what is felt as internal and subjective: an attempt to make public what is essentially private.

Within the context of torture – a different but analogous experience to S/M pain play – agency takes on a special meaning, as a double experience of agency is realised. Pain produced intersubjectively – as it is in torture and most S/M pain play – is experienced at once as internal *and* external. In physical pain, one feels acted upon by both inside and outside: by an external weapon and one's own body. There is no longer the possibility of clearly demarcating what is due to self and what is due to other and this paradoxically may be an important aspect of the appeal of pain play in S/M for with this double experience of agency comes the dissolution of a clear distinction between inside and outside, private and public.

In the context of torture, Scarry (1985: 53) describes the dissolution of the boundary between inside and outside as 'an almost obscene conflation of private and public'. This is because, she argues, it brings 'all the solitude of absolute privacy with none of its safety, all the self-exposure of the utterly public with none of its possibility for camaraderie or shared experience' (p. 53). This experience in S/M, however, offers up quite the opposite: the possibility of absolute privacy made all the more safe by the loss of agency and the presence of a trusted other and self-exposure in the context of another or others to directly share in the experience. S/M pain play thus offers up the possibility of playing with the boundary of inside/outside, private/public such that the peace and sanctity of isolation or threat and thrill of exposure can be experienced in relation with an/other/s.

Disintegration of consciousness

Pain also inevitably involves the destruction of language, our primary source of objectification and self-extension. Scarry points out that before the loss of language, pain first monopolises it, making pain the only subject of speech. With increasing severity and/or prolonged exposure there is then the loss of language and a return to sounds anterior to speech, a return to the sounds of childhood. In torture and also in S/M pain play, the tendency of pain to destroy speech is enacted in obvious and exaggerated form. Through control of power – consensually agreed in S/M – the top can control the slow and steady destruction of language, turning speech and non-linguistic verbalisations on and off at will. The subject of these acts 'gains' the loss of agency, complexly experienced as both inside and outside and the consequent dissolution of the boundary of private and public, finding moments of intense and peaceful solitude and/or moments of intense and thrilling public exposure. With this comes the possibility of the total but temporary destruction of consciousness as the pain obliterates complex thought and emotion, even destroying one's ability to see. Pain takes over one's body, annihilating all else that it was, occupying both inside and outside as it becomes the single omnipresent fact of existence. The world of the tortured is thus closed down – disintegrated – such that the limits of peace and solitude can be found and/or the thrill of exposure and the merging of self and world. The world of the torturer inhabits this space between their still bounded self and the other, feeling the full force of the power and control that this entails, holding the other's consciousness – their world – in their hands. This is likely to be part of the appeal of this role for the torturer, who may come to enjoy the sense of power (and responsibility) that results from living out the world of two people as one.

A fusion of bodily horizons

A further feature of the infliction of pain that Scarry does not describe, not unsurprisingly given her concern with non-consensual torture, is the possibility of what I have previously termed 'a fusion of bodily horizons' (Langdridge, 2005). Merleau-Ponty's (1993) discussion of postural schema highlights the deeply embodied nature of intersubjective experience and the need to recognise that not all understanding comes through language. A person may come to understand their ways of relating through language but much of their experience, and its immediately apprehended meaning, operates outside language. In the context of psychotherapy, I described it thus:

> The therapeutic encounter becomes a dance where therapist and client form a unity, a synchronous back and forth of embodied mutuality. Merleau-Ponty's arguments shift the focus towards the immediate lived presence of two people in contact. Language is one means by which we come to understand. But it is not the only means: meaning also comes through an encounter of flesh with flesh. Another body-subject may draw us near or push us away, capture our interest or repulse us without ever uttering a word. Gadamer (1989) and Ricoeur (1981) talk of the 'fusion of horizons' when a reader comes to appropriate meaning from a text. In the context of appropriating meaning in psychotherapy this needs to be extended to recognise the 'fusion of bodily-horizons'. The bodily-horizons of therapist and client meet and envelop each other within the therapeutic encounter.
>
> (Langdridge, 2005: 96)

S/M and, in particular, the consensual infliction/inscription from/on one to another offers up a very real and visceral way of fusing the bodily horizons of self and other: a fleshly intertwining across a divide of otherness. We tend to hide from the sense of otherness that divides one from another, whilst knowing that it haunts our every move (cf. Heidegger, 1927/1962). There are times, however, when we glimpse this particular truth of existence, having to face up to the flesh and blood reality of knowing we are not unique and yet for some unaccountable reason always a stranger to the other. Jean Genet describes his own experience of this revelation in such harsh beauty that I feel it is worth reproducing at length here:

> Something which seemed to me to be rotten was turning my entire previous view of the world gangrenous. Then one day in a train compartment while looking at the traveller seated across from me I had the revelation that every man is *worth* every other. I didn't suspect that this understanding would lead to such a methodical disintegration – or rather I suspected it obscurely, for suddenly a weight of sadness came crashing down on me which, though more or less tolerable, was still perceptible and would never again leave me. Behind what was visible of this man or farther on – farther and at the same time miraculously and devastatingly close – in this man – his

body and face lacking in grace, ugly in certain details, even ignoble: dirty moustache, the hairs thinning but hard, rigid, sprouting up in nearly horizontal lines above the miniscule mouth, the mouth of someone spoiled, gobs of spit hawked between his knees on to a floor already filthy with cigarette butts, paper, crumbs, everything that made up the dirtiness of a third-class carriage in those days and then, because of his glance which stumbled against mine, I discovered with a shock a sort of universal identity amongst all men.

But that's not it! Things didn't move so quickly nor in that order. First my glance stumbled (not grazed but stumbled) against the traveller's, or rather melted into his. This man had just raised his eyes from his newspaper and quite simply, probably without paying attention, had rested them on mine which in the same accidental way were looking at him. Did he instantly feel the same emotion – and already the confusion – that I did? His glance didn't belong to someone else: it was mine which I met in a mirror, inadvertently and in solitude and forgetfulness. What I experienced I could translate only in these terms: I was flowing out of my body and through my eyes into the traveller's *at the same time he was flowing into mine*. Or rather: *I flowed*, for the glance was so brief that I can recall it only with the help of this verb tense. [...]

What, then, had flowed from my body – did I flow ... – and what had flowed from the body of the traveller?

This unpleasant experience was not repeated again, neither in its immediacy nor its intensity, but its after-effects will never stop sounding inside me. What I understood in the train compartment struck me as a revelation: once the accidents – in this case repellant [*sic*] – of his appearance were put aside, this man concealed and then let me reveal what had made him identical to me. (Genet's 1967 essay on Rembrandt quoted in White, 2004: 461–462)

The pain that results from such a harsh revelation subsides as we once again return to hide amongst the herd and be merely one man [sic] amongst others (Heidegger, 1927/1962). But in spite of this attempt to conceal ourselves from the inextricable otherness of life, we know – in our hearts – that we will ultimately live and most importantly die alone: moments of comfort are rare but can be found, found in the fleshly encounter of one with another, most especially when we find ways to make contact beyond/outside language. Pain is almost inexpressible – always felt first and foremost – and, as such, uniquely available to us to further divide self from other (in the case of torture) or bridge the gap and fuse our bodily horizons in the most real and visceral way (in the case of pain play in S/M). In S/M, bodies speak to each other, merging through the medium of pain, through the transfer of flesh and fluid, power and emotion: speaking outside language and offering that rare thing, a tender moment of togetherness. Of course these moments may occur with vanilla sex too. The tenderness that occurs when lips touch and momentarily, at least, produce a delicious sense of inter-twining across the chiasm of subjectivity (Merleau-Ponty, 1964/1968) is but one such example. Regardless, S/M offers up a highly refined version of such moments of intersubjectivity, where the particularity of such experiences is raised to a fine art.

Genet later came to realise that whilst we may feel lost, distressed and alone when we realise the universal nature of human kind, it is possible to find a way to value the particular, to at least temporarily transcend the universal and thus to return sexuality – broadly conceived – to intersubjectivity. As may be apparent in the quote above, there is a sense in which there is both aloneness and togetherness in the train carriage (although Genet at that time could only identify aloneness). It was much later that Genet himself came to see this through his relationship with a young boy named Hamza and his mother. He found that it was possible to recognise the universal and the particular through love, for whilst his actions may repeat those previously, or simply fade away, emotions live on and through love it is possible to recognise that everyone is the same and also priceless:

> The happiness of my hand in the hair of a boy another hand will know, already knows, and if I die this happiness will go on.
> (*Prisoner of Love* by Jean Genet, quoted in White, 2004: 722)

Conclusions

In this chapter, I have sought to provide some theoretical under-standing of the appeal of pain play in S/M. Given that, for many people, pain is something to be avoided at all costs, the active desire to inflict and/or feel pain, on the surface at least, appears perverse. Psycho-physiological explanations, however, have shown how pain and pleasure need to be understood in context and in particular, how it is vital to examine the meaning of pain for the people involved. In her insightful analysis of torture, I believe Scarry (1985) paradoxically provides a number of reasons why pain play may be pleasurable and actively sought out in S/M. The double experience of agency, the dissolution of inside/outside and the disintegration of consciousness – crucially mediated through consent – provide a number of answers to the apparent paradox of pain play. When supplemented by the possible pleasures that may be experienced through a fusion of our bodily horizons I believe we have a way of looking at S/M pain play that renders understanding possible. Finally, it is worth noting that most critically pain play appears to involve a way of experiencing the limits of one's material-semiotic subjectivity through the exploration of agency and subjection. Through the fleshly intertwining of self and other we may find new boundaries of pleasure that raise the bar on what it is possible to feel.

Notes

1. Scarry (1985) goes on further to examine the structure of war, as well as aspects of pain, that figure in the making and unmaking of our world. My analysis here, however, focuses on her arguments around pain experienced through individual bodies.
2. Whilst there are undoubtedly many similarities between physical and psychological pain there are also some key differences. Notably, in the context of the argument presented here, physical pain is much less amenable to linguistic description than psychological pain (there being a ready vocabulary for this already) and indeed actively destroys language through recourse to sounds anterior to language. It is also worth noting that in many cases psychological pain has a referent quite unlike physical pain.
3. See Langdridge (2006) and Downing (Chapter 8) for more on the complexity of consent with S/M.

References

Ellis, H. (1903). *Studies in the Psychology of Sex*. New York, NY: Random House.
Heidegger, M. (1927/1962). *Being and Time* (J. Macquarrie & E. Robinson, 1962 text trans.). Oxford: Blackwell.
Husserl, E. (1900/1970). *Logical Investigations*, 2 vols (J.N. Findlay, Trans.). New York, NY: Humanities Press.
Langdridge, D. (2005). 'The child's relations with others': Merleau-Ponty, embodiment and psychotherapy. *Existential Analysis*, 16.1, 87–99.
Langdridge, D. (2006). Voices from the margins: SM and sexual citizenship. *Citizenship Studies*, 10(4), 373–389.
Langdridge, D. (2007). *Phenomenological Psychology: Theory, Research and Method*. Harlow: Pearson Education.
Mains, G. (1991). The molecular anatomy of leather. In M. Thompson (Ed.) *Leatherfolk: Radical Sex, People, Politics and Practices*. Boston, MA: Alyson.

Merleau-Ponty, M. (1964/1968). *The Visible and the Invisible* (A. Lingis, Trans.). Evanston, IL: Northwestern University Press.

Merleau-Ponty, M. (1993). The experience of others (F. Evans & H.J. Silverman, Trans.). In K. Hoeller (Ed.) *Merleau-Ponty and Psychology* (pp. 33–66). New Jersey: Humanities Press.

Sack, R.L. & Miller, W. (1975). Masochism: A clinical & theoretical overview. *Psychiatry*, 38, 244–257.

Scarry, E. (1985). *The Body in Pain: The Making and Unmaking of the World*. Oxford: Oxford University Press.

Taylor, G.W. (1997). The discursive construction and regulation of dissident sexualities: The case of SM. In J.M. Ussher (Ed.) *Body Talk: The Material and Discursive Regulation of Sexuality, Madness and Reproduction*. London: Routledge.

White, E. (2004). *Genet*. London: Vintage.

7
The 'Bodily Practices' of Consensual 'SM', Spirituality and 'Transcendence'

Andrea Beckmann

Consensual 'SM' can be related to a variety of broader socio-cultural phenomena and meanings as demonstrated elsewhere (e.g. Beckmann 2001a, 2001b, 2004, 2005; Langdridge & Butt, 2004; Taylor, 1997; Taylor & Ussher, 2001). This chapter focuses on one potential meaning that consensual 'SM' 'bodily practices' (Mauss, 1979) may have, for some practitioners, an understanding of consensual 'SM' as a spiritual practice that might function for some as a site for re-enchantment.

In order to explore this possible interpretation, this chapter will draw on some of the findings of the author's doctoral thesis (University of Edinburgh, 2000). This involved a critical criminological, methodologically mainly ethnographic, social research project in London's 'Scene' of consensual 'SM'. Unstructured but focused interviews as well as participant observations within Scene-clubs aimed at exploring the 'lived realities' of consensual 'SM' and its 'subjugated knowledges' and allowed for empirically 'grounded' insights. A deep contrast between 'scientific' discourses on 'sadomasochism' and the 'subjugated knowledges' of consensual 'SM' was revealed through the 'fieldwork'. The 'harms' that resulted from the dominant discourses that were part of the 'deployment of sexuality' (Foucault, 1990) in terms of concepts of 'self' (for example, as 'deviant', as determined, as pathological) and in terms of the socio-legal reactions towards practitioners of consensual 'SM' became evident.

As part of the 'reflexivity of the research process' (May, 1993, 2001) it became important to adapt the chosen terminology to the findings of my research. As consensual 'SM' aims at the production of pleasure through the empathetic 'play' with 'lived bodies' (Merleau-Ponty, 1968), which is not limited to 'sexual pleasure', the term 'body practice' and/or 'bodily practices' (Mauss, 1979) appeared to be a more adequate term to describe this social phenomenon.

Overcoming our identification of ourselves with 'truth' that shapes our relationship to ourselves as well as others was a central concern of Michel Foucault's life and work (see Miller, 1994), as in the case of 'sexuality' (identification of human beings with their 'sex-desire' or 'genital desire') through a return to 'bodies' and 'pleasures' (by means of e.g. consensual 'SM' and potentially 'transcendental experiences' reached through these practices). Guided by Foucault's project to find out about the way 'truth' is formed in relationships between knowledge and power within social practices (Foucault, 1980), this chapter intends to explore his notion of *the only way* to go beyond this 'truth' ('transcendence') by employing a historio-cultural comparative perspective that facilitates an understanding of consensual 'SM' as a potential spiritual practice. The chapter then engages with an exploration of interdisciplinary sources which have attempted to study a diversity of mystical experiences as well as with sources that confirm the potential for spiritual 'transcendental' and thus transformative dimensions of consensual 'SM' (e.g. Bastian, 2002; Pat Califia, 1994; Thompson, 1991).

The analysis of empirical data derived from the author's own research project within the Scene of consensual 'SM' suggested that consensual 'SM' indeed functions for some practitioners as a spiritual exercise and thus confirms that the notion of 'transcendental experiences' through these 'bodily practices' finds validation in the 'life worlds' of consensual 'SM'.

It is crucial to note that elements of 'SM' and of fetish culture have become part of the capitalist consumerist industry of mainstream society and this will obviously impact on the ways in which the 'bodily practices' of consensual 'SM' are 'lived out' and interpreted, for example capitalism's proliferatory imperative led to the commodification and proliferation of representations of 'kinky sex' (see also Beckmann, 2001a, 2001b). Despite allowing greater access to tools, outfits, clubs and so on, this exploitation cannot in itself be interpreted as representing a greater understanding or respect for these 'bodily practices', as they remain selectively criminalised. A further problematic aspect was discussed by Tyler (2004) who researched the increasing incorporation of management discourses and techniques into 'sexuality' and 'sexual' relations via contemporary mainstream cultural resources (e.g. lifestyle magazines). Tyler argued these eroded and arrested the intersubjective elements of the 'erotic' and suggested:

> Erotic sex, as Rose put it, is clearly about much more than just pleasure; it is a way in which individuals can express themselves and

find an intersubjective release from the fragmenting and alienating effects of organized society (Marcuse, 1955).

(Tyler, 2004: 100)

In this chapter, the aim is to demonstrate that consensual 'SM' practices can achieve this for some of its practitioners.

Consensual 'SM', religion, spirituality and applied mysticism: a historio-cultural perspective

Homophobia may be rampant, but leather phobia is even more so. (...) Much may have been borrowed from the Leather culture in satire, but leather has also borrowed much from our ancestors such as ritualism, tribalism, and rites of passages.

(Bastian, 2002: 73)

This section explores some traditions which appear to have similarities with elements of the concept and ritual of consensual 'SM' as spiritual exercise. The institution of transformation through ritual ordeal and/or sexual ecstasy has an ancient tradition in many cultures and some have striking parallels in the 'bodily practices' of consensual 'SM'.

According to Durkheim (1915/1965), on a collective level, the totemic celebration of a group's own sacred in-group-ness is the most elementary form of religious life. Within the Scene that developed around consensual 'SM', a sense of secrecy and diverse membership procedures, as well as the commitment to a specific code of conduct and a specific philosophy of life, could therefore be seen as elements of the 'religious life' of the Scene. For example, Holt (1993) explicitly linked consensual 'SM' ritual explicitly to the potential for religious experience. On the level of the individual, religion fulfils human needs for identification and recognition, again similar to the functions that consensual 'SM' potentially provides.

Synnott (1993) emphasised the distinction between 'Dionysian' and 'Apollonian' cultural practices that originate in Nietzsche's distinction of Greek tragedies. Whereas the 'Apollonian' cultural practices are associated with the conscious, the rational, the 'life-denying', the 'Dionysian' cultural practices are 'life-affirming' and concerned with passion and ecstasy. 'Dionysian' culture as practised for example by the Indian nations of North America and Mexico valued violent experience and a diversity of means by which humans are enabled to break through the usual sensory routine. Classic examples are the Sun Dance of the

Western Plains and the Peyote Cult of which Starkloff (1974) stated that even though they are based on ancient rites, their development in the late eighteenth and nineteenth centuries fulfilled the purpose of bonding – of bringing the now separated native American tribes back together. In these contexts the sensual, corporal experiences could be at once a personal and a communal spiritual experience of high intensity that was/is functional in the quest for survival.

Parallels to bonding rituals of lesbian, gay and bisexual practitioners of consensual 'SM' that the author observed in Scene-clubs can be drawn. In some of these rituals, the practitioners pierced each others chests at various points and danced, connected to each other by needles, strings and pain, while slowly pulling their pierced skins further and further apart (very similar to the Sun Dance ritual). On a symbolic level this ritual could be read as an intense bonding practice that unites factually disenfranchised members of both the minority groups, with their often prescriptive 'political correctness' (e.g. feminist/lesbian) and/or stereotypical expectations (e.g. mandatory anal sex in gay culture) about 'sex', as well as mainstream culture's socio-political outside pressures of 'normalisation' (see Beckmann, 2001a, 2001b).

Starkloff (1974) states that the tradition of asceticism within the native American cultures should be seen positively as it has provided their people with acquired 'self'-knowledge. Arguably this holds true for consensual 'SM' as well because for many practitioners the aim is to explore the potentials and limits of 'self ' as defined by the 'lived body' (Merleau-Ponty, 1968).

'Dionysus was bound to incite resistance and persecution, for the religious experience that he inspired threatened an entire lifestyle and a universe of values...' (Eliade, 1978: 359). This 'threat' also appears to exist for society in relation to the 'bodily practices' of consensual 'SM' as, for example, symbols and 'technologies of government' are appropriated by its practitioners in order to derive pleasure from them. The 'bodily practices' of consensual 'SM' also imply the transgression of the existing modern scientific 'order of things' (Foucault, 1971) apart from the transgression of the non-consensual 'SM' inherent in Western patriarchal capitalist consumer societies (Chancer, 1992).

Eliade (1978) relates Dionysus also to the totality of life which, on a symbolical level, can be seen to hold true for consensual 'SM' as well as many 'scenes' make use of representations of death and/or use blood and thus also symbolically celebrate a notion of 'life in death'. The 'Dionysian state' represents, and is experienced as, an abysmal loss of 'self', a state of indetermination and of a rupture of the perception of the dualistic, reductionistic modern binarism of 'inside/outside'. Here some obvious parallels can be drawn to the Scene of consensual 'SM', particularly in terms of the practice of 'switching' (e.g. from 'dominant' to 'submissive' role) which implies the swapping of subject/object positions that are usually socio-politically assigned to people without their consent.

This sense of 'indetermination' becomes further evident in terms of the specifically open atmosphere in some of the Scene clubs as captured by Golding (1993) who described the atmosphere at a consensual 'SM' club in London as a space of 'the-impossible-but-actual-limit-to-the-outside/otherside-of-otherness', a location of an exiled identity.

Applied mysticism, detachment, de-centring of 'self' and consensual 'SM'

Ellwood's (1980) reference to Underhill's understanding of mysticism enlightens the relationship between transcendental experiences and consensual 'SM':

> ..., she spoke of mysticism as a quest for truth and reality that goes beyond merely sensory or intellectual spheres, taking on the aspect of a personal passion that must know directly ultimate reality without mediation of mind or sense.
>
> (Ellwood, 1980: 14)

Consensual 'SM' could be interpreted as one form of mysticism in which the 'lived body' and, in particular, its sensuous capacities are used as a medium. This reading would seem to be confirmed, for example, by Vale and Juno's (1989) research with 'Modern Primitives' in which they interviewed people who enjoy 'body'-modifications that do not serve the purposes of 'normalisation' as well as practitioners of consensual 'SM' and explored the diverse meanings 'body' can have for them as an artistic medium.

The mystical significance of detachment was discussed by Staal (1975). 'Detachment is to some extent a prerequisite for the other methods, but it is in turn increased by their practice' (Staal, 1975: 138–139). In terms of consensual 'SM', this detachment could be interpreted to be assured a priori through the artificial, theatrical setting that, perhaps due to its ritualistic appearance, allows individuals to detach from the 'outside world' and to completely enter into the world of a 'scene'.

Within the Christian belief system, medieval devotionalism, flage-llant-processions and so on provide examples of this detachment whereby the techniques for the subjection of 'self' are unconditional obedience, interminable examination and exhaustive confession. Although Michel Foucault seemed fascinated by the Christian ideas of martyrdom and self-sacrifice and remarked 'No truth about the self is without the sacrifice of the self' (Miller, 1994: 324), he rejected the tech-niques applied within the Christian context as well as the focus on the 'sinful body'.

The moral stricture that mysticism is subjected to within the Western world and in Islam hinders a proper understanding and appreciation in terms of this broader and open conceptualisation that appears to match consensual 'SM' practices. In contrast to other religious and/or mystical contexts (e.g. Islam, Christianity, etc.) which reject and/or condemn the 'body' and 'sexuality' on the basis of moral exclusion, 'sexuality' is utilised especially in the tantric traditions of Indian civilisation, here 'sexual' practices are 'utilized in order to bring about greater detachment from the rules of morality' (Staal, 1975: 140).

This view of mysticism also matches Vale and Juno's (1989) sugges-tions as to the reason of the 'revival of the primitive':

> All the 'modern primitive' practices being revived – so called 'permanent' tattooing, piercing, and scarification – underscore the realization that death itself...must be stared straight in the face....Death remains the standard whereby the authenticity and depth of all activities may be judged....All sensual experience func-tions to free us from 'normal' social restraints, to awaken our deadened bodies to life.
>
> (Vale & Juno, 1989: 5)

In terms of the understanding of 'Modern Primitives', mysticism is an active philosophically inspired search for new values and meanings for the individual, as well as for society in general and not a passive act of regression. This view reflects another possible interpretation of the potential broader social meanings that the 'bodily practices' of consen-sual 'SM' might have in contemporary Western capitalist consumer cultures.

In his reflections on the relationship between culture and the indi-vidual, Aldous Huxley suggested that

A culture cannot be discriminatingly accepted, much less be modified, except by persons who have seen through it – by persons who
have cut holes in the confining stockade of verbalized symbols and
so are able to look at the world and, by reflection, at themselves in a
new and relatively unprejudiced way.

(in Solomon, 1964: 31)

As people need to be prepared for the process of 'hole cutting' the
option of the integration of culture comparisons within society's formal
education appears to be valuable but insufficient as the whole of the
person, the 'lived body', must be captured in order to change. In
Aldous Huxley's opinion, the experience of LSD-induced altered states
of consciousness allows for this particular kind of 'training' in that the
highly intense and unusual experiences enable the individual to be more
'open' for change.

The de-centring of the 'self' by means of 'transcendental experiences'
appear to allow for the most fundamental changes in consciousness and
often also result in behavioural changes as all behaviour is learned and
culturally determined, it is changeable. In order to explain behavioural
changes, Timothy Leary (1964) employed the notion of a 'game' to
define 'a learned cultural sequence' (in Solomon, 1964: 98). 'Psychology,
religion, politics are games, too, learned, cultural sequences with clearly
definable roles, rules, rituals, goals, jargons, values' (Leary, in Solomon,
1964: 99). In comparison with sports and consensual 'SM', the problem
with these complex 'games' listed above is that they are less explicitly
games:

Worst of all is the not knowing that it is a game. (…) Culturally,
stability is maintained by keeping the members of any cultural group
from seeing that the roles, rules, goals, rituals, language, and values
are game structures. … Cultural institutions encourage the delusion
that the games of life are inevitable givens involving natural laws of
behavior. These fixed delusions tend to rigidify behavior patterns.

(Leary, in Solomon, 1964: 100)

The game of consensual 'SM' symbolically points to the game-
character of 'normal life' which, in Foucauldian terms, is often determined by socio-political relationships of power that turn rigid and thus
effect 'conditions of domination'. Consensual 'SM' is always clearly a
game with all the advantages of a game, one can start and stop when
one likes (sometimes laid down by contract) and the flexibility of the

game is ensured by the possibility of 'switching' and by the fantasy and empathy developing within the game situation ('scene').

In Leary's opinion,

> ... [the] most effective approach to the 'practical' games of life is that of applied mysticism. Identify the game structure of the event.... The process of getting beyond the game structure, beyond the subject–object commitments, the dualities – this process is called the mystic experience.
>
> (Leary, in Solomon, 1964: 103–104)

This points to the problematic relationship of 'moral' and/or 'radical' feminism' (e.g. Jeffreys, 1993, 2003; Linden, Pagano, Russell & Star, 1982) towards consensual 'SM'. The arguments against consensual 'SM', as well as the occasional selective 'celebration' of lesbian 'SM', suggest that the representations and concepts of societal power relationships, with their explicit and implicit rules, are stabilised and reinforced within the setting of the 'scenes' of these 'bodily practices'. These arguments from 'moral' and 'radical' feminists alike do not try to go beyond the 'game' structures of society and thus promote a positivistic, essentialist view of human beings based on (sometimes selective) socio-political determinism. In a similar vein, the selective approval of BDSM by some Christians (e.g. Sir Gardener for Christian BDSM, http://www.the-iron-gate.com/bdsm_christianity.php, accessed 24 November 2006) between '...a husband and wife in male dominant/female submissive roles...' is clearly only re-inscribing 'bodies' with conventional socio-political power relationships and not 'transcending' these.

Leary lists diverse methods that expand consciousness beyond game limits such as traumatic limit experiences, electric shock, extreme fatigue, sensory deprivation and so on that all 'cut through the game':

> Certain forms of sensory stimulation alter consciousness beyond games. The sexual orgasm is certainly the most frequent and natural, although so brief and so built into interpersonal courtship games that it has lost much of its mystical meaning in the West.
>
> (Leary, in Solomon, 1964: 106)

In Western capitalist consumer society in which orgasms get consumed, counted and chemically achieved, the notion of a mystical experience through orgasm might only survive in a few human beings.

The consequence of 'transcendental experiences' is, according to Leary, the 'unplugged mind':

> Not the 'id'; no dark, evil impulses. These alleged negative 'forces' are, of course, part of the game, being simply anti rules. What is left is something that Western culture knows little about: the open brain, the uncensored cortex-alert and open to a broad sweep.
>
> (Leary, in Solomon, 1964: 106)

One of my interviewees called one of her most intense experiences of consensual 'SM', that to her had a transcendental quality, a 'shamanic journey'. Eliade (in Couliano, 1991) defined shamanism as a 'technique of ecstasy' as opposed to a proper religion. Shamanism consists of a system of ecstatic and therapeutic methods that enable human beings to make contact with the universe of the spirits which exists parallel to the 'here and now' world in shamanistic belief systems. Apart from mere contact, it is attempted to gain the support of the spirits in order to improve the management of individual or group affairs. Norman (1991) pointed to the parallels between shamanism and consensual 'SM' apart from the application of similar methods. Like shamanism the 'bodily practices' of consensual 'SM' can be an ' ... ongoing process of initiation' and a continuous search for new experience and knowledge of 'self' (in Thompson, 1991: 280). As a crucial precondition for a pleasurable 'scene', the 'top' (dominant), often a former 'bottom' (submissive), also ideally has learned to 'control personal spirits' in order to empathise with the 'spirits' of her/his 'bottoms' through the journey of a 'scene' which sometimes, and apparently not that rarely, allows for 'transcendental experiences'. During a 'scene', the 'top', similar to a shaman, makes use of objects that symbolise societal power, for example instruments of corporal punishment of humans or instruments representing the power of the science of medicine over the individual 'body'. These tools function in terms of providing a setting of 'spiritual atmosphere' that is meant to enable the 'bottom' to reach 'ecstasy' and possibly 'transcendental states'.

On the individual level, the experience of 'discrete altered states of consciousness' (Tart, 1975), of 'transcendence' or of 'peak-experiences' (Maslow, 1970) that several interviewees reported and which probably is experienced by many others appears to have a direct impact on the social atmosphere within the Scene as well as on individuals:

Mystical experience has such an inner ring of authenticity that it also authenticates whatever areas of life, indeed whatever life-styles, with which it is symbolically associated. When an individual's life is sufficiently different as to have only questionable social legitimation, this individual naturally craves a corresponding inner authentication. Mystical experience can answer to this need.

(Ellwood, 1980: 142)

Incorporating the 'ineffable' body into empirical research

Martin (2006) noted that there does not exist much empirical research on 'transcendent' 'sexual' experiences and refers to Wade's work (2000) as one of the notable few. Westhaver (2005) also pointed to a lack of incorporation of the 'ineffable body' that appears to be characteristic for much of academic work but especially evident and problematic within the realm of 'sexual' health research and promotion. Consequently '...we exclude an aspect of the subject-ineffable bodily experience, the self shattered in the face of pleasure-that is constitutive of what we are' (Westhaver, 2005: 357)

Horn *et al.* do refer to studies that explored the relationship between sexuality and spirituality (e.g. MacKnee, 2002; Murray-Swank, Pargament & Mahoney, 2005; Wade, 2000) that found that the reported 'peaks of sexual and spiritual connection' did not in all cases involve the experience of orgasm and that

> ...individuals experienced connections with God and with their partner [which] resulted in a breakdown of 'dualism in all forms' that reconciled body and spirit, male and female, human and nature.
>
> (Horn *et al.*, 2005: 83)

As the studies Horn *et al.* referred to were all exclusively concerned with heterosexual relationships and 'vanilla sex' they were quite selective.

The relationship between spirituality and '(sexual) deviance' is thus still a relatively marginalised area in social research. However, there are some sources that do have empirical relevance as these are 'grounded' in experience, for example Califia's book *Sensuous Magic* (1994) defined 'SM orgasm' as 'The reaching of an emotional, psychological, or spiritual state of catharsis, ecstasy, or transcendence during an S/M scene without having a genital orgasm' (Califia, 1994: 151). Further Michel Foucault, himself a practitioner of consensual 'SM', mentioned his aims and hopes for 'transcendence' through these 'bodily practices' several times (Miller, 1994). According to Foucault's own experiences 'transcendental states through 'SM'-practice' are '...potentially self-destructive yet mysteriously revealing states of dissociation...' (in Miller, 1994: 30) that allow a completely different view of the world and open up possibilities for the 'invention' of a new self.

Other related sources that refer to the 'transcendental dimension of consensual 'SM' are to be found in the works of Bastian (2002) as well as Thompson (1991), who both enjoy the practices of consensual 'SM' and have described the possibility of achieving similar states.

'It is little wonder that we sometimes refer to them as religious experiences, because that's what they can feel like' (Thompson, 1991: 172). Under the heading 'New Age leather', Thompson explains the notion of consensual 'SM' as a possible meditation path in more practical detail:

> When leather and S/M scenes were done in a certain way, we achieved a different level of awareness – we felt transformed into someone whom it felt better to be....Some of us referred to it as the 'S/M high'.
>
> (Thompson, 1991: 172)

Michel Foucault believed in the value of experiences and believed that the only way to go beyond our identification of ourselves with our 'sexdesire' was a return to 'bodies and pleasures', to an 'economy of pleasure' not based on sexual norms nor through the liberation of a constructed 'sexdesire' determined by 'scientia sexualis' but rather through '...a creation of anarchy within the body, where its hierarchies, its localizations and designations, its organicity, if you will, is in the process of disintegrating...' (in Miller, 1994: 274). The theoretical relevance of this topic was implicitly already stated by Foucault himself, when he commented on the relationship between 'limit experience' (e.g. 'transcendental experiences through "S/M" ') and the 'history of truth'. Foucault admitted that when starting from some personally transformative 'limit experience': 'it is necessary to open the way for a transformation, a metamorphosis, that is not simply individual but has a character accessible to others' (Miller, 1994: 32).

Within the specific context of my research project the aim was to explore if Michel Foucault's frequent, but rather vague, suggestions about the use of consensual 'SM' for the possible 'transcendence' of culturally learned and internalised categories of 'sex' and 'sexuality' and the possibilities of a new 'mapping' of the 'lived body' involve:

(1) shared motivations and/or experiences of other practitioners of consensual 'SM';
(2) a priori or gained motivations.

Apart from these aims the research tried to explore the quality and the impact of these experiences for the practising people.

The shared view within the literature on 'transcendental experiences' is that the common indicator for such experiences is a highly subjective one: the feelings of the individual. According to Grof (1985), the common determinator of 'transpersonal experiences' is the individual's obviously subjective feeling and impression that her/his consciousness has expanded beyond the 'normal' limitations of the 'ego' boundaries and that during these experiences the dimensions of time and space, which usually give human beings a basic orientation, have been 'transcended'. In order to be able to account for experiential knowledge on transcendental states through the practice of consensual 'SM', access to the subjective experiences of the interviewees had to be acquired. It was crucial to generate and foster a trustful atmosphere between the individual interviewee and me, so that they would feel encouraged to honestly reply to these extremely personal and complex questions. As the conventional scientific world does not engage often with the notion of 'transcendence' there is a lack of discourse, reflected by a lack of adequate language (terminology). Therefore the topic of 'transcendental states' proved to be a difficult one which is represented by its basic criteria ' ... ineffability (it cannot really be described) ... ' (Ellwood, 1980: 15). It was thus going to be 'hard to put into words' for the respondents to the questionnaire.

Wade's research (2000) also employed the taxonomic categories of Grof (1988) as indicators of 'transcendental experiences' while my own research further drew on Grof (1985) and Tart's (1975) characteristics as well in order to probe into this ineffiable arena of human experience. While the rest of my research design was entirely locatable within the ethnographic tradition, I decided to construct a self-completion questionnaire alongside Charles T. Tart's 'Experiental criteria for detecting an altered state of consciousness' (1975: 12, Table 2-1) and Maxwell and Tschudin's 'Common elements of religious and other transcendent experiences' (1990), as this element of consensual 'SM' otherwise would be impossible to research.

The list of Tart's (1975) 'Experiental criteria for detecting an altered state of consciousness' attempts to structure the complex experience of a 'discrete altered state of consciousness' into elements of this experience, thus providing a systematic conceptual framework that enables people to judge about the 'state of consciousness' they are momentarily in. The development of a theoretical framework of questions that are understandable (without being directive and imposing the idea of 'transcendental states through consensual "SM" ') and that would still relate reasonably authentic to experiences of people who have experienced 'transcendental states' in other contexts was my aim for the questionnaire design. While my preference lies with qualitative methods of social research, May reminded me that

> ...questionnaires can tap meanings if adequately designed and piloted and that the divide which is often thought to exist between quantitative and qualitative research, actually 'impoverishes' the aim of understanding and explaining human relations (McLaughlin 1991).
>
> (May, 1993: 88)

This chapter does not allow for a detailed elaboration of all the methodological aspects that were involved in the design of the 'self-completion questionnaire' (these are detailed in my forthcoming book, *Practices of an Unpure Reason*, 2007/2008, Palgrave). Apart from methodological and structural requirements, the other determining factor for the design of a questionnaire is, according to May (1993, 2001), the amount of resources that are available beforehand. In the case of 'transcendental' experiences through the practices of consensual 'SM' there was an absence of former research material or directly focussed theoretical works. Therefore the literature review was conducted in an interdisciplinary fashion, alongside psychological and para-psychological books that deal with the so-called 'transcendental experiences' in other contexts (mainly by Grof, 1985 and Tart, 1975) and literature that deals with 'transcendent experiences' in religious contexts (e.g. Jones, 1991; Maxwell & Tschudin, 1990).

Re-enchanting 'bodies': 'transcendental' experiences within consensual 'SM' 'bodily practices'

The 'bodily practices' of consensual 'SM' appear to provide some practitioners with the possibility of experiencing 'spirituality'. This feature of consensual 'SM' practice is also an element of many diverse religions and mystical belief systems that also involve the 'lived body' as a whole. Consensual 'SM' can therefore satisfy the longing for religious and spiritual experiences for some practitioners and further provide them with the possibility of self-actualisation (e.g. through experience of 'boundary situations', etc.).

The analysis of the self-completion questionnaire, in conjunction with non-directive interviewees and participant observation, revealed that 'transcendental experiences' are part of the sensations searched for in consensual 'SM', even though never as an a priori motivation but only *after* the 'discovery' of them, in other words, as a 'gained motivation'. As only two of the interviewees did not hand back the questionnaire and all the other practitioners of consensual 'SM' that were interviewed could, in one way or the other, relate to the topic of unusual/transcendental experiences through these 'bodily practices', it is possible to conclude that, frequently, the practice of consensual 'SM' appears to include experiences like this. Furthermore it is quite striking to note that the two respondents who could not relate at all to these experiences, and/or did not have very intense or variant experiences, tend to be exclusively 'tops'. It appears as if the 'bottom'-space provides more of a basis for the experience of 'transcendental' phenomena as the degree of detachment from habitual contents that individuals achieve within the ritualised context of a 'scene' is necessarily more completely achievable for the one who inhabits the 'bottom'-space as the 'top' will always need to ensure the safety of the 'bottom'.

This observation is crucial as it underlines that the practice of consensual 'SM' is an inter-relational 'bodily practice' which offers 'bottoms', 'subs' and 'slaves' the possibility to experience 'transcendental states' as they are enabled to let go of the control of the 'internal supervisor' while being 'topped' by a trusted 'dom'. People appear to seek out different 'scenes' and different degrees of sensation in order to match their needs. For some, consensual 'SM' serves mainly as a tool to heighten sensual and 'sexual' experience or as a release of pressure or guilt feelings, while for others the achievement of 'transcendental states' appears to be a core motivation.

While Christianity operates on the basis of a dualistic understanding of mind/body and thus coded 'sexuality' as merely genital,

> ... the literature of sexual theology or embodiment theology has challenged this traditional perception and has suggested that sexuality is much more of an integral and holistic part of the human experience than the activity of genital sex. It is the source of our capacity for

relationship, for emotional and erotic connection, for intimacy, for passion and for transcendence.

(Horn *et al.*, 2005: 81)

The rise of interest in the practice of consensual 'SM' as well as the growing fascination with the Scene ('SM', 'Fetishism', etc.) appears, apart from its current commercial exploitation, to be for some an attempt of individual and collective 're-enchantment' in the sense of the notion employed by Bauman:

> ... postmodernity can be seen as restoring to the world what modernity, presumptuously, had taken away; as a *re-enchantment* of the world that modernity tried hard to *dis-enchant*. It is the modern artifice that has been dismantled; the modern conceit of meaning-legislating reason that has been exposed, condemned and put to shame. (...) The war against mystery and magic was for modernity the war of liberation leading to the declaration of reason's independence.
>
> (Bauman, 1992: x)

The 'bodily practices' of consensual 'SM' are, in many ways, re-enchanting the 'life-world' of its practitioners and can be interpreted as a response to an increasing awareness of the limits of 'progress' and 'reason' and of the dis-enchantment of modernity and consumer culture. The 'body' and 'sexuality' are frequently stripped of any meaning but competitive consumption and 'body image' within the every day world and can acquire new experiential meanings in the context of the 'bodily practices' of consensual 'SM'.

Through the 'desexualisation of pleasure' as well as the necessity of the learning of the 'care of the self' (Foucault, 1990) in the 'scenes' that are played in consensual 'SM', rigid categories of separation are broken down and authentic communication (verbal/non-verbal) is made possible (see Beckmann, 2004).

Consensual 'SM' 'body practices' can be understood as a response of appropriation (of conventionally allocated socio-political roles and relationships of power and powerlessness) which, through sensuous experiences and potential 'transcendental experiences', allow experiential insight into the instability of social constructs of determinisms of power and identity and thus into potentials for change. Practitioners of consensual 'SM' further appear to have a greater potential to realise the 'self' as a 'strategical possibility' (Foucault; in Halperin, 1995: 73) instead of the modern deterministic understanding of 'self' as a fixed unity which allows for the experiential re-inscription of the political.

One of the interviewees appeared to express Foucault's aim of 'abolishing the internal supervisor' and/or the 'panopticon of everyday life' (Foucault, 1976, 1990). Anthony believes in choices that transcend the socially set boundaries not by principle but as a strategy to achieve more freedom:

> We've already lived in a repressive culture anyway, this is why I keep pushing my boundaries to see what works for me, you know what I'm saying? ... I think people have to make their own choices without that power within: you can't do this, you can't do that.
>
> (In. 3, 1997: 3)

The phenomena of 'transcendental experiences' through the 'bodily practices' of consensual 'SM', should thus be regarded as an important aspect of the commitment (Becker, 1960) that practitioners of consensual 'SM' can develop towards their 'plays'. This degree of (religious, spiritual or quasi-religious) commitment of individual 'players' should be taken into account, when the issue of the degrees of 'bodily harm' that serve the criminalisation of certain practices in the context of consensual 'SM'-play is discussed.

Despite the problematic underlying dualistic conception of 'body/spirit' Horn *et al.*'s comments on the importance of pursuing research into the spiritual aspects of embodied 'health' are crucial:

> ...the dimension of embodied spirituality has implications beyond the narrow scope of sexuality/spirituality research. It also addresses the broader dimensions of body/spirit integration (...) Without an understanding of the nature and process of integrating body, mind and spirit, or of the client's level of embodiment, it would be difficult to determine whether the interventions used with a patient or client would facilitate movement towards integration or disintegration and whether they would facilitate healing or contribute to the continuation (and possibly exacerbation) of *dis*ease.
>
> (Horn *et al.*, 2005: 97, 98)

'Transcendence', contextual ethics and the 'care of self'

As discussed above, the occurrence of 'altered states of consciousness' through intense experiences that engage the 'lived body' to such a degree that they might represent 'peak experiences' (Maslow, 1970) provide space for transformations of perception. Maslow who saw 'peak experiences' as the highest form of 'embodiment' (in Spurling, 1977) connected these experiences to an increase of 'self'-awareness. This was clearly reflected in most of the responses to the self-completion questionnaire, as all respondents that experienced consensual 'SM' as spiritual stated that they gained in self-assertiveness and also felt an increase in their ease with themselves.

For Pat who associated her experiences of 'transcendental states' in the context of consensual 'SM' with shamanism (see above), these represented a positive changing point in her life and also an intense way to learn about her 'self': '...it's self-knowledge, it's looking for self-knowledge' (Que. P., 1997: 6). The preconditions of consensual 'SM' in terms of a practice of 'care of the self' (Foucault, 1990) are underlined in their importance here also as an a priori to the experience of 'transcendental states'. This implies the requirement of a constant reflexive mode that informs contextual, relational and personal ethics on the level of the practitioners.

Anthony stated, '...I was willing to let go of the physical body and go more internal. The feelings I can relate all this to is when I was exploring meditation' (Que. 3, 1997: 2). During an interview Anthony referred more explicitly to personal transformation through consensual 'SM': 'basically I found that since I'm having S/M-sex I've become more assertive, in terms of how I relate to people in the wider world. I'm not aggressive but more assertive' (In. 3, 1997: 5). The consensual 'SM' 'plays' altered Anthony's perception of and relationship to 'self' and in turn his interaction with others.

Diabolo noticed changes in himself through these experiences in the context of consensual 'SM': 'I broke the myth of 'normality' in myself and others. I feel more relaxed and flexible about myself and life in general, and less inclined to dichotomies' (Que. D., 1997: 1). This quote comes close to Foucault's (in Miller, 1994) understanding of the transformative potentials of these 'bodily practices' who saw them as a way to discover 'new forms of life', because one's thinking (about the 'self' and its orientation through organising, limiting and hierarchical categories) would get ruptured and shattered through the suffering pleasure obtained in this special 'limit-experience'.

Tom, who aims for 'feeling like a child again' relates differently to himself and life in general after the 'transcendental' experiences he had: '...it's like being a child, watching fireworks for the first time...we all take so much for granted, don't we? (...) It makes me more sensitive and it makes me more caring after' (Que. T., 1997: 3). This can be related to Foucault's notion of 'care of the self' (1990) which describes a continuously reflective attitude that becomes the foundation for a personal yet always contextual and relational ethics.

In *Truth and Eros: Foucault, Lacan, and the Question of Ethics*, Rajchman (1991) explains the notion of the 'concern for oneself ' in the late Foucault:

> ... the eros of this experience of critical thought would not be a sacrificial or renunciatory one; it would not be perfectionist, salvationist or progressivist; and it would not assume the form of inducing people to accept principles or rules known independently of their experience of themselves.
>
> (Rajchman, 1991: 10)

The experimental games of consensual 'SM' allow for the discovery of new intensities, the diverse dimensions and potentials of 'lived bodies' and require the development of contextual ethics, and thus they do have the potential to bring about a 'political spirituality' on a practical level which would involve ' ... questioning through which people might start to depart from the historical limits of their identifications ... ' (Rajchman, 1991: 108). Arguably this notion of a 'political spirituality' has important implications for claims of a privileged position of same-sex attraction in order to facilitate 'transcendence of ego' as claimed by, for example, Johnson (2000).

Within much of feminist theorising the category of 'transcendence' is understood to be 'gendered' and its 'gender' is supposed to be 'male'. In contrast to this perspective, Michel Foucault considered 'transcendence' to be a potential available in and to all human beings. However, he rejected an 'unqualified glorification of transgression' as found in de Sade and noted 'The libertine's nostalgia for a "society of blood", was, in the last analysis a "retro-version"' (in Miller, 1993: 244). Foucault's understanding of 'transcendence' in the context of consensual 'SM' explicitly includes the 'lived body' and cannot be seen as an endeavour to overcome the 'feminine'. Another understanding of 'transcendence' that is not 'gendered' and that embraces the 'body' is offered by Martha Nussbaum (in Kerr, 1997). She provides an alternative reading of 'transcendence', one which is not originating in 'the Augustinian idea of original sin', where ideas about transcendence of human limits seemingly often originate. Nussbaum's framework of transcendence (here read mainly as 'ascent of love') is one that does not alienate human beings from their 'bodily humanity' and offers a version of 'transcendence' that is without the disgust of the 'body' (especially the 'female body') which is fundamental to most traditional notions of 'transcendence'.

Nussbaum's concept of 'internal transcendence' avoids the dangers of aspirations to 'extrahuman transcendence' which certainly matches Foucault's as well as feminist interests. The struggle to transcend the limits of our human condition is for Nussbaum still important but as this should not lead to a rejection of our 'embodied condition', she finds it crucial to conceptualise 'transcendence' in a more fluid manner. Transcending human finitude for Nussbaum is thus to be understood as a '... delicate and always flexible balancing act between the claims of excellence, which lead us to push outward, and the necessity of the human context, which pushes us back in' (Nussbaum, in Kerr, 1997: 21). This understanding of 'transcendence' based on contextuality and fluidity also appears to resemble a lot of the attitudes towards the achievement of 'unusual experiences' that the practitioners of consensual 'SM' voiced within the social world of consensual 'SM'. The goal of 'transcendence' in this perspective, as well as the sense of achievement derived from it, is thus interdependent on our specific 'bodily limits' and the situational context which was also explicitly pointed out by several interviewees. As contextuality and fluidity do not exclude either 'femininity' or the body, this understanding of 'transcendence' is open for all human beings and not 'gendered'.

In the closing words to his book *Chainmale: 3SM*, Bastian stated

> Art imitates life or life imitates art. (...) Possibly, you have guessed by now that this whole Leather thing has very little to do with Leather as defined within erotic parameters, and lots to do with life in more general terms. That may be pretty broad, but when something so profound effects so much of everyday life, it becomes very much a part of existence. It is soul and it is spiritual.
>
> (Bastian, 2002: 112)

This chapter attempted to emphasise this dimension of consensual 'SM'.

References

Bastian, D. (2002). *Chainmale: 3SM – A Unique View of Leather Culture*. Los Angeles, CA: Daedalus.

Bauman, Z. (1992). *Intimations of Postmodernity*. London: Routledge.

Becker, H. (1960). *Outsiders*. London: MacMillan.

Beckmann, A. (2001a). Researching consensual 'sadomasochism', perspectives on power, rights and responsibilities – the case of 'disability'. *Social Policy Review*, 13, 89–106.

Beckmann, A. (2001b). Deconstructing myths: the social construction of 'sado-masochism' versus 'subjugated knowledges' of practitioners of consensual 'SM'. *Journal of Criminal Justice and Popular Culture*, 8(2), 66–95.

Beckmann, A. (2004). Sexual rights and sexual responsibilities in consensual 'SM'. In M. Cowling & P. Reynolds, *Making Sense of Sexual Consent*. Aldershot: Ashgate.

Beckmann, A. (2005). Representing 'healthy' and 'sexual' bodies: the media, 'disability' and consensual 'SM'. In M. King and K. Watson (Eds) *Representing Health: Discourses of Health and Illness in the Media*. Basingstoke: Palgrave Macmillan.

Califia, P. (1994). *Public Sex: The Culture of Radical Sex*. Pittsburgh, PA: Cleis Press.

Chancer, L.S. (1992). *Sadomasochism in Everyday Life: The Dynamics of Power and Powerlessness*. New Brunswick, NJ: Rutgers University Press.

Couliano, I.P. (1991). *OUT of this WORLD*. Boston, MA: Shambhala Publications.

Durkheim, E. (1965). *The Elementary Forms of the Religious Life*. London: Allen & Unwin. Original work published 1915.

Eliade, M. (1978). *A History of Religious Ideas*, Vol. 1. Chicago, IL: University of Chicago Press.

Ellwood, R. (1980). *Mysticism and Religion*. Englewood Cliffs, NJ: Prentice-Hall.

Foucault, M. (1976). *Discipline and Punish*. London: Penguin Press.

Foucault, M. (1971). *The Order of Things*. New York, NY: Vintage Books.

Foucault, M. (1980). In C. Edward (Ed.) *Power/Knowledge: Selected Interviews & Other Writings 1972–1977*. New York, NY: Pantheon Books.

Foucault, M. (1990). *The History of Sexuality*, Vol. 1. London: Penguin Books.

Golding, S. (1993). In excess: An added remark on sex, rubber, ethics, and other impurities. *New Formations*, Spring.

Grof, S. (1985). *Beyond the Brain*. New York, NY: SUNY Press.

Grof, S. (1988). *The Adventure of Self-Discovery*. Albany, NY: SUNY Press.

Halperin, D.M. (1995). *Saint-Foucault – Towards a Gay Hagiography*. Oxford: Oxford University Press.

Holt, D. (1993). Sadomasochism and society. In T. Woodward (Ed.) *The Best of SKIN TWO*. USA: A Richard Kasak Book.

Horn, M.J., Piedmont, R.L., Fialkowski, G.M., Wicks, R.J. & Hunt, M.E. (2005). Sexuality and spirituality: The embodied spirituality scale. *Theology and Sexuality*, 12(1), 81–101.

Huxley, A. (1959). *The Doors of Perception*. Harmondsworth: Penguin.

Jaspers, K. (1951). *Way to Wisdom*. London: Victor Gollancz.

Jeffreys, S. (1993). *The Lesbian Heresy: A Feminist Perspective on the Lesbian Sexual Revolution*. London: The Women's Press.

Jeffreys, S. (2003). *Unpacking Queer Politics: A Lesbian Feminist Perspective*. Cambridge, MA: Polity Press.

Johnson, T. (2000). *Gay Spirituality: The Role of Gay Identity in the Transformation of Human Consciousness*. Los Angeles, CA: Alyson Books.

Jones, J.W. (1991). *Contemporary Psychoanalysis and Religion – Transference and Transcendence*. New Haven: Yale University Press.

Kerr, F. (1997). *Immortal Longings*. London: SPCK.

Langdridge, D. & Butt, T. (2004). A hermeneutic phenomenological investigation of the construction of sadomasochism identities. *Sexualities*, 7(1), 31–53.

Linden, R.R., Pagano, D.R., Russell, D.E.H. & Star, S.L. (Eds) (1982). *Against Sadomasochism: A Radical Feminist Analysis*. San Francisco, CA: Frog in the Well.

MacKnee, C.M. (2002). Profound sexual and spiritual encounters among practicing Christians: A phenomenological analysis. *Journal of Psychology and Theology*, 30, 234–244.

Martin, J.I. (2006). Transcendence among gay men: Implications for HIV prevention. *Sexualities*, 9(2), 214–235.

Maslow, A. (1970). *Religions, Values and Peakexperiences*. New York, NY: Viking Press.

Mauss, M. (1979). *Sociology and Psychology*. London: Routledge and Kegan Paul.

Maxwell, M. & Tschudin, V. (Eds) (1990). *Seeing the Invisible*. England: Arkana.

May, T. (1993). *Social Research*. Maidenhead: Open University Press.

May, T. (2001). *Social Research*. Maidenhead: Open University Press.

Merleau-Ponty, M. (1968). *The Visible and the Invisible*. Evanston, IL: Northwestern University Press.

Miller, J. (1993). *The Passion of Michel Foucault*. London: Simon & Shuster.

Miller, J. (1994). *The Passion of Michel Foucault*. London: Flamingo.

Murray-Swank, N.A., Pargament, K.I. & Mahoney, A. (2005). At the crossroads of sexuality and spirituality: The sanctification of sex by college students. *The International Journal for the Psychology of Religion*, 15, 199–219.

Norman, S. (1991). I am the Leatherfaerie Shaman. In M. Thompson (Ed.) *Leatherfolk: Radical Sex, People, Politics, and Practice*. Los Angeles, CA: Alyson Publications.

Rajchman, J. (1991). *Truth and Eros: Foucault, Lacan, and the Question of Ethics*. London: Routledge.

Solomon, D. (Ed.) (1964). *LSD – The Consciousness-Expanding Drug*. New York: G.P. Putnam's Sons.

Spurling, L. (1977). *Phenomenology and the Social World*. London: Routledge and Kegan Paul.

Staal, F. (1975). *Exploring Mysticism*. Berkeley, CA: University of California Press.

Starkloff, C.F. (1974). *The People of the Centre-American Indian Religion and Christianity*. New York, NY: The Seabury Press.

Synnott, A. (1993). *The Body Social*. London: Routledge.

Tart, C.T. (1975). *States of Consciousness*. New York, NY: E. P. Dutton.

Taylor, G.W. (1997). The discursive construction and regulation of dissident sexualities: The case of SM. In J.D. Ussher (Ed.) *Body Talk: The Material and Discursive Regulation of Sexuality, Madness and Reproduction*. London: Routledge.

Taylor, G.W. & Ussher, J. (2001). Making sense of S&M: A discourse analytic account. *Sexualities*, 4(3), 293–314.

Thompson, M. (1991). *Leatherfolk*. Boston, MA: Alyson Publications.

Tyler, M. (2004). Managing between the sheets: Lifestyle magazines and the management of sexuality in everyday life. *Sexualities*, 7(1), 81–106.

Vale, V. & Juno, A. (Eds) (1989). *Modern Primitives (Re/Search 12)*. San Francisco, CA: Re/Search Publications.

Wade, J. (2000). Mapping the courses of heavenly bodies: The varieties of transcendent sexual experience. *Journal of Transpersonal Psychology*, 32, 103–122.

Westhaver, R. (2005). 'Coming out of your skin': Circuit parties, pleasure and the subject. *Sexualities*, 8(3), 347–374.

8
Beyond Safety: Erotic Asphyxiation and the Limits of SM Discourse

Lisa Downing

> Life is not safe! Life is not benevolent! Life is not consensual!
> There is only living what stretches out before us, honoring our
> chosen moral integrity, for in the end, when all is said and
> done, 'life kills your ass'
>
> (Decker, 1991)

Introduction

Given that sadism and masochism retain the status of mental disorders
in the *DSM-IV* and the *ICD-10*, it is perhaps not surprising that counter-
discourses about SM produced by the spokespeople of SM communities
and support groups and by pro-SM academics, activists and mental
health professionals often promote a rhetoric which attributes liber-
ating and even therapeutic qualities to the practices grouped under the
terms SM or BDSM. In contradistinction to the definition of a paraphilia – a sexual deviation characterised by fixation and compulsion –
pro-SM discourse highlights the role of choice and self-determination in
sadomasochism. The title of a now classic book co-authored by an 'out
Smer', JJ Madeson, and an SM-friendly doctor, Charles Moser, *Bound to
be Free: The SM Experience*, plays on a paradox often attributed to SM
fantasies and behaviours – the fact that in apparent subjugation, pain
and bondage can be found a sense of freedom, catharsis and escape. The
authors describe SM as 'a world of sexual variation, excitement and love,
joy and freedom, limited only by the vast boundaries of the imagination'
(Moser & Madeson, 2002: 17). In this rhetoric, SM itself becomes a form
of alternative therapy, 'freeing' practitioners from repression, anxiety or
limitations. (For more on this discourse, see Barker, Gupta & Iantaffi,
Chapter 12.)

A feature of SM insisted upon with equal frequency as that of freedom is the bond of trust, respect, safety, control and care that exists between those people involved in a relationship of erotic power exchange. The community motto 'Safe, Sane and Consensual', allegedly coined by David Stein (see Stein, 2003), and which forms part of the title of the current volume, neatly encapsulates the spirit of this rhetoric. While some members of the SM community may dispute the usefulness of the motto (more on this later) and while it is not used ubiquitously or always with the same political aims, it is very often deployed by SMers to insist upon the disparity between the content of some SM scenes (bondage, domination, pain, acts of apparent violence, etc.) and the carefully nego-tiated, contractual, respectful context in which they take place. It also serves to demonstrate that the non-consensual violence and abuse that occur in the 'real world' are not self-same with the mediated, eroticised, pleasurable acts that may occur in SM. As Truscott puts it, 'The most common accusation leveled at practitioners of sadomasochism is that we are "violent" [...] Violence is the epitome of non-consensuality, an act perpetrated by a predator on a victim. [...] Despite appearances, consensual sadomasochism has nothing to do with violence' (1991: 30).

However, it is significant that the terms of this rhetoric and the upholding of the spirit of this motto tend to involve the sanctioning of certain forms of behaviour and interaction (those that can be made to fit neatly into its ideology) and the exclusion and indeed condemnation of others, those that fail to meet easily the common definition of 'safe' and 'sane'. (I shall leave aside 'consensual' here, as this opens up a very different area of inquiry.) This article is concerned, therefore, with a consensual, but nevertheless problematic, and therefore often excluded and stigmatised form of behaviour: erotic asphyxiation. The practice of techniques of asphyxiation to induce, facilitate or enhance physical and psychical sensation offers a literal threat to the promise of 'safety', to the extent that its outcome may be accidental death. Pro-SM rhet-oric is consistently concerned with distancing itself from accusations of destructiveness, for the political and ideological reasons outlined above. In a previous article (Downing, 2004), dedicated to a more extreme and conscious form of death-related sexuality – consensual erotic murder pacts, or what John Money has termed the paraphilias of autassassino-philia and erotophonophilia (Money, 1986: 258, 261) – I drew attention to a remark made by Nancy Ava Miller, spokeswoman for the SM support group 'People Exchanging Power'. In response to the highly publicised media case of Sharon Lopatka, an American woman, who met a man, Robert Glass, in an internet chat room and co-planned her own killing for erotic pleasure, Miller stated, 'I don't know what they were doing, but it wasn't S&M. The fundamental rule of the S&M community is to keep interaction "safe, sane and consensual" ' (cited in Jackson, 1996). This statement clearly delineates 'acceptable' behaviour from unacceptable behaviour and defines the acceptable as 'SM'. Since the murder pact in question was consensual, the objection appears to be to the fact that the practice being consented to was not 'safe' or 'sane' in Miller's view. Miller's statement asserts 'SM' as the badge of a single unitary community with its own ideological, moral and regulatory functions and rules. Erotic murder pacts occur relatively infrequently, such that the SM spokespeople who espouse the Safe, Sane and Consensual motto seldom have the embarrassment of having to repudiate these acts and distance the community from them publicly. However, the practice(s) of erotic asphyxiation – also known as asphyxiophilia, hypoxyphilia, breath play or breath control play – feature more commonly in the press (especially when they result in death, as in the widely publicised auto-erotic deaths of British Conservative MP, Stephen Milligan, in 1994 and Australian rock singer, Michael Hutchence, in 1997).

In an interview on consensual physical damage and the law, with Spanner trustee and self-defined gay SM player John Pendall, the interviewee comments, in the context of a discussion of SM safety education programmes, that 'some subjects are almost never covered (such as breath control), despite the fact that a quick search of the Internet will show those activities are popular in private' (Charline & Pendal, 2005: 286). The problem for Safe, Sane and Consensual SMers, then, lies in the frequency with which erotic asphyxiation is publicly associated with SM and the way in which it risks tainting SM with 'destructive' implications that might be used to substantiate the *DSM*'s and mainstream public's assumptions about SM's 'dark side'. Indeed the *DSM* lists 'hypoxyphilia' (literally, love of oxygen deprivation) as a sub-category of 'sexual masochism'. 'Hypoxyphilia' is defined in the *DSM* as a practice which 'involves sexual arousal by oxygen deprivation obtained by means of chest compression, noose, ligature, plastic bag, mask or chemical' (American Psychiatric Association, 1994: 529). (The *DSM*, for some reason, leaves out the most obvious methods of interactive erotic asphyxiation between two or more people – manual strangulation or suffocation – implying, perhaps, the common assumption that most acts of erotic asphyxiation are auto-erotic.) The wish to dissociate SM from danger or destructivity can lead, and has led, to a policy of censorship within community contexts, with regard to activities involving erotic asphyxiation. SM-educator and safety advisor Jay Wiseman, who has written extensively on the medical dangers of erotic asphyxiation notes that 'because of its severe and unpredictable risks, more and more SM party-givers are banning any form of breath control play at their events' (Wiseman, 1997a).

Erotic asphyxiation is the test case I shall use, then, to examine the limits of the Safety and Sanity discourse as it obtains in SM rhetoric. The term 'erotic asphyxiation' (hereafter EA) will be, for the purposes of this article, my default way of describing the practices in question. This is partly because I wish to avoid the pathologising, sexological overtones of the diagnostic labels 'hypoxyphilia' and 'asphyxiophilia' and equally to remain critically distant from the SM lexicon of 'breath play' or 'breath control play', as it is not my intention to represent or voice SM community discourse. However, before proceeding, these latter terms merit some discussion. The term 'play' is applied to 'breath' as it is applied to such terms as 'fire', 'blood' and 'knife', to constitute the category of 'edge play'. 'Play' is the common term for an erotic interaction or scene in the standard SM lexicon since the SM ideology holds that pleasurable practices which involve power exchange and pain are, as Carol Truscott has explained in the quotation I referred to above, examples of role play, designed by mutually consenting partners and distinct from power imbalances in the world. 'Edge play' is a significant and meaningful term, as it suggests both literally extreme activities – playing on the edge of physical safety – and a discursive limit: that which pushes the boundaries of the accepted and included terms of SM and brings SM itself *qua* discourse into focus as a self-regulating social phenomenon.[1]

SM, EA and techniques of exclusion

In this section, I will consider some of the common ways in which EA is debated and treated in SM safety texts, paying attention to the rhetoric of the treatment and the logic underlying it.

Where EA is discussed, the discussion tends to focus on the extent to which one can ensure, with any certainty, that medical safety measures can be put in place to prevent the 'asphyxee' from losing consciousness or suffering permanent brain damage or death from cardiac arrest, in the event of loss of consciousness. The leading name in this debate is Jay Wiseman. In the first of a series of widely published and disseminated articles on the topic, 'The Medical Realities of Breath Control Play', Wiseman writes

I have discussed my concerns regarding breath control with well over a dozen SM-positive physicians, and with numerous other SM-positive health professionals, and all share my concerns. We have discussed how breath control might be done in a way that is not life-threatening, and come up blank. We have discussed how the risk might be significantly reduced, and come up blank. We have discussed how it might be determined that an arrest is imminent, and come up blank.

Indeed, so far not one (repeat, not one) single physician, nurse, paramedic, chiropractor, physiologist, or other person with substantial training in how a human body works has been willing to step forth and teach a form of breath control play that they are willing to assert is acceptably safe – i.e., does not put the recipient at imminent, unpredictable risk of dying. I believe this fact makes a major statement.

Other 'edge play' topics such as suspension, bondage, electricity play, cutting, piercing, branding, enemas, water sports, and scat play can and have been taught with reasonable safety, but not breath control play. Indeed, it seems that the more somebody knows about how a human body works, the more likely they are to caution people about how dangerous breath control is, and about how little can be done to reduce the degree of risk.

(Wiseman, 1997a)

When this article first appeared on soc.subculture.bondage-bdsm, it provoked a great deal of comment and debate in web-based community chatrooms, with exponents of the practice asking for medical proof to refute Wiseman's assertions, leading him to publish a series of four further articles entitled, respectively: 'Breath Control: Is Epinephrine the "Smoking Gun"?' (Wiseman, 1997b), 'More on the Smoking Gun' (Wiseman, 1997c), 'Breath Control: "I Want My Precaution B"' (Wiseman, 1997d) and 'Cumulative Brain Damage from Breath Control' (Wiseman, 1997e). What I find interesting here is that the 'safety' coda continued to be the predominant ethos guiding the majority of the responses to Wiseman's findings, rather than a questioning, or rejection, of the assumption that wanting something dangerous *despite or because of* the lack of a guaranteed safety clause could be a valid version of an ethics of pleasure. The rigidly enforced distinction between the valorisation of *psychical* self-risk in SM (the risk to ego boundaries and the oft-reported sensations of the dissolution of a sense of self in SM scenes) and the vilification of actualised self-endangerment and self-loss in a potential pleasurable death is striking.

Wiseman's second intervention – a genuine attempt to explore whether the kind of reassurance his readers were seeking could be given – looks at the importance of context in determining the physiological effects of hypoxia. He makes use of the analogous cases of forceable police arrests using choke-holds and certain strangulation locks in judo and other martial arts. The tentative conclusion is that there may be a lesser risk of serious or fatal harm being inflicted where the participant is not genuinely afraid or struggling (where less adrenalin is being produced by the body as a result of genuine terror). So, in martial arts, the likelihood of serious damage is statistically reduced. In his first article, Wiseman had told us that 'I have an extensive martial arts background that includes a first-degree black belt in Tae Kwon Do. My martial arts training included several months of judo that involved both my choking and being choked' (Wiseman, 1997a).

Wiseman's conclusion is the one we would by now expect. Since the risk cannot be eliminated altogether, EA is probably not advisable. However, he does not for a moment suggest that martial arts or the other 'extreme sports' he himself enjoys should be subject to similar proscription. Michael Decker, a self-disclosed EA practitioner, whose writing forms the epigraph of this article, offers an account of EA similar to Wiseman's analogy of how the practice might parallel other – socially sanctioned – recreational practices: 'Do I want to die? No. I want to live so I can keep pursuing the pleasures I get from stalking death's intensity. I'm as insane as any other danger seeker, from an Evil Kinevil wanna-be, to a cop, fireman, or soldier, but my motives are easier to understand, self-gratification' (Decker, 1991). Both Wiseman and Decker concur from their different positions that EA and extreme sports share similar risks and similar thrills. However, the unspoken (and probably unconscious) logic of Wiseman's differentiation between the two seems to lie – bizarrely – in the belief that recreational activities involving potential fatal risk are *less acceptable* if the pleasure involved has an erotic component, if self-gratification is their outcome. For a pro-SM sex advisor, this is an odd mainstream commonplace to espouse.

Wiseman's position with regard to EA is articulated most forcefully, perhaps, in his fourth article on the subject, 'Breath Control: "I Want My Precaution B" ' (precaution B being a way of describing safety mechanisms that can be put into practice in most sexual scenes and practices to reduce the health risks – using a condom being the most obvious and frequently occurring example). Wiseman posits that, since there is no foolproof way of ensuring that a practitioner of EA will not die, then 'asphyxiophilia is not just another kink. It is a *qualitatively different practice*, and plays by its own very stark, not-very-forgiving, and often counter-intuitive rules' [my italics] (Wiseman, 1997d). I find this assertion striking. In stating that EA is 'not just another kink', Wiseman makes a crystal clear delineation between the inclusive, community-sanctioned practices of SM and its 'other'. Wiseman presents this difference as a scientific fact (it is qualitatively different because its effect on the physiology is more unpredictable and the outcome more severe than in other 'kinky' practices). While there may be medical truth in this (I have no medical expertise whatsoever and would not wish to comment on the accuracy or otherwise of these findings), my argument here is that Wiseman's distinction is primarily ideological and discursive, telling us as much (or more) about the community self-policing of SM as it does about the physical realities of hypoxia.

While ever the careful distinction is made between activities that are 'acceptable', that are 'properly' SM and those that are outside of it – 'qualitatively different' – Wiseman and others repeat wholesale the logic of the mainstream conservative or medical voice that demonises SM as the dangerous, bad and unacceptable other of healthy, life-giving sexuality. Trying to make *itself* into an acceptable, safe and sane lifestyle, SM rhetoric constructs EA – the death-giving act – as other to its life-affirming good. What I find particularly striking is that the wave of activism in the UK promoted by the Spanner case, involving arguments for the rights of participants to indulge in extreme activity without facing criminal prosecution for actual or grievous bodily harm, has not extended to campaigns for the recognition of the criminal innocence of those whose partners die as a result of EA transactions. Wiseman comments 'I personally know two members of my local SM community who went to prison after their partners died during breath control play' (Wiseman, 1997a), but his response to this is to caution against the practice of the activity by SMers, not to rally to protect SMers choosing to 'play' in this way. The only conclusion to be drawn from this is that this is because their choice to engage in this practice renders them outsiders to the defensible SM identity.

In a recent online interview, David Stein, credited with creating the Safe, Sane and Consensual motto, critiques the way in which what he hoped would be 'the starting point for a continuing community-wide discussion about the elements of an s/m ethics' has developed into a 'credo' which is 'used to define something like articles of faith s/m newbies are expected to absorb...' (Stein, 2003). He deplores the fact that 'the people doing the defining are the kind who do s/m at a very tame, low level of intensity and think that's where the boundaries should be set for everyone'. Stein thus implicitly makes a similar point to mine about the delimiting and policing of the boundaries of SM, such that it becomes a codified, rule-bound practice or religion, something requiring a 'credo' that risks rigidifying into doxa. Later in the interview, Stein also complains that the motto has been used for a purpose that he never intended: to demonise precisely the kind of 'edge play' we are concerned with (though, perhaps significantly, EA is conspicuously absent from his list of examples):

> We *did* intend to draw a distinction and to leave some kinds of sadomasochistic behavior on one side of the line as indefensible while maintaining that whatever fell inside the line *was* defensible ethically and *should* be defended politically and legally. But what we intended to leave outside the line was things like sadistic serial killers and snuff scenes for money, coercive s/m of all sorts, *not* the edgier kinds of consensual play — unless there was a question whether consent was even possible, as with the underage or the mentally unbalanced. We never intended to draw the line to leave out heavy s/m, real pain rather than symbolic pain, blood play, knifeplay, humiliation play, 24/7 Master/slave relationships, and so on. But all these things and more have come under the gun in recent years from self-righteous censors and 'dungeon monitors' *within our community* waving the SSC banner!

While Stein's comments here are broadly along the lines of the argument of this article, he nevertheless continues, like the 'censors' he criticises, to insist that there should be a 'proper' unitary domain that is SM, with a codified catalogue of acceptable practices, a point which I find problematic and to which I will return in the final section.

A recent attempt to address the problem of Safe, Sane and Consensual's exclusion of the edgier elements of SM play is Gary Switch's coining of the acronym RACK (Risk Aware Consensual Kink) as an alternative moniker to highlight the awareness that some elements of SM do carry physical risk, that some degree of physical as well as psychological danger may be part of the pleasure of SM activities and that SM 'players' are informed, prepared and willing to take these risks. Decker's description of the excitement of near-death practices cited above suggests that RACK may get closer to a model of SM that could allow for and include EA than Safe, Sane and Consensual, and yet the very discussion of inclusion or exclusion is itself flawed, as it postulates 'SM' as a container, a self-evident and everywhere self-same unitary entity. I wish to analyse further the problem of the discursive delimiting and self-policing of SM, via a reflection on Michel Foucault's comments on the political value of sadomasochism.

Beyond discourse...?

In interviews with both the mainstream and gay media in the years before he died, Foucault attempted to spell out ways in which certain practices and subcultures might go beyond the historically constructed field of (medical, psychological, legal) knowledge defining 'sexuality' in Western culture and might offer instead new ways of experiencing the 'bodies and pleasures' he had written about in volume one of *The History of Sexuality* in 1976:

> It is the agency of sex that we must break away from, if we aim – through a tactical reversal of the various mechanisms of sexuality – to counter the grips of power with the claims of bodies, pleasures and knowledges, in their multiplicity and their possibility of resistance. The rallying point for the counterattack against the deployment of sexuality ought not to be sex-desire, but bodies and pleasures.
>
> (Foucault, 1990: 157).

Foucault espied in SM (specifically, for him, same-sex leather communities) the potential for constructing an alternative form of community and relationality, which would escape regulatory and normative relations of knowledge and power, by playing with and de-contextualising that power. SM dramatises the elasticity and two-way directionality of power as re-conceptualised by Foucault (a productive and mobile relationship of exertion and resistance, rather than a top-down model of oppression), by enabling players to reverse the roles of dominant and subordinate partner at any given point (unlike in the fixed hierarchies of society) and to stop the unequal power dynamic at any given moment. Moreover Foucault saw in SM a desexualisation of pleasure, by which he meant the possibility of reconfiguring bodily pleasures in ways that are not dependent on the traditional meanings and functions of the genitalia. He also saw it as a means of accessing 'limit-experiences', a term he borrows from Bataille, that is, extreme experiences that push us to the limits of consciousness and shatter rationality (see esp. Foucault, 1998). Halperin has written that practices that encourage the libidinisation of non-genital regions and surprising configurations of pleasure – Foucault's favourite example being fist-fucking – '[decenter] the subject and [disarticulate] the psychic and bodily integrity of the self to which a sexual identity has become attached' (Halperin, 1995: 97). To follow this logic, then, the radical political gesture would be to seek out precisely those bodily acts that are capable of disrupting identities rather than fixing or shoring them up and that thereby undermine the processes of sexual teleology. For as soon as the acts and rules of an identity or a community are codified and fixed, they become part of the field of sexual knowledge from which a radical politics, according to Foucault, must flee.

The establishment of a plethora of gay, bi and straight SM communities in the Anglo-American world, facilitated in recent years by the virtual communitarian possibilities offered by the internet, have resulted in a discursification of SM that often relies on recognisable sexual teleologies and neo-liberal principles, rather than on a philosophy that might be described as radical. When SM borrows from mainstream mental health discourse to justify the benefits of its practices, for example, this seems to stand in contradiction to the Foucauldian idea of SM as a radical reconfiguration, a jamming of the machinery, of sexual knowledge and hierarchies. When SM is given a *useful social function* it ceases to function as a point of resistance and a principle of disruption.

However, the nuances of Foucault's position regarding the political value of the ideas of *community* and *identity* need to be spelt out in more detail. Foucault writes 'the practice of S/M is the creation of pleasure, and there is an identity with [i.e. a personal identity attached to] that creation. And that's why S/M is really a subculture. It's a process of invention' (Gallagher & Wilson, 1984: 29). Here the ongoing creation of an identity through the experience of pleasure (rather than the shoring up of an identity through the processes of subjectivity that arise from the 'discovering' of one's 'true desire', e.g. in psychoanalysis) is accorded a renovating value. However, to the extent that communal and personal identities are defined by a tendency to become fixed, to know themselves and police themselves, to self-identify, they risk calcifying into a lifestyle or an institution, promoting, in Halperin's words, 'new forms of discipline' and constructing 'even more insidious processes of normalisation' (Halperin, 1995: 112). Identity, then, must be precarious. Invention must be willing to open itself to re-invention. Boundaries must not be drawn too soon.

I would argue that SM is currently the site of a political confusion between the radical and the liberal. I have shown in this article how the threat posed by EA, in its liminal capacity, often provides the trigger for the 'normalising' and 'disciplinary' aspects of SM in the discourses I have examined. It points up the conflicted and schismatic nature of SM, by acting as its point of excess. It may be that EA is simply doing something other than that which SM community activists wish the activities they represent and defend to do. The knee-jerk linking of EA with auto-erotic behaviour, in both the *DSM*'s refusal to mention one-on-one strangulation or suffocation as forms of 'asphyxiophilia' and the writings of Jay Wiseman, who states that a very high percentage of 'BDSM-related fatalities' are due to 'some form of autoerotic asphyxiation' and then backtracks to wonder 'if auto-erotic asphyx is, strictly speaking, BDSM at all' (Wiseman, 1997a), suggests the extent to which this pleasure of the body fits problematically with an ideology of intersubjectivity or community. EA, as it is constructed in these discourses at least, whether in its auto- or allo-erotic forms, is not concerned with a safe community. It is rather concerned with radical risk and self-loss – a self-loss moved from the realms of the refusal of the individual and the ego in the sometimes mystical experiences described by SMers, to the literal level of potential bodily death.

Conclusion

This chapter has highlighted the difficultly for many pro-SMers of reconciling an act as a result of which one might very well die with an ethos (Safe, Sane and Consensual Sadomasochism) that co-opts a mental health discourse and assumes the existence of a responsible, self-regulating community. Foucault hoped that SM subcultures might devise ways of relationality that would exceed existing mainstream configurations, that might shatter the field of 'sexuality' and create new pleasures against the grain of utility and the technologies of biopolitics. However, the codes and rules of SM community life, as it struggles to resist discursively the stigmatising epithets attributed to it, reveal the limits of the utopia. The exclusion of EA from SM as 'too dangerous' or 'too destructive' signals the policing function of its own discursive limits that undoes the dissident power of SM to undo sexuality. The tension between the rejection of principles of normativity and conformity on the part of SMers, and the simultaneous wish to refute and indeed *resist* the pathologising discourse levelled against them by asserting the 'good mental health' of its players (in terms defined by the dominant discourses of medicine and psychology), is one that is not easily resolved or overcome.

EA presents a discursive point of resistance to contemporary liberal forms of sexual knowledge, as it thwarts *both* those discourses that argue for the cohesive, binding, relational principles of pleasure embodied in the idea of the sexual community or subculture *and* those that attempt to co-opt and recuperate sex as utilitarian or progressive, whether in the most banal and sanctioned way – for reproducing the population – or in alternative frameworks, such as the positing of SM as radical personal therapy. As far as I know, Foucault never mentioned the pleasures of oxygen deprivation, preferring, perhaps, fist-fucking to asphyxiation. He did, however, speak in an interview about judo, the analogy by which Jay Wiseman explains the dangers of recreational asphyxia. For Foucault, judo stands in for the field of power itself, a technique-bound field in which each movement of attack not only invites but facilitates – births – the resisting response:

> As in judo, the best answer to the opponent's manoeuvre is never to step back, but to reuse it to your own advantage as a base for the next phase... Now it is our turn to reply.
>
> (cited in Halperin, 1995: 114)

In censoring the risky pleasures of EA from its field of inclusion, in seeking to codify it in the very terms of the mental health and safety discourses used to vilify SM itself, the community does not respond but merely accepts and echoes the 'opponent's manoeuvre', parroting it back. In singling out EA as – in Wiseman's terms – a 'qualitatively different practice' that 'plays by its own very stark, not-very-forgiving, and often counter-intuitive rules', SM discourse plays it safe. In so doing, it may be taking one risk too many with its own vital potential for transforming the mainstream sexual field.

Note

1. There is little academic work in existence on EA. Most studies of the phenomenon originate in the disciplines of forensic science and medicine and focus on the post-mortem death scenes of the 'victims' of (usually, but not always, auto-erotic) asphyxiation. The canonical study is Hazelwood, Dietz and Burgess (1983). A more recent full-length study is Sergey and Erlich (2006). A limited amount of sexological and psychoanalytic work on EA exists. The sexologist John Money has written widely on the topic in the context of his study of the paraphilias. An unusual account of a self-confessed 'asphyxio-philiac still living' is Money, Wainwright and Hingsburger (1991). This work, co-authored by John Money and his patient, is saturated with the sexologist's

pathologising perspective. To my knowledge, the only critical account from the perspective of cultural studies, of the relationship between EA and the psychological and medical discourses, is my co-authored article on the subject (Downing & Nobus, 2004), which explores the fascination on the part of forensic experts, psychoanalysts and sexologists with exposing the fantasy structures and behavioural life of 'asphyxiophiliacs' by including images – both pornographic self-representations of wishful, eroticised death and photographs taken by police photographers post-mortem – in their published texts.

References

American Psychiatric Association. (1994). *Diagnostic and Statistical Manual of Mental Disorders: DSM-IV*. Washington: American Psychiatric Association.

Charline, E. & Pendal, J. (2005). Spanner: SM, consent and the law in the UK. *Lesbian and Gay Psychology Review*, 6(3), 283–287.

Decker, M. (1991). *When All Is Said and Done, Life Kills Your Ass. Viewpoints on Asphyxiophilia*. Available: http://www.sexuality.org/l/fetish/aspydang.html. Accessed on 08/03/07.

Downing, L. (2004). On the limits of sexual ethics: The phenomenology of autassassinophilia. *Sexuality and Culture*, 8(1), 3–17.

Downing, L. & Nobus, D. (2004). The iconography of asphyxiophilia: From fantasmatic fetish to forensic fact. *Paragraph: Journal of Modern Critical Theory*, 27(3), 1–15.

Foucault, M. (1990). *The Will to Knowledge: The History of Sexuality, Vol. 1* (R. Hurley, Trans.). Harpenden: Penguin. Original work published 1976.

Foucault, M. (1998). A preface to trangression (D. F. Bouchard & S. Simon, Trans.). In J. Faubion (Ed.) *Michel Foucault: Essential Works 1954–1984, Volume 2, Aesthetics* (pp. 69–87). Harmondsworth: Penguin. Original work published 1963.

Gallagher, B. & Wilson, A. (1984). Michel Foucault: An interview: Sex, power and the politics of identity. *The Advocate*, 400, August 7, 26–30.

Halperin, D. (1995). *Saint Foucault: Towards a Gay Hagiography*. Oxford: Oxford University Press.

Hazelwood, R., Dietz, P. & Burgess, A. (1983). *Autoerotic Fatalities*. Lexington, MA: Lexington Books.

Jackson, J. (1996). *Murder She Wrote*. Cyperpunk Archives, November 12. Available: http://www.joabj.com/CityPaper/murder.html. Accessed on 08/03/07.

Money, J. (1986). *Lovemaps: Clinical Concepts of Sexual/Erotic Health and Pathology, Paraphilia and Gender Transposition in Childhood, Adolescence and Maturity*. New York, NY: Prometheus.

Money, J., Wainwright, G. & Hingsburger, D. (1991). *The Breathless Orgasm: A Lovemap Biography of Asphyxiophilia*. Buffalo, NY: Prometheus.

Moser, C. & Madeson, J.J. (2002). *Bound to be free: The SM Experience*. New York, NY: Continuum.

Sergey, S. & Ehrlich, E. (2006). *Autoerotic Asphyxiation: Forensic, Medical, and Social Aspects*. Tucson, AZ: Wheatmark.

Stein, D. (2003). *SCENEprofiles Interview with David Stein. Sensuous Sadie.* Available: http://www.sensuoussadie.com/interviews/davidsteininterview.htm. Accessed on 08/03/07.

Truscott, C. (1991). S/M: Some questions and a few answers. In M. Thompson (Ed.) *Leatherfolk: Radical Sex, People, Politics and Practice* (pp. 15–36). Boston: Alyson Publications.

Wiseman, J. (1997a). *The Medical Realities of Breath-Control Play.* Available: http://www.leathernroses.com/generalbdsm/wisemanbreathcontrol1.htm. Accessed on 08/03/07.

Wiseman, J. (1997b). *Breath Control: Is Epinephrine the 'Smoking Gun'?* Available: http:// www.leathernroses.com/generalbdsm/wisemanbreathcontrol2.htm. Accessed on 08/03/07.

Wiseman, J. (1997c). *More on the Smoking Gun.* Available: http://www. leathernroses.com/generalbdsm/wisemanbreathcontrol3.htm. Accessed on 08/03/07.

Wiseman, J. (1997d). *Breath Control: 'I Want My Precaution B'.* Available: http:// www.leathernroses.com/generalbdsm/wisemanbreathcontrol4.htm. Accessed on 08/03/07.

Wiseman, J. (1997e). *Cumulative Brain Damage from Breath Control.* Available: http://www.leathernroses.com/generalbdsm/wisemanbreathcontrol5.htm. Accessed on 08/03/07.

Part III
Empirical Research

9
Sexual Fantasies of S/M Practitioners: The Impact of Gender and S/M Role on Fantasy Content[1]

Megan R. Yost

Introduction

Psychologists' perspectives on sexual fantasies have changed dramatically over time. Early psychoanalysts viewed sexual fantasising as a symptom of sexual and psychological disturbance. Freud wrote, 'A happy person never phantasies (*sic*), only an unsatisfied one' (1908/1962: 146), theorising that people engaged in sexual fantasy as a way to compensate for an otherwise unsatisfying sex life. Research has failed to substantiate this point of view, however, and since that time fantasies have come to be regarded as a healthy aspect of sexuality and an activity in which the vast majority of people participate (Hariton & Singer, 1974; Leitenberg & Henning, 1995; Sue, 1979).

In this chapter, I explore the sexual fantasies of S/M practitioners. Because S/M practice involves an appearance of dominance and submission between partners (Weinberg, Williams & Moser, 1984), I was particularly interested in themes of dominance and submission in fantasies. I consider sexual fantasy to be a defining feature of S/M sexuality, so after briefly reviewing the psychological literature on power-related sexual fantasy themes, I discuss various theoretical perspectives that highlight fantasy as an important aspect of S/M sexuality. I then report on the findings of my empirical research on S/M practitioners' sexual fantasies. I situate the results of this study both in terms of gendered sexual scripts and in terms of understandings of gender within the S/M community; thus I conclude by discussing the relationship between gender, sexual fantasies, and sexual identity within the S/M subculture.

Psychological research on power in sexual fantasies

Sexual fantasies are of interest to psychologists due to the potential link between fantasy content and desired sexual behaviour. In particular, research on power in fantasies is quite common, due to a conceptual link between sexual fantasies of dominance and traditional masculine sexual scripts and between sexual fantasies of submission and traditional feminine sexual scripts. Power is eroticised in a gendered way in our society, with male dominance and female submission considered sexually appealing (Byers, 1996).

Not surprisingly, most studies of sexual fantasy uncover consistent gender differences in themes of dominance and submission. Comparison studies show that men are more likely than women to report dominance fantasies (fantasies in which they force their partner to submit to sex; Arndt, Foehl & Good, 1985; Person *et al.*, 1989; Sue, 1979), and women are more likely than men to report submission fantasies (in which they are forced by a partner to submit to sex; Sue, 1979; Wilson, 1987; see Person *et al.*, 1989 for an exception in which men and women were equally likely to report masochistic fantasies).

Thus the traditional sexual script is thought to guide both sexual fantasies and sexual behaviours of men and women. I conducted the present research with an interest in exploring whether the traditional sexual script functioned in expected ways in the fantasies of S/M practitioners.

Theories of sexual fantasy within S/M sexuality

Within S/M practice, fantasy and imagination often play a primary role. S/M practitioners themselves highlight the role of fantasy in their S/M encounters. For instance, Califia, an S/M activist writes, 'The key word to understanding S/M is fantasy. The roles, dialogue, fetish costumes, and sexual activity are part of a drama or ritual' (1981/2000: 172). Similarly John Warren, author of *The Loving Dominant* writes, 'To many who indulge in its pleasures, [S/M] is a cathartic sexual game based on fantasy, a sensual psychodrama' (2000: 9). Dossie Easton and Janet Hardy, authors of many S/M-themed books, use a metaphor drawing on Carl Jung's map of the mind, arguing that S/M incorporates fantasy and the unconscious into sexual play (2004). It is clear that S/M practitioners themselves conceive of S/M practice as dependent upon sexual fantasy.

In addition, ethnographic and survey research with S/M practitioners has consistently found that many people involved in S/M came to this sexuality because of longstanding sexual fantasies of dominance and submission. Scott, in her study of female dominant–male submissive couples, found that a majority of the men cited childhood fantasies of submission as the reason they became involved in S/M; her participants viewed S/M as an opportunity to live out their fantasies (1980). Brame, Brame and Jacobs (1993) describe the common pattern of coming to an S/M identity among their respondents; the typical pattern starts with childhood fantasies that eroticise dominance and submission. In prior research, I asked a sample of 175 S/M practitioners what first attracted them to S/M. Approximately one quarter explicitly cited fantasies of dominance and submission, and another quarter indicated that thoughts of power and sex (obviously fantasy-like) had aroused them since childhood (Yost, 2006).

A number of scholars have theorised that the core or the central definition of S/M is fantasy. Thomas Weinberg (1978) argues that S/M could be defined as 'constructed performance'. Drawing on Goffman's theories (1974), Weinberg claims that S/M occurs within a theatrical frame, in which participants transform what appears to be violence into pleasurable play through 'keying' the behaviour. Various keys are employed by practitioners that give meaning to S/M behaviours; these keys transform what appears to be violence into a mutually pleasurable experience. Examples of S/M keys involve collaborative limit setting (the 'victim' and the 'aggressor' often decide together what will happen) and scripting (practitioners may decide on a particular sequence of events). I would argue that fantasy is the psychological mechanism that enables this theatrical frame. In other words, S/M practitioners are engaging in sexual fantasy to transform a performance of dominance and submission into a personally meaningful and sexually pleasurable experience.

Similarly Patrick Hopkins (1994) suggests that S/M practitioners *simulate* scenes of patriarchal (or power-laden) sexuality. He writes, 'Simulation implies that S/M selectively replays surface patriarchal beliefs onto a different contextual field. That contextual field makes a profound difference' (p. 123). Hopkins explains that participants in S/M do not rape, for example, they do rape *scenes*, in which all participants are aware of the different 'contextual field'. I would argue that in order to create a contextual field that can render otherwise unpleasant activities pleasurable, S/M practitioners employ sexual fantasies; fantasies serve to contextualise the S/M activities.

Terry Hoople (1996) theorises that S/M practitioners attempt to actualise a fantasy relationship through S/M practices. She states, for example, that no one involved in S/M simulates real, actual slavery;

instead participants in S/M actualise a very stylised and historically inaccurate version of slavery which is eroticised. In other words, practitioners create a fantasy of dominance and submission that is sexually arousing and then act out that fantasy in their S/M encounters. Thus Hoople places fantasy at the core of S/M encounters, because sexually arousing fantasies are necessary before an S/M scene can take place.

Research on sexual fantasy and S/M practice

Despite the seemingly central role that fantasy plays in S/M encounters, only one published study to date has examined the fantasies of sadomasochists. Gosselin, Wilson and Barrett (1991), in a study of women only, found that S/M practitioners reported more, and more varied, sexual fantasies than a control group of women. The S/M women fantasised more frequently about three fantasy themes than did controls: sadomasochistic themes (items such as 'whipping or spanking someone'), impersonal themes ('using objects such as vibrators for stimulation', 'intercourse with an anonymous stranger'), and exploratory themes ('sex with two other people', 'homosexual/lesbian activity'). The two groups did not differ on intimate themes ('having intercourse with a loved partner', 'kissing passionately').

The study by Gosselin and colleagues, while documenting important differences between the fantasies of S/M and non-S/M women, is limited in a number of ways. First, of course, it did not include men. Because some surveys indicate that more men than women are involved in the S/M community (Breslow, 1987; Breslow, Evans & Langley, 1986; Herron, Herron & Schultz, 1983), this is an important issue. Also the study was not sensitive to the issue of S/M roles. Surveys of S/M practitioners have found that many participants report a preference for a particular role (being dominant or submissive exclusively) while others report they take a versatile role (switching between dominant and submissive, which is termed 'switch'; Levitt, Moser & Jamison, 1994; Moser & Levitt, 1987). For example, Breslow, Evans and Langley (1986) found that 28% of women and 33% of men preferred the dominant role, 33% of women and 26% of men were versatile, and 40% of women and 42% of men preferred the submissive role. Thus studies of sexual fantasies should be sensitive to issues of role preferences among S/M practitioners.

Finally the method of assessing fantasy content in Gosselin *et al.*'s study was limited. Providing participants with a list of fantasy themes, although easy to administer and analyse, does not yield detailed information about fantasy content. The researchers may have inadvertently left out fantasy themes that were important to participants, so the resulting data may have been incomplete.

The present study

The present study was designed to address these limitations. My goal was to examine the sexual fantasies of S/M practitioners with two research questions in mind. First, does the fantasy content of practitioners vary depending on the individual's gender and self-identified S/M role (dominant, submissive, or switch)? Second, how are fantasies of dominance and submission constructed in terms of sexual pleasure? Specifically I was interested in whether fantasies of dominance and submission tended to also include descriptions of the participant's own or their partner's sexual pleasure. In a previous study using non-S/M participants (85 heterosexual men and 77 heterosexual women), my colleague and I found that men's fantasies of dominance tended to include descriptions of the man's own sexual pleasure, but women's fantasies of dominance tended to include descriptions of her partner's sexual pleasure (Zurbriggen & Yost, 2004). In the present study, I was interested in exploring the relationship between power and pleasure for S/M participants depending on their role identification.

I chose to collect open-ended accounts of sexual fantasies so that participants could fully express their fantasies. I then used a previously developed coding system (Zurbriggen & Yost, 2004) that allowed me to examine, in a detailed way, dominance and submission.

Method

Participants

Participants were 126 men and 138 women between the ages of 19 and 76 ($M = 40$, $SD = 12$). These participants were originally part of a larger pool of 134 men, 152 women, and 6 genderqueer individuals, but because one of the primary research questions concerned the impact of gender on sexual fantasy content, I excluded the genderqueer individuals from these analyses. I also excluded 22 participants because they did not write a sexual fantasy.

Most participants identified as heterosexual (75%), with 19% indicating a bisexual identity and 6% indicating a gay or lesbian identity. Most participants (86%) were White, 5% were multiracial, 3% Latino, 2% Asian, 2% Jewish, 1% African American, and 1% of other racial background. The sample was highly educated: 33% had completed higher education beyond the bachelor's degree, 25% had a bachelor's degree, 19% had attended some college, and all but one participant had at least a high school education.

Procedure

The data reported here were obtained in conjunction with a larger study on power and sexuality (Yost, 2006). Participants were recruited in a variety of ways. Recruitment advertisements were posted on websites that cater to individuals involved in S/M. Also, S/M organisations were contacted, and the officers of these organisations advertised the study to members. In addition, I handed out fliers at the Folsom Street Fair (an annual fair that attracts over 100,000 S/M practitioners) in San Francisco in September 2005. Finally, a printed advertisement was bought in the monthly magazine of the Society of Janus, a large S/M organisation based in San Francisco with members from around the world.

Volunteers contacted me via email or phone. After a brief screening to ensure that volunteers were over 18, involved in S/M, and had access to the Internet, participants were directed to an anonymous, password-protected questionnaire hosted at http://www.surveymonkey.com. All data collection was completed via this online system.

Assessing S/M role

S/M role was assessed both in terms of self-identification and sexual preferences. To assess self-identification, I provided a checklist of S/M roles to participants. The checklist included variants of dominance ('Dominant', 'Master', 'Mistress', 'Top', 'Sadist'), variants of submission ('submissive', 'slave', 'bottom', 'masochist'), and one term indicating that the participant is versatile ('switch'). To assess preference, I asked participants, 'How much do you enjoy being the dominant partner (or top) in BDSM scenes?' and 'How much do you enjoy being the submissive partner (or bottom) in BDSM scenes?' Participants were classified as 'Dominant' if they chose terms from the dominance list but not from the submission list, and if they indicated a strong sexual preference for dominance. Participants were classified as 'Submissive' if they chose terms from the submission list but not from the dominant list, and if they indicated a strong preference for submission. Finally participants were classified as 'Switches' if they chose the term 'switch' or if they chose terms from both the dominance and submission list, and if they indicated a moderate enjoyment of both dominance and submission. Table 9.1 shows the number of participants in each S/M role category, by gender.

Table 9.1 Number of participants according to S/M role and gender

	Dominant	Submissive	Switch	Total
Male	48	42	36	126
Female	20	82	36	138
Total	68	124	72	264

Sexual fantasy measure

Participants were asked to write, in detail, one of their favourite or most frequent sexual fantasies. Participants were encouraged to be as concrete as possible, while letting the fantasy flow along freely (see Zurbriggen & Yost, 2004, for complete instructions).

Dominance and submission

A running text method of coding was used (Winter, 1994). With this method, each sentence was coded for dominance and submission. To control for variations in fantasy length, the total dominance and the total submission score were each divided by the number of words in the fantasy. These scores were then multiplied by 1000 to produce the following: number of images of dominance per 1000 words and number of images of submission per 1000 words.

I scored for dominance and submission whenever there was an indication of one person in the fantasy controlling another: I scored dominance when the self exerted power over another person in the fantasy and submission when another person in the fantasy exerted power over the self. There were seven subcategories of dominance and submission: verbal control, physical control, relationship-based power, and general (e.g. statements about being powerful or powerless). Further information about subcategory scoring is available from the author.

Sexual pleasure

In addition to power, I also coded fantasies for expressions of sexual pleasure. Sexual pleasure was scored when feelings of sexual satisfaction or orgasm were described. Sexual arousal alone did not score for pleasure; rather some indication that the activities provided sexual gratification was necessary. Sexual pleasure was scored as 'self' or 'other' depending on which character experienced pleasure. An example of sexual pleasure-self is, 'It felt absolutely incredible when she started licking my cock';

an example of sexual pleasure-other is, 'I kept rubbing her clit until she exploded in orgasm'.

Results

S/M role differences

Means and standard deviations for Fantasy dominance and Fantasy submission, organised by gender and S/M role, are presented in Table 9.2. I conducted two one-way analyses of variance (ANOVA) to determine whether dominants, submissives, and switches differed in these fantasy themes (see Table 9.3). Overall the highest amounts of Fantasy dominance occurred in the fantasies of S/M dominants, followed by switches, and then submissives. Post hoc analyses revealed that all three groups were significantly different from one another. Conversely the highest amounts of Fantasy submission occurred in the fantasies of S/M submissives, followed by switches, and then dominants. Again, post-hoc analyses revealed that all three groups differed significantly from one another.

To further explore the impact of S/M role and to analyse the impact of gender, I next conducted a mixed measures ANOVA with gender as

Table 9.2 Means and standard deviations of fantasy themes, by S/M role and gender

	Fantasy Dominance	Fantasy Submission
Dominants		
Male	29.2 (26.4)	3.4 (9.6)
Female	30.6 (32.5)	4.3 (10.5)
Total	29.6 (28.1)	3.7 (9.8)
Submissives		
Male	0.0 (26.4)	37.8 (25.2)
Female	0.1 (0.4)	38.5 (22.9)
Total	0.0 (0.4)	38.3 (23.6)
Switches		
Male	12.4 (18.7)	19.9 (29.4)
Female	3.9 (8.1)	31.1 (33.0)
Total	8.2 (14.9)	25.5 (31.6)
All participants		
Male	14.7 (22.7)	19.6 (26.4)
Female	5.5 (16.6)	31.6 (27.2)
Total	9.9 (20.2)	25.9 (27.5)

Table 9.3 Analyses of variance comparing S/M dominants, submissives, and switches on fantasy content

	df	F
Fantasy Dominance		
S/M role	2	73.56***
Error	263	(263.30)
Fantasy Submission		
S/M role	2	47.08***
Error	263	(558.34)

Values enclosed in parentheses report mean square errors. ***$p < .001$.

a between-subjects variable (male, female) and fantasy type as a within-subjects variable (dominance, submission). This 2-by-2 ANOVA was run separately for each group of participants (dominants, submissives, switches). Results of these ANOVAs are presented in Table 9.4 and discussed in the subsequent sections.

S/M dominants

S/M dominants wrote fantasies in which they were the dominant partner more than fantasies in which they were the submissive partner. There were no gender differences, indicating that male and female dominants had the same pattern of Fantasy dominance and Fantasy submission.

S/M submissives

S/M submissives wrote fantasies in which they were the submissive partner more than fantasies in which they were the dominant partner. There were no gender differences, indicating that male and female submissives had the same pattern of Fantasy dominance and Fantasy submission.

S/M switches

S/M switches wrote fantasies in which they were submissive more than fantasies in which they were dominant. Again there was no overall difference between men and women. However, Gender and Fantasy type interacted in the following ways: men fantasised about dominance more than did women, women fantasised about submission marginally more than did men, and women fantasised about submission more than dominance.

Table 9.4   Analyses of variance for fantasies, run separately by S/M role

	df	F
Dominants		
	Between subjects	
Gender	1	.11
Error	66	(345.18)
	Within subjects	
Fantasy type	1	34.69***
G × FT	1	.00
G × FT error	66	(552.43)
Submissives		
	Between subjects	
Gender	1	.03
Error	122	(279.80)
	Within subjects	
Fantasy type	1	286.46***
G × FT	1	.02
G × FT error	122	(281.95)
Switches		
	Between subjects	
Gender	1	.15
Error	70	(456.86)
	Within subjects	
Fantasy type	1	14.78***
G × FT	1	4.84*
G × FT error	70	(729.17)

Values enclosed in parentheses report mean square errors. $*p < .05$, $***p < .001$.

The following examples highlight the gender differences found in S/M switches, showing male dominance (expressed in a stereotypically masculine way) and female submission (stereotypically feminine):

> Most of my fantasies involve bondage and damsel in distress scenarios (i.e., your classic melodrama villain). Usually it involves placing said damsel in a position of distress. On rare occasions it involves freeing her.

> (Male switch)

> My fantasies are 99% sex. There is no roleplaying or costumes or whatever. My role is the guy fucking the hell out of the girl. I guess one of my common fantasies is just really rough sex on a couch with a girl from my imagination, a past lover, or somebody I saw that day.

Lots of hair pulling and dirty talk. A big part of the fantasy is that I don't care about them, and vice versa, therefore, I can treat them however I see fit. They like it though, so it's not as if this is a rape fantasy

(Male switch)

A favorite fantasy is being in my 20s and having sex with a mature, sexually sophisticated man, who introduces me to intercourse in a very slow teaching kind of way. He caresses me all over, introduces me to oral sex. When penetration finally happens, it is very slow and sensuous, giving me time to savor the experience. I am lost in the sensations, and come

(Female switch)

The daydream always comes to me as I drive by large open tree orchards. I imagine myself bound to a tree with hemp rope, my feet barely able to touch the ground. My back is to the tree and my arms are wrapped behind me. The person comes up to me and kisses me savagely. They then blindfold me and begin to use a singletail on my tightly bound tits. I can hear myself giggling from the pain, but trying not to show them how much I am enjoying it. Suddenly they are on me, pressing my body against the tree painfully and sliding themselves inside of me, using my body for their enjoyment only

(Female switch)

Intercorrelations of fantasy themes

Pearson correlation coefficients were computed for the fantasy themes (dominance, submission, sexual pleasure-self, sexual pleasure-other), separately for the three groups of participants. I found that the pattern of fantasy themes varied depending on S/M role.

For S/M dominants, Fantasy Dominance was uncorrelated with Sexual Pleasure-self ($r = -.05$) but positively correlated with Sexual Pleasure-other ($r = .19$), although this latter correlation did not reach standard levels of statistical significance. Tentatively it appears that when S/M dominants fantasise about their own dominance, they tend to do so in a fantasy that highlights their partner's sexual pleasure. For example, a female dominant wrote:

Last night I was thinking of giving my boyfriend a blowjob after tying him up in a chair. He cross-dresses so I was thinking he'd be wearing lingerie and panties. I was thinking about how turned on he'd be, and that *he'd come in my mouth.*

A male dominant wrote:

Dominating my partner in a sensual setting, removing some of her senses via barriers, and teasing her until she cannot take it any more, then giving back her senses (ie: removing blindfolds, restraints, etc) and completing intercourse unrestricted. Each time the fantasy is a little different, as in one time hands tied apart to separate bedposts, one time hands cuffed behind back, but it is always sensual torture, ending with intercourse where her senses have been fully returned just at the point of *her orgasming.*

For S/M submissives, Fantasy Submission was positively correlated with Sexual Pleasure-self ($r = .23$, $p < .05$) but uncorrelated with Sexual Pleasure-other ($r = -.04$). In other words, when S/M submissives fantasise about their own submission, they tend to do so in a fantasy that highlights their own sexual pleasure. For example, a male submissive wrote:

Being controlled, dominated, aroused, and tortured by several dominant women. My arms are tied to hooks in the ceiling, my feet spread apart wide, tied to hooks in the floor. I am blindfolded, being slowly spanked all over. They promise me I will remember them every time I sit down for the next few days. I am tied to a bed, and then the girls take turns to suck my cock while one of them canes the soles of my feet. it drives me crazy until *I'm allowed to cum* which is a mixture of agony, *bliss* and total exhaustion.

A female submissive wrote:

My most common sexual fantasy involves my partner tying me to the bed and then blindfolding me. This allows him to take his time in teasing me. The teasing often involves light touching with his hands, feathers, ice, etc. He then progresses to using a flogger for some more aggressive play. After this he 'forces' his cock in me and after *I come several times* he decides that some anal sex in order. The anal sex is rough and painful with his body pressing me facedown into the bed.

However, for S/M switches, an opposite pattern of intercorrelations emerged. For S/M switches, Fantasy Dominance was positively correlated with Sexual Pleasure-self ($r = .35$, $p < .01$) but uncorrelated with Sexual

Pleasure-other ($r = -.08$). In other words, when S/M switches fantasise about their own dominance, they tend to highlight their own sexual pleasure. For example, a female switch wrote:

> I am a woman, bisexual by nature, and I have alot of sexual fantasies. In this one I am male. I imagine a woman sucking my cock, and speak to her while she is doing it. I am her Top, and give her orders such as when to take me into her mouth or to get down on her knees in front of me. My orders, while firm, are always loving. I imagine *myself coming* on her breasts or sometimes on her ass, so that I can watch the spectacle.

Similarly a male switch wrote, 'Penetrating one submissive girlfriend to conclusion and then making the other *clean her out*' (implying a male orgasm took place within her).

However, for S/M switches, Fantasy Submission was positively correlated with Sexual Pleasure-other ($r = .42$, $p < .001$) but uncorrelated with Sexual Pleasure-self ($r = -.04$). That is, when S/M switches fantasise about their own submission, they tend to highlight their partner's sexual pleasure. For example, a male switch wrote:

> I'm laying on the floor. My shiny black latex covered mistress stands over me, with her booted heel on my chest. My cock is tied up with a leash, and she is tugging on it. I can see up her skirt. She is naked underneath. She sits down hard on my mouth and begins to grind. She continues to pull my cock leash, and tells me to lick her faster. I suck and lick until *she cums on me*, forcing me to lick her clean.

Similarly a female switch wrote:

> Inspired by Story of O: I have been initiated into a society similar to that of the inmates of Roissy. I arrive and am stripped and bound, then prepared according to the whim of the men there (genitally shaved, corseted, dipped in honey, whatever) and then singly and then two or more at a time the men have sex with me (anally, orally, basically anything humanly possible) for several days until *their desires are met*.

Discussion

I had two main goals in this study, both of which involved developing a nuanced understanding of dominance and submission in the fantasies of S/M practitioners. First, I was interested in exploring whether the fantasy content of S/M practitioners varies depending on gender and on S/M role. Second, I was interested in exploring the evidence of sexual pleasure in these fantasies, to determine how fantasies of dominance and submission serve one's own or one's partner's pleasure.

Research question 1: power and S/M roles

First, this study provides evidence that the three categories of S/M identity (dominant, submissive, switch) are meaningful. Recently some S/M researchers have argued that role identification is rare, claiming that S/M practitioners are aroused by power and therefore dominant or submissive roles are unimportant (Beckmann, 2001; Thompson, 1994). However, in this study, I found that there are many people for whom a stable S/M role is erotic, and the eroticism of the role was displayed both in terms of sexual behaviour and in the choice of fantasy content. Also a sizeable number of participants identified as switch and these participants also displayed the eroticism of that role in terms of sexual behaviour and fantasy content. Their fantasies could be seen as falling into an 'in-between' space (expressing more fantasy dominance than S/M submissives, but less than S/M dominants; also expressing more fantasy submission than S/M dominants, but less than S/M submissives). Thus these three roles appear to accurately represent discrete categories of S/M identity.

In addition, for S/M practitioners whose role is stable (i.e. dominants and submissives), S/M role and the content of sexual fantasies are consistent. S/M dominants tended to have fantasies of dominance, and S/M submissives tended to have fantasies of submission. For these two groups of participants there was a complete lack of gender differences in fantasy content related to power, which is counter to decades of research finding clear gender differences in fantasies of dominance and submission (for a review, see Leitenberg & Henning, 1995). On the other hand, for S/M practitioners whose role is fluid (i.e. switches), fantasies conformed to traditional gender-role expectations, where men fantasised about dominance more than did women and women fantasised about more submission than they did dominance.

It is possible that this latter finding was primarily driven by heterosexual participants (27 of the 36 male switches identified as heterosexual, as did 17 of the 36 female switches). With a larger sample of S/M switches who identify as homosexual or bisexual, the traditional gender roles in fantasy might be diminished. In the present study, the S/M switch sample size is small and thus the findings must be interpreted with caution, but analyses showed that even among the homosexual and bisexual switches, women fantasised about more submission than they did dominance (there were no differences among men). This suggests that traditional gender roles may continue to be apparent in S/M switches (perhaps only women) regardless of sexual orientation identity. A larger sample is clearly needed to explore this question more fully.

Fantasies, gender, and sexual scripts

This study raises interesting questions about the source of fantasy content or what individuals rely on to create sexually arousing scripts. The absence of gender differences in the sexual fantasies of S/M dominants and submissives is consistent with the way that many S/M practitioners understand gender within the S/M context. There is evidence from S/M practitioners' writings that the S/M culture defies gender roles. Califia, for example, has written about the gender transgressions that take place in S/M. Califia wrote, 'S/M is so threatening to the established order...S/M roles are not related to gender or sexual orientation or race or class. My own needs dictate which role I will adopt' (1979/2000: 166). Califia argues that although the larger culture assumes that men will be dominant and women will be submissive, in S/M the dominant or submissive roles are freely chosen, without regard to traditional gender expectations of the broader culture. Similarly Taylor and Ussher, in interviews with practicing sadomasochists, found that S/M was understood as 'dissidence' by most participants. This reflected an understanding of S/M as 'deliberately, consciously antithetical to a sexual hegemonic, namely patriarchal heterosexuality' (2001: 302). These participants, then, saw S/M as a place where stereotypical gender roles were reversed or outright rejected. Finally Scott (1980) in her ethnographic study of female dominant–male submissive couples noted the ways in which gender boundaries were transgressed in S/M, and it was the transgression itself that was erotic to many of her informants. Part of the erotic thrill for these couples lay in the taboo nature of men submitting to powerful women.

On the other hand, when S/M practitioners switch roles, gender roles and traditional sexual scripts of masculinity and femininity become important as a guide to what is sexually arousing and explored in sexual fantasy. Perhaps in the absence of a stronger guide for eroticism, gender becomes the main determinant of power-related behaviour.

This finding is consistent with expectation states theory (Berger, Cohen & Zelditch, 1972), which has been used to explain gender differences in communication patterns. When men and women interact in a context where one person has higher status, the high status person engages in stereotypically masculine or dominant behaviours, whereas the low status person engages in stereotypically feminine or submissive behaviours. This happens regardless of the participants' gender. However, when men and women have the same social status, gender becomes the determinant of conversational dominance, with men dominating and women acting in a submissive or supportive role. In other words, gender differences in conversational dominance are *not* evident when people have other social cues to use as a guide for behaviour; it is only in the face of ambiguity or a lack of other status cues that gender becomes the most salient characteristic present. When that occurs, conversational dominance follows a gender-stereotypical pattern.

Although expectation states is a theory of interaction, it may also explain the gender differences in the fantasies of S/M switches (at least for those fantasising within a heterosexual context). A stable S/M role might be the most salient determinant of fantasy content when it is present, but when it is not, gender becomes the most relevant, power-related, determinant of fantasies. In future studies, it would be interesting to explore whether heterosexual S/M switches tend to endorse traditional gender roles in other areas of their lives besides sexual fantasy, and whether heterosexual S/M dominants and submissives rely less on gender stereotypes. Expectation states theory can only comment on heterosexual interactions, because it is based on a man and a woman interacting together; future research might also explore the determinants of fantasy content for S/M switches fantasising within a homosexual or bisexual context. Unfortunately the present research involved too few homosexual or bisexual switches (only 19 women and 9 men) to perform valid comparisons.

Research question 2: power and pleasure

The correlations between fantasy dominance, submission, and sexual pleasure varied depending on S/M role. For switches, power and pleasure followed stereotypical patterns: the person expressing dominance felt sexual pleasure himself/herself, whereas the person who submits provided sexual pleasure to their partner. This corresponds with general cultural ideas about power. It is widely believed that power is self-serving or that people in power will use that power to their own advantage. Similarly, not having power is understood as unfulfilling. Thus S/M switches appear to be drawing upon cultural scripts related to the benefits of power when engaging in sexual fantasy.

On the other hand, for S/M dominants and submissives, power and pleasure followed counter-stereotypical patterns. In fantasy, the person in power tended to use that power to give pleasure to his/her partner, and the person who submits felt sexual pleasure himself/herself. For S/M dominants and submissives, pleasure was experienced in a manner consistent with S/M practitioners' own discussions of these roles. For example, Easton and Liszt discuss the dominant role in terms of focusing on the stimulation and sensations being given to the submissive partner; concern with the dominant's own sexual pleasure often comes after the S/M encounter is over (1995b). Califia writes of the submissive role, 'the pleasures of being done-to – receiving an entire symphony of sensations – are much more obvious than the pleasures of the composer or conductor of the scene' (2001: 140). Thus for many S/M practitioners, providing pleasure is a part of dominance and experiencing pleasurable sensations is a part of submission.

Furthermore this characterisation of S/M (fantasies associating dominance with one's partner's pleasure and submission with one's own pleasure) demonstrates how this sexuality is antithetical to rape. Radical feminists have claimed that the power dynamics played out in S/M are a reproduction of the power dynamics inherent in the crime of rape (Russell, 1982), but the present study challenges this view. Rape has been conceptualised by feminist scholars as 'power-over', which refers to controlling or dominating another person without their consent and with little concern for their well-being (Brownmiller, 1975). Importantly during a rape, the person holding power (the rapist) is more likely than the victim to experience pleasure. In contrast, S/M has been conceptualised by practitioners (Easton & Liszt, 1995a, 1995b) as 'power-with' or empowerment, described as a process in which 'power is something to share, something to use for the enhancement of others' (Miller & Cumming, 1992: 416–417). This reflects a belief that all participants in an S/M encounter give and take power and also give and take pleasure. Thus the way S/M dominants and submissives fantasise about power and pleasure is markedly different from a typical rape scenario.

Conclusions

Practitioners within the S/M community have argued that gender is not the most important factor organising S/M sexuality, and the current study supports this claim. Role identity, not gender, largely determined sexual fantasy content and the location of sexual pleasure. The relationship between power and pleasure in dominants' and submissives' fantasies did not follow that of the general population, rather it was consistent with practitioner's own descriptions of these roles: S/M dominants (male and female) fantasised about dominance and giving their partner pleasure, and S/M submissives (male and female) fantasised about submission and receiving their own pleasure. However, for the third S/M role, switches, a more complicated picture of power, gender, and pleasure was found: fantasies primarily demonstrated male dominance and female submission, with the dominant partner experiencing sexual pleasure himself/herself and the submissive partner providing sexual pleasure to his/her partner.

Sex researchers have traditionally studied differences between participants in regards to gender (and sometimes, sexual orientation). As the present study makes clear, future research with sexual minority groups must be sensitive to subculture-specific personal and social identities. Meaningful identities, beyond gender and beyond sexual orientation, must be incorporated into research design whenever possible, in order to avoid imposing larger cultural norms onto subcultures that conceptualise gender and sexuality in more complicated ways.

Note

1. Portions of this research were presented at the 2006 Annual Meeting of the Society for the Scientific Study of Sexuality, Las Vegas, NV. Data collection was supported by grants from the Psychology Department at the University of California, Santa Cruz. I would like to thank the members of my dissertation committee: Eileen Zurbriggen, Heather Bullock, Raymond Gibbs, and Charles Moser. I would also like to thank Tara Smith for helpful comments on an earlier version of this manuscript.

References

Arndt, W.B., Foehl, J.C. & Good, F.F. (1985). Specific sexual fantasy themes: A multidimensional study. *Journal of Personality and Social Psychology*, 48(2), 472–480.

Beckmann, A. (2001). Deconstructing myths: The social construction of "sado-masochism" versus "subjugated knowledges" of practitioners of consensual "SM." *Journal of Criminal Justice and Popular Culture*, 8(2), 66–95.

Berger, J., Cohen, B.P. & Zelditch, M. (1972). Status characteristics and social interaction. *American* Sociological *Review* , 37(3), 241–255.

Brame, G.G., Brame, W.D. & Jacobs, J. (1993). *Different Loving: The World of Sexual Dominance and Submission.* New York, NY: Villard Books.

Breslow, N. (1987). Locus of control, desirability of control, and sadomasochists. *Psychological Reports*, 61(3), 995–1001.

Breslow, N., Evans, L. & Langley, J. (1986). Comparisons among heterosexual, bisexual and homosexual male sado-masochists. *Journal of Homosexuality*, 13(1), 83–107.

Brownmiller, S. (1975). *Against Our Will: Men, Women, and Rape*. New York, NY: Simon & Schuster.

Byers, S.E. (1996). How well does the traditional sexual script explain sexual coercion? Review of a program of research. *Journal of Psychology and Human Sexuality*, 8(1–2), 7–25.

Califia, P. (2001). *Sensuous Magic: A Guide to S/M for Adventurous Couples*. San Francisco, CA: Cleis Press.

Califia, P. (2000). A secret side of lesbian sexuality. In P. Califia (Ed.) *Public Sex: The Culture of Radical Sex* (pp. 158–167). San Francisco, CA: Cleis Press. (Reprinted from *The Advocate*, December 29, 19–23, 1979).

Califia, P. (2000). Feminism and sadomasochism. In P. Califia (Ed.) *Public Sex: The Culture of Radical Sex* (pp. 168–180). San Francisco, CA: Cleis Press. (Reprinted from *Heresies*, 12, 30–34, 1981).

Easton, D. & Hardy, J.W. (2004). *Radical Ecstasy*. Oakland, CA: Greenery Press.

Easton, D. & Liszt, C.A. (1995a). *The Bottoming Book: Or, How to Get Terrible Things Done to You by Wonderful People*. San Francisco, CA: Greenery Press.

Easton, D. & Liszt, C.A. (1995b). *The Topping Book: Or, Getting Good at Being Bad*. San Francisco, CA: Greenery Press.

Freud, S. (1962). Creative writers and daydreaming. In J. Stachy (Ed.) *The Standard Edition of the Complete Psychological Works of Sigmund Freud*, Vol. 9 (pp. 142–152). London: Hogarth. Original work published 1908.

Goffman, E. (1974). *Frame Analysis: An Essay on the Organization of Experience*. Cambridge, MA: Harvard University Press.

Gosselin, C.C., Wilson, G.D. & Barrett, P.T. (1991). The personality and sexual preferences of sadomasochistic women. *Personality and Individual Differences*, 12(1), 11–15.

Hariton, E.B. & Singer, J.L. (1974). Women's fantasies during sexual intercourse: Normative and theoretical implications. *Journal of Consulting and Clinical Psychology*, 42(3), 313–322.

Herron, M.J., Herron, W.G. & Schultz, C.L. (1983). Sexual dominance/submission, gender and sex-role identification. *Perceptual and Motor Skills*, 56(3), 931–937.

Hoople, T. (1996). Conflicting visions: SM, feminism, and the law. A problem of representation. *Canadian Journal of Law and Society*, 11(1), 177–221.

Hopkins, P.D. (1994). Rethinking sadomasochism: Feminism, interpretation, and simulation. *Hypatia*, 9(1), 116–142.

Leitenberg, H. & Henning, K. (1995). Sexual fantasy. *Psychological Bulletin*, 117(3), 469–496.

Levitt, E.E., Moser, C. & Jamison, K.V. (1994). The prevalence and some attributes of females in the sadomasochistic subculture. *Archives of Sexual Behaviour*, 23(4), 465–474.

Miller, J.B. & Cummins, A.G. (1992). An examination of women's perspectives on power. *Psychology of Women Quarterly*, 16(4), 415–428.

Moser, C. & Levitt, E.E. (1987). An exploratory-descriptive study of a sadomasochistically oriented sample. *Journal of Sex Research*, 23(3), 322–327.

Person, E.S., Terestman, N., Myers, W.A., Goldberg, E.L. & Salvadori, C. (1989). Gender differences in sexual behaviours and fantasies in a college population. *Journal of Sex and Marital Therapy*, 15(3), 187–198.

Russell, D.E.H. (1982). Sadomasochism: A contra-feminist activity. In R.R. Linden, D.R. Pagano, D.E.H. Russell & S.L. Star (Eds.) *Against Sadomasochism: A Radical Feminist Analysis* (pp. 176–183). San Francisco, CA: Frog in the Well.

Scott, G.G. (1980). *Erotic Power: An Exploration of Dominance and Submission.* Secaucus, NJ: Citadel.

Sue, D. (1979). Erotic fantasies of college students during coitus. *Journal of Sex Research*, 15(4), 299–305.

Taylor, G.W. & Ussher, J.M. (2001). Making sense of S&M: A discourse analytic account. *Sexualities*, 4(3), 293–314.

Thompson, B. (1994). *Sadomasochism.* New York, NY: Cassell Press.

Warren, J. (2000). *The Loving Dominant.* Emeryville, CA: Greenery Press.

Weinberg, M.S., Williams, C.J. & Moser, C. (1984). The social constituents of sadomasochism. *Social Problems*, 31(4), 379–389.

Weinberg, T.S. (1978). Sadism and masochism: Sociological perspectives. *Bulletin of the AAPL*, 6(3), 284–295.

Wilson, G.D. (1987). Male–female differences in sexual activity, enjoyment, and fantasies. *Personality and Individual Differences*, 8(1), 125–127.

Winter, D.G. (1994). *Manual for Scoring Motive Imagery in Running Text* (4th ed.). (Available from D.G. Winter, Department of Psychology, University of Michigan, 525 East University, Ann Arbor, MI 48109-1109, USA).

Yost, M.R. (2006). *Consensual Sexual Sadomasochism and Sexual Aggression Perpetration: Exploring the Erotic Value of Power.* Unpublished doctoral dissertation, University of California Santa Cruz.

Zurbriggen, E.L. & Yost, M.R. (2004). Power, desire, and pleasure in sexual fantasies. *Journal of Sex Research*, 41(3), 288–300.

10
On Becoming a Gay SMer: A Sexual Scripting Perspective

Eric Chaline

Introduction

The question addressed by this chapter is how does a man become a gay SMer.[1] By which I do not mean how he formulates the identity of a gay SMer but how his interest in gay SM first makes itself known and how this initial awareness is transformed into lived gay SM interactions.[2] Since the original definitions of homosexuality and sadomasochism in the late nineteenth and early twentieth centuries (Ellis, 1936; Freud, 1938; Krafft-Ebing, 1892), researchers have given a range of answers to this question, but for the most part, these have consisted of constructing culturally universal, unitary and ahistorical theorizations based on biological or psychodynamic pathology.[3]

The move away from disease models of variant sexualities began with the work of Kinsey (1948, 1953), who turned the canvas of sexuality from a stark black and white to shades of grey. It was advanced by the social interactionists (Goffman, 1963, 1974) and symbolic interactionists (Plummer, 1975) and brought to fruition by the social constructionists (Foucault, 1980, 1984; Plummer, 1995; Weeks, 1985, 1995) who succeeded in freeing sexualities and sexual identities, among social scientists at least, from the bonds of biology, essentialism and psychopathology. The caveat 'among social scientists at least' is necessary because parts of the psychiatric establishment (*DSM-IV*, 2000; Weldon, 2002), along with the biological and genetic theorists of sexuality (Wilson, 2000; Wilson & Rahman, 2005), still uphold unitary and/or pathological models of non-procreative, non-heterosexual sexualities and sexual identities.

Sexual scripting

This chapter, and the study whose findings it reports in part,[4] situates itself in the social constructionist tradition but as Brickell (2006) has pointed out social constructionist approaches are diverse, and those he highlights as having particular relevance to the study of sexuality and gender are historicism, ethnomethodology, symbolic interactionism and materialist feminism. This study has made use of several of these approaches, and of one that Brickell specifically mentions: Gagnon and Simon's theory of sexual scripting (1973), which he describes as

> A useful – and somewhat overlooked contribution to the sociology of sexuality. It is relentlessly social, arguing that while the 'private world' of desire is often experienced as 'originating in the deepest recesses of the self', this 'world' in fact emerges at the intersection of social meanings and ongoing processes of self-creation
>
> (2006: 96)

I was first attracted to sexual scripting by its 'relentlessly social' quality and by the central position it gave to human agency while taking into account the effects of social interaction and discourse.

Sexual scripts, like those discussed below, are found within broader sexual narratives. The analysis of sexual narrative has followed several different avenues in the social sciences, the most famous sociological approach being Plummer's (1995) analysis of the sexual story as a subject of study per se, specifically how and when it is told, by whom and to whom. But what is of immediate methodological concern to this study and chapter are not questions of authorship or audience, but the way a sexual script should be interpreted and read. For example, it could be read from the present into the past, as a means employed by the interviewee to describe and make sense of a current sexuality or sexual identity; or from the past into the present, in the order intended by Gagnon and Simon, as a tool to analyse the processes involved in the formation of a specific sexuality or sexual identity. While issues of discursive construction, honesty, memory and the retrospective editing of narratives need to be addressed by any qualitative study of sexuality and sexual identity, for the purposes of this chapter, I have chosen the second and more straightforward approach to scripting theory.

In their initial formulation of sexual scripting theory, Gagnon and Simon proposed two levels: 'intrapsychic' and 'interpersonal' scripting. They later added the third level of 'cultural scenarios'. The three levels correspond, in turn, to the individual, the individual in interaction with others and the social discourses related to sexuality, sexual identity and sexual conduct found in a particular culture or historical period.

Taking as their starting point that nothing is intrinsically sexual, Gagnon and Simon described intrapsychic scripting as an internal process that formed the basis for all sexual behaviour, making it possible for an individual to feel excited about certain practices on the physical, cognitive and emotional level. They defined it as 'The plans and fantasies by which individuals guide and reflect upon their past, current, or future conduct' (Parker & Gagnon, 1995: 190), and which provided 'the motivational elements that produce arousal or at least a commitment to the activity' (Gagnon & Simon, 1973: 14). Intrapsychic scripting defines the selection of roles, material cultures and practices and structures the individual's emotional responses to subsequent interactions. Although they provide guidelines for later interactions, they do not define them.

Gagnon has continued to refine his definition of sexual scripting. An important characteristic of intrapsychic scripts, he explained in an interview in 1995, was that their creation was not the result of a standardized social process. On the contrary, the processes through which individuals found elements and assembled them to create their sexual scripts were unique and accidental. Another quality of intrapsychic scripts that he stressed was that they did not necessarily follow the forms of conventional narrative:

> When dealing with erotic elements in the intrapsychic, we are dealing with a more complex set of layered symbolic meanings which has much more to do with the non-narrative traditions in literary representation and imagery. What is arousing may not be the plan to have sex, but fragmentary symbolic materials taken from mass media or more local experience. Here the proper modes of analysis of mental life should be from a more surrealistic tradition, from poetry or from other sources of more condensed forms of meaning
>
> (2004: 137)

Gagnon and Simon defined the second level of sexual scripting, interpersonal scripting, as dealing with

> The external, the interpersonal – the script as the organization of mutually shared conventions that allows two or more actors to participate in a complex act involving mutual dependence
>
> (1973: 14)

Gagnon added, 'In the case of sexuality, this means specific sex acts' (2004: 118). Simon and Gagnon also defined interpersonal scripts as a reflexive process (1987: 363): 'The representations of self and the implied mirroring of the other or others that facilitate the occurrence of a sexual exchange'. Interpersonal scripts were projections into the interaction order of intrapsychic scripts. Naturally these projections could never be perfect reproductions of the original scripts. The individual came up against reality: what was achievable physically, morally, emotionally and legally in a given historical and cultural context, and he/she also came into contact with the subjectivity of his/her partners.

Simon and Gagnon added the third level of 'cultural scenarios' to take account of the discourses of sexuality that were available within a specific culture or historical period. Gagnon defined them as 'The instructions for sexual and other conduct that are embedded in the cultural narratives which are provided as guides or instructions for all conduct' (Lauman & Gagnon, 1995: 190). These include specific discourses of sexuality within social institutions such as the law, psychiatry, academia and medicine and representations from literature, the visual arts, popular media and pornography. As Simon and Gagnon pointed out, there could be congruence or conflict between the different levels of scripting, depending on the cultural and historical moment or on the development of an individual.

Gagnon summarized the relationship between the three levels of scripting in the following terms:

> Examining sexual conduct from the perspective of scripting allows one to organize and link together what people think, what they do, and how they are affected by the sociocultural context in which they live. Seeing the conduct as 'scripted' on the interpersonal and intrapsychic levels gives the behaviour the quality of a narrative in which conduct is composed of events ordered in time, events that occur with sufficient regularity that individuals recognize that when they occur, often wish to participate in them, and remember them when they are over. At the cultural level instructions for conduct do not stand alone as 'rules' or 'norms' but are rather embedded in narratives of good and bad behaviour, things to be done, things to be avoided
>
> (2004: 169)

To summarize, the key aspects of sexual scripting defined by Simon and Gagnon that are of special relevance to this study are

(1) the accidental and unique nature of intrapsychic scripting; (2) the non-narrative nature of some elements of intrapsychic scripts, as opposed to those of interpersonal scripts and cultural scenarios; (3) the changeability of scripting within a culture, historical period and within the life course of an individual and (4) the congruence or otherwise of the different levels of scripting within a culture or historical period or within the experience of an individual.

Simon and Gagnon did not apply sexual scripting theory to SM sexualities and sexual identities, hence I was curious to see if the pattern they described would fit the findings of this study. I could have found a single pattern, for example, that many of my respondents had suffered from post-traumatic stress disorder in infancy after a long and painful illness, which was one explanation for an interest in SM suggested by Stoller (1991), or that many had been sexually abused as infants, as put forward by Weldon (2002). In the former case, I would have found a form of intrapsychic scripting related to their illness, and in the latter, their development in scripting terms would have reversed the order of intrapsychic and interpersonal scripts. Alternatively, and to imagine the opposite extreme, I could have found no single element shared among the 31 interview respondents.

Sexual scripting and gay SM

This study covers the period from the late 1950s to the present; during this time, the processes of sexual scripting in gay SM were transformed at all three scripting levels. If we look at the cultural scenarios of gay SM at the beginning of the period, both homosexuality and SM were pathologized and criminalized. The situation changed for homosexuality with partial legalization in 1967 and again with the reforms of the Blair government (1997–2007). However, the case of SM remained much more problematic. Although representations of SM became far more common in the popular media (Sisson, 2005), the precedent set by the Spanner case (R. v Brown (1993) 2 WLR 556; 2 All ER 75) criminalized many SM practices (Chaline, 2005b). The available cultural scenarios of gay SM, therefore, were fragmented and contradictory.

Since the early 1970s, however, gay SMers had sources of information (and positive cultural scenarios) about practices other than sexological, legal or psychiatric discourses in the form of how-to manuals, fictions, personal testimonies and histories written by gay SMers themselves.[5] However, until gay SM material became widely available on the Internet in the late 1990s, positive representations were difficult to access for most men. Many who participated in gay SM interactions found the material for their intrapsychic scripts from a variety of sources within mainstream culture. Also, because gay SM interpersonal scripts detailing roles and practices within interactions were also absent or difficult to access, men had to formulate these by a process of experimentation, constructing interpersonal scripts by combining their intrapsychic scripts with those of their partners to evolve workable interpersonal scenarios.

Kamel (1995) suggested that a gay man became a gay SMer by following a six-stage career.[6] While he looked at the American experience in the 1970s and 1980s, it was one of my research aims to see if there was a single or dominant pattern through which men had come to participate in gay SM practices in the UK during the period covered by the study. It should come as no surprise to those involved in the study of sexualities and sexual identities that I could not discern a single pattern, and that there was a great diversity in the way gay men initiated, lived and expressed their participation in gay SM.

In terms of the quantitative findings of the study, the development of an intrapsychic script corresponded to the question about the 'age of first awareness of gay SM' and its subsequent conversion into an interpersonal script, with the question about 'age of first gay SM encounter' in the survey and interviews of participants (see Figure 10.1 for the survey findings).[7] The sample could be divided into two groups: 'early awareness' (<25) and 'late awareness' (>25).

The majority reported 'early awareness', with almost three-quarters of the sample, 37% of whom identified awareness before the age of 15.

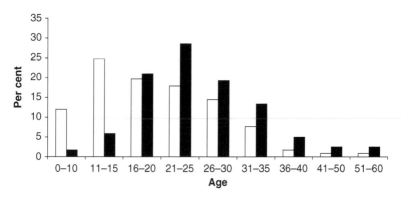

Figure 10.1   Ages of first gay SM awareness and first gay SM encounter (*N* = 119)

This still left a sizeable group of about one-quarter of the sample who reported 'late awareness'. In terms of first gay SM encounter, only 7.6% reported this by the age of 15, with the majority of first experiences occurring above the age of 21 (71.5% per cent). Hence the findings suggested that for many gay SMers, there was a significant gap between awareness and first gay SM encounter. The survey data had nothing to reveal about the processes that had occurred between first awareness and first encounter. The qualitative findings complemented the survey data, by describing the range of source materials for intrapsychic scripting and providing three broad patterns of conversion of intrapsychic into interpersonal scripts.

Sources of intrapsychic scripting

As we have seen above until the advent of mass-market gay magazines, books and of the Internet, cultural scenarios of gay SM were not widely available, especially to the young and those living outside of major metropolitan areas. As a result men who were later going to take part in gay SM practices found the materials to create their early gay SM intrapsychic scripts from a wide variety of sources. These scripts, once created, as Gagnon observed, were not immutable but subject to a reflexive process of 'creation, reorganization, and destruction' (2004: 62).

During the interviews I asked respondents if they could remember what had triggered their first awareness of gay SM. From their responses, I identified seven sources for intrapsychic scripting: (1) mainstream (non-gay and non-SM) visual or printed media, (2) materials (e.g. rubber or leather), (3) found or made objects, (4) physical sensations, (5) childhood games,[8] (6) introduction by partners and (7) visual or printed media with overt gay SM content (in recent years, the Internet has become very important as a source of scripting material). By and large, the first five corresponded to those who had identified an early awareness, while the last two, to those who had reported no early awareness. Different sources could occur in combination – sensations and materials were often paired, for example – but respondents often identified one as dominant over the others. A number of respondents identified elements of intrapsychic scripting that fell into several of the above categories, though these were likely to succeed one another rather than occur simultaneously.

One of the earliest commentators to describe 'leather subculture', Freeman noted that there was no shortage of material for SM fantasies within the mainstream culture of her day. She characterized popular men's adventure magazines such as *Man's Story* , *Man's True Danger* and *Men Today* as 'obsessed with sex and sadism' (1967: 77). In a similar vein, several respondents identified works of mainstream fiction and non-fiction as source materials for early gay SM intrapsychic scripts. Ben (65)[9] remembered that at the age of 14 or 15 he had found a book called *Britain's Wonderful Fighting Forces*, which featured military equipment, including gasmasks, which he found 'terribly, terribly exciting'. But like other respondents who had memories going back to childhood and early adolescence, he said that he did not understand why he was excited and that the excitement was not of a clear-cut sexual nature. Several respondents mentioned scenes from Ian Flemming's James Bond novels, and the eponymous spy, also featured for those remembering scenes from movies, in particular from *Dr No*. Adam (49) recalled being attracted to the uniformed, moustachioed British soldiers in the film *Zulu*, which he had seen as a teenager.

In addition to films and books, materials could originate in comic books and TV programmes. David (47) recounted a pre-pubertal fantasy that he had developed around five or six years of age, which he called 'the Wounded GI'. Based on a comic-book story, it involved him rescuing a wounded American soldier during the Pacific War and caring for him and thus winning his affection. David identified this story as his first awareness because it became the basis of a sexualized post-pubertal fantasy, involving the same situation and characters but with the addition of gay SM elements. TV featured in Chris' (32) pre-pubertal fantasy. He vividly recalled an episode of the TV series *Dr Who* ('Dr Who and the Pyramids of Mars'), which was broadcast in 1975 when he was four and a half. The episode featured 'robot mummies', which he described as 'broad shouldered, deep-chested, very masculine, obviously male', which sandwiched their luckless victims between them and crushed them to death. He associated this fantasy with SM practices such as bondage and breath control (the erotic use of asphyxia) that he subsequently experienced as an adult. While in general masculinity was often a characteristic of the materials recalled by respondents, these did not always have to be obviously male. Harry (40), with no heterosexual history in his sexual career, identified as his first awareness of SM a scene from one of the St Trinian's movies in which one of the schoolgirls was stretched out on a rack.

Unlike the other sources of scripting described below, mainstream media, such as the stories of David's 'Wounded GI' or Chris's 'robot mummies', sometimes exhibited a ready-made narrative structured around masculinity, power-exchange, sensation, emotion and material cultures, into which the individual could ascribe himself a role. However, a structured narrative could not be taken for granted.

Materials were cited by several respondents, though sometimes it was impossible to disentangle the materials from the clothing or objects they were made into. Leather and rubber were common themes, but so were other fabrics such as PVC.[10] Ulli (64) remembered an attraction to leather in his early twenties, when he saw a man dressed in full leather in the street. The following comment shows the link between the material, the idea of power that it embodied and their mutual link with a potential male-to-male interaction:

> I wanted this man: I was attracted by the leather, by the display of strength, the display of power, and, of course, underneath it all was that I would get overpowered by that man.

Frederic (28) remembered an interest in bikers dressed in leather as a teenager, and recalled his reaction during his first visit to a gay shop in his early twenties: 'I remember going to Clone Zone and smelling the rubber and being totally turned on by it'. Alex (29) recalled rubber boots and PVC clothing from his infancy. At the age of ten, he saved up his pocket money to buy himself a PVC outfit from Argos and later acquired other waterproof clothing and footwear. This interest in materials evolved into an early 'pre-sexual' interpersonal script when, at around the age of ten, he would play with another boy, dressing up in the waterproofs.

Paul (56) was so attracted to a 'shiny' PVC raincoat when he was nine or ten that he stole it from school. Later at school, his interest moved to the shiny seat of boy's school uniform trousers, indicating a shift to a nascent interpersonal script that would involve other individuals. Aged 14 or 15, he discovered ads for leather biker clothing in *Exchange and Mart*, through which he purchased a pair of leather jeans, which he used to wear in bed as an aid to masturbation. His interest in leather clothing developed into an attraction for bikers:

> I was thinking, I really want to wear it; then it was, I really want to meet a boy, and it was definitely a boy; maybe I wasn't quite accepting it, but I didn't think I realized that I was gay, just that I wanted to meet these bikers.

Unsurprisingly, as soon as he was old enough and had the resources, he himself became a biker.

Ben, along with his early interest in militaria, was fascinated by a rubber dinghy he had been given at around the age of 14. He recalled, 'You could almost completely enclose it and go into it. In fact you could also shut off the face piece and reduce the air, and I found this terribly exciting'. This interest in rubber, enclosure and controlling the air supply to himself and his sexual partners remained a marked feature of his later gay SM practices. The rubber dinghy also illustrated the difficulty of separating the object from the material it was made of.

Found or made objects formed another class of source materials. Adam, whom we have seen above recalling his interest in the soldiers in the film *Zulu*, identified an earlier sign of his interest in gay SM:

> I think I was aware of being gay and possibly having a slight 'S&My' side to me as early as eight [...] My father was a police sergeant and we always had a lot of uniforms around, and I suppose that interested me.

The uniforms and the representations of the masculine British soldiers in the film, however, were not part of a sexual narrative in which Adam was an actor. His own interpersonal scripts developed much later, when he became a biker. However, it would be possible to make a linkage between uniforms and masculinity, which formed the intra-psychic elements of his early scripts and his later preference for masculine, uniformed (in leather) bikers. John (55), whose first experience of gay SM was at the age of 35, remembered making what he described as homemade 'cockrings' and 'cock cages' when he was aged 13, well before he would have ever been aware of the existence of such items. He mentioned being surprised when, as an adult, he discovered clothing and equipment in sex shops that he had fantasized about as a teenager.

Respondents also reported sensations as indicating their first awareness of gay SM. Ian (24) recounted the experience of accidentally crushing his penis between two magnets at the age of eight, which led to experiments with other sensations. These were not linked to an interpersonal script until much later. He commented:

> It was just sensation. It stayed like that to my first experience, which was primarily to seek someone who could administer that sensation at a level that I could not administer it to myself [...] There was no appreciation of someone else enjoying it.

Two other respondents, Karl (49) and Quentin (45), recalled tying their penises as children. Stimulation of the genitals known as CBT is an extremely popular practice among gay SMers.[11] Neither man was old enough to have access to gay SM pornography; hence, their use of CBT was not experimentation with an existing practice but an accidental discovery.

In the late 1990s, the Internet became a major source of material about gay SM and, as a result, a source of intrapsychic scripting. The difference between this and other forms of material, however, was that it depicted gay SM practices and interactions, providing ready-made scripts.[12] Eric (29) was a case in point. His first experience of gay SM was at 28, and he had begun investigating it around the age of 26. His main source was the Internet:

> When I moved down to London, I got Internet access; I got profiles; then I was on Gaydar[13] for quite a while, and I think it was flicking around there that I began to see [gay SM] profiles. And so became a bit more aware of individuals, what it meant, also the Internet provided me a way of discovering that.

When interviewed, he had not visited any gay SM commercial venues or social groups and had read no books on the subject; his only sources of information were 'reading profiles and looking at porn' online.

The characteristics of the intrapsychic scripting materials given above confirm Simon and Gagnon's description of them as found by accident, often non-narrative and changeable over an individual's sexual career. However, in those with an early awareness of an interest in gay SM, continuity could be observed in scripting, with similar elements, such as specific materials, objects or practices, reappearing in later interpersonal scripts. This did not imply, however, that these elements represented any essential characteristics pertaining to gay SM practices or roles. Once discovered, these elements had been incorporated into scripts over time and elaborated through a process of repetition and experimentation.

Finally I collected evidence that intrapsychic scripts continue to develop even after interpersonal scripts have been formed and interact with them. Alex, who we saw above in relation to his interest in rubber and other materials, described a new and very elaborate quicksand fantasy – a scenario common in many adventure movies in which a character is caught in quicksand – which he wanted to recreate in his back garden.

Conversion from intrapsychic to interpersonal scripting

Gagnon described the process of conversion of intrapsychic into interpersonal scripting in the following terms:

> There exist the erotic mental 'fragments' and 'emotions that are the sources of feelings of the erotic'. These are subsequently encoded into more organized cognitive scripts which form the guides for concrete interactions with other persons
>
> (2004: 138)

The process of conversion was subject to considerable variation among the interview respondents in this study but it was possible to identify three broad patterns: (1) 'interrupted conversion', (2) 'late conversion' and (3) 'direct conversion'. As with the sources of intrapsychic scripting, there is no question of any essentialized or standardized set of patterns of conversion. As we shall see, each pattern exhibited considerable variation.

Interrupted conversion

The first, 'interrupted conversion', which was the most common in the sample with 15 interview respondents, consisted of an early gay SM intrapsychic scripting phase, followed by the development of gay, heterosexual or bisexual interpersonal scripting through non-SM interactions, and at a later date, the experience of gay SM interpersonal scripting and interactions that either replaced or supplemented these earlier interactions. The intervals between the three phases and their duration were highly variable.

In this respect, we should consider the influence of the availability of gay SM materials on the process of socialization and the development of interpersonal scripting. As a rule, the older respondents did not have access to this kind of material. John (55) and his partner Karl (49) both grew up outside of metropolitan areas. Both had early fantasies involving bondage and CBT, and both had long non-gay SM careers before finally embarking on their present lifestyle as full-time master and slave. John did not have any heterosexual experiences, and his first gay SM interaction was through the Blackline telephone chat line in 1984, and his first attendance of gay SM commercial venues were a decade later in 1994.

After initial gay vanilla experiences, Karl was married for 11 years. He recalled that six years into the marriage he had visited a male sex worker and paid him for a gay SM interaction. He recalled, 'I didn't particularly enjoy it because there was no intimacy'. He frequented gay SM commercial venues but did nothing. 'I didn't have the encouragement, the confidence'. It was only later, with the help of a friend, that he managed to come to terms with his desire to become a full-time slave. He met John through a general gay personals website three years before the interview. Although gay SM social worlds had been a presence in both their lives, it played a secondary role in their socialization as gay SMers. It took them many years to make the link between their early intrapsychic scripts and gay SM practices and identities, and they experienced considerable social constraints to their participation in gay SM, which delayed their entry into the lifestyle they later chose.

Mark (72) recalled that as a teenager he had had a strong response to mainstream movie scenes depicting men being restrained and beaten but that it was not a clear sexual response. His first gay vanilla experience was at the age of 20. He continued to be a 'serial monogamist' in gay relationships, and he could not recall any gay SM interactions until the age of 38 when he beat his boyfriend on the buttocks with the stem of a small hand-held flag. The activity caused his partner no real pain, and Mark commented, 'He seemed to enjoy it, and I enjoyed it. But I didn't associate it with SM because I was against SM'.

At the outbreak of the HIV-AIDS crisis in the mid-1980s, he stopped having sex and remained celibate for the next ten years. It was in the early to mid-1990s that a friend suggested that he try SM as a safe alternative to vanilla sex, but Mark was still resistant. Then in his fifties he agreed to visit a gay SM commercial venue, where he had his second gay SM interaction: he spanked a man. The experience had an immediate impact. 'I changed', he recalled. The public nature of the interaction, however, was not significant as he commented that during the interaction he had completely forgotten where he was. He continued with CP activities and then started to learn other gay SM practices from his submissive partners.

Quentin (45) had begun his sexual career at an early age. He had recollections of early sexual experiences going back to the age of between four and six. His interactions were casual vanilla sex until the age of 14 when he met a man who 'tied my bollocks up and shoved a candle up my arse'. His reaction was 'thinking, yeah, this is it'. But circumstances made it impossible for him to have an openly gay or gay SM lifestyle until he was in his early forties. His sexual experiences for twenty or so years were limited to anonymous sex in public places. He described his situation up to the age of 42:

> I realized that I was quite a damaged sexual performer, that all my sexual experience all my life had been closeted, cottage-cruising area quickies, when nothing mattered more than a very quick piece of action for my own personal gratification. I didn't know how to connect with anyone.

Ironically in terms of how some members of the psychiatric profession characterize sexual sadomasochists as dysfunctional and unable to sustain relationships (*DSM-IV*, 2000; Weldon, 2002), it was his discovery of gay SM interactions that enabled him to make a connection with other men:

> And suddenly – and this was only three years ago – it clicked. And the moment that things clicked into place with me in terms of SM were – I was licking his boots [...] And there was no more pleasure than that. And when I was down there, something happened – and it was that moment: suddenly I let go and I relaxed.

Although at the time of interview he did self-identify as a gay SMer, he did not frequent gay SM social worlds but preferred to meet partners by using specialist sites on the Internet.

Frank (59) had early gay sexual experiences with schoolmates and teachers, and he remembered an early attraction to leather and bikers at the age of 13. He did not act upon his interest and had gay relationships until his late twenties when he finally got a bike. He recalled, 'It was getting the bike, then I could get the gear, and then I could give out the signals and start meeting the kind of men I was interested in'. He had his first experience of gay SM with a biker:

> There were toys and things. It was leather. The first time of putting on leather was such an exciting experience. I went back to his place and he dressed me up. It was just very powerful.

Although there was a clear historical dimension to the interrupted conversion pattern, in as much as that before the 1980s, with little information readily available on gay SM practices, it would take time for someone to link their intrapsychic scripts with gay SM practices, identities and interactions, this was not always the case. One of the youngest respondents, Ian (24), also followed this pattern. As we have seen above, his initial interest in gay SM was through self-induced sensations to his genitals disconnected from the participation of another person. He had gay 'coming out' and relationships while at university, and his first gay SM encounter was with an Internet contact who advertised an interest in 'electro'.[14]

Several respondents had had heterosexual experiences before engaging in SM interactions with men. Only one respondent in the sample, Dan (30), had a woman primary partner and described himself as bisexual. He remembered role-play games as a child and enjoying fighting with other boys but his first sexual experience involving SM was with a woman when he was aged 14. His first sexual experience with a man took place during a period in the armed forces, when he reported that he had been 'naturally dominant' with his partner. Ewan (30) remembered early fantasies involving bondage and punishment with boys, but this fantasy life was overlaid by his lived interactions with women that lasted from the age of 15 to 18. And finally Nigel (43) had early fantasies as a teenager that were 'around heavy bondage, rape and control' of himself by other men. He had also been active sexually with boys since the age of 12. Aged 18, he started a long-term relationship with a woman that lasted eight years, followed by another relationship with a woman lasting one year. However, during these relationships he was also fantasizing about gay SM in the submissive role. 'It was something I did but did not think about'. He recalled that he never identified as gay or bisexual at the time, and that his first gay experience took place when he was 25 when he attended a meeting of the social and educational group SM-Gays in London.

While this was the most common pattern among interview respondents, in no way could it be described as a unitary or 'systematized' one. The length of time between what the respondents identified as their early gay SM intrapsychic scripts and gay SM interactions, the forms of intervening interactions and the gender of partners were all variable.

Late conversion

The 11 respondents who fitted the 'late conversion' pattern took a slightly different route. They could not remember any pre-existing gay SM intrapsychic scripting and developed an interest in gay SM at a later stage of their sexual careers being introduced to it by partners or developing an interest independently.

Eric (29), who was just embarking on his gay SM career at the time of interview, had 'messed around' with boys at school and had his first gay experience at the age of 17. It took him 11 years to develop his interest in gay SM and finally act upon it. 'I think it was a very gradual thing: occasional images and thoughts'. He was aware of the existence of gay SM from 'general socialization in the gay scene', and from his mid-twenties he began to investigate more actively by looking on the Internet, first at profiles on general gay sites and then on specialist gay SM sites. He started to 'build up an image of what it would be like but it remained very vague'.

Although he chatted with people online, he did not go through with meetings until he was 28. 'It was like a wank fantasy thing. I'd just go on occasionally and look'. He had finally decided on a meeting when he had found a 'master' whom he found trustworthy, attractive and exciting enough. The intrapsychic scripts that he had developed in his two to three-year period of investigation on the Internet consisted entirely of his playing a submissive role and he still had few ideas of what specific practices he would enjoy.

Roger (43) did not recall any early gay SM fantasies. He came out as gay at the age of 15 or 16 and had a succession of vanilla relationships. It was only in his late twenties that by chance he heard a gay SM interaction in a gay telephone chat room, which, he remembered, sparked his interest. Gay personals sites on the Internet were also getting started at the time, through which he arranged his initial gay SM encounter.

The second most common pattern among the interview sample, late conversion also showed considerable variation. It was possible to see an ill-defined early interest in gay SM in several of the respondents, and, like Eric, they had later actively sought out a gay SM interaction. But others in the group could not identify any evidence of early awareness, and reported being introduced to gay SM by partners.

Direct conversion

The minority pattern in the sample with five interview respondents was 'direct conversion' of gay SM intrapsychic scripting into gay SM interpersonal scripting and interactions without any intervening non-SM phase (though non-SM interpersonal scripting could also develop afterwards).

Bart (45), who grew up in an isolated country area, and still lived outside of a major metropolitan area at the time of interview, evolved his gay SM intrapsychic scripts from mainstream fiction and an interest in bikers and biking, and while he realized he had an interest in men from his teenage years, he chose not to have any sexual interactions, partly because of internalized constraints that made him reluctant to explore gay social worlds and partly because his geographical location made it difficult to meet other gay men.

His first sexual encounter was also his first gay SM encounter at the age of 26, which he described as 'lightweight leather'. He had made the contact through a press ad in a straight biker magazine. He had a few other meetings through print ads, but he related that his sexual career really took off with the development of gay SM phone chat lines:

> From the early 90s onwards, [I was] meeting people off the phone lines and then, of course, the Internet came along [...] Not only could you find people you were interested in but there were websites, places to buy stuff, etc.

In terms of his socialization into gay SM, it was through the transference of his intrapsychic scripts into interpersonal interactions without the mediation of the non-gay SM interactions, or any socialization through gay SM commercial venues (although it could be argued that the Internet and phone lines are an integral though remote part of gay SM commercial social worlds in UK). He learned about gay SM practices from reading books written by gay SMers; he mentioned *The Leatherman's Handbook* (1972), as well as straight articles about SM in *Forum* magazine that 'provided the underpinnings of what people do', and later from his interactions with gay SM partners. Although he never had non-gay SM sexual interactions he did not self-identify as a gay SMer in terms of his identity, nor did he make any efforts to investigate gay SM commercial venues and social groups to any degree, bypassing the socialization process they provided for several other respondents of the same age.

William was another respondent who came to gay SM with no early gay vanilla interpersonal scripting and interactions. Born in the USA, he moved to UK in the early 1980s aged 23, when he immediately found his way to two commercial venues frequented by gay SMers: the Coleherne pub and the London Apprentice pub in East London. William was one of the few men of his age group to have had direct access to gay SM pornography as a university student in the shape of the US gay SM publication, *Drummer* magazine. But he explained that he learned most about gay SM practices from 'a top who suddenly imposed it on me and it felt right – an accumulation of things that just felt right'.

As a coda to this discussion, I should like briefly to pick the issue of identity mentioned in note 2. As Gagnon commented (2004: 299), 'Sexual identity, sexual preferences and sexual behavior are more loosely correlated than ever before and become more so in the future'. This was confirmed in the study sample, as there was no obvious correlation between the age of first awareness, the type of conversion pattern and the degree of later self-identification as a gay SMer. In terms of self-identification, the sample was divided into seven men with partial or episodic identification, 12 with weak or no identification and 12 with strong identification.

Conclusion

To return to the question asked in the introduction, the evidence from the study suggests that there was no single pattern or process in becoming a gay SMer. In respect to both scripting phases, I also had to take into consideration the historical and social factors that affected the availability and accessibility of gay SM-related material to men during different historical periods. It might have taken as little as a few years to as much as several decades for men with early awareness of gay SM but who had no or very limited access to gay SM material to make the link between their early fantasies or practices with gay SM practices and identities. Although in this chapter I concentrated on a realist account of the processes involved in developing a gay SM intrapsychic script and converting it to an interpersonal script, I have not ruled out that sexual scripts, like other types of sexual stories, can also be used retrospectively to make sense of a current sexuality or sexual identity. However, as has already been pointed out, there were no obvious correlations between reported early or late awareness, type of conversion pattern and level of self-identification as a gay SMer among the respondents at the time of interview.[15]

Looking at the source materials for intrapsychic scripting, these could be divided into seven broad types, which could occur singly, in combination or successively in an individual's sexual career. Among those with early intrapsychic scripts, there also seemed to be continuity of intrapsychic elements (materials, objects and sensation-based practices) into interpersonal scripts, even when these had been overlaid by non-gay SM scripting and interaction. Finally intrapsychic elements continued to be created and to influence interpersonal scripting.

Turning to the process of conversion from intrapsychic to interpersonal scripting, there were three patterns: interrupted, late and direct conversion; although the first of these predominated, even within this sample, there was a great deal of variation in terms of the length and type of intervening scripting and interaction. The second most common pattern was late conversion, in which the respondents developed their interest in gay SM as adults independently or were introduced to it by a partner. Again, there was a great deal of variation, as respondents could have developed gay SM intrapsychic scripts prior to interaction or the two levels of scripting could have developed simultaneously, as in the case of introduction through a partner. The third and least common pattern in the sample was direct conversion, with no intervening non-gay SM phase.

This chapter does not claim to give a definitive description of the processes involved in becoming a gay SMer. For one thing, the sample of 31 respondents remains small compared to the total number of men engaged in gay SM practices in the UK; for another, it is the application of a very focused interactionist account of sexual development that does not fully take into consideration the effects of external social constraints and stigmatization. However, I hope it has given the reader an idea of the diverse ways individuals discover an interest in gay SM and convert that interest into lived interactions.

Notes

1. This chapter is part of a sociological study of gay SM in the UK, 1950s to the present. The study concentrated on men who were self-identified as gay and took part in SM practices with other men. In its first manifestation, gay SM was known as 'leather'. Although the term leather was in use throughout the period under study, gay SM social worlds and practices have become distanced from their association with leather material cultures, hence the broader term gay SM was more representative.

2. Earlier studies of SM, including Spengler (1977), Moser and Levitt (1987), Breslow, Evans and Langley (1986), Hunt (1990) and Nordling, Sandnabba, Santtila and Alison (2006) did not address the issue of people who participated in gay SM practices without adopting a gay SM identity because they recruited their respondents from social groups with high levels of identification with SM as an identity and lifestyle. This study made use of a range of recruitment strategies to reach men who were active participants in gay SM both with and without adopting a gay SM identity. Ascribing a specific sexual identity is fraught with difficulties. For this study, I decided on three levels of identification: 'strong', 'episodic' or 'weak', by taking into consideration the following five factors: their own stated self-identification, self-presentation, commitment to gay SM as a lifestyle, commitment to gay SM practices as part of their overall sexuality and engagement in gay SM activism or education.

3. The pathologization of homosexuality and sadomasochism was not the intention of either Ellis or Freud; however, their work, and, in particular, that of Freud, was recast in that light by their later interpreters.

4. The participant-based research consisted of an empirical survey ($N = 119$) and interviews ($N = 31$) conducted between 2003 and 2006; see Chaline (2005a) for a discussion of the preliminary findings of the quantitative element of this study, which also involved observation of commercial venues, social and political groups and private networks in real and cyber space.

5. For e.g. Larry Townsend's *Leatherman's Handbook*, first published in 1972, was mentioned by several interview respondents. It was the precursor of many books written by gay SMers that appeared in increasing numbers, especially from the 1980s.

6. Kamel's six stages: 'disenchantment, depression, curiosity, attraction, drifting, and limiting' begin in adulthood and describe principally the inter-active parts of the process of becoming a gay SMer in a specific cultural and historical setting. This study intended to describe processes that went further back in an individual's life course to what he identified as his first interest in gay SM, which was often of a non-sexual nature, and also to describe processes not necessarily tied to one historical or cultural moment.

7. The average age of the survey and interview sample was 41 years of age (age range 24–72), therefore, many of the participants would have become sexually aware during the 1970s and 1980s.

8. Several respondents mentioned early childhood games, such as cowboys and Indians and card games, which involved tying up and mild corporal punish-ments, as possibly indicating an early interest, but none made a very strong connection, rather they were responding to a prompt from me asking them whether they had had any SM experiences in infancy or childhood. However, it is possible that this kind of play could form the basis for early intrapsychic and interpersonal gay SM scripting. But as most children probably engage in this type of play, it is just as likely that no such link exists.

9. The figure in brackets is the age of the respondent at the time of interview.

10. In his study of SM as a cultural style, Bienvenu (1998) has eschewed the old division between sadomasochism and fetishism to reclassify different media into 'soft' (silk, satin, furs), characteristic of the nineteenth century, and 'hard' (leather and rubber), which he sees a characteristic of twentieth-century SM. The materials cited by the respondents were mostly at the 'hard' technological end of the spectrum.

11. 'Cock and ball torture' refers to a set of practices involving the genitals from simple binding to more complex ones involving equipment. Although the term 'torture' implies only painful activities, this is not actually the case as CBT also includes pleasurable stimulation of the genitals. The survey found that 89% of the sample had tried CBT in the past twelve months and that 70% practiced it in half or more of their interactions.

12. A wide variety of gay SM sites exist on the Internet. The discourses of SM they contain can be commercial, educational, social, individual or political, depending on the kind of site viewed.

13. Gaydar is the largest general gay personals and chat website in the UK (http://www.gaydar.co.uk).

14. The use of electricity in gay SM; electro uses a ranges of devices, from thera-peutic 'tens' unit to more sophisticated specialist equipment.

15. The study found a wide range of personal narrative constructions of gay SM that were developed retrospectively and were used to explain choices of

practices and levels of self-identification. Unfortunately limitations of space prevent me from going into this matter in any detail. I would direct any interested readers to the completed study.

References

Beckmann, A. (2001). Deconstructing myths: The social construction of 'Sado-masachism' versus subjugated knowledges of practitioners of consensual 'S/M'. *Journal of Criminal Justice and Popular Culture*, 8(2): 66–95.

Bienvenu, R. (1998). *The Development of Sadomasochism as a Cultural Style in the Twentieth-Century United States*. Unpublished dissertation, University of Indiana.

Breslow, N., Evans, L. & Langley, J. (1986). On the prevalence and roles of females in the sadomasochistic subculture: Report of an empirical study. *Archives of Sexual Behaviour*, 14, 303–317.

Brickell, C. (2006). The sociological construction of gender and sexuality. *The Sociological Review*, 54(1), 86–113.

Chaline, E. (2005a). Researching sexual difference: A survey of gay SM in the UK. *Lesbian & Gay Psychology Review*, 6(3), 240–252.

Chaline, E. (2005b). Spanner: S/M, consent and the law in the UK, Eric Chaline in conversation with John Pendal. *Lesbian & Gay Psychology Review*, 6(3), 283–287.

DSM-IV (1994, rev. 2000). *Diagnostic and Statistical Manual of Mental Disorders* (4th ed.). Washington, DC: American Psychiatric Association.

Ellis, H.H. (1936 [1903]). *Studies in the Psychology of Sex*, Vol. 2, Part II, *Analysis of the Sexual Impulse – Love and Pain*. New York, NY: Random House.

Freeman, G. (1967). *The Undergrowth of Literature*. London: Nelson.

Foucault, M. (1980). In C. Gordon (Ed.) *Power/Knowledge and Selected Other Writings 1972–77*. Brighton: Harvester.

Foucault, M. (1984). *History of Sexuality I: The Will to Knowledge*. London: Penguin Books.

Freud, S. (1938). *The Basic Writings of Sigmund Freud* (ed. and trans. by A.A. Brill). New York, NY: The Modern Library.

Gagnon, J.H. (2004). *An Interpretation of Desire*. Chicago, IL: Chicago University Press.

Gagnon, J.H. &and Simon, W. (1973/2005). *Sexual Conduct: The Social Sources of Human Sexuality*. Chicago, IL: Aldine.

Goffman, E. (1963). *Stigma, Notes on the Management of Spoiled Identity*. Englewood Cliffs, NJ: Prentice Hall.

Goffman, E. (1974). *Frame Analysis*. Cambridge, MA: Harvard University Press.

Hunt, A.J. (1990). *Gay Men and SM: A Survey of Gay Men Participating in Sado-masochistic Activities*, Project Sigma Working Paper Number 26. London: South Bank Polytechnic.

Kamel, G.W.L. (1995). The leather career: On becoming a sadomasochist. In T.S. Weinberg (Ed.) *S&M, Studies in Dominance and Submission* (pp. 51–60). New York, NY: Prometheus.

Kinsey, A.C. (1948). *Sexual Behavior in the Human Male*. Philadelphia, PA: W.B. Saunders.

Kinsey, A.C. (1953). *Sexual Behavior in the Human Female*. Philadelphia, PA: W.B. Saunders.

von Krafft-Ebing, R. (1892). *Psychopathia Sexualis: A Medico-forensic Study* (trans. of the 7th German ed.). London: C.G. Chaddock.

Lauman, E.O. & Gagnon, J.H. (1995). A sociological perspective on sexual action. In R.G. Parker & J.H. Gagnon (Eds) *Conceiving Sexuality* (pp. 184–213). London: Routledge.

Moser, C. & Levitt, E.E. (1987). An exploratory–descriptive study of a sadomasochistically oriented sample. *Journal of Sex Research* , 23, 322–337.

Nordling, N., Sandnabba, K., Santtila, P. & Alison, L. (2006). Differences and similarities between gay and straight individuals involved in the sadomasochistic subculture. *Journal of Homosexuality*, 50(2/3), 41–57.

Parker, R.G. & Gagnon, J.H. (Eds) (1995). *Conceiving Sexuality*. London: Routledge.

Plummer, K. (1975). *Sexual Stigma: An Interactionist Approach*. London: Routledge and Kegan Paul.

Plummer, K. (1995). *Telling Sexual Stories: Power, Change and Social Worlds*. London: Routledge

Simon, W. & Gagnon, J.H. (1987). Sexual scripts. In J. Geer & W.T. O'Donohue (Eds) *Theories of Human Sexuality* (pp. 363–383). New York: Plenum.

Sisson, K. (2005). The cultural formation of S/M: History and analysis. *Lesbian & Gay Psychology Review*, 6(3), 147–162.

Spengler, A. (1977). Manifest sadomasochism of males: Results of an empirical study. *Archives of Sexual Behavior*, 6, 441–456.

Stoller, R. (1991). *Pain and Passion*. New York, NY: Plenum

Townsend, L. (1972/1977). *The Leatherman's Handbook I*. San Francisco, CA: Le Salon

Weeks, J. (1985). *Sexuality and Its Discontents, Meanings, Myths and Modern Sexualities*. London: Routledge and Keegan Paul.

Weeks, J. (1995). *Invented Moralities: Sexual Values in an Age of Uncertainty*. Oxford: Polity Press.

Weldon, E. (2002). *Sadomasochism*. Cambridge: Icon Books.

Wilson, E.O. (1975, 2000). *Sociobiology: The New Synthesis*. Cambridge, MA: Harvard.

Wilson, G. & Rahman, Q. (2005). *Born Gay*. London: Peter Owen.

11
Playgrounds and New Territories – The Potential of BDSM Practices to Queer Genders[1]

Robin Bauer

In this article I want to examine the potential that BDSM practices have in queering gender as an example of producing social differences and hierarchies and to what extent that potential is transferred to everyday realities. Drawing mainly on an empirical study[2] on the dyke+ BDSM communities[3] in the USA and Western Europe, I will focus on the question why and how this particular scene functions as a social space that is perceived as a safe playground to explore genders.

Introduction

My interviewees and I are positioned within complex social power structures, which influence – if not determine – how we perceive ourselves, our practices and our surroundings. Thus the discourses[4] my interviewees generate in describing their practices and experiences as well as my own analyses represent embodied, *situated* knowledges (Haraway, 1991b). On all levels, my academic work (research questions, field access, manner of conducting interviews, analysis, presenting results, etc.) is informed by my positioning as a white German, queer, polyamorous, BDSM top and transfag with a working class and activist background. Due to certain inclusions, exclusions and my own biography in transition, I am also situated between certain BDSM communities, with roots in the dyke+-scene and faced with only limited acceptance in the gay male scene. Based on my notion of queer politics I have a vested interest in generating valid knowledges about BDSM practices and communities from a queer perspective.

Therefore I conducted 50 interviews with self-identified dykes, trans people, gay men and queers who practice BDSM, addressing them as experts on the topic. For this reason, I chose not to document their individual biographies as a whole, but to hone the focus in regard to their status as representatives of certain BDSM practices and communities (Meuser & Nagel, 1991). Since I have searched for interviewees mostly through personal contacts and community venues, such as mailing lists, my personal political background outlined above has both facilitated and restricted my access to certain groups of people. BDSM queers who don't have access to the Internet or are not in touch with the organized BDSM communities for whatever reason are therefore underrepresented in my research. Although I received a sufficient amount of responses from white people with a working-class background or limited economic resources, and my sample includes people between 20 and 60 years of age, people of color are underrepresented in my sample, which might also have to do with the fact that I'm white myself and that the more formal BDSM communities are dominated by white people, as the white, queer transguy Matt[5] suggests in regard to the local women/trans and queer play parties[6]:

> Most of the play parties I've been to have been really white and also play parties can be really expensive. And I think there's a big issue in terms of class. [...] And also I think the race thing is partly class stuff and it's partly because most of the play parties that I've been to have been organized by white people. And in a lot of ways the queer SM scene has just felt really white. It's sort of coming out of white queer culture.

Therefore my writing on the queer potential of BDSM practices has to be viewed as situated knowledge that is generated in regard to the interviewees' and my position within social power relations and the kind of personal political experiences we have made based on these grounds. In analyzing the interviews I applied a slightly adapted version of the coding paradigm from grounded theory (Strauss & Corbin, 1990). From the wealth of my data, I generated a number of categories through coding procedures, some of which I present in this article.

The dyke+ BDSM communities in Western Europe and the USA

In the USA and Western Europe, BDSM communities are organized around sexual preference and are thus rather segregated. While the gay male and straight communities are quite large, the dyke+ BDSM community is so small that it hardly exists on local levels; instead it manifests itself nationally and internationally at annual gatherings as well as through individual friendships and play partner networks. In the following discussion I will focus on dyke+ communities. A variety of genders and gender expressions are part of that community, including femmes, butches, trans boys and men, dyke boys, genderqueers and transwomen. These are also complimented by identities created and assumed just for play. A number of members of this community have assumed gender identities that transgress the binary gender system, such as genderqueers. While genderqueers do not identify full-time as either men or women, they do not conceive of themselves as in the middle of the spectrum or as androgynous. Their gender is rather fluid (shifting) and multiple at the same time, which means that their positioning within a variety of genders depends on the context.

Queering genders in the dyke+ BDSM communities

Most people who move in (and sometimes out) of the dyke+ BDSM communities share the view that 'SM provides a safe space for people to fuck with their gender and also for their gender identity to be respected' and that gender is 'not at all based on biology, because there are lots of people who don't identify as boys in their everyday life, but within SM context they'll be boys' (Matt), which sets this community apart from the gay male and straight[7] BDSM communities as well as the vanilla dyke/lesbian communities (Hale, 2003). By tracing my interviewees' comments on gender and trans issues in relation to their individual BDSM practices and on the community level, I will try to outline why that is the case.

Queer playgrounds

The frame for queering gender is the construction of a social space that is experienced as a *safe space* (Matt, Eike, Scout, Terry), 'playground' (Connie) or 'field for experimentation' (Jonas). The term 'space' is used to literally refer to the community in a geographical sense (e.g., play party space), but also to the BDSM space as an immaterial entity, as a specific kind of headspace or layer of reality (e.g., a scene/play that is taking place or a state of consciousness that a submissive dives into while playing) that differs from everyday reality (Schütz & Luckmann, 1979: 48f.). What qualifies the space as safe for playing and experimenting with gender is partly due to general BDSM standards and characteristics, such as negotiating and establishing consensuality, communicating, respecting and pushing boundaries and an emphasis on emotional and physical intensity in sexuality, translating sexual fantasies into reality and role play. US-based transgender activist and performer Kate Bornstein sees a connection between BDSM and gender in terms of performativity:

> Sadomasochism intersects with gender at the point of *performance*. We perform our identities, which include gender, and we perform our relationships, which include sex. Transgender is simply identity more consciously performed on the infrequently used playing field of gender. S/M is simply a relationship more consciously performed within the forbidden arena of power.
>
> (1994: 124; *Bornstein's emphasis*)

The concept of performativity thus works differently in BDSM spaces. In contrast to everyday life, in BDSM spaces one can consciously choose and negotiate identities for play. Therefore all participants agree upon the gender one chooses for a scene in a consensual manner, and in this sense BDSM has the potential to become the playground Bornstein and Connie refer to.

Additionally the community excludes certain men, straight and vanilla people who might have prejudices against grown-ups who love to play or might not be able to cope with queer sexualities. This also enhances its value as a safe playground. As the pansexual genderqueer femme Neila points out, this creates a space that is perceived devoid of *predefined* power relations in regard to gender and sexuality, if not in regard to other social power structures such as race or class or, in the words of the dyke Connie, 'dykes and transmen in the [dyke+] SM scene have the possibility to do what is being denied to them in everyday life'.

Exploring gender

The space thus provides its members with the freedom and possibility for self-exploration, especially for *exploring gender*:

> I definitely use SM to explore gender. I mean definitely. Because being in role is almost always a gender thing one way or another and I think just the understanding of role and fantasy automatically – maybe the word automatically I should never use – but I think the space given to role and fantasy, gender is such a natural extension. I think diversity in my own internal community of being happens through SM. As

I recognize different roles in myself, that's an experience of diversity. So if that's something that people are exploring individually, then in the community that would probably be reflected as a common acceptance of valuing diverse expression, because role is fun when it's specific. Role is fun the more clear and specific it is. That's what's hot and so you don't want this medium thing. You want really clearly defined identities.

The venue for exploring gender is often role play because, as the queer, trans masculine genderqueer Firesong quoted above explains, many people find that role play – especially in a DS context – benefits from the specificity of the assumed roles, which includes the gender of the invented characters. Given the social norms surrounding gender, certain roles seem to imply a certain gender. For example, in a military drill scene within a context that started out as a women's community, it may only seem logical for women to impersonate men in certain scenarios. Femmeboy also describes BDSM as opening up a space to explore gender:

> In leather space people have a lot more freedom to explore their own gender(s). For instance, if I'm role playing I could be a girl one day and a boy the other day. Because people are into role playing and taking on different personas in the leather community, it opens up the possibilities for exploring gender. These gender explorations may allow people to discover something about themselves, like 'you know what, wow, I really like living as a boy, maybe I wanna do that for now, but maybe not for my whole life.' And leather space is a place where that possibility can be acknowledged.

Thus self-exploration in role play provides the players with certain *insights* about themselves and about how gender takes on different meanings and functions from the perspective of someone whose gender-wise positioning is different within society than it is for themselves (at least how they would experience a different position). This allows them to experience the situatedness of perspectives, which is a mechanism that the dyke Mistress Mean Mommy compares to reading a book:

> I can't understand what it's like to be a 15-year-old Irish boy in an all boys' boarding school. But I can read the book and have a sense of what it's like. So if you wanna go out and buy a school boy's uniform and wear it and have somebody be the school master and I get to

play it – now I have a sense of what it's like, even as me in my body as a woman. I'll never be a 15-year-old boy. I get to experience what I think a 15-year-old boy would be like. And that might be freeing in some way. Maybe it will give me a different perspective. Maybe I'll suddenly understand something I never understood about young boys.

The experience of *understanding* an identity or a power dynamic is a common and valued theme among BDSM queers and points to the value they place on looking at gender and sexuality from different perspectives as a means of acknowledging and respecting difference, both within themselves and interpersonally. They equally stress the heightening of *consciousness* that BDSM practices trigger: they observe in themselves an increased awareness of or at least an interest in social power structures, including gender hierarchies and norms, in everyday situations. Being very conscious of how certain gender aspects – in the words of the queer, transgendered stone butch Terry – generate 'a lot of play that's gender-based, even if the folks in it are not fluid or are not fucking around with gender'.

New territories

Exploring gender also leads to an *expansion* of gender concepts and identities on individual and community levels or, to use Firesong's geographical metaphor, 'new territories' on the playground of gender. For example, the term *genderfuck* (or fucking with gender) is used to describe activities that aim at creating non-coherent gender expressions in the sense that they deliberately combine elements that are associated with stereotypical (sometimes explicitly exaggerated) masculinity and femininity in our society in a way that is supposed to irritate or confuse onlookers. Interestingly in my sample mostly femmes (or dykes with a feminine appearance) state that they like to fuck with gender, especially through strapping on a dildo while wearing a skirt or other (high) femme attire, as in the situation the high femme Zoe describes:

I used to pack a dick in my toys and I'd be wearing a dick under my skirt and stuff, right? I guess I did that in my thirties, too, it was pretty fun. And I can remember these two guys seeing me on the street, grabbing each other and screaming. And this guy saying 'I like it, I like it, I don't know what it is, but I like it.' (laughs)

While those in the dyke+ BDSM community put a great emphasis on understanding different gender expressions, Zoe's encounter with the two men highlights the role that desire plays as a catalyst for exploring sexual and gender otherness, even if you are not able to comprehend it (yet), or maybe precisely because it questions your usual categories. It also points to the fact that seeing something from the outside without embodying or experiencing it might indeed limit one's capacity to understand a phenomenon. In this sense, the repeated reference to understanding in the dyke+ BDSM discourse could be due to the fact that BDSM is an embodied practice.

Even ftms or the queer dyke fag/butch Lola cite femme genderfucking as one of the main examples how BDSM practices can be politically subversive:

Say two femme women are topping two boys, then sit down and lift up their skirts and the boys suck their dicks. That's very political to me. Because that's fucking with the whole set up of how you expect things to be, how things are portrayed in society, who has the dick, all that. That's really taking back power and shifting it around and doing all sorts of stuff to it and that's very political I think. The act of doing it is political, the act of seeing it is political.

Even though the two boys in Lola's example are either trans identified or playing with gender themselves in that scene, it is the femmes who question the concept of 'who has the dick' in this society, not only bodily but also metaphorically speaking in terms of the phallus as male privilege and power.[8] (The boys, of course, also play an interesting role: being categorized as women in mainstream society implies sexually passivity or submissiveness, but here they perform masculinity for the play, which implies dominance, they then submit to femme dominance. Interestingly they do not rely on dominance or machismo as a typical asset for constructing masculinity, which might also have to do with the fact that they portray boys and not grown up men.)

Queer theoretical and subcultural discourse tends to focus on the supposed subversiveness of female or trans masculinities (in the case of butches, drag kings and certain ftms, less commonly in the case of transsexual men), which simultaneously for the most part disregards the queer potentials of femmes, beyond their being the partners and allies of ftms. My interviews illustrate the significant role femmes play in building and shaping the dyke+ BDSM communities in general, by showing that they do not simply define their femininity in response to their masculine partners, but develop their own, non-mainstream notion of femininity (individually and within discussions among each other),[9] and that they engage in queer sexual practices and embodiments. In this vein, femmeness holds as much potential to queer notions of gender as other queer gender expressions.

Creating subcultural skills

Expanding gender concepts and identities through practices such as genderfucking has the effect of creating (new) *subcultural skills*. I will discuss three of these subcultural skills that my interviewees have repeatedly referred to and described and which seem to be significant in the process of queering gender through expansion: renaming/reassigning, recognition and integration.

Renaming/reassigning

The general BDSM practice of negotiating consensuality has generated specific communication skills about sexual practices, bodily functions, psychological dynamics and sexual fantasies, insofar as they are important for successful playing. Moreover communicating and translating sexual fantasies into play have furthered the importance of psychological dynamics during sexual encounters, and thus to a certain extent decentered the focus on bodies as the core of sexual activity, as the trans-identified genderqueer butch dyke Scout describes: 'And playing in bed in the morning when waking up and fucking, we call it a dick, when I don't have anything on. It's like in my brains and she still comes'. Interviewees insist on the fact that it's really happening 'in the head'. Furthermore it is also central to a lot of BDSM practices to work with and manipulate the body. These general seemingly contradictory characteristics of BDSM provide a starting point for people who are exploring and expanding gender to rename or recode body parts and sexual practices according to the meaning they have for the participants as opposed to heteronormative (outsider) perspectives, while simultaneously reassigning their bodies with gendered meanings that differ from biological or medical assignments. I combine the terms renaming/reassigning to point out that the process entails a simultaneously discursive and material understanding of bodies and sexual practices as 'material-semiotic generative nodes' (Haraway, 1991a: 208). One example of renaming/reassigning is evident in the quotes cited above when Zoe and Lola use the term 'dick' (instead of 'dildo') to refer to a penis that is not permanently attached to the body. While members of the subculture know what it refers to and what it means, communication with outsiders can become misleading at this point. The femme and daddy's girl Lisa realizes that an e-mail correspondence with her long-distance affair, a butch who uses a male name, male pronouns and male terms to refer to her body including her dick, would be misinterpreted by outsiders as a conversation between a biological man and a woman. She recalls a discussion with a gay biological man: 'If you are involved with a butch who wears a dildo then it is with a real dick, it's the same. It was absolutely too much for [him], that these things are also in the head'. Maybe the understanding is again not possible without the actual experience and the subcultural, situated knowledge derived from it.

Scout, who had to undergo surgery in his youth due to an intersex condition, talks about his relationship with his trangender butch sir: 'So, being a boy he was trying to teach me how to have a boy cunt and reassign my body in a way that I could survive in it'. In their 24/7 relationship they consciously worked on inventing new language for their bodies and reassigning 'female' body parts with trans masculine and genderqueer meanings as in the term 'boy cunt', which combines masculine and female elements to create a new meaning.

Recognition

Related to the subcultural skill of renaming/reassigning is recognition. The queer transgender butch Eike recalls a situation,

> where I played at the bottom as a boy, and my partner undressed me and put me in front of a mirror. And for the first time actually I really consciously saw in my naked body an absolutely boyish or masculine body. And after that I had this experience of 'what biology tells us is simply complete bullshit.' (laughs) I see what I want to see and my partners can also see what they want to see.

In this case the act of recognition refers to a certain insight that takes place during a scene and assigns a heteronormatively female-coded body as boyish or masculine, but not as something that is actively sought; it happens rather spontaneously (of course also due to the history and context of the situations). Eike suddenly *sees* themselves differently gendered than before. Seeing is a term that is commonly used by my interviewees, both when referring to seeing oneself, but even more so for seeing others: recognizing somebody else's partial, play or all-encompassing gender identity from the outside, stressing the importance of being recognized as what or who you are. Since Eike interestingly stands in front of a mirror, s/he is able to recognize themselves, so to speak, from the outside perspective. Other interviewees, such as Terry, have also described the function of a play partner as a mirror to reflect parts of one's personality that have not been previously acknowledged before:

> A couple of people that I have been playing with the longest started out kind of like 'I'm a dyke, and I'm in the middle'. But when I looked at them I was like 'I see a boy. How do you feel about me calling you boy?' And by this point they're boy identified in a big way and it's a huge factor in how they see themselves. Is that gender play? I don't know. It probably started out being gender play and now is part of their identity. But it is a factor in how we play together, it is part of the richness that happens, that I could mirror back to them something that they didn't see that they truly feel. And they look back at their life history and they look back at who they are and they're like 'this is who I am.' That I get to show that to somebody in my eyes and in my actions, God, that's hot. (laughs)

Terry's description shows how far this subcultural skill has been developed: it is not only about being able to read someone as the identity they consciously and purposefully express or perform, but it is also a way to recognize, for example through mirroring back one's own akin identity, an identity that has not yet surfaced. This partly invokes, as with Terry, notions of authenticity in terms of a 'true' self, which seem to be closer to a phenomenological approach, as some trans researchers propose, than to a queer-theoretical approach that employs a concept of performativity. Zoe puts it slightly differently:

> I see beauty in people that have never seen the beauty in themselves, and it's really nice to see people bloom into being recognized for being a boy, say. Just being able to mmmmmhh (enjoyably) shine under being recognized for their beauty. And be sort of stunned like 'I've always been told I'm a sport of nature, a freak, and I'm ugly and undesirable', and to have them come into this community that recognizes them: 'you're not an ugly duckling, no, you're a swan, baby.' (laughs) 'No, you're not unattractive, you're a really handsome butch.' (laughs)

This quote shows that recognition does not have to rely on a notion of authenticity, but can also be understood as a subcultural technique that acknowledges the fact that concepts such as beauty are dependent upon context and that the butch/femme, queer or dyke+ BDSM communities have constructed different kinds of gender expressions that generate different kinds of beauty standards. Still Zoe's image of the ugly duckling 'tomboy' in heteronormative culture, who is then recognized as a swan, the handsome butch or boy, by a femme also presupposes that a certain butchness is already unconsciously displayed before one gets into touch with subcultural settings. On the other hand, the BDSM subculture with its role play is equally aware of the performativity of gender. The kind of recognition described here is unique to certain subcultural contexts, since mainstream heteronormative society is not able to see or read gender expressions in this way, because it neither mirrors nor desires queer genders.

Integration

Terry poses the question whether his practices are to be considered as playing with gender or expressing partial identities. He suggests that they started out as play but have become more serious, or have crossed over into everyday reality, implying that exploring gender in BDSM can ultimately lead to developing a trans or genderqueer identity in real life. Indeed, this seems to be a quite common experience; to some extent Scout, Eike, Femmeboy, Firesong, Jonas, Craig, Matt and Mik all report that experimenting with gender within BDSM has helped them sort out their gender identity. As Scout puts it, 'I was also struggling with gender identity issues. And so it entwined, became my identity as a boy and as a leather boy and a tranny boy.' While for some this may result in a relatively stable ftm identity, for others the process of exploring gender is not easily put to an end (however temporary that end may be):

Role play to me is a lot about different aspects of my gender expression and I actually feel it's through those practices that my gender has coalesced. I've been able to kind of get on terms with parts of me that I may have rejected or have been splintered off. I feel role play's been one of the most integrating things I've done.

For the genderqueer Firesong and others, who describe their gender identity as comprised of different parts, personas or nuances, the goal cannot be to attain a singular identity, but to *integrate* the various aspects into their identity.[10] BDSM space offers them possibilities to do that through playing with gender or expressing partial identities in gender-based play. The various aspects may, for example, come out through 'spontaneous combustion' (Zoe), a 'conscious decision' (Femmeboy), certain sexual practices[11] (BJ) or through resonance with your play partner (Petra, Connie): the context influences which part of the identity is dominant. The process of integration is one example for the way that BDSM space spills over into everyday life:

> My gender and sexual explorations affect my every day life, everything I do. One of my intentions is to always be integrating different parts of myself. My life's work is about integration. When I'm interacting and deepening my connections with all different kinds of people in the leather community, when I leave that community, it expands my awareness of the people on the street. And I am reminded to make fewer assumptions about all of who they are.

In this quote, the queer genderqueer Femmeboy speaks about integrating different parts of her personality into her everyday identity. This integration has an effect that goes beyond personal healing; it also changes her views of her surroundings and other people. Therefore experimenting and playing with different partial gender identities as a way of experiencing difference within the self may serve to disrupt the usual normalizing process of excluding the 'other' in the process of identification and open up a queer way of subverting the constant reproduction of exclusionary (heteronormative and other) dynamics. The great acceptance genderqueers and trans people experience in the dyke+ BDSM community can be interpreted in exactly this way, as Firesong does here:

> As I recognize different roles in myself, that's an experience of diversity. So if that's something that people are exploring individually, then in the community that would probably be reflected as a common acceptance of valuing diverse expression.

What interviewees describe as respecting, validating, valuing and celebrating diversity in gender expressions on a community level is therefore a result of the new territories the BDSM space opens up within a specific, gender-segregated context.

Conclusion: straight[12] worlds, queer worlds?

Members of the dyke+ BDSM community assign their gendered BDSM practices with different meanings, as the trans masculine, gay bear and daddy Craig reports:

I'm having an ongoing discussion with my girl about role play, if you're playing role play or not. And I don't feel it's role play, because I feel that I'm just a Daddy. So I don't feel like I'm taking on a role 'I'm in my Daddy role right now.' I'm a Daddy. I just feel like a Daddy most of the time.

For some, it is role or gender *play* and for others it is their (partial) identity as in *being* oneself or expressing certain aspects of one's identity. However, this differs from ordinary everyday identities in the sense that the identity (or role) is more consciously chosen and performed. Interviewees stress the fact that BDSM in dyke+/queer contexts has the effect of increasing consciousness around gender identity issues and social power relations (especially in regard to gender). The queer femme Teresa and others gain sexual pleasure from consciously using heteronormative and sexist dynamics and stereotypes in BDSM interactions:

But a lot of the super nonconsensual power dynamics that exist between straight folks, or just between men and women, like non-trans men and non-trans women, I do eroticize a lot of those dynamics and want to play them out with people who don't actually have those privileges in the rest of the world. Which is a big part of what my sexuality is about for me, masculinity is kind of inherently dominant in the way that I experience it when I'm interacting with someone sexually.

The possibility of actually playing with and experiencing such stereotypes, dynamics or even just the staging of binary genders as pleasurable depends on the fact that in daily life they do not have straight (and male) privileges:

Though there are SM people who I don't know but I see around, the straight ones supposedly, the straight ones who are really well dressed, who wear lots of leather, go to clubs. I don't know these people, and I should know them better before I talk about them. But I see this sort of yuppie consumption of SM culture as being super apolitical in a lot of ways and the way they can play with gender and race – I'm amazed that they have no fucking idea what oppression is. I don't know how they can really engage in healthy SM, when they're not understanding how what they do is different than oppression, because they don't know what oppression is. But the SM community that I experience is a community of other folks who understand what it feels like to be nonconsensually dominated or oppressed, queers and trannies and sex workers and people of color and working class, poor folks who understand that our gender's a creative response to our oppression. And our sexuality's a creative response and a healthy response.

Teresa and others stress the importance of reflecting your situatedness within social hierarchies first to actually being able to consciously play with and perform gender and power in BDSM space. For them, this sets BDSM in dyke+ and queer contexts apart from straight BDSM. MCL, who refuses the category gender altogether, poses the question whether straight BDSM could be labeled as queer: 'If it is partly say strictly monogamous, heterosexual people who practice it, does it have any queer approach at all, since they only mirror what they are in the rest of their lives?'[13]

Many of the interviewees, for example, stopped visiting mixed play parties in the straight BDSM community, because the subcultural skills of renaming/reassigning and recognition have not been developed there (or have been developed there differently in less queer inclusive ways):

if a straight person who doesn't really understand the value of a trans person, if a straight person is watching my trans lover being fucked in the cunt, that person may be perceiving my trans lover's sight as a woman, having breasts. May not be able to construct in his head the body that my trans lover has constructed. And that's very important to me that I'm fucking my lover, his body in a way that is constructing that body, perceiving that body in a way that the person wants to be perceived. And if there're people watching who perceive it differently, I think it would be unsafe.

These differences in subcultures have the effect that queers do not see their identities recognized, respected and valued in straight-dominated spaces, thus they do not provide the kind of safe space or playground that is the prerequisite for exploring, playing with and expressing queer genders, as Femmeboy describes it for her trans lover. Only Mik regards the straight BDSM community in Germany as equally trans friendly and open to gender exploration.

Although my focus in this article has been on the potentials of BDSM practices to queer genders, aside from this potential there are certainly limitations and dangers. Given the fact that there are norms and hierarchies in the dyke+ BDSM community, as some of the quotes have illustrated, the question remains for whom and under what circumstances this social space is actually a safe space and at which times and places it is also illusionary. A few comments for example show, that the dyke+ BDSM space is also not free of conflict surrounding trans and gender issues (let alone other power dynamics). The dyke butch Luise, for example, is repeatedly asked for her male name, although she does not want one. Teresa reports of being accused of fetishizing transmen because her sexual identity includes female and trans masculinities. Femmes are marginalized by the hype around masculinity and some dykes participate in gender play mainly because their partners want to, rather than because they find it especially attractive (Luise, Frl. K), or feel pressured to be able to recognize trans identities, when they really have not learned to (Luise). As much as sexual desire and fantasy is the driving and inspiring force behind exploring genders for some, other desires are inhibited by too much genderqueerness, since the desire for specificity in roles, which Firesong made out to be one of the reasons for triggering gender exploration, can also be satisfyingly fulfilled when sticking to pre-existing everyday identities. Still even those members of the dyke+ BDSM community who do not have the desire to participate in the practices described in this article usually respect and accept the genderqueer and trans roles and identities in their midst.[14]

Even though the interviewees build a bridge between BDSM space and everyday life, for example through integration, in everyday life realities gender is not safe, sane and consensual, as Bornstein points out. Notwithstanding, Eike acknowledges that s/he not only gained gender awareness, but also *gender self-confidence* through gender play, which helps to defend their identity in everyday life.

In summary, the answer to the question why there is such a diversity of queer genders in the dyke+ BDSM scene and why it is unique to that particular community lies within the combination of certain BDSM characteristics and the exclusion of privileged genders (specifically straight and gay 'biological' men), thus creating a social space that is perceived as a safe playground to explore genders. Gender exploration leads to certain insight and awareness on the one hand, especially an embodied understanding of non-heteronormative gender identities. On the other hand it creates an expansion of gender concepts and identities that enables specific subcultural skills to emerge, which I have called renaming/reassigning, recognition and integration. These practices translate to valuing gender diversity on a community level and are partly transferred into everyday life, especially in terms of identities. A transferal of this to other communities and mainstream society, however, remains limited due to heteronormative, sexist and other hierarchical social structures.

Notes

1. I want to thank Marianne Pieper and Volker Woltersdorff for helpful comments on earlier versions of this paper, Erika Doucette for perfecting my English and last, but most, my interviewees for providing me with their time, expertise and ongoing support in this study.
2. For the purpose of this article, I analyzed 31 interviews. All of the interviewees have some connection to the dyke+ BDSM community, except for one, who is only part of the queer community. Nineteen individuals identify predominantly as a dyke or woman, of whom nine also identify as femmes, three as butch and three as transwomen. Three identify predominantly as transgender butch, two as genderqueer, two choose not to identify in terms of gender. Five consider themselves predominantly as transguys. Two members of this sample have proof of an intersex history. In terms of sexual preference, 20 identify as predominantly queer, and three of them also identify as a fag or gay leatherman, ten as predominantly dyke or lesbian and one as gay male. Queer mostly stands for being attracted to other queers, including dykes, trans people and sometimes biologically male gay men (usually excluding straight people). Dyke or lesbian is used by individuals who are attracted only or mostly to women, 'women' usually includes transwomen, and some or all ftms. Their ages range from 20 to 60, and their class backgrounds range from working, middle to upper, both up- and downwardly mobile, some have been previously homeless, six are or have been sex workers and one is a person of color.
3. The women's BDSM scene at this point usually includes self-defined dykes/lesbians, bi/pansexual and queer women, butches, femmes and other genderqueers, who do not necessarily consider themselves women, the whole ftm spectrum, as well as transsexual women (but not mtf transvestites or crossdressers). I therefore refer to it as dyke+ BDSM community, to do justice to both the historical background as well as the identities of the individual members.
4. Epistemologically speaking, I consider the data generated by my interviews as subcultural discourses that simultaneously produce and represent embodied and discursive practices, bodies, identities, power relations and institutions in the social spaces I'm writing about.
5. Names have been changed to ensure anonymity.
6. His observation can be generalized for most broadly accessible straight, gay male and women's play parties in the USA and Europe, if these are not organized privately or by people of color (for people of color).
7. Even though there are mtf transvestites and transsexuals in the straight scene, according to the perspective of the interviewees they are either fetishized or

confronted with other misogynist, sexist and transphobic attitudes, as the use of the term 'forced feminization' illuminates.

8. See Bauer (2005: 81–82) for another discussion of 'cockplay' as a genderfuck activity based on a quote of the genderqueer Femmeboy.

9. For example, the queer femme Mandy started wearing femme attire and learned to fix her car at the same time: 'So I very much wanted to affirm that being a woman and being sexual and being femme did not mean that my brains fell out the bottom of my skirts. But I also wanted to affirm my intelligence and my intellect and my agency and learn to use big tools.'

10. Interviewees (Firesong and Femmeboy) use the term 'integration' themselves, and I have found it an appropriate in vivo code (Strauss & Corbin, 1990) for the phenomenon others describe as well. It bears some resemblance to the Jungian term integration, in terms of embracing the hidden parts; however, the partial gender identities that are integrated into my interviewees' personalities are not necessarily derived from the Jungian shadow. See also Easton in this book.

11. 'Once you stick your fist in my cunt, I don't care what I was doing beforehand, I'm a little girl. If you're fucking me in the ass, I'm a boy.' (BJ, identifies as gay male, with an intersex history)

12. Straight is a term that is used by queers to refer to heterosexuals, as well in the BDSM community to refer to vanilla people.

13. In Teresa's case, her judgment of certain straight BDSM scenes relies on an outsider perspective, as she limits the scope of her comment herself by pointing out that she doesn't know the people she's talking about. MCL on the other hand, is familiar with the straight scene.

14. However, the fact that not a single person in my sample disapproved of the gender diversity in the dyke+ community can also be read as a bias, because transphobic or separatist women would be less inclined to trust a trans researcher.

References

Bauer, R. (2005). When gender becomes safe, sane and consensual: *Gender Play* as a queer BDSM practice. In E.H. Yekani & B. Michaelis (Eds) *Quer durch die Geisteswissenschaften. Perspektiven der Queer Theory* (pp. 73–86). Berlin: Querverlag.

Bornstein, K. (1994). *Gender Outlaw. On Men, Women and the Rest of Us*. New York: Vintage.

Hale, C.J. (2003). Leatherdyke boys and their daddies. How to have sex without women or men. In R.J. Corber & S. Valocchi (Eds) *Queer Studies. An Interdisciplinary Reader* (pp. 61–70). London: Blackwell.

Haraway, D. (1991a). The biopolitics of postmodern bodies: Constitutions of self in immune system discourse. *Simians, Cyborgs, and Women – The Reinvention of Nature* (pp. 203–230). New York: Routledge.

Haraway, D. (1991b). Situated knowledges: The science question in feminism and the privilege of partial perspective. *Simians, Cyborgs, and Women – The Reinvention of Nature* (pp. 183–202). New York: Routledge.

Meuser, M. & Nagel, U. (1991). ExpertInneninterviews – vielfach erprobt, wenig bedacht. Ein Beitrag zur qualitativen Methodendiskussion. In D. Garz & K.

Kraimer (Eds) *Qualitativ-empirische Sozialforschung* (pp. 441–468). Opladen: Westdeutscher Verlag.

Schütz, A. & Luckmann, T. (1979). *Strukturen der Lebenswelt Bd.1*. Frankfurt/Main: Suhrkamp.

Strauss, A.L. & Corbin, J. (1990). *Basics of Qualitative Research. Grounded Theory Procedures and Techniques*. Newbury Park: Sage.

Part IV
Therapeutic Perspectives

12
The Power of Play: The Potentials and Pitfalls in Healing Narratives of BDSM

Meg Barker, Camel Gupta and Alex Iantaffi

Representations of BDSM are becoming mainstream in many Western countries but only within certain tightly policed limits, particularly the heteronormative context. Drawing on Plummer's (1995) notion of sexual stories, Langdridge and Butt (2004) suggest that BDSM is having its 'time' at the beginning of the twenty-first century: there are now communities of support for the telling of shared stories of identity and experience, and BDSM is also becoming more visible beyond these communities, with stories being told in mainstream magazines, television programmes and movies. However, as with the emergence of other sexual stories, such as coming out narratives or those around non-heterosexual relationship recognition, certain discourses are privileged over others and some are completely excluded.

One key narrative, which has emerged recently in accounts of BDSM experience, is that of BDSM play as a safe space to explore issues that might traditionally have been brought to contexts such as counselling and psychotherapy. This 'healing narrative' can be found on BDSM websites (e.g. www.cuffs.com), in BDSM literature (e.g. Easton & Hardy, 2004) and in media representations that extend beyond the BDSM communities in terms of their audience (e.g. the film *Secretary*, the documentary *Sick* and the play *Behind Closed Doors*).

It is clear that some BDSMers see their practices as contributing to a therapeutic technology which enables them to deal with issues such as abuse and discrimination and/or to cope with physical and emotional pain or tension, perhaps as an alternative outlet to self-injurious practices, as the film *Secretary* explicitly suggests. In this chapter, we will consider how BDSM can be conceived as having therapeutic value, challenging traditionally pathologising narratives of BDSM. We will also explore the limitations and constraints of therapeutic discourses and healing narratives in relation to BDSM communities themselves and the wider understanding of BDSM in mainstream culture. Throughout the chapter we acknowledge that terms such as 'healing' and 'therapeutic' are extremely value-laden and consider the implications of them being applied to practices which take place outside the professional medical/psychological domain.

Current discourses around BDSM

Before focusing on healing narratives in particular, it is useful to overview the ways in which BDSM is currently represented by those within and outside BDSM communities and to consider some of the other dominant and available discourses about BDSM, which link with therapeutic discourses in various ways and form a backdrop to newly emerging stories.

Beckmann (2001), Sisson (Chapter 2) and Weiss (2006) all explore the 'mainstreaming' and 'commodification' of BDSM that has occurred in recent years. BDSM-related storylines have been present in films like *Naked Gun 33 1/3* and *Kill Bill* and television programmes like *Will & Grace* and *Buffy the Vampire Slayer* as well as most popular crime series and talk shows. BDSM imagery is present in adverts for Ikea furniture, Muller yoghurt and the 'Keep Britain Tidy' campaign, as well as in high street fashion and songs by popular artists such as Janet Jackson (*Rope Burn*, 1997, track 19) and Britney Spears (*I'm a Slave 4 U*, 2001, track 1). However, commentators within BDSM communities have been cautious in their reactions to this increased availability of BDSM imagery. Califia and Sweeney (1996) write

> While it's nice to have people admire our clothes and to hear jokes about handcuffs during prime time, these media references too often include damaging and dangerous stereotypes about us. When latex, leather, and metallic accessories are taken out of context, we get ripped off so the viewers at home can be titillated.
>
> (p. xiv)

Authors like Beckmann and Weiss have argued that mainstreaming does not simply signify an increased sexual freedom and acceptance of diverse sexual practices. Rather, most mainstream imagery and stories function to normalise certain 'kinky' practices whilst policing against 'real perversions', which are still constructed as pathological, deviant and other. High street sex shops and women's magazines encourage heterosexual women to spice up their sex lives and keep their partners interested with fluffy handcuffs and sequined riding crops, whilst policing the boundaries against 'real' BDSM (Storr, 2003). Mainstream representations of BDSM are of imagery rather than of practices in context, and 'kinkiness' is accepted if it is merely 'playful' and if it takes place in otherwise heteronormative circumstances, without straying further out of Rubin's (1984) 'charmed circle' (e.g. by taking place in a non-heterosexual, non-monogamous, non-romantic or public context). Beckmann (2001) sees the proliferation of BDSM imagery in mass media as part of surveillance culture where people are encouraged to turn their gaze inwards to monitor and control their own (sexual) selves. It is argued that such cultures take people's attention away from those in positions of power and stop them from engaging in political action or critique of legal and medical institutions and other such systems and structures.

Weiss (2006) writes that popular representations of BDSM

> Allow the mainstream audience to flirt with danger and excitement, but ultimately reinforce boundaries between protected and privileged normal sexuality, and policed and pathological not normal sexuality. (p. 105)

However, another perspective could see the construction of a new version of 'good sex', which people should aspire to, as problematic for both those in Gayle Rubin's (1984) 'outer limits' of sexuality (the BDSMers who continue to be pathologised and othered) *and* those within the 'charmed circle'. The latter have to match up to these high levels of eroticism and desire whilst still policing the boundaries against going 'too far'. As Gill (forthcoming 2007) points out, new constructions of experimental and autonomous female sexuality hide a continued message of 'get and keep your man' under a post-feminist veneer of sexual liberation.

Psychological and medical discourses serve to reinforce these boundaries. BDSM is pathologised in the American Psychiatric Association *Diagnostic and Statistical Manual* (DSM-IV-TR) and is also classified as disorders in the F65 section of the international World Health Organization *International Classification of Diseases* (ICD) (Reiersøl & Skeid, 2006). Sexual sadism and masochism are listed as 'paraphilias' (DSM-IV-TR 302.83, 302.84) despite the lack of evidence that BDSMers are any more psychologically unhealthy than others (Gosselin & Wilson, 1980; Moser & Levitt, 1987) and calls for the removal of these DSM categories

(Kleinplatz & Moser, Chapter 4). Medical and psychological discourses permeate the media portrayals discussed above: the talk-show host asks the resident psychiatrist whether the BDSMers present are 'sick'. The crime drama presents attendees at a BDSM club as on a continuum with the 'sexual sadist' serial killer. Such 'expertise' and psychological jargon serves to reinforce the boundary between 'normal' and 'abnormal' sex.

Within the psychotherapy industry, much current training for counsellors and psychotherapists continues to pathologise BDSM. For example, in her guide for counsellors, Hudson-Allez (2005) writes that, in BDSM, 'the lovemap of a person's sexuality [. . .] has been vandalized by actual or vicarious abusive practices' (p. 120) and Crowe and Ridley's (2000) handbook for couples therapists states that

> Prostitution, the use of children for sexual pleasure, *sado-masochistic activities* and other paraphilias, as well as sexual abuse and rape, are aspects of sexuality which can cause much damage to the individual. Relationships can be severely affected and evidence suggests that such behaviour may be passed on to the next generation.
>
> (p. 8, our italics)

We have considered elsewhere the implications for psychotherapy clients of BDSM being equated with coercive sex and considered as pathological, damaging and rooted in childhood trauma (Barker, Iantaffi & Gupta, forthcoming 2007). Here we want to highlight the ways in which psychological and medical discourses mirror, and are mirrored by, those in mass media and popular culture. Also it is important to see the reasons why many BDSMers might not feel disposed to approach conventional medical and psychotherapeutic services.

Narratives emerging within BDSM communities are clearly linked to the dominant discourses around BDSM in the psychology industry and mainstream culture. Taylor and Ussher (2001) and Ritchie and Barker (2005) describe how BDSMers negotiate dominant discourses through countering or challenging some aspects whilst accepting and drawing on others. For example, Ritchie and Barker's participants countered the perception that BDSM is anti-feminist and oppressive to women by discussing their experience of being dominant in BDSM scenes and/or submissive yet in control. However, they also expressed concern about certain practices which were perceived as potentially repressive and damaging (e.g. 24-7 BDSM, rape scenes and age-play). Similarly Taylor and Ussher's participants presented BDSM as consensual (rather than coercive) and playful (rather than serious), drawing lines between themselves and the few BDSMers who went 'beyond the limits' and were pathological (often those who also cut or burnt themselves).

Of course the common BDSM phrase 'Safe, Sane, Consensual' (SSC) used in the title of this book explicitly contradicts popular portrayals of BDSM as dangerous, pathological and coercive (Langdridge & Butt, 2005). Like the participant discourses mentioned above, this alternative to the dominant discourse of BDSM may construct certain practices in a way which is more acceptable, but, like all discourses, it constrains and hinders as well as opens up options and opportunities. It creates a new hierarchy in which certain practices are supported and others policed against, redrawing the line in a different place. For example, SSC suggests that risky practices should be avoided and that only 'sane' people should be involved in BDSM, shoring up problematic constructions of 'mental health versus illness'. It also assumes a shared, simple, liberal understanding of consent, negating the possibility that some might want to 'play' with this (see Downing, 2004 and Chapter 8 in this volume). The more recent term Risk Aware Consensual Kink (RACK, Medlin, 2001) is a response to some of these issues and demonstrates attempts within BDSM communities to negotiate a portrayal which challenges popular negative stereotypes and opens up the possibility of a BDSM sexual citizen (Langdridge, 2006), whilst remaining inclusive of multiple BDSM practices and identities.

These tensions echo those in other non-normative sexual communities (Barker & Langdridge, 2006). For example, claims for citizenship in lesbian and gay communities have often focused around the construction of a 'good gay citizen' who can marry, have children and participate in organised religion. This could be seen as reinforcing the marginalisation of those who practice their relationships in less conventional ways and the reification of a 'damaging hierarchy of respectability' (Warner, 1999: 74). In the rest of this chapter we will introduce the emergence of a 'healing narrative' of BDSM, both within and outside of BDSM communities. We will consider the opportunities afforded by this narrative as well as the hierarchies it may be seen as imposing. We will also explore how this narrative might be seen as resisting and/or drawing on conventional discourses of pathology and therapy.

Emerging healing narratives of BDSM

Below are summaries of four representations of BDSM in recent years which have presented what we have termed a 'healing narrative' of BDSM, where people are taken from a place of psychological and/or physical ill-health to one of emotional stability and/or general well-being through BDSM relationships and practices. The first is a late 1990s television documentary, the second a golden-globe nominated 2002 film and the third an experimental play produced by people within the BDSM community, which toured the Edinburgh festival in 2006. The fourth is the back cover information from the most recent book written by Dossie Easton and Janet Hardy, authors of some of the most popular BDSM literature (e.g. Easton & Hardy, 2001, 2003; see Easton, Chapter 13).

Plot summary for *Sick*: The Life and Death of a Supermasochist (1997)

'Sick' examines the life of the performance artist Bob Flanagan, who died of cystic fibrosis in 1996. A masochist who cultivated the infliction of pain partly as a means to deal with this excruciating fatal illness, Flanagan survived until age 42 and had a lifelong fascination with bondage, ritualized torture and humiliation. He also had a terrific sense of humor about himself. And a good portion of 'Sick' consists of excerpts from videotaped performances in which his collaborator and companion of 15 years, Sheree Rose, lovingly puts him through his paces. Not for the faint of heart.
Stephen Holden, *The New York Times*
movies2.nytimes.com/gst/movies/movie.html?v_id=154580

Plot summary for *Secretary* (2002)

Lee Holloway is a smart, quirky woman in her twenties who returns to her hometown in Florida after a brief stay in a mental hospital. In search of relief from herself and her oppressive child-hood environment, she starts to date a nerdy friend from high school and takes a job as a secretary in a local law firm, soon developing an obsessive crush on her older boss, Mr. Grey. Through their increasingly bizarre relationship, Lee follows her deepest longings to the heights of masochism and finally to a place of self-affirmation.
Sujit R. Varma
www.imdb.com/title/tt0274812/plotsummary

Plot summary for *Behind Closed Doors* (2006)

How much chance does a girl like that have?

She's been abused. That's got to screw her up for life. How can anyone recover from that kind of start?

With a mother who dominates her family with tyrannical violence, Eloise makes a desperate attempt to retain her independence.

Take a 'letterbox' seat for a unique view from behind a doorframe. From here, you'll become one of the shows 'fate-makers', and are able to determine what happens to the central character at key points during the piece.

www.cptheatre.co.uk/event_details.php?sectionid=theatre&eventid=136

See also www.switchtheatre.com/CurrentProductions.asp

Back cover of *Radical Ecstasy* (2004)

For millennia, seekers have used physical and emotional extremes to achieve transcendence and exaltation. Today, many BDSM and leather practitioners are discovering the potential of these practices to reach personal, interpersonal and spiritual goals.

In these pages, top-selling sexuality authors Easton and Hardy document their own journeys into the transcendent realm of kink. They also share techniques that have worked for them to create states of transcendence during solo and partnered sexual and BDSM practice.

As outrageously revolutionary as any sex book published in the last decade, Radical Ecstasy sets the stage for the new millennium in BDSM and sacred-sex practices!

From these examples we can see that there is not just one single emerging 'healing narrative' of BDSM but rather multiple, overlapping 'healing narratives'. In *Sick* we can read the narrative as taking Bob Flanagan from a place of physical pain to one of pleasure, from a limiting disability to a successful career and artistic expression and from a situation where he is controlled (by his family, by the medical profession and by his own body) to one where he is in control.

In *Secretary* the focus is more on mental health and psychological functioning. The story begins with Lee Holloway at a point of 'dysfunction' where she is unable to engage with the world and has to be hospitalised. She is quiet, shy and awkward. The BDSM relationship with her boss takes her to a place of mental health and confidence where she is able to hold down a job, cope with her family, take an active role in relationships with others and eventually form a committed relationship with him. This seems a deliberate reversal of the DSM statement that in paraphilias 'there is often impairment in the capacity for reciprocal, affectionate sexual activity' (DSM-IV, 2000: 567). It is also interesting in *Secretary* that Lee's mental ill-health is signified by self-injury: she cuts her thighs in a secretive and ritualised way. BDSM is fairly explicitly presented as a healthy method of achieving whatever the self-injury achieved, whilst self-injury is something that Lee has to stop completely in order to achieve her 'happily ever after'.

The play *Behind Closed Doors* has two alternative possibilities at the end of each of the first two acts. In the first act we see Eloise physically and emotionally abused by her mother. Her choice over whether to go along with her mother's wishes or not at the end of the first act determines whether she will end up in an equally abusive relationship with her first boyfriend in the second act. The decision to stand up to him or not at the end of this act determines whether the third act finds Eloise in a positive, fulfilling relationship with a man who follows her into a pleasurable BDSM scene with another couple, or whether she becomes an abuser herself, attempting a BDSM relationship but really cruelly abusing her partner in a way which is frowned upon by others in the BDSM community. So this play seems to paint 'good' BDSM as a potential way out of abusive relationships where power imbalance and humiliation are fantasies that are 'played with' in scenes rather than inevitable realities of relationships.

Finally the book *Radical Ecstasy* presents BDSM as more of a spiritual than a psychological journey. The authors, Easton and Hardy, echo some of the previous narratives in their suggestions that BDSM play can help people to revisit past abuse in a safe way to 'travel in the Shadow' (p. 167), according to Jungian metaphor, and to 'find healing' (p. 168) by bringing shame, pain, trauma and taboos to the surface. Examples could be a scene which makes use of terms of hate speech (e.g. abuse around race, sexuality or gender) that have been experienced in 'real life' situations or which replays a specific incident of bullying. Easton and Hardy suggest that healing narratives can be played out in BDSM by scripting scenes that revisit negative past experience but take it from a place of 'pain and victimization to lust and love and orgasm and cuddling' (p. 173). The authors acknowledge that much of the language in *Radical Ecstasy* is more 'religious' or 'poetic' than psychological, and links are made between BDSM and transcendent journeys, spiritual experiences and religious ecstasy.

So it seems that there is not one 'healing narrative' of BDSM but several, using different languages to suggest that BDSM may take a person on a journey from physical ill health to healing, from psychological problems to confidence and happiness, from abuse to positive relationships, from feeling powerless in the face of illness and/or disability to self-control, from painful self-injury to sexual pleasure and from trauma and shame towards enlightenment and transcendence. We have noticed that such narratives are filtering into other media portrayals. For example, a very recent TV series, *House*, showed a dominatrix using BDSM practices to relieve both the physical pain and mental suffering of her submissive.

We will now consider how such narratives may be reflective of the lived experiences of BDSMers and the ways in which they may find them useful, before considering some of the problems and constraints of an overarching narrative of BDSM as healing.

Potentials and constraints of healing narratives

Healing narratives of BDSM can be read as both empowering and problematic, opening up some possibilities whilst shutting down others. Many in the BDSM community see such narratives as reflective of their lived experiences and as accomplishing something politically useful in explicitly countering many of the pathologising discourses around BDSM and putting control in the individual's own hands rather than those of 'experts'. However, this is balanced by concerns that healing narratives may support pathologising discourses by implying that everyone involved in BDSM is damaged and in need of healing. Such narratives could be read as shoring up an 'us and them' dichotomy between the general public and the 'others' who engage in such practices, where BDSM is only for those who are positioned as sick, mentally unbalanced or marginal in some way (queer or disabled). This is also linked to anxiety that healing narratives may exclude anything other than 'therapeutic' BDSM, suggesting that BDSM is *only* valid if it is healing. This could be seen as promoting a single explanation for BDSM practices similar to many of the 'answers' put forward by psychologists and medics and rendering invisible the wide diversity of motivations for engaging in BDSM. Healing narratives could be in danger of constructing a 'good BDSMer' who, like the 'good gay citizen', sits at the top of a new hierarchy above all relationships and practices which do not fit this image, pressurising people to assimilate this rather than embracing a variety of different identities.

Healing narratives as reflective of lived experiences

The first vital point to make is that for many people, ourselves included, the experience of viewing the media portrayals mentioned above is one of resonance and recognition. When we viewed *Sick* with a group of BDSMers, the atmosphere in the room was emotionally charged as we laughed along with the in-jokes and recognised the shared cultural landscape. One of the authors recalled stumbling out of the cinema after watching *Secretary* reeling both from the sense of exposure of having desires and fantasies that had seemed personal and private depicted in such a public arena and from the sense of shared experience at seeing these fantasies reproduced on film. Another remembered being unable to put down *Radical Ecstasy* as each page gave a language to her own hitherto non-verbalised feelings, whilst also rousing desires both old and new. Again this invoked a powerful sense that 'other people do this too', and this felt like a legitimation and validation of her experiences which other texts had only described in the language of damage and pathology.

However resonant they are, these media portrayals focus on the 'spectacular' of healing BDSM. In *Secretary*, healing BDSM is part of the familiar narrative of great romance, with Lee winning her man through her capacity to withstand painful and humiliating scenes. In *Sick*, the context is a struggle with life and death. In *Behind Closed Doors* and *Radical Ecstasy*, many of the scenes are public and the result of much planning and advance negotiation, involving heavy emotions and confrontation of life-long issues for the first time. We see BDSM as 'the big event, the untoward, the extra-ordinary: the front-page splash, the banner headline' (Perec, 1973). Theorists such as Lefebvre (1987) and de Certeau (1984) have called for a turn away from the grand and exceptional towards the 'everyday' as meaningful and useful for exploration and as a potential site of 'resistance, revolution and transformation' (Highmore, 2002: 17). In BDSM research, so far there is certainly a lack of exploration of the everyday experience of practices and dynamics. Here we draw on our own stories to present three more everyday scenes to demonstrate how healing narratives may be woven in to our daily and weekly practices and how they may be a response to everyday experiences of physical pain and disability, depression and victimisation.

My body has betrayed me once again, making me feel useless, old and ugly. I'm still shaking with anger at the thought of you having to do so much for me: cooking, cleaning, helping me get up from the toilet. Not tonight. You knew that when I looked at you, when I goaded you to let your desire for me take you over. Tonight I feel strong as my wrists press playfully against the chains around them, as I arch my body eagerly every time your hand slaps my breasts, hard. You know I can take more than this tonight, as you secure the nipple clamps, tugging on them so firmly that I cannot help but moan, lost in the pleasure of feeling my body so alive once again, so strong. I beg you to let the purple flogger come out of the drawer too. You hesitate but one look from me is enough. Tonight you don't get to decide what's good for me, I do. My hips thrust as you hit my buttocks harder, then harder still. Tonight I am your unbreakable whore. My body is reborn with every stroke. The layers of fragility are stripped away and my unconstrained desire can run wild. And as I lie panting, tingling, aware of every muscle and inch of skin, I see myself reflected in your eyes and, just for tonight, I choose to lose myself in my undisputed beauty as I surrender my body once more to your firm touch.

You've had a hard week. I've had a hard week. You've been on duty 24/7. Everyone wants something from you and you can't possibly please all of them all of the time. I've slipped up, made mistakes and been berated for it at every turn. Constantly feeling like a fool and a fraud. And at the end of all the stress and the craziness you come to me.

I tell you to strip. Make you crouch on the bed on all fours. I stand over you fully dressed in waistcoat and trousers. Hair pulled back. Finally I feel sure of myself. Finally I know what I'm doing and know I can do it well.

I pick up a wooden cane and begin to tap it against your buttocks lightly. For some time there is no audible response but as I pick up the pace I can hear your breath quicken. Eventually you start to moan. I know that your thoughts will still be racing over all the

(Continued)

things you have to do, all the stuff you feel you have to keep in your mind, running over and over each of them to make sure that you don't drop the ball. I hit you harder and harder. Eventually the sensation will be louder than the thoughts. Eventually you will drop down into a dark, soothing space where there is simply the rhythmic pain and the noise of the cane and your own moans echoing down from somewhere above you.

And later still the intensity will build to a point where you break and collapse and the tears come. And then I will hold you in my arms and rock you while we go over each of the harsh things you've been saying to yourself, bring them into the open and let them float away.

So, I'd been in an awful situation, one in which I'd felt a total loss of control, an abusive situation. I was angry, felt weak and fearful and powerless and was in mourning for what I felt was my lost sexual power.

By this I don't mean my power over others, but the fact that the narratives around my sexuality and desires had (probably unusually for a female-born individual brought up in late twentieth century Britain) mainly been a source of self definition, confidence and joy. This is in contrast to longstanding issues of low self-esteem, survivors' guilt and depression.

So, my partner and I set up a scene in which I would be submissive. Ze wanted to help in any way ze could, and this was what I wanted, felt I needed. We both knew that this was extremely risky and discussed the scene and how we'd both feel safe doing it, while cuddling

I 'designed' a scene in which I would be owned, explicitly told that I belonged to hir and had to be available to hir. Ze asked if I was okay to begin, and I said yes.

We lay in bed, and ze put hir hands on me, told me I belonged to hir and that ze could use me in whatever way ze chose. Ze touched my body all over and told me over and over that I belonged to hir, stopped when I was finding it hard to respond and slowly and carefully held me while I cried and cried, for the first time letting out some of the bottled up loss and anger.

Having constructed this position for myself, I found being 'controlled' a huge turn-on and was no longer able to deny the difference between that and my previous experience of being controlled.

In choosing to replicate aspects of the abusive narrative within a consensual context in which I felt in charge, I was able to regain some of my confidence and love for myself and more able to regard the abusive incident as 'belonging' to the attacker.

There is certainly more scope for exploring the everyday of BDSM, preferably going beyond the rather limited medium of textual accounts (Highmore, 2002). However, these stories hopefully make the point that some BDSMers use their practices in daily life in ways which are intertwined with everyday hassles and encounters (no doubt as many of those who do not identify with BDSM may use sexual, sensual and other practices). In each of the above accounts, BDSM is experienced as a practice which may be brought to bear in order to take ourselves from everyday experiences of powerlessness, embarrassment, discomfort, lack of confidence and stress to places where we feel more in control, sure of ourselves, calm and able to manage. We may cope with the everyday work stress of conflicting roles and overwhelming demands by escaping, on our commute home, into a BDSM fantasy of servitude where the rules and associated rewards and punishments are clear. When experiencing everyday victimisation and bullying, we may plan to return to the event later that day within the safe frame of the BDSM scene. In relationships, our partners may learn with us ways to use BDSM to challenge our everyday negative thoughts or to allow flexibility into roles which are in danger of being fixed in terms of power dynamics (for example as 'carer' and 'cared for' in the first story here). It is interesting to note the similarities between these stories and psychotherapeutic narratives, for example, the link to the cognitive therapy practice of challenging negative thoughts in the second story (Gilbert, 1997) or Jungian journeying in the shadow in the third (Easton, Chapter 13). Although, as Heinkin (Chapter 14) points out, it is also important to remember that the frame of BDSM is different to that of psychotherapy with different boundaries, ground rules, aims and agreements between those involved.

Healing narratives invalidating other experiences of BDSM

One danger of articulating such narratives of BDSM as healing is the issue of reception. It may not be the intention of authors of such texts – and it certainly is not ours – to offer up a new justifying orthodoxy of BDSM. However, releasing such stories into the public domain carries with it the risk that people will grasp them for understandable political ends, such as the defence of a stigmatised sexuality.

It is therefore vital to highlight the fact that healing narratives are explicitly refused, or considered irrelevant to, the experience of many BDSMers. All of the authors have experience of mentioning the notion of BDSM as healing to other BDSMers and receiving reactions both of blank incomprehension and of enthusiastic recognition. Some have even regarded the notion of BDSM as healing or therapeutic as antithetical to their own practices, which are described as being about 'fun', 'sex' or 'play'. It seems that healing narratives may suggest that BDSM cannot be something that is simply horny or fun or that it cannot be all of these things at once.

The risk of identifying any narrative around BDSM is that it has the potential to shut off competing narratives. For example, Langdridge and Butt (2004) argue that the narrative of BDSM as 'power play' may invalidate the experience of those who identify their BDSM practices as being primarily or wholly sexual. Similarly, the narrative of BDSM as a fun, playful activity could take away from the possibility of it being something very serious, solemn and ritualistic, or the narrative of it being an intimate thing between close, loving partners could erase and invalidate the potentials of so-called 'casual' or 'professional' scenes (see, for example, Mlle Alize, Chapter 17). We should also point out that none of these are either/or constructs and that many may experience BDSM as being fun *and* serious, healing *and* playful (on different occasions or within the same scene). Some people in our discussions stated that the fact that BDSM practices can be fun is, in itself, a subversive notion, especially when located in the context of having grown up in a culture of sex education where sex was rarely constructed as a fun activity.

Another potential pitfall in privileging healing stories BDSM is the risk of idealising BDSM practices and therefore obscuring negative and/or equivocal experiences. Such stories may leave people feeling unable to share times when BDSM has reinforced negative past experiences or felt uncomfortable or disempowering in some way with others in the BDSM communities, let alone beyond these. As Binnie (1994) warns

While all the time I share a deep suspicion towards censorship...I am also highly dubious of the more utopian claims of activists who advocate and proclaim SM sexualities as the best thing since sliced bread.

(p. 158)

Healing narratives may both counter and support pathologising discourses

One reason for the appeal of healing narratives may be the fact that they explicitly challenge one of the most powerful negative discourses around BDSM, that of pathology. As with 'Safe, Sane, Consensual', discussed earlier, the notion of BDSM as 'healing' involves a conscious inversion of the traditional psycho-medical language of 'harm'.[1]

In this context, a healing narrative could even be seen as threatening the mainstream hierarchies of authority since, instead of going to a counsellor or doctor, the BDSMers choose to take the control, power and responsibility of healing upon themselves. In a society where there is so much trust in the medico-psychological industries, to imply that they may not always have all of the answers potentially destabilises their foundations. In *Sick*, Bob Flanagan stages a scene in which he hangs upside-down, in a hospital gown, aided by medical equipment, reclaiming one of the common treatments for CF as an erotic act. He takes control over his body, which, given that he suffered from cystic fibrosis, represents a wresting of power away from the medical profession.

However, as well as countering the notion of BDSM as pathological, claiming BDSM as healing could also be read as suggesting that those who engage in such practices are in need of healing. This has the potential of reinforcing the very discourses it is attempting to subvert and challenge. For example, people may read such narratives as indicating that all BDSMers have been abused or traumatised in some way, that BDSM is a means to an ends for those who are psychologically damaged and that, as such, it can be discarded once some spurious goal of sanity has been reached. Similarly, in *Sick*, Bob Flanagan's identities as someone living with a terminal illness and as a performance artist could be read as placing him beyond the limits of 'normal' people. It is acceptable for him to grapple with his illness in these ways, where it would not be acceptable for people with more normative identities. Such a reading could reinforce a notion of BDSM as deviant and only appropriate for those at the margins of society, shoring up the pathologising notion that BDSMers are always sick in some way.

Some narratives of BDSM as healing explicitly compare it to other activities, which are usually constructed as pathological, frequently self-injury (e.g. the film *Secretary* and the participants in Taylor & Ussher's, 2001, research). Both BDSM and self-injury can be seen as socially constructed: the activities that are defined within these categories and the ways in which they are viewed by those who practice them and by wider society differ over time and across cultures. Whilst both are currently perceived as pathological by psychiatry and lay people alike, there are many instances of culturally acceptable self- and other mutilation (Babiker & Arnold, 1997), including current Western beautification, body-enhancement and self-adornment practices (Barker, 2005). When talking about BDSM and self-injury, most BDSMers either construct the two as completely different from each other, in terms of the experiences and/or emotions involved (e.g. Taylor & Ussher, 2001) or suggest, as in *Secretary*, that BDSM provides a 'healthier' way of exploring some of the feelings that may have otherwise been released in self-injury. We must be wary of construing self-injury as pathological in opposition to BDSM as non-pathological. This can be seen as perpetuating the myth of a discrete, easily identifiable group of 'aberrant' practices, thus reifying the socially constructed idea of a 'true' and 'simple' distinction between madness and sanity.

Also, like pathologising descriptions of BDSM, healing narratives can be in danger of putting forward one single explanation for why people engage in BDSM practices. Medical and psychological models of human experience often search for one universal cause–effect explanation for human experiences and behaviours in a reductionist fashion instead of seeing any experience or behaviour as having many possible meanings for different individuals (and even within the same individual on different occasions). Bob Flanagan's poem *Why* puts this point across more eloquently and persuasively than any academic reflection could, his answers including

> because it makes me come...because I'm sick; because I say FUCK THE SICKNESS...because of cowboys and Indians...because of my parents; because it makes me feel triumphant...because I've got an active imagination...because it's in my nature; because it's against nature...because it's nasty; because it's fun...because it is an act of courage...because YOU ALWAYS HURT THE ONE YOU LOVE.

> (Flanagan, 1997)

In developing new narratives of BDSM, it is important to be cautious not to suggest one single explanation behind any experience but rather to embrace the diversity of experiences and possible meanings involved.

Conclusion

Exploring healing narratives of BDSM publicly entails a carefully balanced edge-walking, as with other narratives which try to illuminate experiences usually relegated to the margins of the heteronormative society we live in, such as the 'coming out' stories so familiar to those of us who identify as queer in some way. On the one hand, such narratives can be very useful, as some people see their own experiences reflected back to them and validated; on the other they can preclude the possibility of talking about these experiences in alternative ways. For example, coming out narratives (e.g. 'I always knew I was different...') can be seen as reinforcing the notion of heterosexuality as the norm, the undisputed sexual standard from which all other identities can only deviate. As we suggested earlier, we are aware of the danger of creating a 'good BDSMer' narrative, akin to that of the 'good gay' citizen. Therefore, whilst recognising that healing narratives resonate with many people's experiences of BDSM, including our own, we want to be cautious not to create yet another justifying narrative, which renders palatable what is usually seen as unacceptable but only within tightly policed boundaries. Our intent is not to create new hierarchies of abnormality and normality, acceptability and unacceptability but rather to acknowledge yet another dimension of some BDSM practices. As Binnie (1994) states

> Certainly SM is a convenient label for that which is so underresearched and misrepresented. It is important to realize that SM remains a highly nuanced and complex intermeshing of different dynamic communities with the label SM often obscuring more than it illuminates.

(p. 158)

In this chapter, the term 'communities' has also been used as if it were unproblematic, yet many people engage in BDSM practices without ever being part of any communities. We are aware that, for many, BDSM practices are usually firmly located in the private domain. This applies to many medical and psychotherapeutic practices as well. In our culture, there is a certain squeamish factor, which keeps parts of our human experiences, such as pain, bodily functions, emotional distress and many other aspects of physical and mental health, similarly firmly located 'behind closed doors'. Talking about healing narratives of BDSM can therefore be seen as challenging the dominant dichotomous constructs of public/private and out/closeted, hopefully blurring the boundaries of what is considered acceptable to share.

The question we are left with, at the end of this journey, seems to be how we can hold this paradox. For some people BDSM practices can be experienced as healing, yet we are aware that to tell healing narratives can be constraining for others. How can we respect the lived experiences discussed whilst rejecting limiting and disparaging conclusions people may draw from them (e.g. that all BDSMers are fucked up or that BDSM is only justified as a means to mental health)? It is also vital to be aware of the differential power of different discourses (Parker, 2002) and what this means for attempts to work within dominant psycho-medical discourse or to transform it into some emancipation. Langdridge (2006) considers many of the difficulties involved in battles for BDSM citizenship, highlighting the need for strategic use of both citizenship and transgression in putting forward the claims of diverse BDSM communities and practitioners. There are analogies to be drawn with bisexual communities who continue to strategically use an 'identity politics' construction of bisexuals as a quasi-ethnic group demanding rights on the basis of their desire for 'both genders', although this is antithetical to the resistance to dichotomies of gender and sexuality embodied by many of those within the communities (Barker et al., forthcoming 2007). Following from the work of Sprott (Chapter 15) and others, continued research into what various BDSM communities and practitioners wish to claim, and the strategies that they are using in order to do this, will hopefully illuminate how citizenship and transgression can be used strategically in this area also, and the place that healing narratives may occupy within this. As Butler (1993) puts it, the question is not only how discourses injure bodies, but how 'the abjected come to make their claim through and against the discourses that have sought their repudiation?' (p. 224).

Note

1. BDSM practices can also be read by some as questioning the dichotomous construction of healing/harming: much as a doctor may have to be prepared to inflict pain to heal or a therapist may pose potentially painful questions to a client, a scene may involve a dominant or top using painful sensations or emotions explicitly towards a healing purpose.

References

Babiker, G. & Arnold, L. (1997). *The Language of Injury: Comprehending Self-Mutilation*. Leicester: BPS Books.

Barker, M. (2005). Developing an SM awareness tool. *Lesbian & Gay Psychology Review*, 6(3), 268–273.

Barker, M. & Langdridge, D. (2006). Editorial: Special feature on same sex marriage. *Lesbian & Gay Psychology Review*, 7(2), 115–119.

Barker, M., Bowes-Catton, H., Iantaffi, A., Cassidy, A. & Brewer, L. (forthcoming 2007). British bisexuality: A snapshot of bisexual identities in the UK. *Journal of Bisexuality*.

Barker, M., Iantaffi, A. & Gupta, C. (forthcoming 2007). Kinky clients, kinky counselling? The challenges and potentials of BDSM. In L. Moon (Ed.) *Feeling Queer or Queer Feelings: Counselling and Sexual Cultures*. London: Routledge.

Beckmann, A. (2001). Deconstructing myths: The social construction of 'sado-masochism' versus 'subjugated knowledges' of practitioners of consensual 'SM'. *Journal of Criminal Justice and Popular Culture*, 8(2), 66–95.

Binnie, J. (1994). The twilight world of the sadomasochist. In S. Whittle (Ed.) *The Margins of the City: Gay Men's Urban Lives* (pp. 157–171). Aldershot: Arena.

Butler, J. (1993). *Bodies That Matter*. New York: Routledge.

Califia, P. & Sweeney, R. (Eds) (1996). *The Second Coming: A Leatherdyke Reader*. Los Angeles, US: Alyson Publishing.

Crowe, M. & Ridley, J. (2000). *Therapy with Couples: A Behavioural-Systems Approach to Couple Relationship and Sexual Problems*. Oxford: Blackwell.

de Certeau, M. (1984). *The Practice of Everyday Life* [1980, Steven Rendall, Trans.]. Berkeley, CA: University of California Press.

Downing, L. (2004). On the limits of sexual ethics: The phenomenology of autoassassinophilia. *Sexuality and Culture*, 8(1), 3–17.

DSM-IV (2000). *Diagnostic and Statistical Manual of Mental Disorders* (4th ed.). Washington DC: American Psychiatric Association.

Easton, D. & Hardy, J.W. (2001). *The New Bottoming Book*. California: Greenery Press.

Easton, D. & Hardy, J.W. (2003). *The New Topping Book*. California: Greenery Press.

Easton, D. & Hardy, J.W. (2004). *Radical Ecstasy*. California: Greenery Press.

Flanagan, B. (1997). *Why*. Available: http://www.findarticles.com/p/articles/mi_m0425/is_n4_v56/ai_20544724. Accessed on 5/2/07.

Gilbert, P. (1997). *Overcoming Depression*. London: Robinson.

Gill, R. (Forthcoming 2007). Supersexualise me: Advertising and the midriffs. In F. Attwood, R. Brunt & R. Cere (Eds) *Mainstreaming Sex: The Sexualization of Culture*. London: I.B. Tauris.

Gosselin, C. & Wilson, G. (1980). *Sexual Variations: Fetishism, Sadomasochism and Transvestism*. London: Faber and Faber.

Highmore, B. (2002). *Everyday Life and Cultural Theory*. London: Routledge.

Hudson-Allez, G. (2005). *Sex and Sexuality: Questions and Answers for Counsellors and Therapists*. London: Whurr Publishers.

Langdridge, D. (2006). Voices from the margins: SM and sexual citizenship. *Citizenship Studies*, 10(4), 373–389.

Langdridge, D. & Butt, T.W. (2004). A hermeneutic phenomenological investigation of the construction of sadomasochistic identities. *Sexualities*, 7(1), 31–53.

Langdridge, D. & Butt, T. (2005). The erotic construction of power exchange. *Journal of Constructivist Psychology*, 18(1), 65–74.

Lefebvre, H. (1987). The everyday and everydayness. *Yale French Studies*, 73, 7–11.

Medlin, J. (2001). *SSC vs. RACK*. Available: http://www.leathernroses.com/generalbdsm/medlinssc.htm. Accessed on 6/11/06.

Moser, C. & Levit, E.E (1987). An explanatory-descriptive study of a sadomasochistically oriented sample. *The Journal of Sex Research*, 23, 322–337.

Parker, I. (2002). *Critical Discursive Psychology*. London: Palgrave.

Perec, G. (1973). *The Infra-ordinary*. Available: http://www.daytodaydata.com/georgesperec.html Accessed on 5/2/07.

Plummer, K. (1995). *Telling Sexual Stories: Power, Change and Social Worlds*. London: Routledge.

Reiersøl, O. & Skeid, S. (2006). The ICD diagnoses of fetishism and SM. In P. Kleinplatz & C. Moser (Eds) *SM: Powerful Pleasures* (pp. 243–262). Binghamton, NY: Haworth Press.

Ritchie, A. & Barker, M. (2005). Feminist SM: A contradiction in terms or a way of challenging traditional gendered dynamics through sexual practice? *Lesbian & Gay Psychology Review*, 6(3), 227–239.

Rubin, G. (1984). Thinking sex: Notes for a radical theory on the politics of sexuality. In C. Vance (Ed.) *Pleasure and Danger: Exploring Female Sexuality* (pp. 267–319). London: Routledge.

Storr, M. (2003). *Latex and Lingerie: Shopping for Pleasure at Ann Summers*. Oxford: Berg.

Taylor, G.W. & Ussher, J.M. (2001). Making sense of S&M: A discourse analytic account. *Sexualities*, 4(3), 293–314.

Warner, M. (1999). *The Trouble with Normal: Sex, Politics and Social Theory*. Minneapolis, MN: University of Minnesota Press.

Weiss, M. (2006). Mainstreaming kink: The politics of BDSM representations in U.S. popular media. In P. Kleinplatz & C. Moser (Eds) *SM: Powerful Pleasures* (pp. 103–132). Binghamton, NY: Haworth Press.

13
Shadowplay: S/M Journeys to Our Selves

Dossie Easton

Introduction

My understanding of the psychodynamics of role-playing S/M derives from more than 30 years experience in S/M lifestyle, as participant, educator, therapist and lover. I became a formally trained sex educator and peer counselor in 1972 through San Francisco Sex Information, a hotline and now website where trained volunteers offer information and support about sexual issues to the public. In 1974, I came out into S/M and joined the Society of Janus, one of the oldest S/M support and education groups in the USA. I was privileged to begin (and continue) my explorations within an extended family of people who not only played but also studied and researched and discussed (endlessly) the world of S/M, with a very high level of consciousness (see also Barker & Easton, 2005).

I have been a licensed psychotherapist and relationship counselor in private practice with mostly S/M clients for the past 15 years. Before that I interned in the mental health system for nine years and trained in a residential treatment program to work with adult survivors of trauma and child abuse. Before that, I worked for two years at the battered women's shelter in Santa Cruz, CA. I currently serve on the Advisory Board of the National Leather Association's Domestic Violence Project.

With my co-author Janet Hardy (previously known as Catherine A. Liszt) I have written five books about S/M and other sexual explorations: *The New Bottoming Book* (Easton & Hardy, 2001), *The New Topping Book* (Easton & Hardy, 2003), *The Ethical Slut* (Easton & Liszt, 1997), *When*

Someone You Love Is Kinky (Easton & Liszt, 2000) and, most recently, *Radical Ecstasy: S/M Journeys to Transcendence* (Easton & Hardy, 2004). I currently travel around the world to teach about S/M, polyamory and spirituality at conferences and retreats.

I am also a poet, and I believe that truth is often more clearly communicated in imagery than in expository prose, especially truth about our deepest emotions. So I tend to explicate my thesis with stories more than argument and express what I see in metaphor.

During all these years, my understanding of S/M has been informed and enriched by countless wonderful people who have generously shared their thoughts and most intimate feelings as my clients, colleagues, students and lovers. This accumulated experience in the University of Life is the source of my information and the foundation of my authority to speak to you.

One term needs to be defined properly at the outset. When I speak of S/M, I mean safe, sane and consensual; responsibly and consciously chosen adventures engaged in thoughtfully and carefully by people who trust each other and know each other well. In this article, I will be describing S/M scenes as they are practiced by experienced players – some of what is in here may not be appropriate for players who are just starting out.

Discovering Shadow

Some years ago, while we were writing *The Topping Book*, my co-author and I enacted a role-playing scene set in a Victorian workhouse. She was the sadistic matron of this workhouse, and I was a teenage orphan who had been dragged in half-starved from the street where I had been trying unsuccessfully to make my living as a whore. As she lectured me on the errors of my ways, she tied me up and showed me the punishments I would have to endure if I were to break any of her rules. This was a clever device on Janet's part – she likes to play with punishment, and I don't, having survived a childhood where enraged beatings were excused on the grounds that they were punishments for being 'fresh'.

We played for three hours, and I can only describe my subjective experience of those hours as luxurious. Tied up and helpless, whipped and caned, I felt freed to wallow in pathos. It felt like a sort of trance. Indeed we can safely assume that playing with pain in the way that S/M players do is designed to create an altered state of consciousness, perhaps based on endorphins or who knows what neurotransmitters we may yet discover. Many S/M players report that the state of consciousness they experience in play is similar or identical to states of consciousness they experience in meditation or spiritual practice (see Beckmann, Chapter 7).

The next day, still floating in luxury, I found my thoughts wandering back 25 years to a terrible time in my life. In 1968, living as a flower child in the Haight-Ashbury district of San Francisco, I had to flee a battering relationship when I was six months pregnant. My partner of two years had started having psychotic episodes and became violent, crazy and murderous. Later he tried to burn a house down around me and the baby. I was 24 years old.

I had fought my way out the door insisting I was going to get groceries for dinner. He threatened to burn all my clothes so I could never go outside again. I ran and hid in a friend's house and set out to build a new life with nothing but the clothes on my back, in a place where he couldn't find me.

In those first weeks, I often visited an ecumenical ministry in the Haight-Ashbury because they were nice to me and they also had food – for a brief time, their approaching-the-use-by-date free yogurt was my primary source of protein. I am certain that to their eyes I looked terribly pathetic. I still have the scars on my face that would have been healing at the time. But I didn't feel pathetic. I didn't have the luxury to be pathetic. I had a life to build, a baby to care for and how I felt was terribly, terribly angry: angry at a culture whose myths about men and women made battery a common occurrence, angry at the insane Madonna/whore split that drove my partner's violence and very angry at myself for having gotten into such a bad situation in the first place.

I needed that anger. It was the burning fuel that drove me to build a life on my own, as a single mother and as a feminist. The anger gave me strength and motivation to carry on, and I did it well. My daughter is now 37, her childhood was a wondrous adventure and we have a close and loving relationship in the present. That anger also fueled my feminism and made me the therapist and theorist that I am today.

Back then I couldn't afford to have compassion for myself, or so it seemed. I thought 'feeling sorry for myself' would weaken me. I grew up in a family that often quoted 'I cried because I had no shoes until I saw a man who had no feet' and, more ominously, 'I'll give you something to cry about'. Somehow that scene with Janet where I got to be storm-tossed and hurt and sad and pathetic had brought me into a profound feeling of love – the antidote to shame – for my younger self.

In that imaginary Victorian workhouse I learned that compassion begins at home. If I refuse to open my heart to myself, how am I going to be able to open my heart to anyone else? And what more terrible abandonment could I commit than to abandon my own wounded self? It was as if after that scene that I could welcome back a very important part of myself that I had been shunning for all those years.

Jung and Shadow

Now I am a therapist who works with abuse survivors, and I am familiar with how we split off parts of ourselves to defend our psyches against memories and emotions that we experience as intolerable (Jung, 1958). When we can't bear to feel whatever it is that is hurting us, we dissociate it out, bury it, shove it in a pot and put the lid on as tight as we can. Often we do this as children, when our coping skills and understanding are not fully developed and our containers for the emotions we feel are undeveloped, leaving us prone to throwing ourselves down on the floor, screaming and kicking. Later in life, when something comes along that reminds us of what's in the pot – maybe the lid rattles a little – we immediately push that lid down harder. It becomes a pressure cooker, not because the contents of the pot get hotter but because over the years we develop an entire repertoire of ways to keep the lid on that pot, and we press and press until it's ready to explode. I've opened a lot of these pots, in my own therapy and with my clients and learned that when you open a can of worms, it rarely actually explodes. More often what we were so afraid of long ago is no longer scary – perhaps now that we are adults we can see more options or realize that we have obviously survived whatever it was. We actually can take one worm out of the pot, watch it crawl around a little and put it back in and put the lid on that pot till the next therapy session or the next scene. We can develop skills at building containers for trauma.

Jung had another metaphor for that pot, he called it the Shadow. Here is a picture of my oceanic metaphor for my understanding of Jung's metaphor of the contents and construction of the human psyche (based on Jung's, 1964, descriptions). Please think of this as a poetic image, not a diagram, and remember that the map is not the territory. There are no pots in your brain or mine. So here is a picture of a psyche seen as a bit of sky and sea in an eggshell:

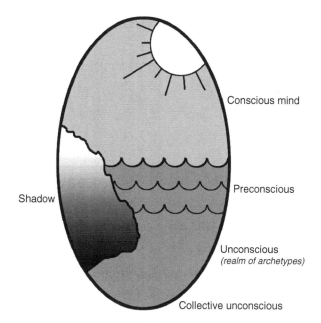

In the sky where the Sun is shining, we can imagine everyday Consciousness: I'm typing on my computer, you are reading in your favorite chair; what we are easily conscious of, brightly lit, no mysteries. Where the drawing shows waves we can imagine what used to be called the Preconscious mind, our partial awarenesses, things we forget most of the time, like our childhoods, or see only in dreams or fantasies. Or perhaps emotional awareness that shifts like the phases of the Moon: the tide-pools of consciousness, only occasionally revealed.

Under the water, much more dimly perceived, is the Unconscious mind that we see only by reflection or by its consequences. There is a cabalistic metaphor that meditation or prayer is like throwing a hook into the dark sea, not knowing what fish you might pull up. This is the realm of archetypes, gods and goddesses, maternal and paternal imagery, our templates for various ways of being human. I do maintain that the roles we play in S/M constitute archetypes. We see them in the movies all the time: Dracula, Cruella DeVille, the Girl in the White Nightie. I have never met a person who didn't recognize the character of Nurse Nasty – she travels in all of our fantasies. These archetypes are the dramatis personae of the psychodramas we enact in S/M.

At the bottom of the ocean, like sunken treasure, Jung placed the gateway to the Collective Unconscious, also called Cosmic Consciousness, which was how he understood our connection to the whole of life: spiritual Consciousness if you will. For our purposes, it is fascinating that he placed this gateway at the very bottom of the diagram. I don't know why he did that, but I do know how it works for me in S/M.

Jung (1928) proposed a realm of Consciousness he called the Shadow, which in our drawing is represented by the iceberg floating on the sea, only a tiny portion visible, most of it below the surface and hidden – the part we believe could sink our ship. The Shadow is the garbage midden of the mind, the imaginary place where we put away everything we have forbidden ourselves to be aware of. We freeze away family secrets, societal taboos, cultural trauma, illness, death, abuse, sex. We split off feelings that are too terrible to bear as if we were promising ourselves: 'I will never ever feel this dreadful feeling again, I won't, I'll kill myself. I'll die. No'. You may notice that open discussions of the horrors of war are often only allowed a generation after the event: to speak of Korea or Vietnam or the Holocaust or the Rape of Nanking a month after it happened might feel impossible.

Jung (1928) first wrote about the personal shadow which comprises everything that an individual's conscious mind would experience negatively and is experienced in dreams and fantasies as a dark same-sex sibling or adversary. This theory was popularized in Ursula Le Guin's (1968) novel *The Wizard of Earthsea*. After World War II, Jung (1951) expanded his theory to distinguish a collective cultural shadow, which is projected onto other races and social groups. Jung (1951) described the challenge of the Shadow as 'recognizing the dark aspects of the personality as present and real' (cited in Campbell, 1971: 145)

In S/M scenes, in role play, in carefully controlled torture, in erotic psychodrama, we can journey into the Shadow in ways that allow us to reclaim parts of ourselves that we have split off. I don't believe that we are ever content with just forgetting trauma or fear or pain, shame or humiliation: when we insist on forgetting we abandon the parts of ourselves that are the most in need of compassion and understanding, much as in the interests of survival I abandoned the part of myself that was so wounded by physical violence. As a therapist, I think consciousness is the essence of healing. If I can create for my therapy clients a safe place in which to be conscious of whatever is troubling them, they will go right ahead and do what they need to do to open up new options and to heal.

S/M is not therapy, it is not remotely the same process and certainly not the same means (see also Henkin, Chapter 14, and Barker, Gupta & Iantaffi, Chapter 12). But it can be therapeutic. When we find ourselves –

or our clients – on such a journey, the question becomes: 'What split-off part of me is trying to come home and how can I welcome it?' As we understand, accept and integrate our various Shadow selves we also understand what draws us to these dark fantasies. S/M people are not alone in being attracted to dark fantasies – the entire culture treasures horror movies, gothic novels and roller coasters. One lover of mine put it very succinctly when she said, 'I know my fantasies have dirty roots'. And how can we grow roses without dirt?

Playing in the Shadow

S/M scenes can be a very carefully controlled form of dirt. We can plan these adventures in advance, so we can pretend to be storm-tossed in our perfectly safe bedrooms. We take these journeys with people we trust – a particular task of the top in an S/M scene is to maintain the container, the vehicle that insures that everyone gets home safely. We get to have limits – my battering partner certainly wasn't worrying about my vulnerability to punishment scenarios, nor did he care very much about my physical safety. My lover never grabs my hair without remembering the bad disk in my neck.

Sometimes we get to meet a part of ourselves we didn't even know was there. I played a scene with my co-author many years ago at a play party in a public dungeon. We had planned a script in which a prom queen (me) gets kidnapped and ravaged by a juvenile delinquent (Janet). I'm always happy when I get to wear one of my prom gowns, and Janet greased her hair back and got a leather jacket and a menacing looking, albeit very dull, knife to threaten me with. The scene went well, and as we worked our way in deeper it also got scary. Janet's delinquent had a seriously hostile and violent energy that we could both perceive. We were safe – other parts of our minds took care of limits and safety and consent, that was all fine. But the characters we played were deeply felt, as we both explored our old tapes about class and resentment and violation. Afterwards, after the rewarding sex that brought us more or less back to ourselves, I was sitting by the buffet replenishing my blood sugar when Janet, now naked, came up to me and asked, in a very small voice, if I could please cuddle her for a while. So we wrapped the erstwhile tough guy in my pink tulle skirts and hugged and stroked till she felt safe again. It is not only bottoms who may need aftercare. That was the first appearance of my co-author's precious inner villain – we have played with him quite happily many times since.

The other person in an S/M scene, top or bottom, provides a mirror in which we can see ourselves in new ways, and it is a validating mirror, a person who finds us desirable and lovable in our most forbidden regions. I remember a scene I played years ago when I was very distressed over having been dumped by a lover I cared a lot about. I was also angry at myself for caring, and I felt terribly inadequate, ugly and old. I negotiated with a friend of mine to top her, and she offered to provide a screen on which I could project all these bad feelings. After all, they weren't about her, and she is a great lover of intensity. After I warmed her up, we dove deeply into caning – me caning her, carefully and ferociously. I felt my rage and self-loathing flowing from my heart down my arm through the cane into her. She was my crucible, together we were melting down this anguish and forging it into something new and bright. As we do in intense play, I would from time to time move up to her face to check in and make sure she was all right. Toward the end of this, when I checked in once again, she turned and looked up at me with a shining face and a huge grin, and said, 'I'm great. I'm fabulous. I love your Shadow'. And in that moment, I loved my Shadow too.

We get to write the script, which also means we get to rewrite the ending. These scripts often start out looking like trauma and end up somewhere else, in sex, in love, in comfort, in orgasm. S/M works by eroticizing these dark stories. We bring our traumas into consciousness and into the flow of eros and give them a healing injection of the life force. This is the ultimate transformation and the real meaning, I think, of sexual healing.

Negotiation

Here's an example of how we scripted a scene to travel in touchy emotional territory. The first overt child/adult scene I ever played was with a man who was also an abuse survivor. We were both terrified, so we talked about how it might work for a few weeks before we felt brave enough to set the date. We decided to write a script that was very different from either of our histories, so he became the teacher at a girl's finishing school, and I was the rebellious teenager who needed to be brought into line and turned into a genteel young lady (efforts at this had been made in my actual adolescence in the 1950s, but I am happy to report they failed). We talked about limits – I felt that face-slapping would remind me too much of my father, so we put that out of bounds. We both felt safer with me as a teenager and decided to think about younger ages at some future time. My lover gave me a spanking over his lap, so there would be lots of skin contact as a way to sneak in nurturing touch and comfort. He told me it hurt him more than it hurt me, and how happy he would be to see me as the sweet young girl he knew was in me somewhere. In the mythic logic of S/M this worked for both of us: for him, because in the story we wrote he was in control of himself, and not replicating one of his father's blind rages. For me, the touch and the absence of rage made it possible for me to sink into a trance. I found myself weeping and repeating. 'I'm sorry, I'm sorry, I want to be a sweet girl!' and somehow that was just right: another way in which I met a part of myself from the past and came to terms with her.

Playing with power

I have heard S/M described as 'Power play for fun rather than profit'. That makes a lot of sense to me. We spend a lot of our lives struggling with power – empowering ourselves, acquiring financial and social power, ensuring that our power can be passed down to our children and so on. Very serious stuff. In S/M, we *play* with power, in a metaphorical reality that has real consequences in terms of how we see ourselves and each other, but not so much in how we enlarge our bank accounts or climb the corporate ladder. It helps to see S/M adventures as characterized by power that is shared rather than taken or given up. We play roles that polarize the apparent power, which has an amplifying effect, so that by sharing our power in this way we wind up with a total increase in power all around.

What are the scripts and stories that we explore in S/M? Many scenes provide an opportunity to experience something that is rare or impossible in the everyday world. (Janet likes to point out that if she really were the villain of her fantasies she would be in jail.) We can script a scene so we get to be our precious inner villain or, equally forbidden, our precious inner victim. We can be child, parent, brat, hero, bully, betrayer, betrayed, cops, criminals, prisoners, interrogators, priests – the possibilities are endless.

We can also get to feel a particular emotion: rage, pathos, grief, shame, cunning, predatory, helpless, hapless, omnipotent. A friend of mine once set up a scene with four gay men she knew. She asked them to tie her firmly to a padded table so she could struggle as hard as she could while they flogged her and shouted every insult they could think of that men have shouted at women – cunt, bitch, on the rag and so on. What she wanted to experience fully was her rage, and so she did, screaming and struggling, yelling back, a burning ball of fury safely tied to the safely padded table. They played it through till they were all exhausted, and my friend felt she had accomplished her purpose to completely express her rage at the sexism she had been subjected to all her life. Note that she specifically chose gay men as her tormenters – heterosexual men might have been a little too threatening.

Some scenes provide the opportunity to explore gender (see also Bauer, Chapter 11). You may have noticed my pronoun dysphoria as I talk about my co-author Janet she, and her precious inner villain, he. Every professional dominatrix has a closet full of oversized lingerie and size 13 high heels and a make up kit to go with them. Forced feminization is a popular fantasy among the straightest of men – for some this may provide an opportunity to be vulnerable and to be welcomed and desired in that vulnerability, very forbidden territory for most men in the regular world (Mlle Alize, Chapter 17).

Some scenes offer an ordeal: a challenge, the chance to be confronted with extremely intense stimulation and either triumph over it or surrender. I recently played Wicked Witch to my friend's Hansel. Hansel is a butch woman who was referred to as he during this scene. He was being an utter brat, pulling his little sister's hair, yelling at the witch, arguing with everything – so I tied him to the wall, and let him argue all he liked. Hansel in the real world is a person who almost never bottoms, so I was aware that we were treading on vulnerable turf. After the warm-up, with Hansel still securely fastened, I turned up the heat and caned his back into welts and blisters till he stopped raging and got quiet, went limp, hung his head and said he couldn't take any more. For some reason my intuition told me that we shouldn't end this scene in Hansel's defeat, so I looked him in the eye and declared, 'I want five more'. In our language, that means I wanted to hit him five more times very, very hard. There was long silence, and Hansel nodded and gave his consent, looking utterly terrified. I took each stroke singly, gave him plenty of time to feel it, to scream and thrash and then feel the endorphins pumping as the pain receded. (Please note: if I had seen him unable to manage the sensation I had the option to hit more lightly or on less sensitive skin, but that wasn't necessary this time.) When the five were done, I took him down and hugged and cuddled him, telling him what a brave boy he was and how happy I was that he had given me more than he thought he could. Thus his defeat became his triumph. In a different scene, we might have gone for surrender and offered the experience of succumbing, giving up, letting go to fall into a safe landing place.

In dominance and submission, the drama is more around offering and receiving orders, commands and control. Submissives may feel taken care of, appreciated, competent, selfless, entirely outside of themselves, and in the trance the meditators think of as letting go of ego. Dominants may feel nurturing and nurtured, enlarged, loved, get a chance to be taken care of without having to be small.

Fetish is a word we use for objects of both sexual and spiritual cathexis, a symbolic thing with sensual properties (fur, silk, golden grails) that connect us to energies larger than ourselves, a way of traveling into trance.

Pain itself carries us into an altered state of consciousness not that different from runner's high, only higher that we usually attribute to neurotransmitters like endorphins. Pain as a path to spiritual journeying is familiar to us in flagellation and sun dance and body-stress religious rituals in many cultures around the world. This is pain that is very different from breaking your toe. We tend to use pain that arrives in one intense flash and then gets better, better, better, like the strike of the cane or the quick pierce of a needle. Some people in S/M explore prolonged pain, but that is less common and to my mind more advanced play. I consider myself to be an endorphin adept, and I still like my pain in the smash and recede mode.

Some of the most forbidden stories we explore are enactments of cultural trauma. Remember my friend's reenactment of sexism? Scenes are often constructed to give their members an opportunity to live out experiences that they or their ancestors may have had – imprisonment, torture, slavery, rape and so on. Let me share a bit of poetry I wrote about a proposition that was once made to me:

My friend Susannah tells me she dreams
every day. She dreams of her body, lashed to a wagon wheel and
flogged to the blood
by an ice blonde with steel eyes,
    in the cotton, on the plantation
        where Susannah's grandmother
            slaved.

Susannah told me that whenever she found a Nordic number who thought it would be nifty to play Simon Legree, she got to wondering what this white person would get out of it and how it would turn her on and that opened up some really scary possibilities so Susannah had not, at that time, ever actually played out this fantasy. I found this a terrifying proposition and could not see myself becoming the brutal slaver of my friend's fantasy – tops have limits too, you know. I do hope she has found a way to live her dream and discover what wisdom waits for her in that fire.

Spiritual journeys

Finally, some scenes are deliberately designed as spiritual practice, traveling into the Collective Unconscious on vehicles of intense stimulation, giddying power and total trust between participants. Such rituals often involve piercing, because opening the skin is a way to open emotionally and spiritually to an expanded consciousness. We have written our most recent book, *Radical Ecstasy* (Easton & Hardy, 2004), about this. It is my experience and my understanding that all sex that is connected, consensual and conscious is spiritual, that we share our spirits in all of our intimate encounters. But there is particular and radical ecstasy in finding that gateway by delving into our Shadows; and truly radical to use S/M roles and stimulations to travel to the roots of our emotional realities and the core of our sense of identity, deep under the dark earth to suck up some mysterious nourishment ... and find out what blooms.

References

Barker, M. & Easton, D. (2005). On tops, bottoms and ethical sluts: The place of BDSM and polyamory in lesbian and gay psychology. Meg Barker in conversation with Dossie Easton. *Lesbian & Gay Psychology Review*, 6(2), 124–129.

Campbell, J. (1971). *The Portable Jung* (R.F.C. Hull, Trans.). New York, NY: Penguin Books.

Easton, D. & Hardy, J.W. (2001). *The New Bottoming Book*. California: Greenery Press.

Easton, D. & Hardy, J.W. (2003). *The New Topping Book*. California: Greenery Press.

Easton, D. & Hardy, J.W. (2004). *Radical Ecstasy*. California: Greenery Press.

Easton, D. & Liszt, C.A. (1997). *The Ethical Slut*. California: Greenery Press.

Easton, D. & Liszt, C.A. (2000). *When Someone You Love Is Kinky*. California: Greenery Press.

Jung, C.G. (1928). *Instinct and the Unconscious*. Collected works, Vol. 8. Princeton: Princeton University Press.

Jung, C.G. (1951). *Aïon: Researches into the Phenomenology of the Self*. Collected works, Vol. 9. Princeton: Princeton University Press.

Jung C.G. (1958). *The Undiscovered Self*. London: Routledge.

Jung, C.G. (1964). *Man and His symbols*. New York, NY: Doubleday.

Le Guin, U.K. (1968). *The Wizard of Earthsea*. New York, NY: Bantam Books.

14

Some Beneficial Aspects of Exploring Personas and Role Play in the BDSM Context[1]

William A. Henkin

> The self divided is precisely where the self is authentically located.... Authenticity is the perpetual dismemberment of being and not-being a self, a being that is always in many parts, like a dream with a full cast. We all have identity crises because a single identity is a delusion of the monotheistic mind.... We all have dispersed consciousness through all our body parts.... Authenticity is *in* the illusion, playing it, seeing through it from within as we play it, like an actor who sees through his mask and can only see in this way.
>
> James Hillman, 'The fiction of case history', *Healing Fiction*, p. 39

> Whereas mechanical acting makes use of worked-out stencils to replace real feelings, over-acting takes the first general human conventions that come along and uses them without even sharpening or preparing them for the stage ... never allow yourself externally to portray anything that you have not inwardly experienced and which is not even interesting to you.
>
> Constantin Stanislavski, 'Action', *An Actor Prepares*, p. 36

Prologue

The activities that fall under the heading of BDSM are not new in history nor are they new in the lexicon of psychology. But for most of the years psychodynamic theory has held sway, and in the absence of any significant research to support or contradict the position, they have been

regarded by mental health professionals as developmental psychopath-
ologies (e.g., Stekel, 1963, 1964 [1929]), even when they neither cause
participants distress nor interfere with their healthy functioning in other
areas (American Psychiatric Association, 1987a,b, 1994, 2000).

I will begin this paper by defining three terms relevant to the concept
of role play and personas in a BDSM context. Thereafter I will offer
two perspectives concerning the development of personas, suggest why
personas might be important aspects of BDSM that can lead participants
to personal growth and related benefits, and conclude with some discussion about the risks, as well as the rewards, of BDSM role play.

Three salient definitions

Role, persona, and archetype

As I use the term, a *role* is a part or a character, like femme fatale,
awkward schoolboy, prom queen, or tough guy, that a person tries on
as he/she might try on a suit of clothes. It might fit or it might not. It
does not fit if it has no resonance for the actor: it feels either wholly
external or simply wrong. A person might be able to fake the part, as
he/she might wear unsuitable or ill-fitting clothes, but it fails to engage
the actor who is, therefore, unlikely to choose it again. If a part does
fit, on the other hand, the actor feels as if he/she might actually live
this character's life. Such comfort in a fit suggests the role is something
more: it might be a persona.

A *persona*, as I use the term, is not a role adopted from outside images
and worn like a suit of clothes, but is rather a state of mind or a single
facet of someone's personality expressed as a whole, if limited, personality: a full expression of an ego fragment, for example, that emanates
from a person's authentic experience. Some psychologists use the term
subpersonality to identify a persona (e.g., Rowan, 1990).

Whether personas are innate features of our deep selves (Assagioli,
1965) or spring from historical areas of unresolved emotional trauma
(Herman, 1992) they coalesce around what Jung (1964) called *archetypes*:
the general and universal forms of which many personas are our particular expressions. Sometimes a role is archetypal in itself. The wicked
stepmother is a classically archetypal role, for example, and her behavior in fairy tales, such as thwarting her equally archetypal innocent
daughter, is an archetypal fantasy (e.g., Woodman, 1985). But the fact
that a role is archetypal does not mean it fits *my* archetype: the heroic
prince may fit me better than either mother or daughter. As we can

discover our own personas from the roles we adopt to fulfill our fantasies and the comfort with which they fit us, so we can learn about our archetypes – and about who we are – from the personas that emerge in our personal explorations.

From Civil War re-enactments to conventions of the Society for Creative Anachronism to costumed teens at cult movies like *The Rocky Horror Picture Show*, people in many subcultures and interest groups negotiate parts for role play in order to act out mutually enjoyable fantasies. The most significant difference between those sorts of play-acting and the sexual theatre of BDSM is that in BDSM people generally act out ideas about power dynamics they find erotic.

How exploring roles in a BDSM context can be beneficial

Acting out a fantasy with one or more consenting partners can be a useful way for people to encounter those of their own feelings, thoughts, beliefs, attitudes, and behaviors they might ordinarily keep hidden, even from themselves. In this way all sorts of theatre games can be windows through which people may come to know themselves (Blatner & Blatner, 1988; Moreno, 1943, 1959, 1969; Perls, 1969).

Even the act of negotiating a BDSM scene may be beneficial. Considering how I will perform a role and learning to draw on aspects of myself to fulfill parts that might otherwise be mere play-acting (Blatner, 2006) can help shed light on who I am both alone and in relationship. For example, in DS role play, negotiation can help to separate someone who believes himself/herself to be submissive from someone who is actually a bottom or from someone who wishes to be a pet or from the good boy or girl who deeply wants to please. Being a bottom or a good girl may look like submission, but it is not. The good girl's agenda is to be perceived as being good so she can reap the relevant rewards; the pet's agenda is to be prized and pampered, which is reward in itself; and the bottom's agenda is to have his/her own needs met; but the submissive's agenda is to fulfill the Dominant's agenda. The corollary, of course, is to distinguish among Dominant, Top, sadist, Master or Mistress, and someone who just wants his/her way and gets it by being bossy or domineering.

Clinical experience confirms that when a person fantasizes by oneself the process tends to be circular: the fantasy goes around and around in one's mind, and with no feedback or new information from outside the loop the person remains stuck in the repetitions. The fantasy may please the fantasizer over many months or years, but where there is no process, neither psychological progress nor growth is likely. When the person brings the fantasy into real time and explores it with another person, however, the interaction can open some doors of perception (e.g., Assagioli, 1965; Berne, 1961).

How people learn about their personas

We cannot know if the seeds of our personas exist in our natural personalities as infants, but we can observe two ways they develop: through natural evolution and through conscious creation.

Natural evolution

In the *Introductory Lectures on Psychoanalysis*, Freud (1963 [1913]: 339) likened the process of human development to an early nomadic tribe that moves from one place of domicile to another. '[W]e may be certain,' he wrote,

> that the whole of them did not arrive at the new location. Apart from other losses, it must regularly have happened that small groups or bands of the migrants halted on the way and settled at these stopping-places while the main body went further.

From his researches as a neurologist he found evidence to support his hypothesis that this kind of 'lagging behind at an earlier stage' occurs throughout nature in individuals and species alike; he defined it in human development 'as a *fixation*... of the instinct' (Freud, 1963 [1913]: 340).

Whether or not we think in terms of fixation, psychodynamic understandings of personality from psychoanalysis to object relations to trauma theory proceed in the belief that the child is father to the man or mother to the woman: that the way the child learns to behave, so the adult will behave in fact; and generations of clinicians of various theoretical orientations have concurred that what we learn as children affects, influences, shapes, and determines the adults we become in ways that start so early, root so deeply, and persist so thoroughly in our habits, personalities, and ways of living that we never even start to realize we weren't just born that way (e.g., Freud, 1963 [1913]; Herman, 1992; Kernberg, 1966; Klein, Heimann, Isaacs & Rivière, 1952/1985; Kohut, 1985; Ross, 1994; Winnicott, 1945).

Some events that shape us are unremarkable; others we experience traumatically, whether we define the event as bad (e.g., being mugged) or good (e.g., winning a substantial prize), because they contain more input than we can process as they occur in real time. While we are liable to remember some traumas, we may forget others; and as Ian Hacking observes, it was Freud who 'made us all aware of how forgotten trauma could act upon us' (Hacking, 1996: 77).

Real-time events may re-engage or 'trigger' traumas that are unresolved (American Psychiatric Association, 2000; Miller, 1984 [1981]), some of which we can identify through body memory (Feldenkrais, 1977; Johnson, 1977; Rolf, 1977). For example, if as a child I behaved in some way for which I was shamed by my parental figure and if I was unable to process my feelings of shame so they persisted, then when I feel a similar sort of shame about any other form of embarrassment many years later, I might feel an echo of the same embarrassed flush to my cheek, the same tightening in my gut, the same clenching of my jaws and sphincters, that I felt at or in reaction to the original shaming; but once I become aware of the connection I can begin to distinguish my adult, present-time feelings from my unresolved historical reaction to the event (Lowen, 1958). It is a cornerstone of psychodynamic theory that resolving the early trauma is a precondition to resolving later feelings (e.g., Miller, 1981 [1979]).

A principal benefit of BDSM role play is that it can enable people to become aware of such incidents simply by pursuing their erotic interests. The introspection that ideally precedes negotiation, the negotiation itself, and the actual play that follows can all enhance self-awareness because each step encourages players to pay attention to what they want and, if they will, to the reasons or impulses beneath their desires. Examining those reasons leaves people freer to choose and less liable to simply do what they have always done without reflection. When the lover of a well-known therapist and writer on the subject of alternate sexualities noted that she knew her fantasies had 'dirty roots' the author asked, 'how else would you grow roses?' (Easton & Liszt, 1994: 89).

Conscious creation

Under another name, Sybil Holiday, now a clinical hypnotherapist, was a famous burlesque artist from 1968 until 1980; her many acts expressed such archetypal images as a hippie flower child, an SM dominatrix, and a 1950s' burlesque queen. During the 1980s and 1990s she was a well-known professional dominatrix and teacher in San Francisco's leather community. She had performed many roles in the theatre and was already aware of an erotically dominant persona in private life. Yet, working as a pro-domme challenged her to play intimately with someone with whom she had talked by phone for only half an hour and had never met and who walked in the door five minutes before they were supposed to be erotic together. She concluded she needed a separate dominant persona for her professional life – and so she created one.

There were many activities the professional Mistress Cybelle enjoyed in which Sybil took no interest. Sybil found bondage boring, for instance, but Cybelle found satisfaction in taking people on intricate bondage journeys. The longer Cybelle plied her trade the more particular Sybil became, distinguishing what she liked from what she was willing to do professionally, and each aspect lived by her own boundaries. Mistress Cybelle was not an evolution, then, but rather was Sybil's conscious, deliberately developed creation.

Even before creating Cybelle, Sybil discovered she was good at being a nurturing erotic Mommy. Then, as she reports,

> inner Mommy evolved into Mommy Sybil; and as Mommy Sybil started to evolve, my Inner Child began to find it safe enough to come out as well; so by creating one part I made it safer for other parts to speak up. When I discovered I had an Inner Mommy I also discovered how to create a persona.
>
> (Holiday, 2006)

Co-consciousness

To become a whole, integrated human being, it helps to be intimately familiar with our own personas. We can become *co-conscious* when we explore ourselves through real-time play.

The term 'co-conscious' was coined by Morton Prince, one of the first researchers into multiple personalities in the USA (Prince, 1906). By now, a century later, its use refers not only to a process in resolving dissociative identity disorder (American Psychiatric Association, 2000), but also to any simultaneous awareness of the multiple moods, states of mind, complexes, or personas embodied in a single life, and even in a single moment. An experience of co-consciousness makes it very clear, for example, that even when an inner child is frightened, an inner adolescent may be angry, one inner grown-up may be concerned, and another may be protective, all sort of stacked up simultaneously in the same psychic space. Once a person is aware of living through a co-conscious moment it is never quite as easy as it was before to identify completely with just one of state of mind (Hillman, 1983), so this simultaneous awareness makes it easier for an individual to choose a mode of being at any given moment, regardless of the conditions he/she passes through. In this fashion, co-consciousness is also useful for identifying and choosing role-playing parts in BDSM encounters.

The risks of role play

I have proposed that there are rewards available in exploring personas and role play in the BDSM context, and that chief among these rewards is enhanced self-awareness. Certainly, however, role play cannot guarantee psychological safety any more than do other methods of seeking self-awareness. But greater knowledge does permit a person to minimize the risks entailed, whether those risks are encountered in person or less directly, as on the telephone or on the web.

In person

One kind of risk, which I call 'doing therapy in the dungeon' (Henkin & Holiday, 2004 [1996]: 103–108), usually involves a Dominant or other Top trying to 'fix' some real or imagined failing in a submissive or other bottom; sometimes the sub tries to fix the Top, and occasionally either party might try to fix himself/herself.

In basic SM courses, experienced players often talk to novices about negotiating *everything*, from age play to water sports. But in more advanced courses experienced players generally acknowledge that such extreme negotiation may often take the fun right out of the play. While politically correct, a clear, complete negotiation can eliminate the risk of edges in favor of safety. Yet, whether bringing someone to a party in a collar and on a leash or addressing a player's fear of knives, a great deal of BDSM not only represents play at someone's edge but is actually *about* the edge: A can tell B to get a cup of coffee and B can obey, but because they have produced no tension, they have also produced no excitement. Telling B to fetch the coffee under various forms of consensual and erotic physical or psychological duress makes the effort a very different task. Since playing at *some* edge is part of what makes BDSM exciting, it is inconceivable for experienced players to imagine that this sort of risk will not occur from time to time – usually deliberately and willingly, and sometimes successfully. But the risks must be acknowledged.

One risk players encounter involves someone – usually but not always the bottom – going or being taken beyond his limits, and perhaps not even knowing there was a limit to go beyond. In such a situation a young persona, or 'inner child,' may be elicited, simply because going past one's

limits is generally stressful and all people are liable to regress emotionally under stress. Since greater stress implies at least the possibility of
greater regression, a player may experience himself/herself as exception-
ally vulnerable or fragile under those kinds of circumstances.

It may appear that addressing deep-seated traumas can be readily
accomplished in scene because BDSM play is *designed* to be intense,
and intensity can be both extremely cathartic and extremely intimate.
But catharsis is more likely the beginning than the end of trauma
resolution, which makes the risk more potent. Even trained, experienced psychotherapists can never really be neutral in their feelings and
thoughts about someone they have played with; they can never be
available to someone on the regular sort of schedule a therapist must
be to their clients; they will never be able to do without some sort
of emotional reciprocation from a lover or play partner, as they will
and must where a client is concerned; they will never have no vested
interest in their love or play relationships, as they must have with
their clients; nor, finally, does their profession have a place in their
play time.

Certainly people can learn about themselves in BDSM play, which is
the thrust of this paper. But the general purpose of BDSM play is to
take erotic pleasure in a particularly intense form of intimacy, while the
purpose of psychotherapy is to discover, explore, examine, resolve, and
heal trauma, as well as to learn about and develop oneself as a person.
While some people find pleasure being in therapy, it is a very different
kind of pleasure than is available in BDSM. Most accomplished Tops will
be able to bring most accomplished bottoms to a point of catharsis, but
none I have ever known has been ready, willing, or able to devote the
requisite hours, months, or years to work through the catharsis he/she
has engendered.

Since there are risks and dangers inherent in some forms of BDSM play,
it is imperative that players be aware how scenes can go awry and be as
prepared as possible for emergencies. To that end it is very useful to read
the community books that cover these topics in some detail (e.g., Henkin
& Holiday, 2004 [1996]; Jacques, 1993; Moser, 2006 [1999]; Wiseman,
1993); to know basic first aid and CPR through courses sanctioned by
organizations like the Red Cross; to know other experienced players they
might be able to call on for advice, assistance, and/or support; to know
community resources such as local BDSM organizations and the Kink
Aware Professionals list (KAP) at http://www.ncsfreedom.org/kap/. If a
player has a therapist it is useful to know how to reach the therapist and
be willing to make the call, even if only to leave an alert message for

later response. And, of course, for true emergencies players must know how to reach their local police, fire, and hospital emergency rooms.

In the event these resources are needed there is neither any point nor any value in permitting fear or embarrassment to stop the call: the organizations exist to serve the whole population, not just the vanilla world, and it might surprise both players and non-players to learn how many of their public servants are players too. Besides, almost no one trained to deal with serious emergencies has not already seen a greater variety of embarrassing problems than are ever liable to crop up in a scene.

Online and on the phone

Different sorts of risks are associated with playing online, in chat rooms, or over the telephone than are associated with playing in person. It is difficult to 'fix' much in cyberspace, and the impossibility of presence and follow-through are apparent to anyone who wishes to avoid them. Nonetheless, people can talk on the phone when they cannot meet in person, and the Internet has proved a great boon to the diffusion of BDSM knowledge, allowing people who otherwise would not even have known where to turn for information and play partners to find both, to discuss methods of play, learn about safety issues, post their profiles, and respond to those of others. And just as ignorance is the enemy of awareness, so knowledge is its ally.

For better and for worse the net is not vetted, however, and there is no way to verify much of the information disseminated there. It is important for novices to avoid – or at least not to get hooked by – the legions of porn sites that also advertise BDSM opportunities until they know what they're really looking for. After all, while anonymous role play can provide a vast window for exciting fantasies, no one can be sure that the person in the chat room who claims to be the *Great Master Oz* with a stable of 49 slaves has ever even seen a real whip or collared a real submissive. It is not even possible to know that *Esteemed Mistress Whosis* is female, or that *pretty barely legal submissive sally* isn't a someone very different from the persona she presents, whose online role play may be neither honest nor consensual. The uncertainty that is built into this kind of activity on the web can be eased as the novice player becomes more sophisticated and adept. Sites such as those associated with established organizations like the Society of Janus (http://www.soj.org/) or The Eulenspiegel Society (http://www.tes.org/) are generally reliable, contain useful information, and have links to other valuable sites.

Conclusion

As people in theatre have long known, and as drama therapists have described extensively, role play is one way to learn about who we are. Even in role play, however, it has often been difficult to explore sexuality in our journeys toward wholeness because sex is poorly understood in our society both by the general public and by psychological professionals.[2] As a result, sexual expression is frequently suspect, and often gives rise to fear of and anger toward individuals who talk about it, write about it, or otherwise represent it in any but legal, moral, or academically restrained clinical terms.

Yet, where circumstances dictate that even a modicum of awareness be paid to the nature of a sexually charged performance, as is exemplified in BDSM role play, an individual may discover aspects of himself/herself that are deeply and personally meaningful as personas. And among those personas some that are archetypal can be transformative and even critical to the development of a whole, integrated self, with all parts present, accounted for, and fully accountable as only a complete human being can be.

Notes

1. An earlier version of this paper was the basis for a presentation at a conference of the American Association of Sex Educators, Counselors, and Therapists (AASECT), San Francisco, CA, 4 February 2006. In that presentation I was joined by Sybil Holiday, CCHT, who did not participate in writing this paper, but who contributed substantially to its development, whose remarks form part of its narrative, and whose efforts I am grateful to acknowledge. My thanks also to Susanna Bonetti of the Psychoanalytic Institute of San Francisco for her valuable research assistance.
2. Only one course in human sexuality is required to become a licensed psychotherapist in the State of California, for example.

References

American Psychiatric Association (1987a). *Diagnostic and Statistical Manual of Mental Disorders* (3rd ed., revised). Washington, DC: American Psychiatric Association.

American Psychiatric Association (1987b). *Diagnostic and Statistical Manual of Mental Disorders* (2nd ed.). Washington, DC: American Psychiatric Association.

American Psychiatric Association (1994). *Diagnostic and Statistical Manual of Mental Disorders* (4th ed.). Washington, DC: American Psychiatric Association.

American Psychiatric Association (2000). *Diagnostic and Statistical Manual of Mental Disorders* (4th ed., text revision). Washington, DC: American Psychiatric Association.

Assagioli, R. (1965). *Psychosynthesis*. New York, NY: Penguin.

Berne, E. (1961). *Transactional Analysis in Psychotherapy*. New York, NY: Grove.

Blatner, A. (2006). *Role dynamics: An Integrated Approach to Psychology and User-Friendly Language*. Available: http://www.blatner.com/adam/level2/roletheory.htm. Revised 2 May 2006.

Blatner, A. & Blatner, A. (1988). *Foundations of Psychodrama: History, Theory, & Practice*. New York, NY: Springer.

Easton, D. & Liszt, C. (1994). *The Bottoming Book*. San Francisco, CA: Greenery Press.

Feldenkrais, M. (1977). *Awareness Through Movement*. New York: Harper & Row.

Freud, S. (1963 [1913]). Some thoughts on development and regression – aetiology, Lecture XXII, *Introductory Lectures on Psychoanalysis* (Part III). The standard edition of the complete psychological works of Sigmund Freud, Volume 16. New York: Norton

Hacking, I. (1996). Memory sciences, memory politics. In P. Antze & M. Lambek (Eds) *Tense Past: Cultural Essays in Trauma and Memory*. New York, NY: Routledge.

Henkin, W.A. & Holiday, S. (2004 [1996]). *Consensual Sadomasochism: How to Talk About It and How to Do It Safely*. Los Angeles, CA: Daedalus Publishing Company.

Herman, J.L. (1992). *Trauma and Recovery*. New York, NY: Basic Books.

Hillman, J. (1983). *Healing Fiction*. Woodstock, CT: Spring Publications.

Holiday, S. (2006). Some beneficial aspects of exploring personas and role play in the BDSM context. Presentation for the American Association of Sex Educators, Counselors, and Therapists (AASECT), San Francisco, CA, 4 February 2006.

Jacques, T. (1993). *On the Safe Edge: A Manual for SM Play*. Toronto: WholeSM.

Johnson, D. (1977). *The Protean Body*. New York, NY: Harper & Row.

Jung, C. (1964). *Man and His Symbols*. New York, NY: Doubleday.

Kernberg, O. (1966). Structural derivatives of object relationships. *International Journal of Psychoanalysis*, 47, 236–253.

Kink Aware Professionals, http://www.ncsfreedom.org/kap/.

Klein, M., Heimann, P., Isaacs, S. & Rivière, J. (1952/1985). *Developments in Psychoanalysis*. London: Karnac.

Kohut, H. (1985). *Self Psychology and the Humanities: Reflections on a New Psychoanalytic Approach*. New York, NY: Norton.

Lowen, A. (1958). *The Language of the Body*. New York, NY: Collier MacMillan.

Miller, A. (1981 [1979]). *The Drama of the Gifted Child: How Narcissistic Parents Form and Deform the Emotional Lives of Their Talented Children*. New York, NY: Basic Books.

Miller, A. (1984 [1981]). *Thou Shalt Not Be Aware: Society's Betrayal of the Child*. New York, NY: New American Library.

Moreno, J.L. (1943, 1959, 1969). *Psychodrama*, Vols 1–3. Beacon, NY: Beacon House.

Moser, C. (2006 [1999]). *Health Care Without Shame: A Handbook for the Sexually Diverse and Their Caregivers*. San Francisco, CA: Greenery Press.

Perls, F. (1969). *Gestalt Therapy Verbatim*. Lafayette, CA: Real People Press.

Prince, M. (1906). *The Dissociation of a Personality: A Biographical Study in Abnormal Psychology*. New York, NY: Longmans, Green.

Rolf, I. (1977). *Rolfing: The Integration of Human Structure*: Santa Monica: Dennis Landmann.

Ross, C.A. (1994). *The Osiris Complex: Case-Studies in Multiple Personality Disorder*. Toronto: University of Toronto Press.

Rowan, J. (1990). *Subpersonalities: The People Inside Us*. New York, NY: Routledge.

Society of Janus, http://www.soj.org/.

Stanislavski, C. (1936). *An Actor Prepares*. New York, NY: Theatre Arts.

Stekel, W. (1963, 1964 [1929]). *Sadism and Masochism*. New York, NY: Grove Press.

The Eulenspiegel Society, http://www.tes.org/.

Winnicott, D. (1945). Primitive emotional development. *International Journal of Psychoanalysis, 26*, 137–143.

Wiseman, J. (1993). *SM 101: A Realistic Introduction*. San Francisco, CA: Greenery Press.

Woodman, M. (1985). *The Pregnant Bride*. Toronto: Inner City Books.

Part V

Bridging the Academic/Activist Divide

15
CARAS: An Initiative to Link Alternative Sexuality Communities and Academic Researchers[1]

Richard A. Sprott and Robert V. Bienvenu II

For the purpose of public health research, a community has been defined as 'a group of people with diverse characteristics who are linked by social ties, share common experiences, and engage in joint action in geographical locations or settings' (MacQueen *et al.*, 2001: 12). In recent decades sexual subcultures have become increasingly coherent communities organised around particular sexual practices and identities. The most prominent example is the gay community, which in the early twenty-first century has achieved a high level of social and organisational development.[2] Other sexual minority groups have also developed social networks and organisations that meets criteria for a 'community'. An example is found in the Bondage-Discipline-Sadism-Masochism (BDSM) subculture, which has had a supporting social–organisational infrastructure since the 1930s in the USA (Bienvenu, 1998; Jacques, 1996; Rubin, 1994; Townsend, 1972). Today the BDSM community exists as an organised subculture of practitioners who are linked through informal social networks, formal organisations, businesses, political advocacy organisations, community archives, and specialised health resources.[3]

Scholarly and community accounts provide evidence that most members of the BDSM community experience their participation as positive and enjoyable, and community norms strongly enforce an ethical framework that emphasises principles of consensuality and safety in BDSM erotic play (Baldwin, 1993; Bannon, 1992; Bean, 1994; Brame, Brame William & Jon, 1993; Midori, 2005; Rinella, 2003; Sandnabba, Santtila & Nordling, 1999; Weinberg, Williams & Moser, 1984; Weinberg, 1995). However, BDSM remains a misunderstood phenomenon in the broader society. Sexual behaviours found in the BDSM community are subject to classification as psychiatric disorders and have been criminalised in areas ranging from obscenity law to assault (American Psychiatric Association, 2000; De Grazia, 1969; Thompson, 1994; White, 2006). Less formally, members of the BDSM community share a vulnerability to stigma and social sanctions that can have negative personal and professional consequences (see Kleinplatz & Moser, 2006).

Communities that are referenced in research, whether the study is framed at the group or individual level, become stakeholders in the outcome of such research. In recent years the concept of *community-based research* has taken root in many academic disciplines, as a means to involve subject communities directly in research (e.g. Mittelmark, Hunt, Heath & Schmid, 1993). At its core a community-based approach involves active collaboration and sharing of responsibility and power between academic and non-academic partners in research. There are a number of dimensions to such collaborations; Israel, Schulz, Parker and Becker (1998: 178–180) define the following as 'key principles of community-based research':

(1) Recognises community as a unit of identity
(2) Builds on strengths and resources within the community
(3) Facilitates collaborative partnerships in all phases of the research
(4) Integrates knowledge and action for mutual benefit of all partners
(5) Promotes a co-learning and empowerment process that attends to social inequalities
(6) Involves a cyclical and iterative process
(7) Addresses health from both positive and ecological perspectives
(8) Disseminates findings and knowledge to all partners.

The degree of collaboration between researchers and communities can vary along a spectrum that ranges between community dialogue, which may involve informal discussion with someone who is a community member, to a full community partnership, which can entail formal collaboration between researchers and community members in all phases of the research process, from protocol development to dissemination of final results (Sharp & Foster, 2000).

A formal mechanism for facilitating such collaboration is a Community Advisory Board (CAB). The CAB has become an established part of public health research and is incorporated in research programs funded by major institutions such as the US National Institutes of Health (Cox *et al.*, 1998). A CAB is a committee or other review group that 'is composed of community members who share a common identity, history, symbols and language, and culture' (Strauss *et al.*, 2001: 1940).

CABs represent the subject community in discussions with researchers and can serve a variety of roles. These include community assessment and feedback on proposed research, development of shared goals and values guiding the research, and, as appropriate, formal community consultation and consent (Blumenthal, 2006; Dickert & Sugarman, 2005; Strauss *et al.*, 2001). The role of CABs in the research review process, including their role in assessment of potential *group-level* harms to subject communities, has been favourably discussed in the bioethics as well as the research and advocacy literatures (Cox *et al.*, 1998; Levine, 1986: 90–91; Melton *et al.*, 1988; Quinn, 2004). As noted below, a CAB entitled the CARAS Research Advisory Committee (RAC) is an integral part of CARAS's organisational structure and mission. Over time, the CARAS RAC is expected to play a positive and facilitative role in research addressing BDSM and other sexual communities that may elect to work through CARAS.

In sum, there are many benefits for both researchers and community members from community-based research collaborations. Community-based research empowers community members and can help the research process in tangible ways by enlisting the experience and insight of knowledgeable community experts when designing research and interpreting results. Community-based organisations can bridge academic and non-academic cultures and help to translate research issues to a form that will be meaningful to subject populations. Community-based research can also directly help researchers by facilitating access to subject communities to recruit subjects and collect data and/or samples needed to conduct scientific studies and other forms of scholarly research. Finally for research that has group-level implications, community consultation affords an ethically sound process for maximising the protection of research subjects and their communities.

Enter CARAS

The Community-Academic Consortium for Research on Alternative Sexualities (CARAS) began as a presentation given by co-author Sprott and licensed clinical social worker David Ortmann in April 2005 at the ninth annual Leather Leadership Conference (LLC) in Phoenix, AZ. The presentation addressed a community need for a clearinghouse to provide current information about research and clinical topics addressing BDSM.[4] Discussions among LLC participants that immediately followed broadened the concept to include some form of research advisory role, in part to address a perception among community members that most of the existing literature was either hostile to BDSM or poorly focused on issues that are relevant to the BDSM community. Some community members expressed frustration regarding research that they perceived to yield little information of interest and that consistently seemed to be years or decades behind current developments within the community.[5] These discussions not only made it clear that there was support for research within the BDSM community, but also conveyed a sense among community members that scientists were not doing a particularly good job of selecting topics for research and addressing the needs of the community.

Objectives of this analysis

CARAS emerged from these discussions and from its inception has embraced a model of active collaboration between academic researchers and non-academic members of alternative sexual (alt-sex) communities served by CARAS. As of March 2007, this includes primarily the BDSM community, with an ongoing initiative to address the feasibility of including polyamory and swinger groups. In the remainder of this chapter we highlight a subset of issues that have been focused topics of discussion, negotiation, and occasional heated debate, as CARAS has developed. We focus on the following issues that emerged early in conversations about what CARAS would do and how the organisation would be structured:

- How does a partnership between alt-sex community members and academic researchers address issues of bias in research?
- What ethical issues arise out of a partnership between alt-sex communities and academic communities?
- What communication issues arise out of a partnership between alt-sex communities and academic communities?
- What identity issues arise for an organisation that attempts to blend two very different cultures, the alt-sex community culture and the academic culture?

In particular, the issue of bias was a major concern, both from the academic community's concerns of validity and reliability in science and from the BDSM communities' experience of stigma and prejudice. Bias is a major concern to both groups, but for different reasons – and the question of how these different positions in regard to bias will unfold in a partnership was a significant topic in early discussions.

The analysis presented here was conducted as a case study, based on the fact that CARAS is a unique case (Stake, 1995; Yin, 2002). A unique case rationale exists when the person or organisation is 'so rare that any single case is worth documenting and analyzing' (Yin, 2002: 41). CARAS is the first of its kind, as a community–academic partnership between BDSM community and the academic community.

Methodology

To address the questions defined above, multiple sources of evidence were gathered. The data sources included the following:

- Archival data: including CARAS newsletters, brochures, mission statements, email exchanges, meeting minutes, forum/chat exchanges, business plans, articles of incorporation, press releases[6]
- Interviews: open-ended interviews with organisers of CARAS about these research questions
- Participant observation: CARAS business meetings, presentations at conferences, meetings with community organisations
- Interview and observational data were gathered between April 2006 and November 2006. Archival data cover the period between April 2005 and November 2006.

Analysis

Content analyses were conducted on these data. The emphasis in the analysis is on the description of these issues: from the perspective of the participants, how do they conceptualise ethical and identity issues, communication issues and concerns about bias? Themes were identified for each of the research questions, and then a systematic comparison of those themes across all available data was conducted, to capture how well particular themes accounted for the data, and whether there were any disconfirming data.

Part of the analysis included coding for source of the data (Boyatzis, 1998; Miles & Huberman, 1994). In the coding framework, the following categories were used to organise different perspectives in the analysis and will be referenced in the discussion below:

CARAS Partners refer to individuals or organisations that are formally affiliated with CARAS. This includes individuals who have identified themselves as part of the internal administration of the CARAS organisation (team leaders, officers of the corporation), academics or researchers who have formally applied for professional membership in CARAS or community members that have formally applied for membership in CARAS.

Community Members refer to people who are self-identified as having an alternative sexuality and active in alt-sex communities, but who have not officially joined CARAS as individuals.

Researchers/Scholars refer to academics or researchers who are not members of CARAS.

Results

Following a year of informal coordination between April 2005 and April 2006, CARAS was formally incorporated in May 2006 as a not-for-profit organisation in the State of California with a mission 'dedicated to the support and promotion of excellence in the study of alternative sexualities, and the dissemination of research results to the alternative sexuality communities, the public, and the research community.' CARAS currently has a Board of Directors with nine seats, some of which are designated as 'academic' expertise and some as 'community' expertise. In March 2007 CARAS is organisationally divided into three functional teams, under which discrete projects are organised that address specific organisational functions or research areas: the Information Clearinghouse Team, the Research Advisory Team, which includes the CARAS RAC, and the Development Team. An executive staff headed by an Executive Director (Sprott) oversees the overall operation of CARAS, but the organisation has adopted a decentralised model that allows projects, which may be geographically dispersed, to proceed with considerable autonomy. CARAS currently has two geographic centres of activity, a CARAS 'West' centred in the San Francisco Bay area and a CARAS 'East' centred in the Washington, DC metro area.

In discussions that led to the creation of this structure and CARAS's current activities, the following issues were addressed.

How does a partnership between alt-sex community members and academic researchers address issues of bias in research?

The conversations and communications among the CARAS partners and communications between CARAS and the wider community reflect two themes when it comes to bias: concerns about *community benefit* and concerns about *respect from academia*.

Community benefit

The wider community and CARAS partners often discussed the consequences of research for the community. In particular, the concerns were about poor quality research being used by social authorities that interact with alt-sex communities, resulting in discrimination. Another concern was the lack of research or credible information about alternative sexualities. Community members felt that this lack of knowledge about alternative sexualities impacts the development of community practices and identities, as well as fosters discrimination against alternative sexuality communities.

CARAS brochures and discussions highlighted this issue as a reason for creating and participating in an effort like CARAS:

> Very little credible research and the lack of accurate statistical information have left the alternative sexuality (alt-sex) communities in the dark.... A basic role of CARAS is to have an important and positive role in legal, scientific and public policy debates.
>
> (CARAS community brochure #2, 1 Nov 2006)

> The idea goes something like this: By providing a center for communication between community organisations and academic/scholarly researchers, we can help them do a better job by giving feedback on their research proposals, by cooperating with researchers who are doing good work (not biased or potentially dangerous work to us), and by proposing our own lines of research on questions that matter most to us.
>
> (CARAS partner email to community organisation, 27 May 2006)

> Too much sex research is just ignored at this time. Too much bad research is out there.
>
> (CARAS partner email, 1 Nov 2005)

> The need for good, quality research is apparent – in the absence of sound scientific facts on alternative sexualities, people will continue to penalise and stigmatise us, enforce policies and laws against the expression of alternative sexualities, and give us poor quality health care. And without good scientific facts, our efforts to educate and

socialise others interested in the scene will be hit-or-miss and not as powerful as we would like.

(Community member email, 26 May 2006)

Respect from academia

On the other side, there were conversations and statements made that highlighted the concern about CARAS being respected by academics and seen as legitimate from the perspective of the larger academic community. This concern also involved the issue of potential bias affecting validity in research:

> If the group is not respected, the researchers will just bypass the group.
> (Internal CARAS partner email, 1 Nov 2005)

> Is this group going to be taken seriously in its capacity to make a determination of 'scientific merit'?... [W]hat exactly qualifies such a group to make that determination? If the research ends up getting published anywhere meaningful, it will have to pass muster with a journal's editorial review board, and then (if published) it will come under the critical eyes of colleagues who, it could be argued, are way better qualified to determine 'scientific merit' than [CARAS]... a group generated from within the kink world itself... will be seen to be.
> (Community member email to CARAS, 7 May 2005)

The main solution to address the academic credibility question was articulated mostly as a need to be seen as a professional, scientific organisation, and not an advocacy organisation, political organisation, or community educational organisation. The guiding idea among the CARAS partners was that adhering to established professional and ethical guidelines of conducting science ('good science') would address the concerns about credibility and bias on both sides:

> I think that we can be both an academic center of excellence and a group within the larger kink communities. In fact, I think it serves us better to be both. In my experience, people of alternative sexualities are reluctant to come forward and be studied, or even talk about their experiences honestly. If [CARAS] should encounter this, our being a part of, and having a reputation within, the community for having

its safety and integrity in mind, we are in a strong position to address and overcome this reluctance.

(Internal CARAS partner email, 20 Sept 2005)

Another guiding idea was that the community–academic partnership model would have to more actively address questions of the benefit of research to the studied communities than has been traditional in academic circles. This guiding idea might be seen as a move towards 'advocacy,' which raises concerns about bias again. The primary CARAS partners shared a belief that 'good science' can address the questions of bias, because the scientific method and scientific endeavours have built-in processes for correcting bias, if applied conscientiously.

What ethical issues arise out of a partnership between alt-sex communities and academic communities?

One ethical issue was articulated early in the formation of CARAS as an organisation – the issue of *privacy* and confidentiality on the part of community members. It was recognised by CARAS partners and the administrators of CARAS that it is a common practice, especially among heterosexual BDSM community members, that pseudonyms are used to both claim an alternative identity and to protect one's legal identity, disclosure of which could lead to personal or professional harm. It is common to attend a convention, educational forum or 'play' party and see role names such as 'Mistress R' or 'slave D' or folkloric names such as 'Pan' appearing on name tags and registration forms. This cultural practice and the likelihood that community members would want to protect their anonymity seemed to clash with the professional practices of science and academia, where transparency and openness are normal and perceived as necessary for the progress of the discipline and the establishment of authority and authenticity. The issue was not clearly divided along academic and community lines, however, as some community members argued that use of real names should be a requirement for even community participants, and some academic members felt that this would be ethically indefensible:

CARAS (academic) partner A: This organisation cannot force people to 'out' themselves as a condition of membership. They need to be able to participate and contribute with full confidence that the organisation will respect and protect their privacy.

Community member B: We're trying, I hope, with CARAS to move forward to an open dialogue about alternative sexualities (i.e. moving up to the level of a public, respected academic organisation), not to perpetuate the current hidden, and thereby viewed as perhaps sleazy, nature of them (i.e. not moving back to the practices of a hidden, self-protecting subculture). To that end, I feel that the overriding, fundamental principle that guides CARAS must reside in honesty and transparency, not retrovision and perpetuation of old practices. We should always refer back to that principle whenever we have to make a decision about how to operate and what requirements are put upon members (who join (i.e. provide money) of their own free will).

I fervently hope that the purpose of CARAS is to be an academically-oriented organisation to help both academics and the subculture as a whole, not a community-based organisation of kinksters for the purposes of play, politics, or, even, BDSM education. The benefits, not least of which is moving forward with openness about kink, to the CARAS itself and the societies CARAS serves (i.e. the kink subculture and society at large) in my view VASTLY outweigh the potential harm to an individual who has not been coerced into paying a membership fee.

(CARAS partners' email exchange, 15 Oct 2005)

After lengthy discussions, the CARAS Board of Directors adopted the following policy statement 'CARAS Policy on the Use of Legal Names':

CARAS recognises many members of alternative-sexuality (alt-sex) communities perform community work, including work with CARAS, without disclosing their legal names. CARAS further recognises that many individuals within alt-sex communities work under established pseudonyms (by 'established pseudonym', we mean a pseudonym that has been established for some public use other than to work with CARAS). While CARAS membership entails disclosure of one's legal name via the CARAS membership form (this information will be safeguarded under the CARAS privacy policy), participation in CARAS does not necessarily entail public disclosure of one's legal name.

It is CARAS policy that CARAS supporting members or representatives of CARAS member-organisations need not disclose their legal names.

CARAS professional members who participate in CARAS activities are expected to disclose, to other CARAS participants, the name under which they perform their professional duties.

Board members and select top-level CARAS staff (the Executive Director, the IC Team Leader, the RAC Team Leader and the Development Team Leader), are expected to allow either their legal names, or an established pseudonym, to be disclosed in relation to their CARAS duties.

Each member of the CARAS Research Advisory Committee (RAC) is expected to provide either a legal name or an established pseudonym for use in non-public RAC activities.

(CARAS internal document, 31 Mar 2006)

The tension between public use of legal names and protection of individuals from institutional stigma and respect for privacy is an ongoing ethical issue in this academic–community partnership. It highlights how identity and ethics intertwine in the context of stigmatised sexual practices and an actual clash between the academic culture, in which real identifies are used, and the alt-sex community, in which pseudonyms are frequently used. CARAS's initial attempt to respond to these ethical issues emphasised 'roles' – people who act in their professional role in association with CARAS will be required to use legal names, but people who act in 'community' roles in association with CARAS will not be required to use legal names. A second emphasis has been that community pseudonyms have a public 'history' in the community – this emphasis on one function of 'names' addresses concerns of establishing authority and authenticity, transparency and openness, without the use of formal legal names. CARAS, in attempting to bridge these two communities, is an organisation at the forefront of exploring such issues of ethics and identity.

What communication issues arise out of a partnership between alt-sex communities and academic communities?

Communication became a significant concern for CARAS – because the organisation is an attempt to bring together different communities, the language choices for organisational communication become an issue of lengthy and intense examination and discussion.

One area where this became important was the title of the organisation. The issue of title is also examined in the next section, on identity issues. Early suggestions for the name of the consortium had used the word 'kink' in the title. This brought up many issues about the use of language to facilitate communication:

> Here we're revisiting a discussion we had a few months ago about the most appropriate name for this organisation, given the mission and constituencies involved (primarily kink community and scholarly, with others from time to time). One axis of this discussion emerges from the organisation's interstitial role – it is envisioned as a community-based organisation that will bridge the space between kink subcultures and those conducting scientific research addressing these subcultures. In framing the organisation emphasis on either side leads to different sensitivities. As a community-based organisation, to incorporate language that reflects the community of origin is to make a statement about identity and commitment to serve that community (and here, 'kink' does have historical grounding with early practitioners and a lineage distinct from that of medical classificatory frameworks). This occurred, for example, with the choice of 'Leather Archives of Museum' rather than something akin to 'Archive of the Paraphilias.' With an academic emphasis, the tendency will be to conform to established conventions and to avoid language or connotations that are outside of academic discourse.
>
> (CARAS partner email, 12 Jun 2005)

In developing the first brochure to announce and explain the organisation, a brochure that targeted the alternative sexuality communities, the issue of language choice was highlighted. Here is an excerpt offering two different perspectives, the first from a researcher and the second from a community member, responding to the brochure:

> Throughout the brochure, there is a mix of colloquial terms (kink) with more academic terms (Alternative Sexualities). It should be consistent and the scientific terms should be used throughout.
>
> (Researcher/scholar, 1 Nov 2005)

> I think that, to be successful, this organisation would have to keep in mind that the language used to reach the general public is necessarily going to be different from the language used to reach researchers. . . . I noticed a few people frowning in puzzlement as they read through

the mission statement that XX handed out at [community organisa-tion]. I think the pamphlet does quite a good job of expressing the organisation's serious mission and of reaching researchers and people who work with research. But I think that you have to recognise that phrases like information clearinghouse and 'interactive data manage-ment system' and 'searchable bibliography of references germane to the study of kink' and 'summaries of the review actions of the Research Advisory Committee' are simply not going to be understood by the average layperson.

(Community member, 10 Jun 2005)

A comment from one of the CARAS partners highlighted the inherent difficulties and ambiguities in language choice for alternative sexuality communities, especially when one is attempting to bridge communities transnationally – and the power of language choice by CARAS to affect the development of dialogue:

I feel that it is worth pointing out that the terms of kink/leather/ bdsm/fetish/whatever self-description vary pretty widely from place to place. Further, a successful KLBFW institution will itself influence the language. For this reason, I hope that the board will choose terminology with the understanding that, if [CARAS] is generally successful, their choice will likely be deemed acceptable.

(CARAS partner, 29 Sep 2005)

Interviews with several of the community members who are involved in the CARAS organisation and community members who are on the Board of CARAS also highlighted the inherent difficulties in academic discourse vs. community discourse. One CARAS partner commented that when the academic researchers began talking during the first Board meeting, he noticed the use of jargon which he did not share and often had to guess at what was being communicated (and had to confirm his understanding later, after the meeting).

The issues of name, jargon, and language choice all point to the fact that an ongoing concern for CARAS will be 'translating' – taking concepts and meaningful distinctions that are created in alternative sexuality communities and communicating that to researchers, to improve the quality of their research, and taking concepts and mean-ingful distinctions created in academia and communicating that to alternative sexual communities and the larger public.

What identity issues arise for an organisation that attempts to blend two disparate cultures, the alt-sex community culture and the academic culture?

The first identity issue was the name of the organisation. There were many lengthy discussions about the name. At one point, a list of 16 different names had been generated. For example, in addition to the name CARAS eventually selected, some of the candidate names were

Kink Research Centre
The Centre for the Scientific Study of Alternative Sexualities
Academic Society for the Study of Kink/BDSM Sexuality
Kink Research Clearinghouse.

The issue of an appropriate name took several months to resolve:

I am of two minds on this issue of organisational title, and so I am still discerning. My current thoughts: if we go with the more formal/traditional/academic kind of title, I would definitely argue for 'sexualities' and, with [another CARAS partner], I don't want this to be US centric from the start. On the other hand, there is definitely a sense of connection and ownership for those in these alternative sexuality based communities/circles when they see one of their own words in the title of an organisation: Leather Archives and Museum, for instance, does this to a certain extent, and I think Kink Research Centre would do this too. The main reason I want to be part of this effort is because I believe it is very important and scientifically sound to give a voice to those who are studied, to empower them to study themselves, etc.

(CARAS partner email, 18 Sep 2005)

I am still weighing the options between this name and our original name with 'Kink' in it – I am persuaded by the historical roots aspect and the 'why hide, haven't we had that enough' aspect.

(CARAS partner email, 25 Sep 2005)

On 4 October 2005, the CARAS partners voted and decided, with one dissenting vote, to use the name 'Community-Academic Consortium for Research on Alternative Sexualities'. The shared intention was to stick to more academic language, in light of the need to bring in academic researchers to the organisation's mission, and to distinguish this organisation from other community organisations which serve the alternative sexuality communities in very different ways.

Another concern mentioned was that alt-sex community organisations' lack of a professional reputation would keep community members from participating in a research organisation like CARAS, if it were seen as just another community organisation:

> One problem is that often the community organisations for alt-sex communities are not considered 'professional' enough for people to donate and support monetarily – this lack of professionalism hurts efforts to conduct research.
>
> (Minutes from Research Roundtable, 19 Oct 2006)

> I liked the intent of this organisation and thought it would be a scholarly approach to inquiring into and discussing kink issues/informing the larger scientific community primarily about kink issues from a scholarly perspective. It seems to me to have 'slipped' considerably toward becoming just another leather/kink organisation.
>
> (Community member email to CARAS,
> 25 Mar 2006 – this exchange was part of concern that
> the first slots filled on the Board of Directors were community
> expertise members rather than academic expertise members)

Issues of identity were intertwined with concerns about bias, authority, transparency, professionalism and the need to bridge different communities – to position this organisation to serve a unique set of needs for both alt-sex communities and for the academic community.

Conclusion

The formation of CARAS as a community-based organisation that attempts to bridge alternative sexuality communities and academic researchers has been greeted by many BDSM-identified people as a much needed development. It has also been greeted by researchers as a much needed boost in terms of professional networking and as a development that will increase access to alt-sex communities for scholarly research. In the first 20 months of the formation of this community–academic partnership, issues of community benefit, respect from academia, privacy and transparency, jargon and 'cross-cultural' communication and professional identity have been discussed and debated by CARAS partners, outside community members and researchers/scholars. It remains to be seen if such a partnership will endure, but it is clear from these early beginnings that the path to becoming a stable bridge between the BDSM community and academe will depend on a rigorous adherence to scientific practices and mores and a continual monitoring of the balance between academic vs. community voices.

Notes

1. The authors would like to thank Jonathan Krall for comments on an early version of this paper.
2. On the historical and sociological development of this community see, for example, Chauncey (1994), D'Emilio (1983), Duberman, Vicinus and Chancey (1989), Nardi and Schneider (1998).
3. Prominent examples of BDSM community organisations include The Leather Archives and Museum, which was founded in Chicago in 1991 and houses the largest dedicated collection of community archival materials; see http://leatherarchives.org. The National Coalition for Sexual Freedom, an educational and advocacy organisation based in Baltimore, MD, was founded in 1997 and hosts a number of projects supporting the BDSM community and other alternative sexuality groups; see http://ncsfreedom.org.
4. The Leather Leadership Conference (LLC) is an organisation dedicated to education and the development of the BDSM community. The LLC holds an annual conference that brings together community leaders for presentations and discussion of topics such as fundraising, event management, legal issues, and current trends in politics and scientific research. See http://leatherleadership.org.
5. For example, in these discussions community members familiar with the social science literature complained of an inordinate number of academic studies that focus on topics such as frequency and distribution of sexual practices – how many people like to be spanked and tied up. In contrast, community members mentioned possible research topics they deemed to be more relevant today, such as the activities of community organisations including LLC and the NCSF or the proliferation of service (Domination-Service-Submission or 'DSS') and gender-referenced (e.g. 'boi') roles that are being actively created and explored in the context of BDSM relationships.
6. The majority of these data have been archived and are accessible on the CARAS website (http://www.caras.ws).

References

American Psychiatric Association (2000). *Diagnostic and Statistical Manual of Mental Disorders: DSM-IV-TR* (4th, text revision ed.). Washington, DC: American Psychiatric Association.

Baldwin, G. (1993). *Ties that Bind: The SM/Leather/Fetish Erotic Style: Issues, Commentaries and Advice*. San Francisco, CA: Daedalus.

Bannon, R. (1992). *Learning the Ropes: A Basic Guide to Safe and Fun S/M Lovemaking.* Los Angeles, CA: Daedalus.

Bean, J.W. (1994). *Leathersex: A Guide for the Curious Outsider and the Serious Player.* San Francisco, CA: Daedalus.

Bienvenu II, R.V. (1998). *The Development of Sadomasochism as a Cultural Style in the Twentieth-Century United States.* Unpublished dissertation, Indiana University, Bloomington, Bloomington, IN. Available for download: http://americanfetish.net.

Blumenthal, D.S. (2006). A community coalition board creates a set of values for community-based research. *Preventing Chronic Disease,* 3(1), A16.

Boyatzis, R.E. (1998). *Thematic Analysis and Code Development: Transforming Qualitative Information.* Thousand Oaks, CA: Sage.

Brame, G.G., Brame William, D. & Jon, J. (1993). *Different Loving: An Exploration of the World of Sexual Dominance and Submission.* New York, NY: Villard Books.

Chauncey, G. (1994). *Gay New York: Gender, Urban Culture, and the Making of the Gay Male World, 1890–1940.* New York, NY: Basic Books.

Cox, L.E., Rouff, J.R., Svendsen, K.H., Markowitz, M., Abrams, D.I. & Terry Beirn Community Programs for Clinical Research on AIDS (1998). Community advisory boards: Their role in AIDS clinical trials. *Health Soc Work,* 23(4), 290–297.

D'Emilio, J. (1983). *Sexual Politics, Sexual Communities: The Making of a Homosexual Minority in the United States, 1940–1970.* Chicago, IL: University of Chicago Press.

De Grazia, E. (1969). *Censorship Landmarks.* New York, NY: R.R. Bowker.

Dickert, N. & Sugarman, J. (2005). Ethical goals of community consultation in research. *American Journal of Public Health,* 95(7), 1123–1127.

Duberman, M.B., Vicinus, M. & Chancey, G. (Eds) (1989). *Hidden from History: Reclaiming the Gay and Lesbian Past.* Markham, ON: New American Library.

Israel, B.A., Schulz, A.J., Parker, E.A. & Becker, A.A. (1998). Review of community-based research: Assessing partnership approaches to improve public health. *Annual Review of Public Health,* 18, 173–202.

Jacques, T. (1996). *Alternate Sources* (2nd ed.). Toronto, ON: Kink, Ink.

Kleinplatz, P. & Moser, C. (Eds) (2006). *Sadomasochism: Powerful Pleasures.* Binghamton, NY: The Haworth Press.

Levine, R.J. (1986). *Ethics and Regulation of Clinical Research.* London: Yale University Press.

MacQueen, K.M., McLellan, E., Metzger, D.S., Kegeles, S., Strauss, R.P., Scotti, R., et al. (2001). What is community? An evidence-based definition for participatory public health. *American Journal of Public Health,* 91(12), 1929–1938.

Melton, G.B., Levine, R.J., Koocher, G.P., Rosenthal, R. & Thompson, W.C. (1988). Community consultation in socially sensitive research. Lessons from clinical trials of treatments for AIDS. *American Psychology,* 43(7), 573–581.

Midori (2005). *Wild Side Sex: The Book of Kink.* Los Angeles, CA: Daedalus Publishing.

Miles, M.B. & Huberman, A.M. (1994). *Qualitative Data Analysis: A Sourcebook of New Methods* (2nd ed.). Thousand Oaks, CA: Sage.

Mittelmark, M.B., Hunt, M.K., Heath, G.W. & Schmid, T.L. (1993). Realistic outcomes: Lessons from community-based research and demonstration programs for the prevention of cardiovascular diseases. *Journal of Public Health Policy,* 14(4), 437–462.

Nardi, P.M. & Schneider, B.E. (Eds) (1998). *Social Perspectives in Lesbian and Gay Studies*. New York, NY: Routledge.

Quinn, S.C. (2004). Ethics in public health research: Protecting human subjects: the role of Community Advisory Boards. *American Journal of Public Health*, 94(6), 918–922.

Rinella, J. (2003). *Partners in Power: Living in Kinky Relationships*. Oakland, CA: Greenery Press.

Rubin, G. (1994). *The Valley of the Kings: Leathermen in San Francisco, 1960–1990*. Unpublished dissertation, University of Michigan, Ann Arbor.

Sandnabba, N.K., Santtila, P. & Nordling, N. (1999). Sexual behavior and social adaptation among sadomasochistically-oriented males. *Journal of Sex Research*, 36(3), 273–282.

Sharp, R.R. & Foster, M.W. (2000). Involving study populations in the review of genetic research. *Journal of Law, Medicine and Ethics*, 28, 41–51.

Stake, R.E. (1995). *The Art of Case Study Research*. Thousand Oaks, CA: Sage.

Strauss, R.P., Sengupta, S., Quinn, S.C., Goeppinger, J., Spaulding, C., Kegeles, S.M., *et al.* (2001). The role of Community Advisory Boards: Involving communities in the informed consent process. *American Journal of Public Health*, 91(12), 1938–1943.

Thompson, B. (1994). *Sadomasochism; Painful Perversion or Pleasurable Play?* London: Cassell.

Townsend, L. (1972). *The Original Leatherman's Handbook*. Beverly Hills, CA: LT Publications.

Weinberg, M.S., Williams, C.J. & Moser, C. (1984). The social constituents of sadomasochism. *Social Problems*, 31(4), 379–389.

Weinberg, T.S. (Ed.) (1995). *S & M: Studies in Dominance and Submission*. Amherst, NY: Prometheus.

White, C. (2006). The spanner trials and the changing law on sadomasochism in the UK. *Journal of Homosex*, 50(2–3), 167–187.

Yin, R.K. (2002). *Case Study Research: Design and Methods* (3rd ed.). Thousand Oaks, CA: Sage.

16
Turning the World Upside Down: Developing a Tool for Training about SM

Meg Barker

During the past three years in which I have been researching and publishing work on SM (e.g. Barker, Iantaffi & Gupta, forthcoming 2007; Ritchie & Barker, 2005) I have been asked to provide training sessions on the topic in a number of contexts (e.g. with health professionals, sex therapists, counsellors, people involved in film certification and members of lesbian, gay and bisexual community groups). In addition to this I have incorporated sessions about SM into my teaching with undergraduate and postgraduate students studying courses on human sexuality, mental health and clinical psychology.

One major issue that I have faced in running such teaching and training sessions is how to get past the blocks that many people have around SM due to the dominant discourses that are likely to have constituted most of their previous exposure to the topic. Mainstream media depictions and everyday perceptions of SM are largely negative, perpetuating psychiatric and legal perspectives of SM practices as pathological and on a 'slippery slope' towards criminal behaviour (see Barker, Gupta & Iantaffi, Chapter 12). It seemed necessary to challenge some of these 'taken-for-granteds' before I could present research material about the experiences and needs of people in the SM communities and others who engage in SM practices. I wanted to encourage students and trainees to reflect critically on their existing assumptions about SM, loosening some of their existing constructs before making other alternatives available to them (Burr & Butt, 1992).

In the teaching and training that I have previously carried out on other aspects of sexuality (particularly lesbian, gay and bisexualities (LGB)), I have frequently used existing exercises which have been designed to get participants questioning their assumptions and revealing them as just one way of constructing the object under consideration rather than as 'fact' (e.g. Butler, 2004; Rochlin, 1977, outlined below). Many of these resources have been developed as part of a tradition of lesbian and gay awareness training within equal opportunities, medical and educational contexts (Peel, 2002). However, I could find no past awareness-raising sessions on SM. Most workshops about SM take place in SM community contexts with people who are either already involved in SM or who are strongly considering it (e.g. Kinkfest, 2005, 2006). They tend to focus on introducing attendees to SM techniques and how to use these safely. There is little material available aimed at introducing people outside the SM communities to SM.

In her overview of lesbian and gay awareness training, Peel (2002) mentions that trainers often use exercises within training in order to encourage attendees to realise their existing stereotypes, gaps in their knowledge and so forth. Bertram and Massey (forthcoming 2007) also write about using such exercises as pedagogical tools in a higher education context. This seems important because higher education has been described as a site of 'thundering heteronormativity' (Epstein, O'Flynn & Telford, 2003: 102), where heterosexism and homophobia are still commonplace and non-normative sexualities continue to be silenced and excluded in both textbooks and lecture material (Barker, 2007). Snyder and Broadway's (2004) analysis suggests that such exercises may also be useful in the context of school teaching because of the 'pervasive acceptance of heteronormative behaviour' there, which 'privileges students that fit the heterosexual norm, and oppresses through omission and silence those who do not' (p. 617).

Bertram and Massey (forthcoming 2007) discuss their reasons for using exercises like Rochlin's (1977) 'heterosexuality questionnaire' as pedagogical tools. Amongst these they include the development of critical thinking skills in students in order to flatten the hierarchy between them and the teachers. They also talk about the goal of shifting scrutiny away from subordinate to dominant groups (in this case from LGB people to heterosexuals). Feminist authors, lesbian and gay activists and queer theorists have all employed such techniques to put their points across in particularly powerful ways which may amuse and relieve readers on the 'inside' whilst simultaneously engaging and discomforting those on the 'outside' by encouraging empathy and the imagining of oneself in a very different societal position. This encourages normative populations to reflect on their positions of privilege and the ways in which oppressive hierarchies are perpetuated (Fine, Weis, Powell & Wong, 1997; Garber, 1994).

Such exercises aim to increase awareness of the perceptions, positioning and treatment of marginalised groups by drawing attention to the constructed nature of divisions of sex, gender and other related categories. Social constructionist writers have pointed out the cultural and historical specificity of current understandings of sex and sexuality by making comparisons between different time periods and societies (e.g. Burr, 2003). Kimmel (2006) explicitly draws on discourses of cultural comparison in his 'anthropological field study' of a 'Nacirema' subculture: 'Tarfs'. By using anagrams and anthropological jargon he presents common American fraternity practices as unfamiliar, bizarre and 'other'. By the time the reader has understood the trick they have already engaged critically with the material (in the way they might when reading about some foreign tribe) and questioned the practices, particularly realising the homosexual elements in what is often promoted as a particularly macho version of heterosexuality.

In the case of sexuality, a major goal of exercises is to show that normative heterosexuality itself is culturally and historically constructed (Weeks, 2003) and to show the impact of a person's own standpoint on the kinds of questions they ask (and don't ask). Exercises often point such social constructions out by imagining parallel universes, alternative realities and carnivalesque 'worlds turned upside-down' where conventions and rules are reversed in a way reminiscent of the early modern 'feasts of fools' (see Oldridge, 2005).

Examples of tools which challenge stereotypes and myths by envisioning what life would be like if these were reversed include the much used heterosexuality questionnaire, attributed to Rochlin (1977), which asks respondents questions such as: 'what do you think caused your heterosexuality?', 'is it possible that your heterosexuality is just a phase you may grow out of?' and 'is it possible that all you need is a good gay or lesbian lover?' This enables them to imagine an alternative reality in which heterosexuality was treated as homosexuality is, in this one, encouraging empathy and drawing attention to the problematic assumptions that lie behind common views of homosexuality. Butler's 'homoworld' 'attempts to give heterosexuals a taste of what it would be like to live outside of the dominant norm regarding their sexuality' (2004: 15). It describes a day in the life of a heterosexual person who lives in a world where homosexuality is the norm, saturating everyday conversation and popular representations in the way that heterosexuality does in our world. For example,

Arriving at work, one of the admin staff is showing pictures of her holiday she just took with her girlfriend in Lesbos. As you join the group to look at the photos you get asked 'Where did you take your last holiday?' Do you admit it was Corfu, a destination well known for its heterosexual holidays, and do you say who you went with?

(p. 15)

and

Finally you reach your home tube station and as promised your boyfriend is there to meet you. You feel a flood of relief at seeing him, realising how tired you are. But do you greet him with a kiss with all these people still around? As you walk home you both have to walk down a quiet street. You start to hold hands, glad of the contact. However, unexpectedly a group of youths rounds the next corner and you let go. Did they see the contact? Are they going to say anything, heckle you? Worse still, is this a potentially violent situation? You both stare at the floor as you walk past.

(p. 17)

Sedgwick's (1993) essay, 'How to Bring Your Kids up Gay' similarly invites the reader to imagine a world where same-sex sexual desire was valued and parents would look for self-help literature to help them to encourage it in their children. Rothblum's (1999) 'friendship planet' exercise turns monogamy on its head by imagining a planet where people treat lovers as we do friends and vice versa (so they look for one true friend, deny themselves friendships on the side, try to avoid friendliness with inappropriate people and have a number of uncomplicated lover relationships). Steinem's (1978) essay asks her readers to imagine a world where men menstruated, suggesting that menstruation would become something to boast about and celebrate with rituals, with national research bodies to find cures for PMS and to provide free sanitary protection.

I wanted to begin my own workshops and teaching sessions on SM with a comparable exercise which would help attendees to become aware of their existing assumptions about SM and to begin to challenge these. I felt that it would be more powerful if attendees saw for themselves the problems with the common myths around SM rather than me telling them directly that these were problematic. Specifically I wanted to highlight some of the popular misconceptions around SM (see Barker, Iantaffi & Gupta, forthcoming 2007; Bridoux, 2000), for example, that

SM always involves extreme amounts of pain or lasting damage, and that it is violent, non-consensual and unsafe. Like Moser and Kleinplatz (2005), I decided that it would be useful to contrast SM practices with culturally acceptable practices like sport and leisure pursuits to challenge participant's criteria for deeming SM dangerous, wrong, sick or otherwise troubling.

First I developed an exercise along the lines of Rochlin's (1977) questionnaire (described in full and discussed in detail in Barker, 2005). In this the reader is presented with 13 descriptions of 'scenes' and asked to decide, for each one, whether they would be concerned or not if a friend revealed taking part in this activity (for therapist training, 'friend' was changed to 'client'). Examples of scenes include

> An individual pays a stranger to carefully insert sharp pieces of metal into parts of their body. This leaves permanent scarring and sometimes results in infection.

and

> A small group of people arrange to meet in a private space in order to watch others role-playing being raped, humiliated and tortured. They find this an enjoyable way of spending their evening.

Generally I get the participants into groups of three to look at four or five of the scenes in detail. They then feed back to the rest of the class which they found most disturbing and why. This leads to a useful discussion of issues such as levels of informed consent, negotiation, physical and mental harm, sexual context and power differences, which tend to be some of the criteria used to make these judgements. Usually one or two students will realise the 'trick' of the exercise at some point. Like the practices described in Kimmel's (2006) article, the scenes are mostly descriptions of commonplace activities that a non-kinky heterosexual person might take part in (tattooing, watching a thriller, going on a stag night, wearing high-heeled shoes, etc.) Three are real SM scenes, taken from my research, but these are almost never the ones that are picked out as problematic. Once this is revealed the group discusses how activities are socially constructed as acceptable or unacceptable and this leads into a critical consideration of the construction of SM practices as pathological and/or criminal.

I also often use Moser and Kleinplatz's (2005) article as a follow-up exercise because this applies the American Psychiatric Association

Diagnostic and Statistical Manual criteria (see Moser & Kleinplatz, Chapter 3) to heterosexual behaviour in order to show that heterosexuality could just as easily be categorised as a paraphilia as SM since it often leads to distress (they consider sexual dysfunction, affairs and divorce, for example).

In addition to these materials I wanted to develop more of an explicit 'world turned upside down' exercise along the lines of Butler's (2004) 'homoworld' or Rothblum's (1999) 'friendship planet'. As several authors in this volume have pointed out (e.g. Weait, Downing), SM authors and activists often draw comparisons between SM and sporting activities when campaigning for the legal rights of SM practitioners. The healing narratives of SM discussed elsewhere in this book (Barker, Gupta & Iantaffi) also sometimes sound rather similar to the claims made about the positive physical and psychological impact of 'good exercise'. Given my own rather positive perspective on SM (and a lifelong perplexity at the mass appeal of participation in, and watching of, sporting events) I tried to imagine a world in which the way we viewed SM and the way we view sport were reversed. The following is what I came up with. I hope that I, and others, can begin to incorporate exercises such as this and the one published previously (Barker, 2005) and to evaluate how these are responded to and which prove the most useful in achieving the kinds of aims discussed above. I would welcome any feedback from any colleagues using these, or other, exercises.

THE DAILY KINK

Get whipped into mental and physical shape for the summer: PM urges us to learn the ropes from our Olympic boys and girls

Today we welcome our UK team of Olympic SMers home from Madrid where they have been demonstrating their expertise in a number of different events, achieving gold in Japanese Rope Bondage, boot-worship and co-topping. This in the same week that Britain's Manchester Fetishists romped home from the States with the world cup, which was gladly passed over to them by the exhausted California Leathermen after a strenuous and nail-biting four hour session. TV viewers can catch a re-run of the event this Saturday following the human-pony chariot racing on ITV.

Prime Minister Tina Blur greeted the Olympic team along with a crowd of thousands when they arrived back at London Heathrow this morning. At a later press conference she encouraged the public to learn from these role models and to ensure that they build a range of SM activities into their weekly routine. A recent report to the ministry of health confirmed that even a leisurely daily spanking increases the average lifespan by three years. In a passionate speech Blur spoke of her own Sunday meditation sessions in a rubber sleep-sack. 'It is every citizen's duty to ensure that they maintain a healthy and happy body and mind,' she said. 'Periods of needle play and flogging release endorphins and raise heart rate as well as providing a valuable emotional release'. The PM also spoke of the team-building potential of group-based role-play. She recommended that business people engage in brief role-reversal sub-dom scenes during their lunch-break to relieve work-related stress and to aid manager–employee relations.

There are plans to build an even larger play-stadium at Wembley to accommodate the growing number of internationally renowned professional SMers who are keen to use the venue. Top SMers pull in salaries of several million pounds. Number three seeded cane-sub Jan Pindle, who courageously endured 350 strokes to bring home bronze from Madrid, is rumoured to earn at least ten million a year. He recently said 'I would like to see a move towards the kind of SM-camps they have in the US to train students to become professionals'.

Unfortunately, a group of extremists have attempted to taint these recent successes by forcing their agenda into the public arena once more. The 'sports' contingent wasted no time in latching onto the PM's rousing speech. The PM said that this was 'a vain attempt to convince a weary public of the legitimacy of their bizarre activities, by drawing some kind of comparison between them and popular SM pursuits'.

The Daily Kink have heard of one group who meet in secret to pound each other in the head until one or other is rendered unconscious. Almost as concerning are the underground 'rugby' afternoons whose depraved 'scrums' frequently result in broken limbs and brain damage which our overworked health services are then expected to treat. Another minority group suspend themselves from dangerous heights with ropes and harnesses: a practice resulting in several deaths every year.

(Continued)

Shockingly, participants in these marginal activities experience *no* form or sexual or sensual pleasure as a result. Given this lack of any normal reason for such behaviours, we asked Professor Jane Dollar of Yile University to explain. 'Clinical studies have shown that most "sports" practitioners have been damaged by early experiences of abuse,' Prof. Dollar claimed. 'Competing for leather-encased sacks of air has clear Freudian undertones and may well be a result of arrested development'.

Martin Blackhouse is a campaigner from a national group which is fighting for a complete ban on all 'sports' or 'sports-related' activities. 'We are battling to tighten legislation so that prosecution will be much easier in these cases,' Martin said. 'The dangers involved in "sports" are severe. We are concerned about what will happen if children get access to footage of activities like "American football" and attempt to copy them. There is also clear evidence that taking part in "sports" is the start of a slippery slope leading to increased levels of aggression and violence'.

The Daily Kink managed to conduct a private interview with an anonymous 'sportsman'. 'Jack', as we will call him, was seduced into 'boxing' at a young age. He showed us his private collection of the peculiar satin costumes and oversize gloves that 'boxers' are expected to wear. Jack's involvement in 'boxing' led to him becoming involved in 'bare knuckle fighting' and he has been present on two occasions where somebody was beaten to death. No more evidence is necessary to prove that 'sports' are extremely dangerous activities which are only practiced by sick individuals. The claim by 'sportspeople' that they consent to take part cannot be taken seriously. As Prof. Dollar says, 'The so-called consent of mentally unstable persons cannot be taken account of in a court of law'.

To conclude on a more positive note, recent university statistics show that SM-studies is now the fourth most popular course taken in the UK, with many students also specialising in SM-physiotherapy and SM-massage, learning the skills necessary to prepare professional SMers for scenes and to deal with the occasional minor injuries that result from more strenuous practices. We truly are a nation of SM-lovers!

References

Barker, M. (2005). Developing an SM awareness tool. *Lesbian & Gay Psychology Review*, 6(3), 268–273.

Barker, M. (2007). Heteronormativity and the exclusion of bisexuality in psychology. In V. Clarke & E. Peel (Eds) *Out in Psychology: Lesbian, Gay, Bisexual and Trans Perspectives*. (pp. 86–118) Chichester: Wiley.

Barker, M., Iantaffi, A. & Gupta, C. (forthcoming 2007). Kinky clients, kinky counselling? The challenges and potentials of BDSM. In L. Moon (Ed.) *Feeling Queer or Queer Feelings: Counselling and Sexual Cultures*. London: Routledge.

Bertram, C.C. & Massey, S.M. (forthcoming 2007). Queering dialogue: safety and discomfort in a lesbian, gay, bisexual and transgender psychology course.

Bridoux, D. (2000). Kink therapy: SM and sexual minorities. In C. Neal & D. Davies (Eds) *Pink Therapy 3: Issues in Therapy with Lesbian, Gay, Bisexual and Transgender Clients* (pp. 22–34). Buckingham, UK: Open University Press.

Burr, V. (2003). *Social Constructionism*. London: Routledge.

Burr, V. & Butt, T. (1992). *Invitation to Personal Construct Psychology*. London: Whurr Publishers.

Butler, C. (2004). An awareness-raising tool addressing lesbian and gay lives. *Clinical Psychology*, 36, 15–18.

Epstein, D., O'Flynn, S. & Telford, D. (2003). *Silenced Sexualities in Schools and Universities*. Stoke on Trent: Trentham Books.

Fine, M., Weis, L., Powell, L.C. & Wong, L.M. (Eds) (1997). *Off-White: Readings on Race, Power, and Society*. New York, NY: Routledge.

Garber, L. (1994). *Tilting the Tower: Lesbians Teaching Queer Subjects*. New York, NY: Routledge.

Kimmel, M. (2006). Ritualised homosexuality in Nacirema subculture. *Sexualities*, 9(1), 95–105.

Kinkfest (2005). Available: http://www.unfettered.co.uk/kinkfest2.htm. Accessed on 29/7/05.

Kinkfest (2006). Available: http://www.unfettered.co.uk/kinkfest2/kinkfest/. Accessed on 31/1/07.

Moser, C. & Kleinplatz, P.J. (2005). Does heterosexuality belong in the *DSM? Lesbian & Gay Psychology Review*, 6(3), 261–267.

Oldridge, D. (2005). *Strange Histories: The Trial of the Pig, the Walking Dead and Other Matters of Fact from the Medieval and Renaissance Worlds*. London: Routledge.

Peel, E. (2002). Lesbian and gay awareness training: Challenging homophobia, liberalism and managing stereotypes. In A. Coyle & C. Kitzinger (Eds.) *Lesbian and Gay Psychology: New Perspectives* (pp. 255–274). Oxford: BPS Blackwell.

Ritchie, A. & Barker, M. (2005). Feminist SM: A contradiction in terms or a way of challenging traditional gendered dynamics through sexual practice? *Lesbian & Gay Psychology Review*, 6(3), 227–239.

Rochlin, M. (1977). *Heterosexuality Questionnaire*. Available: http://www. pink-practice.co.uk/quaire.htm. Accessed on 29/7/05.

Rothblum, E. (1999). Poly-friendships. In M. Munsen & J.P. Stelbourn (Eds) *The Lesbian Polyamory Reader* (pp. 71–84). New York, NY: Harrington Park Press.

Sedgwick, E.K. (1993). How to bring your kids up gay. In M. Warner (Ed.) *Fear of a Queer Planet* (pp. 69–81). Minneapolis, MN: University of Minnesota Press.

Snyder, V.K. & Broadway, F.S. (2004). Queering high school biology textbooks. *Journal of Research into Science Teaching*, 41(6), 617–636.

Steinem, G. (1978). If men could menstruate. *Ms. Magazine*, October 1978.

Weeks, J. (2003). *Sexuality*. London: Routledge.

17
Who Is in Charge in an SM Scene?
Sophia

In this article I will be looking at the complex power structures within a BDSM scene or relationship. I am writing on the basis of my own experience and observations as a practicing BDSMer over the last two decades, primarily in the bisexual and queer BDSM communities in London and the north of England.

BDSM is very important to me and is a core part of my sexuality; it has played a major role in all my serious sexual relationships throughout my adult life. I identify as a switch, but most commonly – and much prefer to – play as a bottom, as I find it much more visceral and enjoyable. However, when I do top, which is frequently, I think that the thrill of taking someone where they want to go and then bringing them back again safe and happy is too beautiful for words. The majority of my play occurs within a relationship or with close friends, though I will sometimes play casually, for example at a play party.[1] I almost never play at clubs because I find that the atmosphere lacks intimacy and also because I'm a bit deaf and they are generally too loud for me to hear what my partner is saying. I'm bisexual, and while I have no preference as to the gender of my partners I mostly play with other bisexuals or queer people rather than with heterosexuals.

My BDSM practice is firmly based around the concept of SSC – 'Safe, Sane and Consensual' – shorthand for playing with informed consent and full awareness of associated risks and attempting to minimize same, and BDSM as a life-enhancing and, above all, fun thing for all involved.

A look at the kind of relationships and scenes that are commonly found in BDSM fiction can offer a misleading picture of the ways that BDSM tends to work in real life. From reading such material one might get the impression that the usual situation is that the partner is exclusively dominant, the other is exclusively submissive and further that the dominant partner is in complete control of the submissive and directs the relationship, sexual practice and activities within it in accordance with their own desires. There is little or no input from the submissive partner, save to fulfil the dominant partner's wishes.

As this prevalence in BDSM fiction suggests, this kind of structure is a very hot fantasy for many people, and for a sizeable percentage of submissives it is a *beau ideal* of what they'd like if their fantasies came true. However, in my experience, opinion is much more divided on whether such a relationship is desirable – or even possible – in real life. Many, perhaps most, including myself, who love the fantasy know that they'd hate it in reality. While relationships based on the model described above do exist, they are very rare in consensual BDSM practice.

Equally misleading to the outside observer can be watching actual BDSM play between partners. One might see one partner in chains and another wielding the whip, but this can conceal a multileveled power structure within the scene that is far more complex than meets the eye.

In a consensual BDSM relationship the core concept is that of what has sometimes been called 'power exchange' (Langdridge & Butt, 2004). One partner, the submissive or bottom, must give up some or all of their power and control over what happens to them to the dominant or top. This might be for the duration of an individual scene (maybe hours or just minutes), in the context of the sexual side of an ongoing relationship, possibly more generally and at the extreme even extending to the control of the submissive's daily life by the dominant partner.[2]

The degree of power given up will be the result of an agreement between the participants generally referred to as negotiation. For most people what they negotiate will fluctuate from time to time depending on the circumstances, who they are playing with and, most particularly, the level of trust that they have in a given partner. In some ways the exchange of power is very real, in others it is illusory.

Negotiation, whether open or hidden, is the key to successful consensual BDSM. It's the fundamental building block for building up the trust that is essential for power exchange to take place. Negotiation could be thought of as agreeing what's on the menu and establishing the social contract under which the BDSM activities will take place.

The participants will agree such things as areas of mutual interest and respective dislikes (which, considering the range of activities that come under the heading of BDSM, is obviously very important!), roles (for example who will top and who will sub), possibly themes for a scene (classic Dominatrix and Slave? Kidnappers? the Tough Sergeant and the Squaddie?), specific activities (perhaps a given scene is to be a play-piercing,[3] flogging or CBT[4]-orientated event), the level of vanilla sexual contact – if any – and procedures for physical and emotional safety (such as safe-words) and talk about any relevant medical conditions (e.g. asthma). The aim of negotiation is to ensure that the needs of all partners are met and everyone comes away safe and happy. Negotiation is essential not only when players who are unfamiliar with each other are planning a one-off scene but also when they have a long-term partnership. Within the context of a healthy BDSM relationship it is a naturally ongoing process.

It should be noted that the setting of limits, in particular, setting up safety structures, is equally important to the dominant as the submissive, though it may seem otherwise as the submissive is the one in physical jeopardy and, to an extent, more at risk of emotional damage. Dominants have limits too, some matters of taste and areas that they don't wish to go to for any number of reasons, some connected with their responsibility and duty of care for the physical and mental well-being of the person who is subbing to them. The consequences of a failure in this regard may very well be catastrophic.

The ways people approach negotiation vary greatly according to personal taste and the perceived requirements of the situation. For instance, the potential players may be negotiating a one-off scene with each other, organizing activities within their sex-life and checking in to make sure mutual needs are being fulfilled or perhaps planning to explore something new. Negotiation is most often done verbally, by casual discussion and mutual agreement, though some people prefer to do it in a more formalized way, particularly when playing with someone new for the first time, for instance by the swapping of negotiation lists (typically a document listing activities and preferences, sometimes with 'yes', 'no' and 'maybe' options). Most often negotiation takes place prior to play and indeed some sections of the BDSM community insist that it should always be done this way to ensure minimum risk for things going wrong.

It is expected that negotiated limits be adhered to strictly and not exceeded. A dominant who deliberately ignores or goes beyond agreed limits will quickly find themselves classed as untrustworthy, even dangerous, and will probably be ostracized if word gets around. Negotiation can, of course, never remove the absolute right of any participant to withdraw consent at any time.

It is, however, very common for consensual BDSM to take place without an explicit negotiation prior to play or for it to be done in only the most cursory way, for example 'no permanent marks, safe sex, SSC, no scat,[5] don't mess with the hair'. Situations where this might occur include where people meet at a club or a play party and decide to play impromptu, in the context of an ongoing relationship or perhaps where a given dominant has a reputation for doing a certain activity well and the prospective submissive requests that. Frequently too, negotiation may be deliberately avoided or unacknowledged; this can happen for a number of reasons, most often in my experience because of a feeling that too much planning can make the event seem cold or, particularly in the case of submissives, because it breaks the spell, the illusion of submission – in fact the fantasy that I described at the beginning of this article.

In such situations negotiation will still take place, the difference is that it is unstated and actually becomes part of the internal dynamic of the scene. The onus then is on the top to discover where the limits of play for the submissive lie, using a variety of techniques, either overtly, perhaps for example by asking questions of the submissive within scene, or to explore using their experience, great caution and a keen eye on the submissive's reactions to discover empirically what is likely to be well received.

The submissive meanwhile is the centre of the top's attention; it all revolves around them. This is one of the fundamental dichotomies of BDSM: the submissives have given up their power, are serving their dominant's every whim and desire, but in fact it's an illusion. The power is exchanged, but so is the responsibility that goes with it. Bottoms also have a key advantage over their tops: they can immerse them- selves in what's happening in the scene, maybe float on their endorphin high, in a way that the tops simply cannot as they always have to keep control, making sure that the submissive is safe and in a good headspace; checking a piece of bondage isn't going to cut off circulation, noting when a cold house is going to make a flogging hurt far more, knowing when to go much harder, when they are approaching their submissive's limits and most vitally when a hug and a cup of tea is the best thing.

While the top is in control of events, they must focus on the responses of their submissive in order to ensure the scene's success and the emotional and physical well being of their partner. This is of course true for all consensual BDSM scenes, previously negotiated or not (and even in the case of 'no safe-word' scenes[6] or relationships), and the ability to do this is the beginning of what makes a competent top.

However, even the most skilled, experienced and aware top cannot create a successful BDSM scene alone; they must have the active co-operation and help of the bottom. Just as the top has responsibility, so too does the bottom and it's an equally important one. They must communicate with their partner. It is essential for them to provide their partner with the honest feedback they need to work with, before, after and especially during play. They also have a duty both to their partner and themselves to retain awareness of their physical and emotional state and inform their partner of any issues that arise. A BDSM scene is in some ways akin to a conversation and it is one all parties involved must participate fully.

So, to summarize, who is ultimately in charge in a BDSM scene? In truth it's a balancing act. In some ways the top is in charge, tops have got the power, they give the orders and get to fulfil their desires (and those of their partner!) within consensually agreed limits, but in some ways I'd argue it's the power of the ship's pilot, turning the wheel to sail the ship into a harbour. But the captain set the course and chose the harbour: that person is the bottom.

Notes

1. A play party is a party usually held at a private home, typically on an invite-only basis. It's a party where BDSM play can take place, and provides a safe space for it to do so. By no means all the guests will necessarily play; there is just the opportunity to do so in an accepting environment.
2. This is sometimes called total power exchange (TPE) or '24/7'. In a TPE relationship, dominance and submission go beyond the bedroom door. The submissive partner might be expected to focus their sexuality purely on fulfilling the desires and needs of the dominant rather than their own and they will have no choice as to the direction of the relationship. They may also be expected to behave in a submissive manner at all times, 'in role' so to speak 24 hours a day, 7 days a week (sometimes enforced by elaborate protocol and rules of behaviour). All important decisions about the relationship and the submissive's life will be made by the dominant. Such relationships are very difficult to pull off, partly because of the demands of society, but mostly for the stress that it puts on the top, and the difficulties in communication to maintain the relationship both for BDSM and in the wider sense. This doesn't mean that no such relationships exist of course, but that they are rare and it is my contention that they are more fantasy than reality.
3. Play piercing is using medical hypodermic needles to create temporary surface piercings on the body. It creates an incredible endorphin high for the recipient and can be visually very impressive. Done by a skilled practitioner using appropriate safety methods, it is a low-risk art.
4. CBT is cock and ball torture: torture of the male genitals, typically by binding, pulling, squashing, using needles, hot wax or a variety of fiendish purpose-made devices. Great care is needed!
5. Scat is play involving faeces.

6. A 'no safe-word scene' is a BDSM scene in which the submissive agrees to give up the use of their safe word (thus implying that they have given up the chance to veto what will happen to them), typically for a limited – and usually short – period.

References

Langdridge, D. & Butt, T. (2004). The erotic construction of power exchange. *Journal of Constructivist Psychology*, 18(1), 65–74.

SM and Sexual Freedom: A Life History

Grant Denkinson

In this piece I am going to illustrate how SM and sexual freedom activism have intertwined in the context of my life so far as a UK SMer. The piece is sparsely referenced because much communication was spoken or on-line and rarely recorded in publicly available archives. Sometimes we simply didn't think to. A medium we could consider evanescent encouraged candor. We often didn't want to make intimate – and following Spanner possibly illegal – acts a matter of public record (see Weait, Chapter 5). At the time, my activism more often aimed to influence the future than chronicle the past. Analysis from one event or action produced lessons for the next rather than weaving rich histories. I suspect that there are copies of messages on many hard drives in dead machines or on obsolete magnetic media but these hardly constitute a well-maintained library. Events that I organized or attended were often bubbles of time and space (Bey, 1991) where people joined, had their lives transformed and then dispersed. Regular groups had a high turnover of people who came just a couple of times, never to be seen again. I hope they found what they wanted or were at least inspired in their search.

Personal history

I was always into kink. Alone, my early story worlds and dreams contained many examples. I neither worried about nor discussed my fantasies. As with many of Chaline's participants (Chapter 10), stories from television or children's books fuelled my masturbation from childhood through adolescence. I was curious about pornography and classmate conversations but found that neither related much to me. Always single, I had unrequited obsessions towards women and fuzzy cravings for male closeness as yet uncategorized as attraction. Frustrated and lonely, I figured I was still young. I had a naive libertarian sense of sexual ethics.

At university I gained Internet access and was part of the proliferation of SMers telling their stories online (Langdridge & Butt, 2004). Initially this was not the now familiar image-based, porn-rich version, but text-based sharing, arguing and information. Decentralized newsgroups carried messages worldwide to be read by any number of anonymous eyes, many of whom were 'lurkers' and never wrote themselves. I found out that people really 'did this stuff' and, more importantly, did it in an ethical way enjoyed by all parties. An article by a submissive woman in our student newspaper told me that I had some kinky peers. I began to work around censorship via free US servers and even looked at a few slow-loading pictures late at night. Before the web and search engines I typed words to like-minded others using Internet Relay Chat and 'talkers' modified from multi-user game sites. I was proud to avoid being tagged as one of the ubiquitous horny net geeks and moved between Internet 'places' as I was trusted with where to find more.

It was time for this to be real. I spent my first 'munch' social in a London pub, quietly avoiding being seen as a clueless 'newbie'. Weekend drinking and chatting with friends sometimes included slightly kinky horseplay which I watched turned-on but uncomfortable with boundaries far from my ideals of direct and open negotiation and clarity of consent. I wanted strong sensations, particularly after drinking. Hot food, physical exertion or using sewing needles had to suffice. Being defensively sensitive to touch and having felt physically sick at pornographic images of real abuse I was attracted to the careful SM negotiation I had read about. I also craved the creation of a safe space where I could lose control.

After getting over the surprise of kissing a man among friends who cared for happiness, not sexual orientation, and sure of a continuing attraction to women I started calling myself bisexual. Being a frustrated activist type who often had more energy and anger than focus I was happy to have a new area to be activist in and a clearer vision of potential enemies. Aspects of my life, friendships and queer and SM sexualities felt like different worlds and their integration was uncomfortable for me, often provoking a strong craving for privacy balanced with choosing to be out. I made a quick decision to be out on-line too and chose to always make my full name available. I felt scarily exposed and it certainly inhibited what I wrote but I always felt like I was bravely doing the right thing.

I met my first girlfriend flirting over banner knots at London Pride. Joining her in trying polyamory[1] seemed an entirely reasonable proposition. Two retired men also became lovers of mine and their stable and conversational home taught me how relationships could work, challenged me to know what I wanted and to express it and gave me hope for growing older. I've been in poly relationships ever since and haven't seen a good enough reason to change to monogamy.

I wasn't sure if I would like pain as a bottom until my first experience. After a minor panic over a pulled muscle I keep the experience as a treasured memory. Amongst people who could negotiate and had a nuanced and wide understanding of what sexual/sensual interaction could include I felt much more open to trying to be the sexual being I wanted to be, bulldozing my own awkwardness at times. While often speaking of explicit negotiation, much of my own was in the context of a shared SM culture but actually quite implicit and more of the form 'take things slow with no surprises and check in'. Some experiences were too intense for me and I ran away. Most I wanted to repeat. I regret none of them.

I was already being active promoting free speech and privacy (Zimmerman, 1999) and when I heard about a new group 'Digital Diversity': 'a group of individuals who aim to use the Internet and its technologies to promote communications between lesbian, gay and bisexual people, and to provide services that use those technologies' (Whitfield, 1998), I expected to become part of it. I entered my first gay bar, a Holborn bear hangout, and talked about encryption with other queerfolk. I thought the Spanner case and historical and current persecution of homosexuals meant we should be wary of mass surveillance (see Chaline, Chapter 10, and Weait, Chapter 5).

I'd found my local bisexual group in Nottingham and eventually got to the London-based SM-bisexuals group after missing it due to many pleasant distractions. SM-bis was a unique pansexual group for anyone interested in SM. I took regular trips down to London to be there, often having time to reflect on my 'differentness' as I walked home in the early hours when most people were asleep in bed. Anyone who was at the group when I arrived became a respected elder in my eyes and it took me some time to know that some of them had arrived only shortly before me. I started going to national and international bi get-togethers which have become regular fixtures in my diary (Barker & Yockney, 2004). At BiCon I could be 'me' and 'at home', keeping in touch with friends introducing others to ideas and sometimes new sensations.

I confidently attended Countdown on Spanner, SM-Pride marches, and Dungeon in the Sky parties. I remember most queuing to get into the venue with what could genuinely be referred to as an assortment of people, the crush of wall-to-wall leathermen inside, quiet chats over coffee away from the maelstrom, crashing out for a few hours and eating chips at some friends' house and then a late crowded party. The marches were small but had good people and when the London tour buses cruised past I'd shout that we were one of the sights. I found myself hanging out at fetish fairs with people from the Sexual Freedom Coalition (SFC, 2007) and gradually helping organize events with them. I agreed to join the organizing team. I learned some of the histories of the organization and of their sometimes friendly, sometimes inexplicably hostile, interactions with others. Internally to the SFC we had frank and sometimes heated while respectful discussions. As the name implies, the SFC are a coalition and have broad and radical aims. We created some mass actions and parties and also worked behind the scenes writing letters, offering advice or giving political parties a framework for debate.

SFC actions had several aims. Often awareness was one of them, such as bringing a cause to the attention of those who could do something about it or generating wider public and press notice. We've had many people under the umbrella of sexual freedom and rather than just accept they didn't necessarily have much in common, we've run conferences to facilitate them making connections. One important thing we have done is to ground some of the endless debate about tactics in actual actions. We can defend the idea of play spaces but until we put them together we don't know all of the issues which might come up and can't address them.

Some community activities could have been controversial if more widely known. I was most impressed with a shop that served as a social hub for SMers. There was a young guy there, under-age, whom they were happy to have hang out. They were clear that he could not be anyone's partner: he was just getting good information and being around people who could understand him.

Several times in different organizations I came across impressive activists who were good at making things happen in the face of apathy or opposition and were effective solo leaders with big address books. This did sometimes make them hard to work with in a team both getting resources aligned with joint group decisions and transferring knowledge, skills and contacts from one over-stressed person to a team. The busiest times may have most benefited from delegation and yet were the hardest time to organize that.

Current issues in SM activism

I consider myself anti-sexist and appreciate feminism in a somewhat ignorant way. I'm so glad that a small and vociferous group of SM women have stood up for the idea that SM is not inherently anti-women (see Ritchie & Barker, 2005). I've had good conversations with feminist women, both SMers and not, about prosecuting rape and whether legalizing SM could reduce convictions still further than the low levels they are already at (Harrower, 1998). Marks on the body can be used as evidence of a struggle and therefore a woman not having consented to sex. If the same marks could be explained as consensual SM then such evidence could be less reliable. I am concerned about this but still think that taking away competent adults' rights to consent to sex (whether for fun or money) or SM pushes already dodgy industries further underground and is disempowering by taking away the voice of those who most need to be heard.

I've found that some people become more open to experimenting with their own gender and the choice of gender of those they choose to play with through SM (see Bauer, Chapter 11). I dare say that some people – once they are outside of the white-picket-fence heterosexual monogamous box – may consider various forms of sexual expression. I avoid some on-line SM fora due to outbreaks of homophobia although I've never had a problem taking a boyfriend to any club or munch nor had more than jokes from gay men against kinky sex. The bitterer arguments in the bi community over SM seemed to have happened before my time.

Unfortunately some people are great on consent when it comes to SM or sex but don't take the same responsibility for their actions as smokers. Breathing has sometimes been an issue for me and I wonder what self-harm I'm willing to put myself through to be in contact with other kinky types and/or activists. Experiences abroad do make me look forward to the upcoming smoking ban in the UK.[2]

In the UK we still have censorship laws based somewhere between archaic moralism and genuine if misguided paternalism. Some is just ignorance of human sexuality and variation encoded into the power to use violence towards individuals by the state or at least open the way for blackmail or police victimization. The flexibility of the censorship laws makes them unpredictable and also harder to combat since they can be said to vary with society's mores (Home Office, 2007). The Internet has worked around a lot of this but people seem to be so used to it they have stopped questioning why adult materials should be censored at all.

Consent is a mess in law. You can put your life at risk on a mountain, get punched in the head until you have brain damage in a boxing ring or head out to a warzone and yet a love bite could be illegal after the Spanner precedent. Later cases dropped have muddied it for SM even more. Practically the police no longer prosecute SM but this could change and we need a change in law. There is a clear difference between loving and desired sex and rape. The same difference is clear between abuse and SM. Why is this not obvious to everyone?

Recently there has been a so-called consultation on 'extreme pornography' (Home Office, 2006). This started with an admission of there being no good evidence that pornography causes actual violence but went on to conflate 'violent' images with child exploitation and proposed to ignore consent no matter how actual. This further undermines the difference between fact and fiction (will they now propose locking up those who read Agatha Christie in case they are moved to murder? – If you want to find the books most cited by murderers to justify their acts look in a religious setting). The consultation went as far as to suggest criminalizing all deviant sexuality (Backlash UK, 2007). Observers cannot necessarily see the difference between an act of violence and people enjoying (or acting out professionally) an SM act. They need to know about consent and what SM is and have the transparency and understanding of real-life power abuses to tell the difference. We can manage to tell that a blockbuster film about shooting people isn't real and doesn't harm the actors nor overly harm educated viewers. Why does sex fuck up people's understanding?

Notes

1. Polyamory (poly) refers to a relationship set-up which involves openly having multiple romantic and/or sexual relationships (see Barker, 2004).
2. See Barker (2005) for a consideration of the social construction of different kinds of 'harmful' activities.

References

Backlash, UK (2007). *Backlash*. Available: http://www.bbc.co.uk/dna/actionnetwork/G2073. Accessed on 5/4/07.

Barker, M. (2004). This is my partner, and this is my... partner's partner: Constructing a polyamorous identity in a monogamous world. *Journal of Constructivist Psychology*, 18, 75–88.

Barker, M. (2005). Experience of SM awareness training. *Lesbian & Gay Psychology Review*, 6(3), 268–273.

Barker, M. & Yockney, J. (2004). Including the B-word: Reflections on the place of bisexuality within lesbian and gay activism and psychology: Meg Barker in conversation with Jenni Yockney. *Lesbian & Gay Psychology Review*, 5(3), 118–122.

Bey, H. (1991). *T. A. Z.: The Temporary Autonomous Zone, Ontological Anarchy, Poetic Terrorism.* Available: http://www.hermetic.com/bey/taz_cont.html. Accessed on 5/4/07.

Harrower, J. (1998). *Applying Psychology to Crime.* London: Hodder & Stoughton.

Home Office (2006). *New Offence to Crack Down on Violent and Extreme Pornography.* Available: http://press.homeoffice.gov.uk/press-releases/crack-down-on-pornography. Accessed on 5/4/07.

Home Office (2007). *E-petition on Obscenity.* Available: http://petitions.pm.gov.uk/OpposeCensorship/. Accessed on 5/4/07.

Langdridge, D. & Butt, T.W. (2004). A hermeneutic phenomenological investigation of the construction of sadomasochistic identities. *Sexualities, 7*(1), 31–53.

Ritchie, A. & Barker, M. (2005). Feminist SM: A contradiction in terms or a way of challenging traditional gendered dynamics through sexual practice? *Lesbian & Gay Psychology Review, 6*(3), 227–239.

SFC (2007). *Sexual Freedom Coalition.* Available: http://www.sfc.org.uk/. Accessed on 5/4/07.

Whitfield, N. (1998). *Digital Diversity.* Available: http://www.diversity.org.uk/index_o.html. Accessed on 5/4/07.

Zimmerman, P. (1999). *Why I Wrote PGP.* Available: http://www. philzimmermann.com/EN/ essays/WhyIWrotePGP.html. Accessed on 5/4/07.

Experiences of a Pro-Domme

Mlle Alize

Introduction

Professional domination is an often misunderstood field. The casual observer will likely lump anyone engaged in this activity with other sex workers, like prostitutes or exotic dancers, without realizing anything but the most superficial aspects of the occupation. This comes as no surprise. However, even many hardcore members of the BDSM community and professional domination clientele do not fully understand its nature. They may understand their own particular desires and feel comfortable in the environment, but there is much more to the profession than personal fantasy. A professional dominant must possess a vast array of knowledge on a multitude of topics and then use this to craft a scene which meets her client's needs. All the while, there is a tremendous amount of responsibility to ensure that this is accomplished in a safe setting. The dominant must also attend to her own needs to maintain emotional and physical well-being.

So how do you classify professional domination? There is no doubt that it is a bona fide profession that requires training for technique as well as a solid understanding of human sexuality and a true interest in kink. It could also be viewed as a glamour industry, similar to acting, in that a small number of people are very successful financially but the majority are just making do. One can also view professional domination as a service profession. Some dominants do not view themselves as sex workers and become incensed if it is even suggested. Others, however, not only see themselves as sex workers, but also as 'service tops' where they provide a service to the paying submissive. At the lower echelons, professional domination has a large turnaround as many dominants quit when they are not able to meet their financial goals or find they are unprepared for the rigors and nature of the field. At the high end it can provide a challenging and rewarding lifestyle for the long term.

Preparing for a session

Professional BDSM sessions can be very intricate and do require advance planning in order to be successful. Prior to any session, the play space must be cleaned thoroughly. All surfaces and implements that have come into contact with a client should be disinfected with hospital grade products. Anything that has come into contact with bodily fluids should either be discarded properly or sterilized. It is a professional dominant's responsibility to ensure that her clients do not contract any type of infection due to sub-standard cleaning.

The first part of the session setup is the email or phone introduction. This is the initial contact by a prospective client seeking an appointment and detailing his/her requests. At this point, the dominant discusses the scenarios that are being requested and asks a few questions to better understand the client. It is at this junction that she decides whether to accept the client or not. This interaction should be honest and frank and not in character.

The next step is the brief in-person meeting that comes right before the session. Normally these in-person meetings allow more insight into the client as well as a better understanding of their needs. The discussion at this point should centre around trying to understand the client better as well as interacting with them on a human level. The questions that should be asked relate to medical history, hard limits, whether marks are permissible or how the client wants to feel after the session amongst other things. The dominant should have the client explain everything in detail because the more information the dominant has, the more prepared she will be. If a client asks to be humiliated, then knowing what he/she finds humiliating is important. The same applies if a client asks for something like 'medium'-intensity corporal punishment. Since everyone has different thresholds, knowing what range you are dealing with is important. Safe-words should also be discussed and set.

Client and session classifications

Clients and their session requirements come in all sorts of different flavours and there is no 'one size fits all' solution. A professional dominant should be able to read her clients and after conversing with them, she should be able to identify not only their needs and fantasies, but also their head-space. The relationship between the dominant and the client is contingent on the type of client she is dealing with. In some cases, the dominant evolves into a confidante and healer.

BDSM play can be loosely divided into nine technical categories, all of which may be combined to create a scene:

Sensation play: This can range from light and sensual to very intense. Implements may be used to create different sensations.

Bondage: This incorporates all aspects of bondage to include leather, rope and anything else that may be used to restrain the submissive.

Medical play: This incorporates all medical role-play as well as scenes incorporating sounds, catheters and any other medical instrumentation.

Role-play/fantasy: This includes all role-play scenarios like teacher/student, boss/secretary. It generally revolves around scenarios where the 'tables are turned' on the submissive.

Gender play: This may be privileged cross-dressing where the submissive loves to be dressed up as the opposite sex or it may be forced where the submissive is forced into being dressed as the opposite sex. Sessions generally go beyond just cross-dressing and often require the submissive to assume the qualities and mannerisms of the opposite sex.

Age play: This includes infantilism, and sessions revolve around treating the submissive as a baby, while the submissive acts as a baby.

Dominant fetish: This includes scenarios where the dominant uses the submissive's fetishes to tease them and control them in the scene. These fetishes may include rubber, feet or shoes and so on.

Humiliation: This includes all scenarios where the dominant humiliates the submissive whether verbally, physically (spanking, dildo play, golden showers) or by making them perform humiliating tasks. It is the dominant's duty to find out exactly what the submissive finds humiliating as this can vary from person to person, and in some cases what is deemed humiliation to one person may actually be a reward to another.

Training: This involves all sessions that include training elements whether it is training a submissive to be a slave, maid, animal or object.

Along with the above technical categories, scenes can have different styles. The dominant should be able to tweak her style to match her client's needs. The list developed by Diane Vera which is included in The Lesbian SM Safety Manual is titled 'Kinds of Masochism and/or Submission' and includes the following:

Adversarial: These are scenes where fear is incorporated and power-lessness is eroticized. These often include situations that the submissive would really hate in real life such as rape, kidnapping and so on.

Reverential: In these scenes, the masochists or submissives hold the dominants in high regard and have a positive attitude towards them. It is reminiscent of chivalry and is very person focused.

Macabre humour: This session type combines fear and amusement. There may be some elements of resistance but the general tone of the submissive is scared and eager along the lines of 'you wouldn't do that to me mistress', but eagerly awaiting the punishment.

One may wonder where a professional dominant would get training to properly administer to her clients. There are several ways to gain such knowledge. A prospective dominant can approach an established professional or a house of domination and serve as apprentice until she is adept. While serving as an apprentice, a prospective dominant may be asked to switch so that she is exposed to what her future clients would be feeling. Another approach is to attend a 'school' as well as workshops in order to pick up techniques and skills. Finally some dominants end up learning from a submissive they have a relationship with, whether a friend or a significant other. Whichever approach is chosen, a lot of practice and time is required before taking on clients as some activities can be dangerous if a dominant is not capable. Small things such as testing the temperature of hot wax before using it or making sure that all electric play is below the waist can go a log way in helping to avoid a disaster.

Clients can also be loosely grouped into several categories that may also be combined together, and the dominant must be able to correctly identify the category or categories into which each client fits. The five main categories developed by William A. Henkin for clients are:

Fetishist: This person is fixated on an object or an action and requires that object or action to be engaged. This would include foot, rubber or nylon fetishists.

Masochist: This person needs intense sensations in a session that might be deemed painful by others. These sensations can be created via implements such a crops and floggers as well as TENS units and wands.

Submissive: This person seeks to give up mental control.

Pet: This person seeks to give up both mental and psychological control. Pets like to be treated with love and kindness as one would with a real pet.

Slave: This person seeks to give up not only mental and psychological control but emotional control as well. The slave enjoys being controlled completely by the dominant and not having to think.

Within the slave and submissive categories are several sub-categories as well. Slave types include novice, SAM, servant and captive. A novice is a slave without much experience, a SAM is a 'smart arse masochist' who wants to ultimately please but needs a lot of attention and also needs to be overcome. They may also attempt to goad the dominant to perform a particular action, hence the term SAM. A servant slave is one whose mission is to please and is capable of being mentally present despite being turned on and can actually perform functional tasks assigned to him/her. Finally a captive slave is one who needs to be overcome both mentally and physically.

There are also many varying degrees of submission that a professional dominant will encounter. In an essay in The Lesbian SM Safety Manual, Diane Vera describes "Nine Degrees of Submission" as the following:

Non-submissive masochist or kinky sensualist: This person does not view himself/herself as a submissive at all. He/she is just into the sensation play.

Pseudo-submissive (not slave): This person plays at being a submissive but does not want to be a slave. He/she enjoys humiliation and other roles but not servitude.

Pseudo-submissive (play slave): This person likes to pretend to be a submissive and slave and enjoys feeling subservient; however, such play is done on his/her own terms which have been negotiated prior to the session. This category may also include fetishists.

True submissive (not slave): This person really loves giving up control but only temporarily (for the duration of the session) and within the pre-negotiated limits. He/she gets satisfaction from submission to the dominant in ways other than serving and seeks direct pleasure as opposed to deriving pleasure from pleasing the dominant.

True submissive (play slave): This person really loves giving up control but only temporarily (for the session) and within the pre-negotiated limits. He/she loves being used by the dominant and likes to serve but only when doing fun activities as opposed to practical ones.

Uncommitted short term (but more than play slave): This person likes to give up control and wants to serve the dominant for both practical and fun tasks but only at certain times and not in a 24/7 scenario. In this situation the slave has the final say when he/she serves.

Part-time consensual (real slave): This person has an ongoing commitment to the dominant and regards himself/herself as their property. He/she serves in all aspects but will have a life outside their service to the dominant, whether it is a job or a relationship.

Full time live-in consensual slave: This person exists solely for the dominant's pleasure and needs. He/she gives up a huge amount of power in return for being regarded as the dominant's prized possession and/or significant other. Very few limitations exist in this scenario and it can be likened to that of a committed couple living a D/S lifestyle.

Consensual total slave:- This person gives up complete control to the dominant. This is more of a fantasy situation and really does not exist outside cults.

The classifications listed are by no means intended to be set in stone, and people may or may not fit into one or more descriptions. Professional dominants will tend to have clients who come from the first three categories in that they are only submissive in a session and that the session is almost always on their terms. Once the negotiation is over and the discussion has yielded the necessary parameters of play, it is time to start the session.

Conducting the session

An ethical professional dominant has obligations to herself as well as her clients. She is the guardian of her client's mental and physical well-being while they are in session. Her actions can have a huge impact on their psyche and thus she must always act accordingly. A professional dominant should be centred and have self-knowledge and confidence. Her personal issues should never be taken out on her clients, and she should always assume responsibility for the scenes in which she participates. Needless to say, a professional dominant knows the difference between what is consensual and what is not; she respects her clients' boundaries and hard limits and she never sessions while angry or mentally unbalanced. The goal is to provide a session that is not only safe, sane and consensual at all times, but also tailored to suit the clients' needs while respecting everyone's boundaries. A well-rounded dominant is knowledgeable about most scenes even if they are not her favourites. She is able to develop her own style of domination and is comfortable with her philosophy about submission, slavery and superiority.

Dominants have different ways of starting their sessions, whether it is having the client undress or kneel, or anything else they may desire. I usually have my clients undress and kneel on a cushion while I change into my clothes. I enjoy making them wait for the sound of my heels on the floor as I walk up behind them. Generally it is at this point that the client is collared; however, collaring does not apply to every session. If the client is not submissive and is only interested in a fetish scene or sensation play, then the dominant may choose to skip the collaring. I enjoy using different collars depending on the scene. A cross-dresser may get a pink ribbon, while a pet may get a dog collar. The collar symbolizes the transfer of power from the submissive to the dominant. It also symbolizes the dominant's burden of ensuring the submissive's well-being. In my sessions, I like to explain the symbolism of the collar to my clients, and I make sure to tell them that only I should remove the collar at the end of the session.

A session should consist of three parts: a start, a peak and a wane, and these should flow into each other smoothly. Elements should be built upon as the intensity is increased and the client is drawn deeper into the play space. A good dominant should be able to teach her clients breathing techniques that will enable to them to relax into the sensation. She should always stay connected to the client and be able to read their body language as she proceeds with the scene. Should anything unexpected arise, the dominant should always remain calm and avoid panic.

Post-session responsibilities

Aftercare at the conclusion of a scene is an often ignored element. While some clients like to be dismissed with a swift kick to the rear and nary a word, most clients are vulnerable at this point in time – especially when scenes are intense and thus require warmth and compassion afterward. This is where the dominant and submissive revert to being equals, and the dominant can take on a nurturing role. I usually express gratitude to the client and affirm their gift of submission. Many times a hug, though not always necessary, is a nice bridge back to the real world. Offering the client a shower with clean towels and some tea or other revitalizing drink is a nice touch and is always appreciated.

In the professional realm where it is always cheaper to hold onto an established client than establish a new one, feedback is very important. Feedback may be done after the session or via email at a later date when the session has sunk in. A good professional dominant takes notes and keeps them in mind for when the client returns.

Effects of professional domination on the dominant

Professional domination can be very emotionally draining. The dominant is always 'on' during a scene as she is responsible for her clients' well-being. She must be able to get into her submissive's head and take him/her to sub-space, and this can be very taxing as it requires a lot of mental effort and awareness. Some clients are more emotionally demanding than others and may dump their burdens on the dominant. In such scenarios, meditation can be very beneficial in dispelling negative energy.

Professional dominants must make sure that they do not overbook themselves. Seeing too many clients in a day can lead not only to a burnout, but also to sub-par sessions. As a rule, an hour should be the absolute minimum time between two sessions, This time is necessary in order to clean the play space and to be able to shed the emotional entanglements created by each scene, especially when switching from a heavy intense scene to a light playful one.

A professional dominant should make sure that her needs are taken care of outside her paid sessions. She should never use her time with clients to administer to her needs.

Conclusion

It should now be obvious that professional domination requires a large skill set to be successful. A wide knowledge of BDSM, human nature and a certain amount of business savvy are crucial. While these requirements may seem daunting to some, the profession can be a very satisfying one to those willing to put in the time and effort to learn them.

Total Power Exchange in a Modern Family: A Personal Perspective*

Rachel Green

The term 'Ds' might mean different things to different people, I am using it here to refer to Dominance and submission in a total power exchange (TPE) dynamic where one (or more) people in a relationship give their personal power freely to another. The popular SM guide, *Screw the Roses, Send Me the Thorns*, defines TPE as 'the empowerment of the Dominant BY the submissive's surrender to His/Her control. The power exchange is consensual and should be well negotiated. The depth of power yielded by the submissive is equal to the level of responsibility assumed by the Dominant' (Miller & Devon, 2002, cited on Fetishopedia, 2005). The care of the dominant for their submissive in such an exchange occurs not only in the bedroom but also in the safety, attention and support afforded to the submissive in everyday life, in some cases as far as including money, property, decisions and careers. TPE is not slavery, and either party may always ask for clarification and/or time out to reassess their needs. I feel it is important to consider TPE as on a continuum with the power dynamics inherent in relationships more broadly. It seems to me that many couples, whether in opposite or same sex relationships, will recognize that one of them takes more control than the other. This too is a power exchange, though not necessarily a complete one. The division of responsibilities in any relationship may indicate underlying currents of a power exchange; one partner, for example, might choose to allocate responsibilities as they see fit, whilst another accepts the decisions thus made.

In my own situation, Ds is combined with polyamory, so multiple partners are involved. In polyamorous situations a hierarchy of

---

* This piece was first published as Green, R. (2005). Total power exchange in a modern family: A personal perspective. *Lesbian & Gay Psychology Review*, 6(3), 279–282. Thanks to the BPs for permission to reprint this article.

control develops, with one person or couple having control over the relationships of and between the others. I have found that an openly acknowledged Ds relationship can smooth many difficult areas, where the abdication of control allows partners of the dominant person to accept their guidance for the benefit of all. This is by necessity a generalization, because there are many other issues that need to be worked through before non-monogamous relationships become stable, not least of which is the jealousy that one member of the unit will feel towards another when it appears that the power dynamics are unbalanced or that X receives more attention than Y. In my experience, such problems need to be worked through by all the parties involved, though if the trust in the dominant party is correctly placed and earned, these difficulties can be addressed and worked through. A good example of this hierarchy in my own situation is the 'marital' bed, hand built to sleep three. As two of us were an established couple before the third joined us as a submissive, her third of the bed is slightly lower than the rest as a permanent reminder of her submission to us. She wouldn't have it any other way.

The place of SM in wider culture

There are many influences in our society to guide people onto the path of 'normal' vanilla relationships. As soon as we are born we are bombarded by messages from the media, and those around us, to conform to gender stereotyping and heterosexual monogamy. I feel that it takes a great deal of courage to step outside of socially enforced boundaries to venture into relationships outside of the stereotypes. Gay sexuality still attracts negative attention and stigma, and the exploration of sexuality outside the accepted 'norm' can lead to many difficulties. Although being gay is no longer seen as a crime or disorder (at least in the UK), the same-sex relationships I am involved with still invite suspicion from our neighbourhood, particularly from members of the church and those who feel threatened by them. Until the repeal of Section 28 of the Local Government Act, schools were prohibited from 'promoting' homosexuality and gay family relationships were labelled as 'pretend', and we still feel the legacy of this, for example in recent calls for local governments to ban the inclusion of books promoting gay positive literature in school libraries.[1]

In my experience, those who openly embrace fetishism and sadomasochism are stigmatized even further, being instantly labelled as 'perverts' and relegated to a similar pigeonhole in society as child abusers and serial killers (see, e.g., the positioning of SM with sadistic rape and paedo-philia in the American Psychiatric Association's *DSM IV-TR*, 2000, and the links made between SM and serial killing in the popular TV series *Wire in the Blood*, 2002). Even though sadomasochism (SM) is widely practised by consenting adults behind closed doors and in adult-only clubs, to participate in SM is to invite condemnation by the culture that surrounds the practitioners. This demonization and pathologization has led to an underground subculture. However, the recent trends in club wear have done much to promote acceptability of the fetish scene. It is now possible to purchase collars, cuffs, handcuffs and even whips from formerly disapproving high street stores (see Beckmann, 2001). Many practitioners of SM would not even think the term applied to them, and that tying a partner to the bed with silk scarves or the purchase of a pair of fluffy handcuffs was merely 'amusingly kinky' (see Storr, 2003, for an in-depth analysis of the way Ann Summers shoppers talk about such purchases and practices). I feel that it would serve SM activism well to show that most practitioners of such kinky games, and by exten-sion, SM, have merely utilized a way of engaging in great sex. It is not necessarily 'scary and deviant' but can equally be 'fun and normal and happy'.

Incorporating Ds into a modern family

A relationship that includes TPE relationships can also include children, but I feel that awareness of SM practices should be managed carefully in relation to children because of the continued pathologization and demonization highlighted above.

In my case, the dominant partner is a woman with children who has taken two permanent female partners to share the same living space, and a number of semi-regular submissives, of both sexes, who join us for periods of time from a weekend to a fortnight to learn the dynamics of submission in a 24/7 family situation. Although hesitant at first, the children soon learned to both accept and value the new family set-up. Rules were given by the biological mother and filtered down throughout the rest of the new non-nuclear family. The children found that there was always an adult to talk to about anything they wished, and that they had access to a wealth of help and information that was not available previously. One adult had a thorough knowledge of English, another of Mathematics and another of sports, for example. There was always someone to watch over them, to cook for them and to provide for their needs. Also the multiple income sources from those adults who worked increased the well-being of the family as a whole, both materially, in the purchase of a bigger house or second car, and spiritually, in the provision of holidays and outings. If children received a 'no' from one adult, they would work their way up the hierarchical chain, but the buck stopped with the dominant adult. When Mum said no, it was a definite no! The respect, trust and honesty that such a relationship demanded were a good platform for the children to learn personal values. Although they were never privy to the outward trappings of Ds, other than the necklaces that the adults wore, I feel that the respect shown towards their mother taught them the values that they would need to be responsible adults themselves.

Problems came when the children were faced with external pressures. Neighbours would occasionally be jealous of the affluence and structure of the family and cause a nuisance by writing to the local authorities. Visits from social welfare officers would result in glowing reports of the contentment of the children, and schools were impressed by the diversity of the children's home life and education, especially when one or more of the parents were able to help the school via the PTA. Other problems for the children came as the result of peer pressure. Their classmates did not believe that they had 'more than one mum' and often ostracized them as 'different'. Again, when the adults engaged in the local community showing that they were just people like any other, and well-adjusted ones at that, the pressure on the children to conform to majority views subsided.

Conclusion

I feel that it is more than possible to integrate alternate lifestyles into the modern family, but the people involved must be very certain of their aims. Sadly it still seems to be that the best policy at present is to keep everything that does not adapt to the over-riding society morality behind closed (and preferably locked) doors. Being gay is no longer a crime, and it is possible to complain if you are discriminated against because of it. Being polyamorous, however, is far less accepted. It does not matter, it seems, if everything of an adult nature is behind locked doors, for it crosses a distinct line of social mores relating to monogamy. The course we have chosen, at least until legislation referring to polyamory is revised, is to adopt a distinct couple as the public face of the relationship when it comes to issues such as parenting. It is possible to obtain a residence order from the family court, giving all the adults in the relationship parental responsibility for the children, but people have to be prepared for a long battle to obtain one.

I feel that adult pursuits, particularly those pertaining to SM, must always be behind locked doors and locked bookcases. A five-year-old may well ask an innocent question to a teacher that has disastrous consequences for the family unit. In our case we try not only to be honest with the child, but also to be aware of their maturity. If they are old enough to ask the question, they are probably old enough to be given some sort of satisfactory answer. I feel that my seven-year-old showed a very healthy attitude, for example, when she said 'when I grow up, I'm going to buy a house with my boyfriend or girlfriend'.

Note

1. See, for example, 'Gay Times removed from college': http://www.thefileroom. org/html/650.html. 'Harry potter book ban': http://www.sundayherald.com/ 35279. 'Schools 'gay Month' fury': http://www.thesun.co.uk/article/0„2-2005031608,00.html

References

APA DSM-IV-TR (text revision) (2000). Available: http://www.behavenet. com/capsules/disorders. Accessed on 21/5/04.

Beckmann, A. (2001). Deconstructing myths: The social construction of 'sado-masochism' versus 'subjugated knowledges' of practitioners of consensual 'SM'. *Journal of Criminal Justice and Popular Culture*, 8(2), 66–95.

Califia, P. (1988). *The Lesbian S/M Safety Manual*. Rev. Ed. Denver, CO: Lace Publications.

Miller, P. & Devon, M. (2002). *Screw the Roses, Send Me the Thorns*. Connecticut: Mystic Rose Books. Cited on Fetishopedia (2005). Available: http://www.fetish-school.com/frames/02_tools/a_fetishopedia/contentFrame.htm. Accessed on 5/8/05.

Wire in the Blood: Mermaids Singing (2002). Revelation films for ITV, screened in 2003, directed by Andrew Grieve.

Storr, M. (2003). *Latex and Lingerie: Shopping for Pleasure at Ann Summers*. Oxford: Berg.

Author Index

Subject Index

'Leather', as synonym for SM traces, 48
lesbian, 16, 19, 25, 26, 28, 30, 34, 49, 54, 63, 82, 185, 267, 268, 269, 285
level of vanilla sexual contact, 279

masochist, 51, 293
medical play, 292
medium-intensity corporal punishment, 291
'Modern Primitives', 108, 109

nacirema, 269
National Coalition of Sexual Freedom (NCSF), 27
   National Violence and Discrimination Survey (1998), 28
Negotiation, 230–1
no safe-word scene, 280, 282
non-SM relationships, 44, 50
non-submissive masochist or kinky sensualist, 294
'normal' sexuality, western clinicians perception of, 61
'normal' vanilla relationships, 299
normative heterosexuality, 269
novice, 294

Obscene Publications Act 1959, 85
obscenity
   criteria for, 23–4
   'SLAPS' test, 24
Offences Against the Person Act 1861, 73
   see also Operation Spanner
Operation Spanner, 73–4, 78–9, 82, 165
   judgement given, 75

pain
   attempts (medicine) to voice pain, 94
   destruction of language, 98
   difference between SM and torture, 95
   experienced as pleasure, 92; chemical 'high', 92; psycho-physiological explanations, 92–3

inexpressibility, 93–4; finding language for, 93–4; power as consequence to, 94–5
infliction: torture *v* SM, 95–6, 97
intentionality in pain, 94
internal and external, 97; dissolution of inside/outside, 102
lack of a referent, 94
and SM: consent to, 95; eroticising pain, 95–6
as union for SM, 101
paraphilias, 62, 205, 210
part-time consensual (real slave), 295
personas
   co-consciousness, 240–1
   conscious creation, 239–40
   natural evolution, 238–9
pet, 294
physical harm
   law and consent in, 72
   law's approach to, 73
   possibility of framing, by law, 73–4
   and SM, 72–6
play parties, 25, 26, 184, 185, 229, 257, 277, 280, 281
play-piercing, 279, 281
polyamorous situations, 298–9
polyamory, 284–5, 298
power exchange, 279
power play, 231–4
prevalence of SM, statistics, 62
privacy, 80
   claims and freedom, 81
   in English and European Human Rights law, 81
   right to respect/right to privacy, 81
private behaviour, claims of privacy in, 81
professional BDSM sessions, 291
professional domination (Pro-domme), 290–7
   categories: adversarial, 293; macabre humour, 293; reverential, 293
   and degrees of submission: consensual total slave, 295; full time live-in consensual slave, 295; non-submissive masochist or kinky sensualist, 294;

Printed and bound in the United States of America